YUN DONG-JU

DITTA: Korean Humanities In Translation

Series editors: Young-mee Yu Cho, Jae Won Edward Chung, and Pil Ho Kim

"Ditta" in Korean means stepping on or over, pressing into shape, or overcoming an obstacle or failure. These usages aptly capture the uneasy yet provocative coexistence of translation's tropes of passage and metamorphosis, and translation's role as a vital site of worldbuilding. DITTA: Korean Humanities in Translation provides a unique and sustaining venue for the English translation of overlooked Korean sources across literature, language, history, religion, philosophy, arts, and popular culture. Each book includes a foreword by noted scholars underscoring the significance of the author and their work within Korea and beyond.

Song WooHye, *Yun Dong-ju: A Critical Biography*. Translated by Flora M. Kim

Kim Soom, *No Hand Held Mine: Stories—"Granny Wild Goose" and "The Root's Tale."* Translated by Joon-Li Kim and Doo-Sun Ryu

Moon Tae-jun, *Flatfish: Poems*. Translated by Brandon Joseph Park

YUN DONG-JU

A CRITICAL BIOGRAPHY

SONG WOOHYE

Translated from the Korean by Flora M. Kim
Foreword by David Krolikoski

RUTGERS UNIVERSITY PRESS

New Brunswick, Newark, and Camden
London and Oxford

Rutgers University Press is a department of Rutgers, The State University of New Jersey, one of the leading public research universities in the nation. By publishing worldwide, it furthers the University's mission of dedication to excellence in teaching, scholarship, research, and clinical care.

This book is published with the support of the Literature Translation Institute of Korea (LTI Korea).

Library of Congress Cataloging-in-Publication Data

Names: Song, U-hye, author. | Kim, Flora M., translator.
Title: Yun Dong-ju : a critical biography / by Song WooHye ; translated from the Korean by Flora M. Kim.
Other titles: Yun Tong-ju p'yŏngjŏn. English
Description: New Brunswick : Rutgers University Press, [2025] | Includes bibliographical references.
Identifiers: LCCN 2024058623 | ISBN 9781978841697 (hardback) | ISBN 9781978841680 (paperback) | ISBN 9781978841703 (epub)
Subjects: LCSH: Yun, Tong-ju, 1917-1945. | Poets, Korean—20th century—Biography.
Classification: LCC PL991.96.T6 Z8713 2025 | DDC 895.71/3 [B]—dc23/eng/20250531
LC record available at https://lccn.loc.gov/2024058623

A British Cataloging-in-Publication record for this book is available from the British Library.

Yun Tong-ju p'yŏngjŏn by Song WooHye was first published by Yŏrŭmsa in 1988. This English language translation is based on the third and most recent Korean language edition, published by Sŏjŏng Sihak in 2014.

References to internet websites (URLs) were accurate at the time of writing. Neither the author nor Rutgers University Press is responsible for URLs that may have expired or changed since the manuscript was prepared.

∞ The paper used in this publication meets the requirements of the American National Standard for Information Sciences—Permanence of Paper for Printed Library Materials, ANSI Z39.48-1992.
rutgersuniversitypress.org

CONTENTS

FOREWORD

Yun Dong-ju: A Critical Biography (*Yun Tong-ju p'yŏngjŏn*) by Song WooHye (1947–) was first released in 1988 by the publisher Yŏrŭmsa. It received a warm reception from critics—feted by the likes of poet-scholar Ch'oe Tong-ho, among others—as well as from general readers. Song subsequently issued multiple revised editions, the first in 1998 upon the book's tenth anniversary, and the next in 2004. Flora Kim's English-language translation is based on the third and most recent Korean-language edition, which was released by Sŏjŏng Sihak in 2014. This current publication is the first time this seminal study has been made available in English.

Readers may be surprised to learn that Song is not a scholar of Korean literature but a novelist and essayist by trade. Although not formally trained as a historian, she had previously researched Gando, the Northeastern region of Manchuria where Yun Dong-ju was born and raised, in relation to the Korean independence movement. It is likely for this reason that the poet Ch'oe Ha-rim (1939–2010), who at the time was serving as Yŏrŭmsa's chief editor, commissioned Song to undertake this formidable project.

Yun Dong-ju: A Critical Biography served as the basis for the 2016 biographical film *Dongju: The Portrait of a Poet* (*Tong-ju*), which studiously restaged the life of the titular poet in atmospheric black-and-white images. Although the film's director Yi Chun-ik (1959–) and screenwriter Sin Yŏn-sik (1976–) deviated from the historical record in several places, they followed Song's lead in centering the film's narrative around the relationship between Yun Dong-ju and his cousin Song Mong-gyu (1917–1945), a firebrand whose ties to the Korean independence movement were likely the reason he and Yun were arrested by Japanese authorities in 1943.

In English-language academia, the author study has somewhat fallen out of vogue. This is especially the case within the field of East Asian studies, primarily due to publisher concerns about the marketability. Few East Asian authors are perceived to have obtained the international currency of their Western counterparts. In South Korea, this is not an issue, and author studies about canonical writers like Yun Dong-ju continue to be released at a steady pace.

The scope of *Yun Dong-ju: A Critical Biography*, however, is broader than a conventional author study. Song dedicates a significant number of pages in her hefty volume to Yun's friends and family, major geographical locations, and the social and political concerns of the poet's life. In this respect, it is as much a portrait of an era and a region as it is of the poet. The book bears comparison to *Yi Kwang-su and His Era* (*Yi Kwang-su wa kŭ ŭi sidae*, 1986) by literary historian Kim Yun-sik—a magisterial three-volume study of Yi Kwang-su (1892–1950), the controversial author of the seminal novel *The Heartless* (*Mujŏng*, 1917), who has often been described as "the father of modern Korean literature."

The granularity of detail included in *Yun Dong-ju: A Critical Biography* is unmatched among similar studies. Song was able to uncover so much material by conducting a series of interviews with Yun's living acquaintances that serve as the basis for the book's countless anecdotes. These interviews have been supplemented by extensive archival research. Song includes snippets of Yun's early writing—his first poems for adults and ditties for children—providing readers with a sense of his development as an emerging young writer. She also contextualizes Yun's most well-known poems within the individual stages of his life. The intersection of biography with literary analysis serves as a firm reminder of the sober realities that Yun confronted as a colonial subject, hardships that he miraculously transformed into art.

Song is openly apprehensive when discussing the potential influence of socialism on Yun Dong-ju. There is little to no evidence that Yun was ever interested in leftist ideology. However, socialism did play a major role in intellectual culture during the colonial period.[1] During the mid-1920s, KAPF (Korea Artista Proletara Federatio, 1925–1935)—a coalition of leftist writers—was a central force in the Korean writing establishment before its eventual dissolution at the hands of the Government-General of Korea, who believed socialism to be an immediate threat to its authority. Communism also had a significant presence in 1930s Manchuria when Yun was an adolescent. Song's trepidation about socialism should be understood in the context of contemporary South Korean politics, where it remains a perpetual boogeyman, a legacy of division and the Cold War. Leftist literature, as well as writing by authors who relocated to North Korea after liberation, were banned in South Korea until the 1980s.

In many respects, Yun Dong-ju is the epitome of a national poet (*minjok siin*), a moniker used by South Korean scholars to refer to poets who embodied national sentiments in their lives and literature. Han Yong-un (1879–1944), a Buddhist monk and public intellectual, is another example of a prototypical national poet: He was imprisoned for his leadership role in the March First Movement and later penned *The Silence of Love* (*Nim ŭi ch'immuk*, 1926), a celebrated collection of poetry about loss during the colonial period. (Song notes that Yun owned a copy of *The Silence of Love*, a telling detail.) Yun's status as a national poet is colored by tragedy, namely his untimely death in a Fukuoka prison, which cast him as a martyr in collective memory. The unassuming beauty of his verse, which is written in a lucid, almost childlike voice, has made his poetry a longtime fixture of school textbooks. Although Yun admired modernist poets like Chŏng Chi-yong (1902–1950), he inherited none of the latter's characteristic abstruseness. The accessibility of Yun's poetic language has contributed to his widespread appeal. Novels and plays, as well as the aforementioned feature film, have been produced to commemorate Yun, transmuting the humble story of a literary prodigy into a national tragedy.

In its resemblance to a hagiography, *Yun Dong-ju: A Critical Biography* might seem like a prototypical example of the mythmaking process in action. And yet Song's meticulous attention to the contours of Yun's life also works to complicate the conventional image of the national poet. If the recurring celestial imagery of Yun's poems imparts a sense of universality to his verse, the encyclopedic detail of *Yun Dong-ju: A Critical Biography* dissembles the impression that Yun's experiences were in any way prototypical of his generation. Although he is considered to be the quintessential Korean poet by many South Koreans, Yun spent only four short years on the peninsula when he was a student of Yŏnhŭi College, the institution that would later become Yonsei University. The majority of his life was instead spent abroad in Gando and Japan. It is perhaps for this reason that Yun continues to be embraced by international readers, especially by diasporic Koreans in China, Japan, and elsewhere, who have informally adopted him as one of their own. His story, in this sense, means different things to different people. And now, thanks to the efforts of Song WooHye and Flora Kim, it is yours to discover.

David Krolikoski

TRANSLATOR'S NOTE

One of the first issues a translator faces when translating from Korean is which romanization rules for proper nouns and bibliography should be used. In academia, McCune-Reischauer (MR) is the norm, while the most widely used system everywhere else is Revised Romanization (RR). While this biography is a meticulously researched book that is now the authoritative biographical work in the studies of Yun Dong-ju, its intended readership was by no means limited to academics, and neither should its English version be so. Therefore, unless another form of transliteration has been firmly established for a particular name, such as Park Chung Hee or Yonsei University or the last name Kim, I employed the RR system for the most part for better readability and easier recognition of Korean names and words that may already be known to the reader.

With that in mind, the following notes are necessary:

1. My endnotes are denoted by "—Trans."; otherwise, the notes are the author's own. I only added "Author" to a few endnotes within quoted texts to clarify that they were the author's endnotes. Likewise, within the text, occasional short parenthetical information that I supplied is denoted by "Trans," while the author's own in parentheses and brackets would appear without notation.

2. For the ease of reading and understanding, I translated the titles of books and articles into English for the most part. The names of the publishers and authors, as well as titles of periodicals, are Romanized. The translated titles are quite literal and can easily be translated back to the original Korean, such as *Baekbeom Diary* = 백범 일지 and *Sky and Wind and Star and Poem* = 하늘과 바람과 별과 시. In rare cases, however, the title is both transliterated and translated: *Nodakdari Chorok Durumari* (An Old Ox, a Green Overcoat). In the bibliography, each source is listed alphabetically as appearing in endnotes, followed by the original script and corresponding romanization in MR for searchability.

3. Non-Korean geographical names, corporate names, and personal names were transliterated according to the usage of the country of their origin—for example, Tianjin (rather than Cheonjin), Rikkyo University (rather than Ipgyo University), and Yanagihara Yasuko (rather than Yangwon Taeja). There are exceptions where the use of Korean pronunciation of the non-Korean name is warranted for historical or contextual reasons. Thus, some names of places in China were kept in Korean transliteration, such as Yongjeong, Haeran River, and Nakyang. However, I frequently denoted the original pronunciation in parentheses as well. Also, 북간도 was translated as North Gando ("north" in the name was usually translated, as in North Hamgyeong Province).

4. Certain terms were idiosyncratic, and I used a translator's judgment. I chose to translate 전문 학교 as "junior college" even though the meaning is not the same as what it means currently. Several terms were used for 독립 운동가: "independence movement fighter," "freedom fighter," and "resistance fighter," depending on the context. Some Korean terms were kept in transliteration, usually in italics—for example, *naeseon ilche*.

5. All passages quoted by the author, including poems by Yun Dong-ju, were newly translated by me even if translations of those passages were available. In so doing, I hoped to achieve a kind of uniformity and consistency in the style of writing while minimizing copyright issues. Exceptions include a short poem by Sappho titled "One Girl" quoted in chapter 7 (Dante Gabriel Rossetti's translation), Turgenev's poem titled "The Beggar" in chapter 7 (Constance Garnett's translation), and Bible passages (King James version).

6. The author did not give citations for her personal interviews, which are not dated. Throughout the book, I cited "Author's personal interview with ____ (undated)" from the context. The list of interviewees appears at the end of the bibliography.

7. This book is a translation of the entire main text of the Korean version but does not include supplementary materials such as Yun's chronology and several prefaces and afterwords that were added as new editions were published. From many images with the author's

comments that appear within the Korean text, I curated nineteen images for this book.

Lastly, the text used for this translation is the 2018 ninth printing of *Yun Tong-ju Pyŏngjŏn* by Song WooHye, published by Sŏjŏng Sihak in 2014 (3rd rev. ed.).

YUN DONG-JU

CHAPTER 1

Birth of the Poet

THERE IS A SAYING, "Peace without honor is no peace," which has proven to be true in the history of Korea. When imperial Japan annexed the Korean Empire, the dishonorable peace enjoyed by the empire dragged its people down to a world of calamity. In this dark time of calamity was a poet sent by God. This book is about that poet.

Born During World War I

All through the summer of 1917, soybean stalks grew thick and green everywhere in the vast fertile land of North Gando. And as these stalks absorbed the glorious continental sunshine of autumn, the soybeans ripened to perfection. The Koreans in that part of China favored using Chinese words and called the soybeans *baektae* (white beans—Trans.). Literally every Korean in North Gando grew *baektae*, and they were all waiting to harvest the beans, which would then be sold to "Gurapa"—what they and Koreans in the homeland called Europe, based on the Korean pronunciation of the Chinese transliteration. With the money from these sales, their lives would become more abundant, as they had been in the past few years.

Already in its fourth year, the First World War—which started after a Serbian assassinated Archduke Franz Ferdinand of Austria and his wife on July 28, 1914—was being fought in earnest in Europe. Countless wars dotted the history of mankind, yet it was the first time in human history that all major powers of the world took sides and fought on all fronts.

The war affected not only those countries and peoples directly involved in it but also the bystanders, like Koreans. North Gando's soybean production and its export to Europe were connected to this war, as was described by Kim Shin-muk (b. 1895), a very close friend of the Yun family and mother of Reverend Mun Ik-hwan: "During the European War, they couldn't farm there, I guess.... We produced a tremendous amount of soybeans. As soon as the harvest was over, the grain merchants collected them all to send to Europe."[1] As if it had happened yesterday, Kim Shin-muk recounted in detail what happened in North Gando around the time Yun Dong-ju was born: "Usually, the grain merchants only bought soybeans. Many Koreans made much money by growing soybeans then. And they'd buy more land and build a bigger house and move. Dong-ju's family also did well. Of course, his family was quite affluent, to begin with."[2]

In 1917, however, it was not just beanstalks growing in the vast soybean fields that pleased those in the large tile-roofed home of Elder Yun Ha-hyeon (1875–1947) in Myeongdong Village, North Gando. The truly gratifying event was that Kim Yong—wife of Elder Yun's only son, Yun Young-seok—was expecting a child. The couple had married in 1910, but their firstborn daughter died soon after she was born. In their eighth year of marriage, she finally became pregnant again. This was the happiest of times.

Just as the beanstalks flourished in the fields, the baby thrived in the womb. On December 30, 1917, the baby—a handsome and healthy boy—was born. Professor Yun Il-ju, the poet's brother, described his household as follows:

There were four of us: Dong-ju, my elder sister Hye-won, myself, and my younger brother Gwang-ju, born in Yongjeong. The house in Myeongdong where the three of us were born stood out in the village. It was a large tile-roofed house. Plum trees lined the front yard, and when you stepped outside the large tile-roofed gate, you'd see vegetable gardens and the threshing yard. To the north of the house was an orchard of thirty-or-so apricot trees and plum trees. Outside the eastern gate was a well and a large mulberry tree. From the well, one would see in the north-east, a church on the side of a hill and its bell tower that was mounted on a dead tree. In the south-east were school buildings and Sunday school buildings that looked too large for the small village.[3]

The birth of the first son in the Yun family was an event the family had been anxiously awaiting. Overjoyed, the new father gave his son the childhood name of Hae-hwan, a combination of the pure Korean word *hae* (the sun) and the Chinese character *hwan* (to shine brilliantly).

Perhaps it was the father's wish that his firstborn son shine brilliantly like the sun, or maybe it symbolized his sentiment that this long-awaited child radiated like the sun just by being born. Perhaps it was both. Either way, the baby would grow up and be called "the National Poet" by succeeding generations.

According to Reverend Mun Ik-hwan (b. 1918), the only surviving friend from Yun's elementary and middle school days at the time of this writing,[4] Yun Dong-ju used the childhood name Yun Hae-hwan until 1931, the year he graduated from elementary school, not only at home but also at school. Only after starting Eunjin Middle School did he adopt the official name Dong-ju.

The "Gurapa War" finally ended with Germany's surrender in November following Yun Dong-ju's birth. Afterward, Europe no longer imported Manchurian crops. Consequently, in North Gando, each house was buried in bags of unsold soybeans. Some grain merchants who had acquired large amounts of soybeans went bankrupt.

Such were the circumstances surrounding North Gando around the time Yun Dong-ju was born. However, there were other grisly, critical events besides the ongoing war and its aftermath. The most significant event was the Russian Revolution of 1917. The Russian Empire, a participant in World War I, collapsed, replaced by the Soviet Union. Its change from absolute monarchy to the Soviet Union greatly affected numerous nations, both tangibly and intangibly. Siberia, North Gando's neighbor, also went through a transformation. The battles between the Red and White armies, the Czech troops' stay in Siberia, and the dispatching of British, American, French, Italian, and Japanese troops to Siberia—all these events were repercussions of the tidal wave called the Russian Revolution. North Gando could not avoid its effects either. Geographically and politically, it was too close to Russia.

Another grave event in 1917 was the death of Yi Sang-seol, a freedom fighter. To North Gando Koreans, the Russian Revolution, shocking as it must have been, could be externalized as one of the outside historical events. However, the death of the revered patriot Yi, who had been a confidential emissary of King Gojong to the Hague Peace Convention of 1907,[5] was a heavy blow to the Koreans in North Gando. It weighed down on them to the depths of their soul.

Yi Sang-seol, former second-in-command in Uijeongbu (the highest governing body of the Joseon dynasty—Trans.), had been an essential figure in the history of Koreans in North Gando since the turn of the century. In 1906, before the demise of the Korean Empire, Yi arrived in Yongjeong and established Seojeon School, the first Western-style educational facility in North Gando. It is said that he used all his private means to operate the school, which became the cradle of patriotic, anti-Japanese education for Koreans there.

After Yi Sang-seol was sent to Hague with Yi Jun and Yi Wi-jong in 1907 under the secret direction of King Gojong, Seojeon School eventually closed its doors. The Korean judiciary, which had become the puppet of Japan, sentenced Yi Sang-seol to death after a default trial for going to The Hague as the king's emissary (vice emissary Yi Jun and special emissary Yi Wi-jong were given life sentences). For North Gando Koreans, Yi Sang-seol was the greatest of patriots.

Yi Sang-seol died of an illness on March 2, 1917, during exile in Nicholisk, Siberia. He was forty-eight years old. His last words to the comrades at his bedside—Yi Dong-nyeong, Yi Hui-young, and Baek Sun—were heart-wrenching: "Comrades! We must achieve independence! How can my soul return to Korea after leaving this world without achieving it? Cremate my body, burn all my possessions, spread ashes in the sea, and do not hold a memorial."[6]

This testament was faithfully obeyed. They piled up wood by the Amur River, cremated him, and spread his ashes toward the northern sea. Even the remains of his bones were ground to powder and blown away. All his belongings were collected and burned into ashes.

The year 1917 was also momentous in the history of Korean literature. Chunwon Yi Gwang-su wrote the novel *Mujeong* (*The Heartless*—Trans.).[7] According to Professor Kim Yun-shik, "Not only is *Mujeong* a monumental literary work that opened the gate to the modern Korean novels, but it is also a monumental masterpiece reflecting the writer's entire life."[8] The fact that Yun Dong-ju was born in the year *Mujeong* was published—what kind of symbolic meaning does it hold in the poet's life?

These events serve as flares that illuminate the identity and core of the era into which Yun Dong-ju was born, casting their long shadows during his lifetime and up until his death. Perhaps the images of the shadows became synthesized in Yun's life.

When he was born in Manchuria, which served as the grain house during World War I, the flames of the communist revolution were blazing; the freedom fighter who gave his lifetime to Korean independence turned into cold ashes in a foreign land; and modern Korean literature opened its grand door. And when he died in prison in Japan during World War II, his body was cremated in that foreign land; his ashes were spread over the tranquil waters of the Korea Strait; and his literary works became a gigantic and brilliant torch that pushed away the ravaging darkness created by colonial Japan. Yun's works, like Yi Gwang-su's, became a new monument in the history of Korean literature. Among the historical events that affected his life, only the Russian Revolution did not have a significant effect, even though it indirectly caused the Yun family to move from Myeongdong to Yongjeong.

Now let us trace back Yun Dong-ju's genealogy.

The Family Tree

The Yun family's lineage is from Papyeong, Gyeonggi Province. The official name for the branch of Yun, as recorded in its genealogy book, is Papyeong Yun Clan of Gwanbuk, Hamgyeong Province.

The late Professor Yun Il-ju, the poet's brother, records the genealogy of his family as follows:

This statement is based on my memory, as well as testimony of the few surviving elders of my family, the family genealogy (*The Genealogy of the Papyeong Yun Clan of Gwanbuk, 1929: Hoeryeong*, Volume 4, from National Library of Korea, which is identical to what our family kept in our hometown and whose last entry is "Dong-ju"), the student registry of Dong-ju kept at Yonsei University, the eulogy and profile handwritten by Kim Yak-yeon for the funeral of our grandfather's brother Yun Deok-hyeon (d. 1941), and some relevant photographs.

Our family comes from the Papyeong Yun clan. According to the genealogy registry, it stems from the Lord Boryeong branch, which originates from the Lord Moonjeong branch. The first ancestor of the Hoeryeong branch was Bu-gae, the mayor of Boryeong District. He was banished to Hoeryeong in North Hamgyeong Province in the Year of the Third Rat (1456), during the reign of King Sejo. For the next five hundred years, his descendants spread in the Hamgyeong provinces, and we are the twentieth generation. That is how we were called to be the "Hoeryeong Yun" clan. When I was small, I thought that our grandfather came from Hoeryeong. My great-grandfather (1844–1906), however, resided in Sangjang-po, Dongpung-myeon, Jongseong-gun, North Hamgyeong, and moved from there to Jadong, North Gando when he was 42, with four sons and a daughter.

At the time of the move, my grandfather Ha-hyeon (1875–1947), the oldest of the four boys, was eleven, and Deok-hyeon (1878–1941), the second oldest, was eight years old, which makes the year 1886.[9]

The eldest of Yun Dong-ju's family known personally by the surviving relatives and friends in South Korea is his great-grandfather Yun Jae-ok (1844–1906), a seventeenth-generation offspring of Lord Boyeong. Those who knew him remembered him as a tall, handsome man of impressive physique. It was Yun Jae-ok who immigrated to North Gando with the family.

Before moving to North Gando, Yun Jae-ok lived in Sangjang Village, Dongpung District, Jongseong County, Hamgyeong Province. In 1886, when he was forty-two, he crossed the Tumen River with his wife and five young children—four sons and a daughter. He settled in Jadong in North Gando, across from Jongseong.

After moving to the wide open but sparsely populated North Gando, Yun Jae-ok farmed diligently to till the land. He was a good farmer, and the land of North Gando was agreeable, making him prosperous. By the time he arranged a marriage for his eldest son Ha-hyeon, he was considered a "rich man," which was the highest praise for a farmer.

At the time of Yun Jae-ok's relocation, immigration to North Gando had not yet been common, even from the North Hamgyeong Province. Yet he moved to a foreign land and became successful. If this were to prove his strong will, an episode concerning his death demonstrates his fun-loving character.

In 1900, Yun Jae-ok moved from Jadong to Myeongdong Village and stayed prosperous. In 1906, however, just eleven years before Yun Dong-ju's birth, he died as a result of a swing accident during the Chuseok holidays. It was a custom in the area that grown-up men also enjoyed swinging. Thus, even though Yun Jae-ok had already reached the mature age of fifty-two, he got on the swing, fully dressed in his white coat and horsehair hat. After a couple of turns, he fell off the swing and ended up passing away. His funeral was a great event that stayed in people's memory for years to come. Later, in the 1960s, when the bloodbath of the Cultural Revolution swept China, his tomb was dug out. If expensive accessories had been found in the coffin, the descendants would have been accused of being the exploiting class and condemned; fortunately, that was not the case, and they were spared.

If Yun Jae-ok, the first-generation immigrant to North Gando, was a man of strong will and fun-loving character, his eldest son, Yun Ha-hyeon, was known as a gentleman of the highest caliber and generosity. Like his father, Yun Ha-hyeon was a tall, impressive man who was deeply respected for the greatness of his character.

Reverend Mun Ik-hwan, Yun Dong-ju's closest childhood friend, remembered Yun Ha-hyeon as follows: "In my opinion, among all the elders of Myeongdong, Elder Yun Ha-hyeon was the most extraordinary person, even more significant than Reverend Kim Yak-yeon, who was called 'the president of Eastern Manchuria.' Elder Yun was a person of great magnanimity and confidence. Despite his lack of formal education, he was greatly respected in Myeongdong, a place of scholars. He was elected as a church elder, too. With his great character, he would have achieved remarkable deeds had he received more education."[10]

As stated earlier, Yun Ha-hyeon, at age eleven, moved with his parents to Jadong in North Gando and grew up there. He married a daughter of a Kang and had his only son, Yun Yeong-seok (1895–1962), at age twenty. Later, two daughters, Shin-yeong and Shin-jin, were born. Yeong-seok and Shin-yeong were born in Jadong, and Shin-jin in Myeongdong.

Yun Yeong-seok was a third-generation immigrant in North Gando, and by then, the Yun family were no longer simple farmers. Though respected for their impressive physique and character, Yun Jae-ok and Yun Ha-hyeon received little education; on the contrary, Yun Yeong-seok was of a delicate constitution and received a formal education. Thus, he looked quite different from his father and grandfather.

In 1909, Yun Yeong-seok began receiving a "new" (Western—Trans.) education at Myeongdong School. In 1913, he went to Beijing with four other students to study, becoming a "Beijing student" envied by others. He was only eighteen years old then. However, he had only graduated from Myeong-dong Middle School and could not enter college yet. It is certain that he did not go to college in Beijing, but it is not clear where he studied. After coming back from Beijing, he became a member of the faculty at Myeongdong School, his alma mater.

In 1923, he again went away to study, this time to Tokyo. It is said that he did not attend a college there but rather studied English at a small institution. His relatives say that he had a "poetic inclination." Not only was it so in daily conversations, but his diction was poetic when he said public prayers (a selected person praying aloud on behalf of the congregation during a Christian worship service).

Another episode supplements this reputation. After the infamous Great Kanto earthquake struck on September 1, 1923, false rumors of Koreans setting fires or poisoning the wells spread, resulting in mass murders of insanity when the Japanese lost all reason and began killing Koreans indiscriminately. Such vicious rumors are thought to have been disseminated by the Japanese government, using innocent Koreans as the scapegoat to appease the crowd, who had become extremely anxious and angry over the disaster.

The news of the massacre reached North Gando, and the Yun family was engulfed in fear, not knowing if Yun Yeong-seok was safe. His wife, Kim Yong, who had been rather sickly, became even weaker at around this time. One day a telegraph arrived. Only a short phrase was written: "Neyba mine-doh." It was from Yun Yeong-seok. The family was confused. What did this mean? Someone finally figured out that it was a Japanese-style transliteration of the English expression "Never mind," to mean, "Don't worry." Only after this explanation was everyone at ease.

It was the kind of episode seen on a multicolored woodcut print. From a land of massacre steeped in the odor of innocent blood, where a person could be impaled by a bamboo spear just because he was Korean, flew in two words like a small butterfly: "Never mind!" Perhaps he had used the transliterated English phrase to hide the fact that he was Korean. At any rate, such an idea was extraordinary and highlighted his poetic qualities. Yun Dong-ju was the magnificent summit of a structure built on the foundation of such ancestors.

Here, it is important to mention another person: Song Mong-gyu (1917–1945), who was born in the home of Yun Dong-ju three months before the poet's birth.

In the spring of 1916, Yun Yeong-seok's sister Shin-yeong (1897–1966) married Song Chang-hui, who taught the Korean language at Myeongdong School. They lived in the Yun house after marriage, and on September 28, 1917, their first child, Song Mong-gyu, was born. In three months' time, elder Yun Ha-hyeon had two grandsons, both of whom would grow up to be handsome and smart. As there had been no births for a long while in the Yun household, these were significant events for the family. When Song Mong-gyu was five, his family moved to their own house.

The two babies born in the house of Yun Ha-hyeon in 1917 maintained a very special relationship throughout their lives. Even identical twins could not have such connected lives. Besides being born in the same house, three months apart, they spent most of their school days together. They went to Japan together to study, were arrested and tried in the same city, and served a prison term in the same prison, during which they died within nineteen days of each other. Throughout their entire history, they shared life and death. Thus, Song Mong-gyu is a key figure in the study of Yun Dong-ju.

CHAPTER 2

Myeongdong

The Place of Freedom Fighters

GENERALLY, A TOWN is formed naturally, spontaneously. If its surroundings are beautiful, its water clear, and its terrain advantageous, houses can be built there, and a community can be born. However, this was not the case with Myeongdong, which was formed artificially. Its special characteristics originate in Manchuria's unique history.

A Korean Town in China Established in 1899

The Qing dynasty, established by the Manchu, ended the era of the Ming dynasty. Afterward, Manchuria became a special sacred district of inviolability. The Qing government regarded Manchuria as the birthplace of Qing's First Emperor and prohibited non-Manchus from entering the land.

Korea's Joseon dynasty had to adhere to the policy. Under its laws, crossing the Yalu or Tumen River to Manchuria constituted a serious crime punishable by death. The fallow land became fertile after hundreds of years of disuse. As the Qing dynasty began to decline, outsiders started moving in. By the 1880s, the Qing government had abolished the prohibition against entering Manchuria and even established policies for Manchurian pioneers.

Around the same time, the Joseon government also abolished the law against crossing the river. As the number of immigrants increased in Gando, Yi Beom-yun was appointed in July 1903 as overseer of Gando to govern and protect Koreans there.

Apart from Qing's establishment and history, North Gando had been an old territory of the Korean kingdoms of Goguryeo (37 B.C.–A.D. 668—Trans.) and Barhae (698–926—Trans.), which were home to many Koreans, as relics and artifacts from that area have shown. For example, in the fortress of Seongja (Chengzi—Trans.) Mountain, where the Haeran (Hailan—Trans.) River meets the Buerhatong River, they excavated red rectangular tiles with rectangular stripes from what had been Goguryeo, and tiles with finger designs from what had been Barhae, along with coins from the later Jin and Song dynasties of China. This tells us that the fortress was built during the reign of Goguryeo and was used for defense by Barhae and other Chinese dynasties.

The name "North Gando" reflects the peculiar history of the region, resulting from the Qing dynasty's prohibition on entering the land. When the crime of entering Manchuria was punishable by death, Koreans crossed the Tumen River by boat, using the excuse that they were going to a *gando*, or an "in-between island" (an island in the Tumen River). However, they secretly landed across the river in the fertile land of their ancestors. Drought and famine afflicted them continuously in the narrow and barren fields of northern Korea, but across the river, the land was so rich that it seemed to grow abundant crops with little work. They would set fire to the grassland to make the land tillable, and after seeds were sown, they would not even need to weed until harvest.

To them, "Gando" was a code word that referred to the continent across the river. At first, that is what they called the land north of the Tumen River; later on, north of the Yalu River was called "West Gando," and north of the Tumen River was called "North Gando." (Some used a different Chinese character—*gan*, "to cultivate"—when they recorded the name North Gando.)

Through the Ministry of Interior's Order No. 4, published by Secretary General Yi Dong-nyeong on December 23, 1919, the Provisional Government of the Republic of Korea in Shanghai confirmed these customary names used by laypeople as the official administrative names. Order No. 4 was a law that enacted the rules regarding the election of the Provisional Congress of the Republic of Korea. It set forth the number of representatives of the Congress from each electoral district, such as "three from West Gando, and three from North Gando."[1]

Myeongdong Village was established on February 18, 1899. On that day, 141 members of twenty-two households—all of them belonging to four clans led by scholarly leaders in the Hoeryeong and Jongseong areas near the Tumen River—left their homes and crossed the Tumen to settle in North Gando.

Three clans were from the city of Jongseong: forty members of the Nampyeong Mun clan, led by leader and scholar Mun Byeong-gyu; thirty-one members of the Jeonju Kim clan, led by Mencius scholar Kim Yak-yeon; and seven family members of Nam Do-cheon (born Nam Jong-gu), who was Kim Yak-yeon's teacher. In addition, sixty-three members of the Kimhae Kim clan, led by Kim Ha-gyu of Hoeryeong, joined the three clans. Kim Ha-gyu (Mrs. Kim Sin-muk's father) had read the *Book of Changes*, studied Sirhak, and participated in the Donghak Revolution of 1894.[2]

The newly established Myeongdong Village was an area that had previously belonged to Dong Han, a wealthy Qing landowner, but the families had sent a vanguard earlier to purchase the land.

When the families arrived, the land was distributed among them in proportion to the money each family had contributed. A notable thing, however, was that they set aside a piece of land as "education fields" before dividing it. The income from the land was to be used for schools.

Mun Byeong-gyu, Kim Yak-yeon, Nam Do-cheon, and Kim Ha-gyu were scholars who had private schools in their hometowns. After their immigration, Mun and Nam, who were past sixty, retired from teaching. Thirty-eight-year-old Kim Ha-gyu, thirty-two-year-old Kim Yak-yeon, and Nam's son Nam Wi-eon established three schools, like the legs of a tripod. With proceeds from the so-called education fields, they bought classical Chinese textbooks and taught children.

According to the testimony of the late Mun Jae-rin (1896–1985)—great-grandson of Mun Byeong-gyu and father of Reverend Mun Ik-hwan—these scholars had specific purposes for immigrating to North Gando. These were, as told to Mr. Mun by Mr. Kim Yak-yeon:

1) To sell the barren yet expensive fields of Joseon, purchase the fertile land in Gando, and become prosperous by farming it;
2) To make Gando our territory through mass immigration; and

3) To educate our young and produce talents so that we can save the
homeland from a declining fate.[3]

With such clear purposes, the first thing they did in the new place was to
dedicate a piece of land specifically for educational funds. Clearly, they were
forerunners and pioneers of the Korean nation. But did they achieve their
goals? Certainly. A well-meaning goal can be a victory in itself, and they prepared the ground that later bore the fruit.

First, they achieved prosperity.

As for the second goal, such an acquisition plan seemed a naïve desire when
seen from the geopolitical perspective of the cold international politics of the
time—almost fantastical, in fact. Yet they did not fail. Many Koreans who
shared the same thought created a Korea within the borders of China. And
this is neither a metaphorical expression nor merely a psychological concept.
As the governing body changed hands from Qing to the Republic of China to
the People's Republic of China in the span of over a hundred years, they stead-
fastly persisted in the land, resulting in the establishment of the Yanbian
Korean Autonomous Prefecture in China.

Regarding the third goal of producing talents, again, they accomplished
it. Aside from many notable Koreans from the region, Yun Dong-ju alone
proves it.

So let us now examine the geographical traits of Myeongdong and their
relationship to the Yun family.

When the Qing landowner Dong Han owned the land, it was called the
Dong Family Region or Pigeon Rocks. (By the town border toward Yongjeong
(Longjing—Trans.), three large boulders stood, roosted on by pigeons; Koreans later called them Monk's Coat Rocks.) When Koreans settled there, names
started changing, beginning with small village names, such as School Village,
Dragon Rock Village, Snake Village, Jangjae Village, Sunam Village, Seho Vil-
lage, and Joong'young Village. Later, the name Myeongdong Village included
the entire area of all these smaller villages.

The Yun family moved to Myeongdong in 1900, the year following the initial migration of the four clans. It is unclear why the family moved from
Jadong, where they had settled comfortably in 1886, to the newly established
Myeongdong. One likely possibility is that the Yuns had become close with
the residents of Myeongdong, who had evacuated to Jadong, which was very

close to the Tumen River, at the start of the Boxer Rebellion (1899–1901—Trans.). The Boxer Rebellion was a peasant militia uprising with an anti-foreign agenda that began in Shantung, which then spread to northern China and even to North Gando. There were three Catholic churches in North Gando, and they were all burned down by the hands of the Boxers. It is said that the Qing military, dressed in red uniforms, chased after them to Myeongdong, shooting rifles.

For whatever reason, the Yun family sold their assets in Jadong and moved to Myeongdong, where they were considered one of the most affluent families in town. The eighteen-member household included Yun Jae-ok and his wife, their four sons and daughters-in-law, and two other relatives.

In the personal history of Yun Dong-ju, the Yuns' move to Myeongdong was a momentous event, because ten years after, Yun Young-seok married Kim Yong from town, and Dong-ju was born several years later.

Kim Yong (1891–1947) was a stepsister of Kim Yak-yeon, who was one of the leaders of the original immigrants. Kim Yak-yeon's mother died when he was young, after which his father married a woman from a Shim family. The stepmother gave birth to four children, and Kim Yong was the only daughter. By the time of their immigration, the father had passed away, but Kim Yak-yeon crossed Tumen with the remaining family: his stepmother, his wife and two children, his three brothers, a sister-in-law, and Kim Yong, who was eight years old.

A daughter from a scholarly family, Kim Yong would come to be known as a ladylike and generous woman, and she and her father-in-law, Yun Ha-hyeon, were equally praised for their character. Kim Yong was also talented in sewing, and many of the brides in town would ask her to sew their bridal gowns for them. She did it not for the money but as a favor, because her sewing skills were coveted. Her only flaw was her frail health, which afflicted her throughout her life.

Characteristics of Early Myeongdong Culture

If "culture" can be defined as products of the inner minds of humans and phenomena that accompany them, Myeongdong had its own unique culture. With dramatic changes brought on by the passage of time, it underwent three conflicting periods. At first, Myeongdong was a town of pure Confucian traditions. The acceptance of Christianity in 1909 inaugurated the middle period. The final period began in 1929 with the emergence of communism.

In each period, not only the town's external culture but also the essence of the townsfolk's lives were transformed. These transformations were prompted by internal elements in the town as well as by the historical circumstances that created them. Spatially, Myeongdong residents were exiles in a foreign land who dreamed of the independence of their homeland, and the changes were prompted by their status as exiles.

During the first period of Myeongdong—that is, the ten years between 1899, the year of immigration, and 1909, the year of the conversion to — Christianity—three cultural characteristics reigned supreme: (1) Confucian traditions represented by ancestor worship and persistent status identity, (2) unique linguistic culture, and (3) educational fervor.

Examining the first characteristic, it is important to note that the central figures of the settlers were scholars; Myeongdong began as a community of thorough Confucian traditions. Shaman ceremonies were seldom seen there, and the most important event in each clan was *jesa*, an ancestor ritual. Demonstrating the community's heavy emphasis on *jesa*, testimony by Reverend Mun Ik-hwan states that before the family's conversion to Christianity, his great-grandmother—the eldest matriarch in the family—took painstakingly elaborate steps for the ritual. Grains were set aside at harvest, and sweet rice grains were carefully handpicked and spread on a clean sheet over a straw mat to dry. Afterward, the rice was put into a separate mortar to be pestled and made into rice cake. Cooked rice was also made from the choicest crops. While making the dishes, women washed their hands frequently in a basin of lye water they had prepared. All preparations were done with the utmost care and attention.

Such emphasis on the *jesa* ceremony and persistent status identity were two sides of the same coin, manifested in various ways. For instance, when the ceremony was given to a deceased family member on the anniversary date of death, there was a complex system of status distinction. *Jesa* of a deceased mother who had remarried was not observed. In the case of a deceased second wife, it was observed on her anniversary, along with her deceased husband, but she would not be included in the husband's on *his* anniversary. And this was on top of the regular ceremonies on holidays. Thus, if a man had married twice, his *jesa*, aside from the holiday ceremonies, would be on three dates: the day he died, the day his first wife died, and the day his second wife died. The first wife's *jesa* would be on two dates: the day she died and the day her husband died, whereas the second wife's would be only on the day she died. Indeed, it was complicated.

The distinction between legitimate and illegitimate children was also very strict, and the two were not allowed to stand side by side during the ceremony. "Illegitimacy," however, was a delicate matter. First, offsprings of concubines were naturally illegitimate. Second, offsprings of a widow who remarried were also regarded as illegitimate. Thus, when a widower married a virgin, their children were legitimate, but if he married a widow, their children were illegitimate. Such distinctions were well established in everyday life in Myeongdong. The town told a story of a young virgin who was arranged to be married to a man who was born of a remarried widow. She lamented, "I feel as if I am about to drink water out of the lid of a chamber pot."

These Confucian traditions would end abruptly in 1909, when the town accepted Christianity and the people's fundamental mind frame changed altogether.

The second and third characteristics—unique linguistic culture and educational fervor—are different from the first one in nature. These characteristics were handed down from residents' pre-immigration lives in Jongseong and Hoeryeong in Hamgyeong Province and consistently continued even after they became Christians. Thus, we will examine the Yukjin (Six Bases—Trans.) culture of Hamgyeong Province, in which these characteristics were rooted.

People from Hamgyeong Province were known to have strong and forceful temperaments. Perhaps this was due to the barren terrain and rough climate of the area. Nevertheless, King Taejo Yi Seong-gye (1335–1408—Trans.), the founder of the Joseon dynasty who had spent his childhood in Hamgyeong Province, is said to have pronounced, "Do not hire people from Gwanbuk because they are difficult to manage."

Calling Hamgyeong Province "Gwanbuk" ("north of a hill"—Trans.) originates from its being north of Cheollyeong-gwan. Cheollyeong is a soaring hill located between Anbyeon-gun, South Hamgyeong Province, and Hoeyang-gun, Kangwon Province. It appears in a *sijo* written by the great politician and wit Oseong Yi Hang-bok (1556–1618—Trans.) during the reign of King Seonjo: "Dear clouds who stop at the tall Cheollyeong to take a nap."

The fort built on Cheollyeong was Cheollyeong-gwan. Because of King Taejo's precepts, those from the north of Cheollyeong-gwan were kept out of high government positions.

In King Sejong's time, a new chapter was added to its history. General Kim Jong-seo (1383–1453—Trans.) reclaimed the North Hamgyeong Province, which had often been under attack by the Jurchens, and established Yukjin, or Six Bases (Gyeongwon, Gyeongheung, Puryeong, Onseong, Jongseong, and Hoeryeong). This became a turning point for the area. Even though General Kim Jong-seo's reclamation of the northern border was an outstanding achievement, problems arose after the establishment of Yukjin. For the bases to operate, they needed people to live and work there. No respectable citizen, however, was willing to leave his hometown and migrate to the border facing the Jurchens. Out of necessity, the government started sending convicts and the lowly caste to Yukjin. A great migration took place in exchange for a pardon.

A rise of status accompanied this geographic move. The life of a convict or slave was no ordinary life. Just by moving to a new place, however, they could simply throw off their heavy yoke and embrace an exceptional new opportunity.

People with such peculiar experiences formed a unique culture with their own singularities, chief among them their weaving. The hemp made in the region was called Yukjin *jangpo*. The dictionaries describe it as "excessively long hemp cloth from Yukjin in North Hamgyeong Province."[4] The word "excessive" hints superbly at the originality and uniqueness of Gwanbuk's Yukjin culture.

Another distinctive feature of Yukjin culture was its language. Until the end of the Joseon era, they maintained the phonetic sounds of King Sejong's time with little change in their everyday speech. This was probably because they lived in a closed society, not interacting with other parts of the country after their migration to Yukjin during Sejong's reign.

On this point, I had a very interesting conversation in 1985 with Reverend Han Jun-myeong (1907–1999—Trans.), Yun Dong-ju's teacher at Myeongdong Grade School and a former professor at Jungang Theological Seminary. Born in Daegu, North Kyeongsang Province, Han Jun-myeong had had a keen sense for languages from childhood and was fluent in seven languages, including Hebrew, Greek, English, and Japanese. His father,

Han Woo-seok, a doctor of Chinese medicine, had a brother who immigrated to Hawaii and worked for some time in San Francisco at a newspaper for Korean immigrants, *Sinhan Minbo*. In Hawaii, however, he suffered serious burns in a fire and subsequently contracted Hansen's disease. Dr. HanWoo-seok summoned his brother to come back to Korea to convalesce but then became concerned about contagion when his small children kept clinging to their uncle. After agonizing over it, he moved the family to Gyeongju and then permanently immigrated to faraway Manchuria in the spring of 1919.

The family first went to a place called Seojeon'gol near Namyangpyeong, then settled in Myeongdong in early September 1919. Han Jun-myeong, who was twelve years old at the time, was taught at Myeongdong Grade School by Yun Yeong-seok, Yun Dong-ju's father.

After arriving in Myeongdong, Han Jun-myeong was extraordinarily impressed by the very gentle sound of Korean that the residents spoke:

How mild, soft, and beautiful their spoken words were. I can scarcely describe it. It was a peripheral dialect mixed with old Korean. The pronunciations were so gentle. In southern parts of Korea, "horses ('mal'—Trans.) and cows ('so'—Trans.)" are referred to as "maso." Residents of Myeongdong used the extinct vowel sound between "a" and "eo." So they would say, "maushyo." They'd pronounce chan-song-ga (hymns—Trans.) "chanshyong-ga," too. Old Korean pronunciations. When Mr. Kim Yak-yeon asked his son, "Did you put horses and cows in the barn?" it came out like, "Ya, maushyo-reul yeo-eon-nya?" It was just so gentle and beautiful. Really beautiful.[5]

Reverend Han marveled that their etiquette and manners were second to none. Most Myeongdong residents were related to each other by marriage; when they greeted their in-laws in the streets, their polite words of respect were also extraordinary. He added, "Southern *yangban* cannot compete with their gentle, sincere ways of speech and manners. I suspect that Hoeryeong and Jongseong people are descendants of those who were exiled there during the Goryeo dynasty."[6] Reverend Han did not know the historical background of the Hoeryeong-Jongseong area and merely guessed that the vowels used in the Goryeo era were preserved there. Actually, when you read chapter 87 of *Yongbi-Eocheon-ga* (*Songs of Flying Dragons*—Trans.), published two years after the invention of the Korean alphabet during the reign of Sejong, you see the vowels described by Reverend Han:

> Sa-ho-naun han-shyo-raul du-son-ae ja-bau-si-myeo
> Dau-ri-ye peo-dil mau-raul neon-jeu-si chi-hyeo-si-ni
> [He grabbed a big struggling cow with his two hands
> Gently pulling a horse falling from the bridge.]

The first edition of Yun Dong-ju's posthumous poetry collection *Sky and Wind and Star and Poem*, published after liberation, contains a eulogy titled "Knock If You Are Outside the Window" by Yu Yeong, a friend from Yonhui College. A verse from it reads, "Your Yongjeong dialect, never harsh even in rough winds,"[7] which tells us that Yun Dong-ju's gentle pronunciations also left an impression on his friends.

People from Yukeup, which consisted of Musan, Hoeryeong, Jongseong, Onseong, Gyeongwon, and Gyeongheung, had different accents from those of seaside cities Gilju and Buryeong. Myeongdong people's keen sense of language can be glimpsed in the following conversation between Mrs. Kim Sin-muk and her son Reverend Mun Ik-hwan, who were from Yukeup.

> MUN: Anyway, when listening to you and father, I get the feeling that people from Yukeup looked down on those from the seaside towns like Saeup and Haejin.
> KIM: Haejin people would say, "beon-jin-da," and saying "ji" was looked down on.
> MUN: How did they say it in Yukeup?
> KIM: "Beon-din-da."[8]

When I asked Mrs. Kim what "beondinda" means, she said it means "to turn over." It is the same meaning, then, as "beon" (*dwiwihyeo*) in the first line of the famous Chinese poet Du Fu's poem in seven-syllable lines, "Friendship in Poverty." Korean pronunciation of the Chinese characters are "Beon-su-jak-un-bok-su-u," which *Dusi Onhae* translates as:

> Sonaul dwiwihyeo gureumeul jitgo sonaul eopdeorihyeo biraul haunani
> [They turn a hand up to make clouds and turn it over to make rain.][9]

"Dwiwihyeo" is "dwijibeo" in modern Korean. The "d" sound changes to the "j" sound in front of the vowel "i," which is one of the phenomena of palatalization. Because of more frequent contact with the outsiders than the inland, coastal towns accepted these phonological changes more readily.

Another example of palatalization is the word for sunrise. It is written as "haedo*di*" but pronounced as "haedo*ji*." Such a phonological phenomenon would be looked down on by Myeongdong residents should they hear it now. Yun's being born in a place with heightened linguistic senses must have affected the formation of his linguistic sensibility as a poet.

Let us now examine the third cultural characteristic, educational fervor.

The fervor for academic reverence was not exclusive to Yukjin; the whole of Hamgyeong Province shared it. It was not just about moving upward by passing the *gwageo* exam, the yearly civil examination for government jobs. Learning was considered a basic human condition. This, in fact, was a fierce rebuttal to the mainstream *yangban* culture that focused on learning to pass the *gwageo* exam to obtain a high government position with power.

Baekbeom Kim Gu visited Hamgyeong Province in 1895.[10] He later wrote in his *Baekbeom Diary* about the educational fervor he found in the area:

> More than anything, I marveled at the education system in Hamgyeong Province, which was superior to Hwanghae Province and Pyeongan Province. Even in indigent villages filled with thatch-roofed houses, libraries and schools were tile-roofed. I saw in Heungwon area that a *seodang* had three teachers, each teaching elementary, middle, or high-level classes. For an old-fashioned *seodang*, it was a rarity. A drum and a bell were at each end of the *seodang*'s hall. When the drum was beaten, students started reading, and when the bell was rung, they rested. Bukcheong, in particular, is famous for its reverence for knowledge, even in Hamgyeong Province. When I passed it by, there were over 30 living *jinsa* [those who passed the first-level state examination—Trans.] and seven government officials who had passed the higher-level examination. Truly, a place of intellects, I exclaimed.[11]

This unique trait characterizes the people of Hamgyeong Province. One might say that they chose "pure" academic paths because they had little chance of obtaining power in government. Considering their peripheral societal situation, Reverend Han Jun-myeong admired their high manners and etiquette. Perhaps these are by-products of their academic training, which was pursued even in the absence of practical gain.

Myeongdong Village Adopts Western Education and Christianity

The first Western educational institution in North Gando was Seojeon Seosuk, established in October 1906 in Yongjeong (Longjing—Trans.). The former Prime Minister Yi Sang-seol, accompanied by Yi Dong-nyeong, Yi Jun, Jeong Sun-man, and Pak Jeong-seo, had gone to Yongjeong and established the school in the biggest house there—that of Choi Byeong-ik, the Catholic church leader. Catholics in North Gando had received large sums of money from the Qing government as compensation for damages caused by the Boxer Revolution of 1900, and they had each bought a large parcel of land and built a large home.

Yi Sang-seol used his private means to pay for the school's expenses, paying out of pocket the teachers' salaries, books, and even stationery items. He enforced a thorough nationalistic, anti-Japanese education, offering classes in arithmetic, history, geography, international public law, constitutional law, and Chinese characters. There were over seventy students, among whom were Kim Hak-yeon and Nam Wi-eon from Myeongdong. The following year, however, Yi was selected as King Gojong's secret envoy to the Hague Conference on World Peace in the Netherlands. This was a big blow to the operation of the school. Only a few months after Yi's departure in April 1907, Seojeon Seosuk closed its doors.

Around the same time, Myeongdong residents showed a great enthusiasm for Western education. Concerning its background, one episode particularly stands out: Kim Ha-gyu, one of the major leaders of Myeongdong immigration, had a relative named Kim Do-shim. When an endemic broke out in Hamgyeong Province in the spring of 1907, Kim Do-shim and his fourteen-year-old son became sick. When they were on the brink of death, Kim's wife bled her fingers and cut out meat from her thigh to revive them. She died shortly thereafter, while Kim and his son returned to health. Kim Do-shim was determined to convince the government to bestow "virtuous ladyship" upon his late wife. He asked Kim Ha-gyu to write the letter and walked 1,000 *ri* to Seoul, carrying the letter to the Department of Treasury. His request was granted. However, the officials noticed that the writing was that of a great scholar and sent Kim Do-shim back with a letter appointing "the scholar Kim Ha-gyu as the 'President of North Hamgyeong Educational Promotion Society.'" The appointment was accompanied by an order: "Start a new Western education, as the old knowledge is now useless." According to the testimony of Kim Shin-muk, Kim Ha-gyu's daughter, the order arrived with "a great bundle filled with notices and rules on scrolls of white paper and things like that," and that was the first time she had ever seen white wood-pulp paper. It was the summer of 1907 when Kim Do-shim arrived in Myeongdong. Hearing the news, people gathered at the Kims' house. With the doors wide open because of the hot weather, they read what was sent from Seoul and sent the message out in all directions.[12]

What does this episode mean?

In 1905, the Korean Empire was forced to sign the shameful Eulsa Treaty (or Japan-Korea Protectorate Treaty—Trans.) with Japan. Not only the Korean government but also common people in North Gando were aware of the mighty power of Japan. Only with this fact as a premise can the nature of this episode be understood clearly.

North Gando Koreans were eyewitnesses to the power of Japan that won the Sino-Japanese War (1894–1895) and the Russo-Japanese War (1904–1905). To their minds, the only difference between the Japanese then—whom they used to call "savage little islanders"—and the Japanese now was their acceptance and learning of Western culture and civilization. Indeed, the shock received from the Eulsa Treaty forced upon them by the might of Japan had been tremendous. That is why the Myeongdong leaders, hard-core Confucians as they were, accepted without objection the Korean government's order on the white wood-pulp paper to "start a new Western education." They simply set aside Confucian studies, to which their whole lives had been devoted, into the category of "old studies" and opened their minds wholeheartedly to the unknown "new studies."

After Seojeon Seosuk in Yongjeong closed down, Myeongdong leaders launched into action. They merged their three Confucian schools into a new Western educational institution called Myeongdong Seosuk. Pak Mu-rim (born Pak Jeong-seo), a former Seojeon Seosuk teacher, was invited to become the first principal of the school. Kim Yak-yeon in Myeongdong Village took the position of vice principal. After a while, the school's name was changed from Myeongdong Seosuk to Myeongdong School to give it a modern feel. It officially opened on April 27, 1908. On that date every year, various events, including sports competitions, were held to celebrate it.

No source clearly points to the origin of the name Myeongdong when the Myeongdong Confucian scholars established the new Western educational institution. Seojeon Seosuk in Yongjeong came from Seojeon Fields, the name for Yongjeong and its surrounding region. But in the case of Myeong-dong Seosuk, the school's name came first; Myeongdong Village was named after its school.

Myeongdong appears to originate from the first line of *Great Learning* (one of the *Four Books*, along with *Analects*, *Mencius*, and *Doctrine of the Mean*): "Daehak-ji-do jaemyeong myeongdeok." I suspect that the verb "myeong" (illuminate) was taken from this line, which means "The way of great learning is in illuminating shining virtue," while "dong" is from Korea's byname, Dongguk (Eastern Country).

From long ago, the sobriquet Dongguk had been used frequently because Korea was a country east of China. The name had the convenience of dia-chronic acceptance because it was based on the country's geographic condi-tions rather than periodic conditions and categories, as were the names of kingdoms such as Goguryeo, Shilla, Baekje, Goryeo, and Joseon. Thus, the word "Dongguk" is found in many titles about subject matters distinctive to Korea: *The Bibliographical References of Dongguk* (King Yeongjo, Joseon), *The History of Wars of Dongguk* (King Munjong, Joseon), *The Abbreviated History of Dongguk* (King Taejong, Joseon), *The Atlas of Dongguk* (King Seongjong, Joseon), *The Collected Writings of Yi Sang-guk* [Yi Gyu-bo—Trans.] *of Dong-guk* (King Gojong, Goryeo), *The Standard Phonology of Dongguk* (King Sejong, Joseon), *The Geography of Dongguk* (King Seonjo, Joseon), *The Chronological History of Dongguk* (King Seongjong, Joseon), and so on. Coins circulated during the Goryeo dynasty also bore names like Dongguk Jungbo and Dong-guk Tongbo.

If this presumption is correct, Myeongdong, as the name of an educational institution of Western knowledge, contains the meaning "nurturing the tal-ents who would illuminate Korea." When interpreted in accordance with the first line of *Great Learning*, the name means "The way of Western learning is in illuminating Korea."

A point should be made here. Yun Il-ju, the poet's younger brother, pre-sumed that the character "dong" in "Dong-ju," the name given by their father, came from Myeongdong.[13]

This presumption seems incorrect because the character "dong" probably originates from the *Book of Changes*. "Dong" refers to *jin'gwae*, one of the eight trigrams in the *Book of Changes*, and "jin" means "firstborn male." Thus, in royal families, the term for crowned princes was "Donggung." Because Yun Dong-ju was the firstborn son of the Yun family, the character "dong" was used, followed by "ju," their *hangnyeol* character.[14]

When Myeongdong Seosuk opened, its maintenance was to come from the educational land that had been set aside during the land distribution at the time of immigration. It was a small-scale start with the purchase of an eight-room house. Two of the rooms were opened up to make a staff office, and the other rooms were used as classrooms.

Under the principal Pak Mu-rim, Kim Yak-yeon was appointed vice principal and Mun Chi-jeong the finance director. Kim Hak-yeon and Nam Wi-eon, who had received a Western education at Seojeon Seosuk, were employed as teachers. However, their training at Seojeon Seosuk had lasted less than a year. The school needed to quickly acquire qualified teachers. Notices were sent everywhere to find teachers of Western education but to no avail. At one point a man named Go Yeong-bal came to the school, claiming to be such a teacher, but was quickly chased away after his ignorance was exposed.

In 1909, however, with the hiring of a twenty-five-year-old teacher by the name of Jeong Jae-myeon (a.k.a. Jeong Byeong-tae, 1884–1962), the school finally got on the right track.

The father of Reverend Dr. Jeong Dae-wi (1917–2003—Trans.), the former president of Kunkuk University and of Hanshin University, Jeong was a fervent Christian and patriot from Sukcheon, South Pyeong'an Province. He had studied at a Christian Western educational institution called Cheongnyeon Hakgwan in Seoul and had also joined Shinminhoe (New People's Association—Trans.), a clandestine patriotic organization led by Yi Dong-hwi, An Chang-ho, Yang Gi-tak, Kim Gu, and Jeon Deok-gi.

After his training in Seoul, Jeong taught at Bogwang School in Wonsan. Shinminhoe, however, advised that Jeong reconstruct the educational work in North Gando started by Yi Sang-seol. Jeong took the advice, resigned from the Bogwang post, and moved to North Gando.

Jeong first went to Yongjeong to restart Seojeon Seosuk. Under disadvantageous circumstances, however, including the presence of and pressure from the Gando Police Office in Yongjeong, overseen by the Japanese Resident-General of Korea, the work did not go as planned. Thus, he turned his eyes on Myeongdong School, built spontaneously by the villagers to start a Western education.

The Confucian scholars in Myeongdong welcomed Jeong heartily, as he seemed to be true to the name of a Western education teacher, and vigorously requested that Jeong start teaching there. Jeong had one precondition to his acceptance that Bible studies be a required class for students, and the students attend Christian worship.

This was a revolutionary request in the town of traditional Confucian scholars. The leading Confucian scholars of Myeongdong Village gathered to discuss the issue. After a few days of discussion, they decided that a true Western education teacher must be procured even with that condition. Here, one can feel the intensity of their fervor for Western education.

As soon as Myeongdong Village accepted his request, Jeong began his employment. This is how Western education and Christianity took off together in Myeongdong Village.

Around that time, Shinminhoe was working on the nationalistic education of North Gando Koreans, secretly forming the North Gando Education Corps. Jeong was the corps' leader and field officer, and Yi Dong-hwi and Yi Dong-nyeong were its consultants. Corps members' living expenses were funded by a designated financial officer, who donated from his private means. That financial officer was Yu Heung-won, whose son was Yu Il-han of Yuhan Co. Ltd.[15] Yu Heung-won faithfully carried out his responsibility to the end of his life.

The relationship between Shinminhoe and Myeongdong School has not been thoroughly evaluated, as academic research on Shinminhoe's activities is insufficient. However, North Gando's Myeongdong School is representative of the schools that were operated under the philosophy and influence of Shinminhoe, such as Osan School of Jeongju, Daeseong School of Pyeong-yang, Bochang Schools (under the management of Yi Dong-hwi), and Shin-heung School of West Gando.

After Jeong Jae-myeon's appointment in 1909, the school was newly organized. Pak Mu-rim retired from the position of principal. Kim Yak-yeon succeeded as principal, and Jeong became the vice principal. Jeong's contribution was remarkable. He brought in a group of outstanding teachers, including such luminaries as the historian Hwang Ui-don, whose daughter became the first female judge in Korea; the Korean language scholar Jang Ji-yeong; Pak Tae-hwan, who wrote the introduction to Ju Shi-gyeong's seminal grammar book *Urimalbon*; and Waseda University–trained jurist Kim

Cheol, all of whom were spirited independence activists. The middle school curriculum was created in 1910. Students came from all directions. When the teachers and students heard the news of Korea's demise after the Japan-Korea Annexation Treaty on August 29, 1910, they gathered at the school and cried out loud. The scene of historian Hwang's wailing and lamenting was engraved in people's memory.

Myeongdong School's education of women was truly ahead of its time. Yi Dong-hwi visited Myeongdong in March 1911 for a Christian revival assembly, and a girls' school started that spring. Teachers at the boys' school also taught girls. Soon, Jeong Jae-myeon's sister Jeong Shin-tae and Yi Dong-hwi's daughter Yi Ui-sun came to the school to teach girls. Jeong Shin-tae taught the Bible, and Yi Ui-sun taught music, sewing, and science. Like her father, who supported women's rights, Yi Ui-sun emphasized the need for women's education and women's contribution to society.

The Christian Culture of Myeongdong

How almost all of Myeongdong residents became Christians makes a fascinating story. The sole credit for this win goes to Jeong Jae-myeon's commitment and strategy.

At first, Jeong's Bible lessons and worship services were only for the students. According to Reverend Mun Jae-rin, who was Jeong's student then, the students would break out in laughter when they heard "Amen" in prayers because it sounded to them like "eum-mae" (cows' mooing—Trans.). After school, the children would mimic the novel worship ceremony among themselves, letting the adults at home guess how these *yesu jaengi* (Jesus-mongers—Trans.) worshiped their god.

After a while, with a complete understanding of the risk involved, Jeong proposed new terms, stating that he'd leave Myeongdong unless all adults attend the worship together. He probably felt that he had already won their hearts with his merit and character. The residents were greatly disconcerted when Jeong seemed ready to pack up and leave. Again, after a few days of discussion, a quiet revolution took place. To keep Jeong, the villagers decided to convert to Christianity.

Thus, sometime in May or June 1909, a Christian church was established in Myeongdong Village. The renowned Confucian scholars of Myeongdong took their families to church to worship, learning the Bible from the youthful teacher. An eight-room house was purchased as the church building. In those days, unrelated men and women were strictly separated, with the men's and women's seats separated in an L shape, where they could not see each other. Jeong stood in the middle and led the service.

One question to consider here is, Did Myeongdong residents convert to Christianity only to keep the Western education teacher there? In order to answer, we need to examine the history of North Gando Korean society to which Myeongdong belonged.

Currently, a kind of fantastic image of North Gando as the land of freedom fighters is the general public perception. But this is far from the real history of North Gando. Looking into North Gando Korean society up to the point of 1909, when Myeongdong's Christian culture began, we can categorize it into four periods:[16]

1. Qing government's rule and tyranny (from the beginning of immigration to 1903)
2. Protection of immigrants by Gando Governor Yi Beom-yun (1903–1905)
3. Qing's rule again (1905–1907)
4. Infiltration of Japanese power through the installation of the Japanese resident-general's Gando Police Office: Qing's administrative system *hyangyak* and Japan's counterpart *sajang* coexisted, fiercely opposing each other over the administration of Koreans in Gando (1907–1909)

From the outset of their immigration history, North Gando Koreans were subject to the tyranny of Qing officials and landlords. They were coerced to change their hair and attire to the Manchu way and suffered disadvantages and undue pressure as tenant farmers. The despotism of Chinese translators, empowered by their Qing employers, was tremendous. As for Myeongdong, however, the group of immigrants had paid the Qing landowner the purchase price of the land before moving in, and they did not suffer as much. Yet they were not exempt from it. Even Myeongdong could not avoid incidents like the case of Kim Byeong-wae, who had tried to swindle a resident in a land sale. Outraged, Kim Ha-gyu and his relative Kim Seon-cheon denounced Kim Byeong-wae, who was eventually sentenced to a prison term. After serving the term, however, Kim Byeong-wae gave away his daughter to a Qing, and with his newly endowed power, schemed an act of revenge against Kim Ha-gyu and his relatives. In the end, they suffered imprisonment before they were released.

The first time North Gando Koreans felt at ease was when the pro-Russian Gando Governor Yi Beom-yun resided there, making his influence felt. But it was only a temporary arrangement when the Russian force occupied three eastern districts east of Shanghai Pass: Fengtian Sheng, Jilin Sheng, and Heilongjiang Sheng. European and American world powers dispatched troops to the Qing when the Boxer Rebellion of 1900 inflicted damages on them. Russia did not miss the opportunity either. Under the pretense of protecting the construction of the Chinese Eastern Railway (connecting Heilongjiang to Jilin to Vlodivostok), Russia executed a large-scale dispatch and took over the three eastern districts. By April 1903, it had advanced all the way down to Yongam Port, by the lower Yalu River in Korea. However, Japan likewise harbored an ambition to enlarge its territory there. The two countries' collision resulted in the Russo-Japanese War, which broke out in February 1904. The following year, Russia, now defeated, retreated from Manchuria. Yi Beom-yun could no longer protect Koreans in North Gando. In fact, he could not even safely stay there, so he left for Siberia.

These were the circumstances to which Myeongdong Village was exposed. Mrs. Kim Shin-muk vividly remembered seeing "Russian soldiers suddenly entering" her yard where she and other members of the family were threshing crops in the autumn of 1904.[17]

Under such circumstances, dramatic incidents would openly take place. For example, Kim Seon-cheon, who was related to Kim Ha-gyu, was a soldier in Yi Beom-yun's troop. After Yi's troop was disbanded, Kim Seon-cheon, who had not yet fled, was arrested by Qing officers and sentenced to death. They put him on a cart and took it to the fields toward a scaffold, singing. They were going to tie him up there and behead him. Suddenly, a whirlwind hit the scaffold, knocking it down. They raised it, but another whirlwind knocked it down again. Seeing that, they stopped the execution, fearing that the gods were sending a message not to kill this man. Afterward, they demanded fines for Kim Seon-cheon's life. His eight cousins, including Kim Ha-gyu, sold fields and cows and whatever else they could to pay them. Kim Seon-cheon was released after a severe flogging, and he left for Siberia when he had recovered. These were the events that Myeongdong residents had experienced firsthand only twelve years before Yun Dong-ju was born.

In 1907, the Japanese entered North Gando, establishing the Gando Police Office of the Resident-General of Korea, further complicating the situation. Koreans were now stuck between Qing and Japan. Qing, with the *hyangyak* local administrative system, and Japan, with the *sajang* administrative system, existed side by side, each claiming the right to manage Koreans' lives.

This was the situation when Jeong Jae-myeon demanded that Myeongdong residents accept Christianity, and it seems likely that they would have considered the advantage of securing the political asylum guaranteed by Christianity.

Christianity, which had advanced to the Chinese continent, was not only a religion but also an empire without walls, like an organism. And it was the kind of organism whose injury would bring unfailing and prompt retribution to its perpetrator. Wherever a Western missionary was murdered, his motherland dispatched troops to the place.

In November 1897, the murder of two German priests in Juye, Shandong Province, led to the German troops' Jiaozhou Bay landing. The Boxer Rebellion of 1900, which significantly harmed the Catholics in China, resulted in the dispatch of imperial troops from America, England, Japan, Germany, France, Italy, and Austria, and subsequently the siege of Beijing. The Qing government had to give in to the demands of the European and American powers and could barely appease them by compensating for the damages not only to the Western and Chinese Catholics but also to North Gando Koreans.

In the end, religion had become a bridgehead for imperial invasion. However, that was from Qing's point of view. For Koreans in Gando who suffered from the Qing's oppression and tyranny, that side of Christianity could function as their faithful protector and refuge. Under the terrifying talons of the Japanese invasion, their motherland was a candle in the wind, but they were even worse off in Gando, with no sovereign power to protect them. They had nowhere to turn to, and it was enticing that, simply by converting to Christianity, the powerful European and American countries would take the role of guardians.

How great was European and American power? Even the ferocious Japan could not overwhelm it, as they witnessed in the Sino-Japanese War that had taken place before their eyes. As a result of its victory, after shedding countless people's blood, Japan was given the Liaodong Peninsula. Yet when Germany, France, and Russia became involved and demanded the land, Japan quietly gave it back. In view of the fact that North Gando Koreans were suffering in between the powers of Qing and Japan, their relationship with Christianity can be explained by the saying "The enemy of my enemy is my friend."

Without examining the time period and the geopolitical background, the myth that the dignified Confucian scholars of Myeongdong rushed to convert to Christianity only because of the young Western education teacher's threat of leaving the school sounds like a frivolous comedy.

At the same time, the situation kept changing, as can be seen in the following series of events:

September 1909: Gando Treaty between Qing and Japan
October 1909: Patriotic martyr An Jung-geun's assassination of Ito Hirobumi
August 1910: Japan's annexation of Korea
October 1911: Xinhai Revolution (Chinese Revolution—Trans.)
January 1912: Establishment of the Republic of China
February 1912: The fall of the Qing dynasty
March 1912: Inauguration of Provisional President Yuan Shikai

In the whirlwind of violent upheavals, Myeongdong embraced Western education and Christianity, progressing continuously. A rural farming movement, which conformed to Shinminhoe's philosophy and was led by Jeong, transformed the village. Myeongdong School also changed. Students came from all directions to the school and were taught by excellent teachers. Besides North Gando students, Koreans sent their children from Korea and Siberia.

Myeongdong became one of the most famous places in North Gando, and the social status of Kim Yak-yeon, as the school's principal, also rose in North Gando society. It was as if the sun were rising, breaking through the darkness.

North Gando Korean society had a groundbreaking event in 1912, only five years before Yun was born. Ganminhoe, a Korean autonomous governing body, was formed for the first time in the history of North Gando immigrants.

This was made possible when a group of representatives was sent to see Provisional President Yuan Shikai (1859–1916—Trans.), who held the real power in the newly formed Republic of China. After negotiating the terms, Yuan gave permission. Kim Yak-yeon was elected as the president of Ganminhoe, which meant that he was the top leader of ethnic Koreans, who made up 70–80 percent of the North Gando population. Kim Yak-yeon was soon nicknamed "the President of East Manchuria." However, Ganminhoe was disbanded by the Chinese government in 1914 when it gave in to the pressures of Japan; the good times lasted for too short a period.

Among the numerous changes Christianity brought about in Myeongdong, external improvements were significant. More important, however, was the fundamental shift in people's mindset. This change, triggered by the fact that they had accepted the Christian perspective on human equality, resulted in their doing away with status consciousness. Following the Christian doctrines, they also abolished *jesa*. When compared with the previous cultural climate of the Confucian traditions, this was revolutionary.

Breaking away from status consciousness was most clearly shown when they started giving proper names to women. Girls would typically be called by childhood names, like Gomannye, Gaettongnye, or Gopdani.[18] After marriage, they were called by their hometown names, such as Hoeryeong-daek (wife from Hoeryeong—Trans.), Jongseong-daek, and Sadong-daek. After their conversion to Christianity, however, they started giving proper names in Chinese characters to daughters, as they had been doing for sons. Moreover, many girls' names began with the Chinese character *shin*, which means "faith."

During our interview, Mrs. Kim Shin-muk immediately recited over fifty names of women she knew whose names began with Shin: Ju Shin-deok, Kim Shin-jeong, Kim Shin-u, Mun Shin-gil, Yun Shin-yeong, Yun Shin-jin, Yun Shin-hyeon, Kim Shin-hui, Han Shin-hwan, Han Shin-ae, Nam Shin-hyeon, Nam Shin-hak, and so on.[19] These women were all born around the same period.

What this meant was that Myeongdong residents declared that women and men were all brethren of equal position in their faith, breaking down the walls among them of family background, pedigree, age, and intimacy. In addition, women having the same kind of names as men was a realization of gender equality.

The Christian doctrine that "all human beings are equal as the children of God" was explicitly realized in Myeongdong residents' daily lives, which exemplifies the core of Myeongdong's Christian culture.

"Our family moved to Myeongdong in late August of 1919," stated Reverend Han Jun-myeong. His testimony shows what Myeongdong's Christian culture at its peak looked like to those from elsewhere: "We found a nice community when we got there. The church and the school were large, the roads were wide and straight, and there was a cooperative, too. . . . Even then, most houses had a sewing machine. On Sundays, the church would be packed with over two hundred people. They were all into their children's education."[20]

During this period, Myeongdong was also famous as a base for the independence movement in the entire North Gando area. After twenty years of this period, Myeongdong Village's period of communist infiltration would begin.

Yun Dong-ju at Myeongdong Grade School

It was in this period of independence that Yun Dong-ju was born and raised. His parents became Christians before his birth, and he was brought up as a Christian. He received infant baptism and was recorded as a member of the church.

At age eight, Yun started Myeongdong Grade School. The poet Kim Jeong-u, Yun's schoolmate, remembered Yun when they were first graders: "When we were in Korean class together in first grade, the Korean textbook was mimeographed, called *Spurting Spring.* I still remember vividly, he'd recite with a clear, ringing voice, bobbing his head, 'Add a "giyeok" to "ga" to make "gak" and add a "nieun" to "ga" to make "gan,"' as if reciting *The Thousand Character Classic.*"[21]

Since its establishment, there were many significant events at Myeongdong School. First was its physical improvement. A new Western-style brick building replaced the old one in 1918. Next, the school produced a great many talents dedicated to the Korean independence movement. In fact, Principal Kim Yak-yeon himself was one of the leaders.

After Ganminhoe was disbanded in 1914, the spirit of Korean society and its independence movement took a downturn for a while. After the end of World War I, however, it was set ablaze again. Especially for a year and a half, from the March First Movement in 1919 to the Battle of Bong'o-dong in June 1920 to the Battle of Cheongsan-ri in October 1920, when a large number of Japanese troops were dispatched to Manchuria, North Gando was the place for freedom fighters. In these exploits, Myeongdong School graduates played a remarkable part. Consequently, the Japanese army took revenge on its quest for the so-called Great Gando Liquidation. On October 20, 1920, the Japanese military set fire to Myeongdong School, reducing it to ashes. This was a day before the Battle of Cheongsan-ri began. Japan's very first reprisal against Koreans in Gando was to burn down the school, evidence of the Japanese hatred of Myeongdong School as the lair of *futeisenjin* (delinquent Joseon people—Trans.).

Nevertheless, the Japanese army in Myeondong could not rampage as they wished. They only burned down the school and an adjacent empty house belonging to Ma Jin (a famous freedom fighter) before they left. No one was killed. This was the first of a series of events called the Gyeongshin Massacre, Japan's horrific retaliation against Korean civilians. So why was no one in Myeongdong Village killed or even beaten by the Japanese army? This was because Myeongdong was a Christian community that had a large-scale church and a Christian school. The Japanese, in their own terms, were being cautious about potential troubles with Western powerhouses.

One episode connected to this explains the thought process. On their way to burn Myeongdong School, the Japanese army encountered Philippe Perris, a French Catholic priest, near Myeongdong. The army asked him to write an affidavit stating that he was not affiliated with Myeongdong School. In addition, only after making sure that the school had no affiliation with either Americans or the English did the army go on to burn the school down. As Myeongdong School was Presbyterian, it had no affiliation with the Catholic missionary. The affidavit written in English by the French missionary remains in the Japanese records.[22] It reads as follows:

> Myodo school has no relation to me.
> Philippe Perris
> Missionnaire Apostolique

In 1922, the school was restored to its original form with the damages paid by the Japanese government. After 1920, however, Myeongdong School's glorious reputation began to wane. This was because Yongjeong, a transport hub, became the center of North Gando's Western education after the Canadian missionaries set up mission schools: Eunjin Middle School and Myeongshin Girls School. Yongjeong also had Yeongshin School, Dongheung School, and Daeseong School, which predated the new mission schools. Students now went to Yongjeong instead of Myeongdong.

The fall of Myeongdong School, which had once been the training school for freedom fighters, is partly due to its location in a remote area. Moreover, the spirit of the independence movement in the whole of North Gando was dampened after Japan's retaliation and massacre there in 1920. Many freedom fighters and those involved in the independence movement fled North Gando, exiling to Siberia or mainland China.

To make matters worse, the infamous draught during the Year of the First Rat (Kapjanyeon) caused a poor harvest in 1924, and the school faced serious financial difficulties. Consequently, in 1925, the year Yun Dong-ju entered Myeongdong Grade School, the middle school closed its doors and only the grade school remained, attended by children from Myeongdong. Some records about Yun Dong-ju state that "Myeongdong Middle School was forcefully shut down by the Japanese," but this statement is incorrect.

Time spent in Myeongdong Village and Myeongdong Grade School carries a significant meaning in Yun's life. He spent fourteen years there, more than half of his short life of twenty-seven years. Moreover, his character and poetic sensibilities were formed there.

In Yun's life, no other days were as beautiful and abundant as the days spent in Myeongdong in all aspects, including the natural and residential environments and even in political situations. We shall first survey the natural environment of Myeongdong and look into his grade school years.

The surrounding nature of Myeongdong is described well by the poet Kim Jeong-u, Yun's classmate and cousin:

I shall explain what Myeongdong's natural scenery was like. It was a large, but cozy village surrounded on all sides by mountains. A gentle crescent-shaped hill screened behind the village to its east, north, and west. To the north-west, three brotherly rocks called Monk's Robe Rocks stood high, shutting out northwestern winds and forming a magnificent view. Behind them was a mountain fortress that was thought to be a battleground for our ancestors, where artifacts like old arrows were discovered from time to time. The area surrounding the three brother rocks was also Myeongdong residents' park. Changbai Mountains, which sprouted from the east, formed a vein towards the southwest, with Wufeng Mountain and sharp peaks called Spoke Rocks as a starting point. Those high mountains and steep peaks sprawled in the front of the village, scraping along Monk's Robe Rocks.

When spring came, the hills of the village would be filled with azaleas, wild apricot blossoms, mountain cherry blossoms, peonies, trumpet lilies, pasque flowers, and few-flower coneheads. In the willow forest stream by the riverbank, catkins were in full bloom. The village was a paradise covered in flowers and fragrance. Summertime was covered in pastoral green, and autumn was rapturous with the reds and golds of the foliage from the hills and fields far and near, along with the golden fields of ripened grain.

Winter scenery was even more impressive. Thin limbs of bare trees from the hills and fields would wail as winter winds blew over them, and on snowy nights of glittering silver, jade-hued icy streams meandered, receding into the valley by the Monk's Robe Rocks. They were indeed exquisite views. On days of heavy snowstorms, herds of roe deer and wild boars would descend into town looking for food. On such days, the entire village would turn into a scene of wild excitement. Winter in Myeongdong Village was made up of unforgettable memories of spinning birch tops, sledding, skating, and following around pheasant hunters with falcons. . . .

Dong-ju's house belonged to the school village, and his family was on the affluent side. Only a few households farmed rice in that big village, and his was one of them.

His house was the first one at the mouth of the school village. By the foot of hills thickly wooded with oak trees stood the church building and two houses, and his house was the front one. His house, facing south, was a sizable tile-roofed house. To its left and right and behind it was a not-so-big orchard. Through the back door, a well could be reached. The well, deeper than a hundred feet, was famous for its refreshing water. His poem "Self Portrait" may have been inspired by this well. Dong-ju and I used to pick and eat the berries from mulberry trees that fenced the orchard, draw water from the well to wipe our mouths and shout into the well to hear the echoes.

Toward the main street, out of the big front gate of the house, he would have always seen the rays of the sun that had risen over the Dog Rock and followed him shine behind the cross on the church steeple above the thick oak forest. The cross must have penetrated his heart, just as the nails pierced Jesus on the cross. Together we went to Sunday school and on Christmas Eve, gathered at his house, for it was near the church, and stayed up all night to practice carols and make confetti. Thinking about those times of caroling while walking on the snowy roads, clad in layers of warm clothes and bucket hats and dog-hide oversocks, I feel infinitely happy even now. "The rays of the sun chasing me / Are hanging on the cross / On top of the church // The steeple is so tall, / How did they climb so high?" Whenever I read "The Cross," I remember the beautiful, picturesque scenery around the church behind Dong-ju's house and our childhood memories associated with the church.[23]

Kim's writing beautifully describes the surroundings of the olden days of Myeongdong as a painter paints on a canvas.

It is curious to wonder what Yun was like as a young student, growing up in such surroundings. When asked about Yun's grade school memories, Reverend Han Jun-myeong, Yun's fourth grade teacher, chuckled quietly and said:

Dong-ju was very mild-tempered. He was so gentle. He'd break into tears frequently. . . . If someone scolded him a bit, tears would well up in his eyes. When some friends said mean things, too . . . Ha, ha. He was talented. His marks were pretty good, too. But whenever he couldn't answer a question, tears would well up. Song Mong-gyu, who was then called Han-beom, was well-spoken and full of surprises. The two always sat together at the same desk. Mun Ik-hwan was the best-looking kid. . . . Dong-ju's grandfather was the wealthiest man in town. He had a lot of fields. He always kept a horse in the house and rode it on outings. Even sent his son to study in Tokyo.[24]

Yun's childhood image in Reverend Han's memory is clear: the heir apparent of a rich old man who rode a horse, a tenderhearted boy, gentle and smart.

Let us further examine Myeongdong Grade School, attended by Yun. First, the school's song should be mentioned. Here are the lyrics (transcribed from Mrs. Kim Shin-muk, class of 1914):

The White Mountain aloft, and the blessings abundant
In the Land of Hanbae-geom
The grand visions and seeds planted by him
I will raise them and grow at my Myeongdong[25]

The words have firm, determined meanings. The song resolutely claims sovereign power over the land, insisting that the land belongs to Korea's ancestors and that their descendants carry on the vision. During my interview with Mrs. Kim, she said: "The school song had four verses, but now I only remember the first verse. The tune was borrowed from the hymn, 'God Is Our Refuge Strong,' you know? That's it. To the music of the hymn, we sang our school song." Mrs. Kim then sang the hymn for me, which she said was often sung in Myeongdong. I knew the hymn, and while I listened to her singing it, the words deeply resonated with me, as if something spoke inside me.

The lyrics of the hymn are reproduced here. As both the hymn and the school song were sung often, thinking about both sets of lyrics to the same tune may be another way of understanding Myeongdong. The hymn is also in four verses. Readers unfamiliar with the hymn would recognize the tune, as it is also used as the United Kingdom's royal anthem, "God Save the Queen." Disciplined and solemn, it is a superb piece of music.

> God is our refuge strong; let all who suffer wrong find welcome here
> Here, though earth no more, though oceans rage and roar
> And break the mountains o'er, we shall not fear
>
> Peoples and nations shake when raging heathen, their malice felt
> But once a single word of our Lord's voice was heard
> A greater thing occurred: the earth did melt
>
> Our God, the Lord of all, our help our tower tall, will not us fail
> To earth's remotest shore He makes wars rage
> No more sword, spear, the tools of war can naught avail
>
> Our Lord, great God above, saves us in power and love; Praise ye the Lord!
> Though grief and pain strife, sharp woe and bitter strife,
> Our refuge and our life Is our Lord God.[26]

Yun, of course, sang the school song. And every Sunday, during Sunday school, he must have sung the hymn.

What kind of place, then, was "my Myeongdong" school that made it a "refuge strong"?

When considering the quality and concept of schools at that time, Myeongdong School was top-notch. The school even had a brass band in the 1910s and boasted a tennis court. The brass band, in particular, actively performed at community events. Extant records show that in 1913, when Gando Korean society's spirits were elevated by Ganminhoe's autonomous activities, the band took an active role in the Dano Festival at the intramural sports tournament held on the sandy beach by the Yanji Bridge in Juzijie. Moreover, when mass demonstrations for independence unfolded in gruesome bloodshed in Yongjeong on March 13, 1919, Myeongdong School's brass band took the lead. Its heroic activities are recorded in the history of the Korean independence movement. On November 15, 1919, *Dongnip Shinmun* (*The Independent*—Trans.), the newspaper for the Provisional Government of the Republic of Korea, established in Shanghai, China, reported testimonies of the participants of the Yongjeong demonstrations: "How is it a crime to hail in one voice? How did all these lives arrive at death? Here and there, corpses are crisscrossing, and blood is welling. I wailed aloud. Many joined me. A gale continues to roar, blinding my eyes. The trumpet sounds of Myeongdong School students lined up in the field sing a plaintive tune, moving men's hearts to grief."[27]

At that time, Principal Kim Yak-yeon had left for Siberia with Jeong Jae-myeon to attend an independence movement conference as North Gando representatives. In their absence, the remaining teachers and students were fiercely active on the scene of demonstrations.

Consequently, Myeongdong School suffered ordeals inflicted by the Chinese government under the pressure of Japan. First of all, Kim Yak-yeon, upon returning from Siberia, was arrested by the Chinese police and imprisoned for over two years. Additionally, Myeongdong School suffered financial damages and was subsequently shut down. *Dongnip Shinmun* reported the situation on January 22, 1920: "Among them, Mr. Kim Yak-yeon was jailed in the Chinese Police Department.... Myeongdong Boys School and Girls School suffered damages of over 7,000 in Daeyang (Chinese currency—Trans.) and was ordered to close down by the Chinese government as a result of Enemy Japan's interference."[28]

Myeongdong School was shut down for a period of several months. Reverend Han Jun-myeong witnessed the situation when he enrolled in Myeongdong Grade School after his family moved there in early September 1919. "They said a Myeongdong School student was killed during the demonstrations, and the Chinese officials shut the school down. So, the big school building was empty, and students were studying at someone's house. Chinese soldiers were keeping posts there so that the school was not used, probably because of the pressure of Japan. Later on, the school reopened. But the school was burned down during the Great Liquidation of the year of the White Monkey, and for a while, we had to continue our studies in a private house."[29]

In October of the Year of the White Monkey (1920), the Japanese set fire to the school during the Great Gando Liquidation. This fire was a snare that sought to paralyze its victims. How did this powerful snare affect Myeongdong?

Myeongdong had been a place of freedom fighters, shining pure and clear, but over time, its brilliance started to wane as darkness appeared, greedily gobbling up its beautiful rays of light, reducing their luminosity. What was this darkness, and how did it work? Simply put: Myeongdong School taught Japanese to its students.

One of the errors that most Yun Dong-ju researchers commit is the notion of Myeongdong School's unflinching anti-Japanese sentiments. Upon hearing the testimony that Myeongdong people called Japan "Walbon" instead of "Ilbon"—because Japan did not deserve the use of the Chinese character for "the sun" ("il," 日) in its name, the character for "speaking" ("wal," 曰) would do—researchers quickly presume that Myeongdong School did not teach Japanese. But that was not true. By 1921, Japanese was in its regular curriculum, taught by a qualified Japanese language teacher. This change occurred as a result of the burning down of the school.

After Principal Kim Yak-yeon returned from Siberia and was imprisoned, church elder Kim Jeong-gyu stepped in. The Great Liquidation took place during Kim Jeong-gyu's term. After the school burned down, Kim Jeong-gyu took out loans and built a small wooden structure on the school field so that the school could operate. In 1921, Kim Yak-yeon was released. After two years of imprisonment, he resumed his position and was constantly raising money to pay back the loans. At the same time, he met and negotiated with a powerful Japanese man named Hidaka Heishiro, who was in North Gando then. Kim Yak-yeon demanded that Japan return Myeongdong School to its original state, since the Japanese army had burned it down.

Hidaka seemed receptive to the idea but under one condition: inclusion of Japanese language education in Myeongdong School's regular curriculum. Kim Yak-yeon accepted. Subsequently, an identical brick building was built on the previous site of the school by Japanese workers, funded by the Japanese government, and Japan sent a Japanese language teacher, a Korean man named Yi Gyu-seok.

The extant Myeongdong Grade School graduation photograph of Yun Dong-ju shows the rebuilt brick building in the background.

Yi Gyu-seok, who left after a few years, was succeeded by none other than Han Jun-myeong. Thus, Han knew the background story behind the inclusion of Japanese in Myeongdong School's curriculum. He also explained how he had become a Japanese language teacher. Han graduated from Myeongdong Grade School and enrolled in Eunjin Middle School (a four-year degree). After graduating in April 1926, he received a request from Myeongdong School to teach Japanese that September. He accepted the post as a teacher of Japanese and music. Han was also Yun's fourth grade homeroom teacher.

When asked about the accuracy of the hitherto unknown fact of Japanese language education at Myeongdong School, Reverend Mun Ik-hwan confirmed it: "Yes. Myeongdong School, too, taught Japanese. The students would call it 'Walbon' language, not 'Ilbon' language." He also reminisced, "I remember, once, my Japanese test score was very low, and I was severely scolded by Mr. Han."[30]

It might seem a curious circumstance on the surface. However, the relationship between the rebuilding of Myeongdong School and Japanese language education closely resembles that of Jeong Jae-myeon's continued stay at the school and the conversion to Christianity in Myeongdong. Myeongdong School had given in to Jeong's demand that Bible studies be a required class for students and that students attend Christian worship.

However, as seen previously, the episode of Jeong Jae-myeon was not simply about retaining a Western education teacher. It was also a strategy for the Myeongdong people to seek their autonomous position and solutions as Koreans in North Gando under dual pressures from Japan and Qing.

It was the same with the Japanese language education. It cannot be considered a grave surrender of integrity, succumbing to Japan's demand for Japanese education in exchange for the restoration of the brick school building. When Yun and his classmates enrolled in Eunjin Middle School in Yongjeong in 1932, all the textbooks were in Japanese. That was the reality of North Gando's educational system. Without knowing Japanese, it would have been impossible to pursue higher education.

Thus, it is fair to conclude that by including Japanese in its curriculum, the school compromised in order to seek a realistic and insightful response to the fact that the Japanese language dominated in the overall educational system. At any rate, the tumultuous experiences of the Myeongdong people should be looked on squarely without exaggerating, beautifying, or self-debasing. Only by doing so can we properly read into the pains, sorrows, and struggles experienced by colonized subjects living in a foreign land.

In the olden days of the school, gym classes were taught by a former military officer of the Korean Empire. Singing military songs for independence, the students were trained like soldiers with wooden rifles. Myeongdong School had been overflowing with patriotic, militaristic spirit.

By the time Yun attended, however, the atmosphere had changed along with the changing times. The school was more inclined toward a literary education. Three languages were taught: Joseoneo (Korean—Trans.), Chinese (required by the Chinese government's 1915 Education Law), and Japanese.

Yun's class consisted of boys of literary interests, as revealed in the poet Kim Jeong-u's recollection:

In fourth grade, Dong-ju subscribed to a monthly children's literary magazine published in Seoul. His first cousin and classmate Song Mong-gyu was also interested in literature. Mong-gyu subscribed to the magazine *Children*, also from Seoul, and Dong-ju subscribed to *Kids' Life*. Neighborhood kids borrowed the issues after they were done with them. Two boys in a remote Manchurian village subscribing to Seoul periodicals was a great deal. It influenced others there, and the monthly periodical *Samchonri* was circulated among young people, too.

Entering fifth grade, at Dong-ju and Mong-gyu's suggestion, we decided to publish our monthly magazine using a mimeograph. We collected and edited writings but did not know what to call the magazine. So we consulted Reverend Han Jun-myeong (currently a professor at Central Seminary), our homeroom teacher and revered by us. He praised us and suggested the name "New Myeongdong." So we published a few issues of *New Myeongdong*.

Perhaps because we were all interested in literature, the school gave each of us as a graduation present a copy of the poetry collection *Night on the Border* by P'ain Kim Dong-hwan.[31]

Yun Dong-ju graduated Myeongdong Grade School on March 20, 1931. The class of '31 consisted of fourteen boys. Afterward, Yun enrolled in sixth grade at a Chinese grade school in Dailazi, the capital of Helong Prefecture. According to Kim Jeong-u, four of the graduates went there, including him, Yun Dong-ju, Song Mong-gyu, and another classmate. Kim Jeong-u dropped out, but the other three walked over two miles to school each day. The memories from the school are reflected in Yun's poem "A Night of Counting Stars," in which he names each shining star Pae, Gyeong, or Ok, as "exotic names" of Chinese girls.

Myeongdong Pervaded by Communism

"Yes, it was really scary then." With these words, Reverend Han Jun-myeong began describing the period in which communists gained great power in North Gando: "There were rumors of 'this person killed here' and 'that person killed there' after each night. And the victims were mostly schoolteachers. There was a rumor that the communists sentenced me to death, too."[32]

Myeongdong Grade School in Myeongdong Village, a home of nationalists, was also swept over by the storm. The school belonged to Myeongdong Church and was operated as a kind of church school. Typical of a Christian school, classes began each day after a worship service.

Socialists, however, were planning to separate the school from the church and make it a "people's school." Things were getting fierce beginning in 1928, and by 1929, communists had taken over the school. Assemblies, speeches, and instigations followed, making commotions in the process of taking over.

"They made critical remarks in all matters," commented Reverend Han, giving a few examples. When the school prepared the students for solos at the school presentations, the socialists opposed, making sarcastic remarks. "Chorus is better than solos. It's more democratic." According to Reverend Han: "Mr. Song Chang-hui, Mong-gyu's father, sympathized with them somewhat. Mr. Yun Yeong-seok, Dong-ju's father, was leaning that way, too. They attended church but were not passionate Christians."[33]

Principal Kim Yak-yeon, once called "President of East Manchuria," was powerless against the challenge that came with this new ideology. He let the school be taken from him by socialists. A rumor circulated that when he stepped down, he mourned the absence of Reverend Mun Jae-rin (Reverend Mun Ik-hwan's father). "If Reverend Mun were here, I'd try to fight them, but without him, what would I do even if I won?"[34] Mun Jae-rin devoted himself to Christianity after the Gando Massacre in 1920. He became an elder at age twenty-six, attended Pyeongyang Presbyterian Seminary, and was ordained as pastor. In 1928, he went to Canada to study at Toronto University on the Canadian Presbyterian Mission's scholarship. Reverend Han Jun-myeong clearly remembered the day of the takeover: "When Myeongdong Grade School became a 'people's school,' I was driven out. It was the spring of 1929, April, to be exact."[35] After that, he became an itinerant pastor to do mission work.

Kim Yak-yeon turned sixty in 1928. When he lost the school to socialists the following year, he made a new resolution. He went to Pyeongyang and enrolled in a three-year seminary program at a Presbyterian seminary. Yet after just one year, the seminary ordained him as a pastor. This was a very exceptional action. In 1930, Reverend Kim Yak-yeon returned as the pastor of Myeongdong Church. The fact that a man in his sixties acted with such determination shows how great his shock was from the rise of communism and the harm it caused.

The life of the people's school, however, was short-lived. The Chinese government had already planned to absorb private schools in North Gando as prefectural schools, and in September 1929, an administrative order was issued, stating that all private schools operated by Koreans in North Gando were to be forcefully merged into prefectural schools. The Chinese government claimed that this was to prevent the Japanese government from involving itself in education in China under the pretense of educating its colonial subjects. In any case, for Korean private school owners, it was robbing their schools in broad daylight.

Joseon Ilbo had a headline on September 14, 1929: "Yanbian's Joseon Schools Merged to Public Schools Based on Laws on Private Schools." Thus, Myeongdong Grade School had to be converted to a prefectural school under the jurisdiction of Yanbian's education bureau.

There is an interesting testimony about Myeongdong School's change to a people's school. Apparently, Song Mong-gyu took part in the process. During our interview, Mrs. Kim Shin-muk recollected:

KIM: At that time, Han-beom (Mong-gyu's childhood name) gave a
hand. He went out in front of a crowd and gave a speech that the
school should become a "people's school." He must have taken his
father Song Chang-hui's view.

AUTHOR: In the spring of 1929, Song Mong-gyu was only twelve,
beginning fifth grade. Did he really make a speech?

KIM: Yes, he did, too. Han-beom was always strong-minded. Even at
that age, he made speeches to adults without hesitation. He was
quite a good speaker, too.[36]

This is an important fact, as it is also indicative of Yun's ideological journey.

Once I attended an interview between Professor Yun Il-ju, Yun's younger
brother, and a Japanese interviewer. One of the interviewer's questions was:
"How did Yun Dong-ju view leftist ideas? As you know, at that time, leftist
ideas widely circulated among the intellectuals. Moreover, he studied in
Japan."

The question was quite befitting of someone from Japan, where various
ideologies, including communism, coexist on an equal basis. It was certainly
a novel question, even refreshing. Having been brought up in and hardened
by a thoroughly anticommunist nation, I would not even imagine such a
question about the "national poet of purity." It directly asked about the connection between Yun Dong-ju the intellectual and the time he lived in. It is
said, "If you're not a communist at the age of twenty, you don't have a heart; if
you're still a communist at the age of thirty, you don't have a brain." Although
Yun Dong-ju was also a child of the times, Professor Yun Il-ju answered cautiously, like the academic that he was: "There's been no evidence whatsoever
that Yun Dong-ju had leftist ideas. So we can assume for now that he had no
connections with them."

In fact, nowhere in the records about Yun Dong-ju is his involvement with
leftist ideas. The National Diet of Japan enacted its first Maintenance of the
Public Order Act in 1925. The statute prescribed that a crime is constituted
under the law when activities are accompanied by either of two intentions:
(1) to change the political system of Japan, and (2) to deny the private property system. Denying the private property system (espousing communism)
was made as serious a crime as conspiracy to overthrow the government.

Until Japan's defeat in World War II, this was the will and vision firmly held by imperial Japan's Bureau of Public Order.

However, there is no mention of leftist ideas in the reports by Japan's Special High Police (a secret unit that exclusively dealt with ideology-related crimes), which interrogated Yun, or in his trial transcripts. Such absence proves that Yun was not at all involved in leftist ideology because all his writings were confiscated when he was arrested. Under the protocols at the time, if anything suspicious was found among his writings or his belongings from a house search, it would have become another indictable offense and been reflected in interrogation reports or trial records.

Under these considerations, I suddenly became intrigued by Yun's relationship with Marxism. As an intellectual of that time who could not have been ignorant of Marxism, even as a mere mental exercise, what was his understanding of or feelings toward it? At the time, no materials to shed light on this question had been found. I was still curious about this when I heard the testimony about young Song Mong-gyu's actions during the process of Myeongdong Grade School turning into a people's school, when communism infiltrated Myeongdong Village. From this, one might guess at the form of Marxism that Yun personally encountered.

Regarding the communist ideology and its effect on North Gando, the aftermath of the Russian Revolution of 1917 had no immediate effect. In ideological aspects, North Gando was detached from the international trend. Even though the Korean resistance army would purchase weapons from the Red Army from time to time, nationalism was always the ideological mainstream. All of the independence movement organizations, whether big or small, were nationalistic, such as the North Gando Korean People's Association, whose foremost leaders were Christians. Its commander in chief, General Hong Beom-do, was engaged in an armed struggle against Japan. Another organization was the Northern Road Military Corps, whose principal leaders were followers of Daejongism (religion of Dangun—Trans.) and whose commander in chief was General Kim Jwa-jin. Like the leaders, lay members of North Gando Korean society were also nationalists in ideology.

The ideological foundation, however, gradually started to shift after the Battle of Cheongsan-ri in October 1920 and the subsequent massacre by the Japanese, and communism started to gain its power.

There are various reasons for this shift. First, to avoid running into the Japanese punitive forces, the freedom fighters of North Gando fled to Siberia. During their stay, some of them were influenced by communism, and they later became a channel through which communism was directly imported.

Second, while most countries, even China, were indifferent to the Korean freedom fighters, only Lenin gave them material and emotional support, such as aid in the form of 40,000 rubles, a fortune then. Thus, many believed that the Soviet Union was on their side. The special envoy sent by the Provisional Government of the Republic of Korea in Shanghai brought the great sum of money from Moscow. Some of the money was later used for holding the National Representatives Convention in Shanghai, and this was enough to confirm people's belief. This, too, became a catalyst for the spread of communism.

The third factor was the despair felt by Koreans during the Gando Massacre. When a large number of Japanese troops crossed the border in October 1920, the freedom fighters all fled to Siberia after only a few days of battle in the ravines of Sandaogou (Battle of Cheongsan-ri—Trans.) and Toudaogu, Helung Prefecture, leaving civilian Koreans behind, fully exposed to the cruelty of the Japanese punitive forces and as helpless as if their hands and feet were bound. These Koreans became the victims of appalling massacres and arson. Watching their family and neighbors being murdered, with no one to turn to, they despaired. They had been abandoned there like orphans. The Gando Massacre was not a mere backdrop for the fancy rhetoric decorating the Battle of Cheongsan-ri. Because of those piercing and agonizing experiences, North Gando Koreans became drawn to the communist ideology and comradeship of bonding people of all nations regardless of ethnicity or race. Overlooking them, one cannot explain the psychological background that brought on the rapid ideological changes in North Gando after the massacre.

Fourth, the North Gando Korean poor were suffering greatly. Many had gone there carrying a bundle on their back because they could not make a living in Korea. But many of them ended up as tenant farmers of Chinese landowners and lived a life of continuous disadvantage and exploitation. Many *Donga Ilbo* and *Joseon Ilbo* articles from the 1920s testify to the sad realities of North Gando Korean society, reporting about miserable Joseon tenant farmers who were left with empty hands after a whole year of hard work because of the Chinese landlords' tyranny. To people in such circumstances, communism must have literally sounded like the gospel.

Fifth, the more despairing a situation is, the greater the longing for a new world will be. Intellectual curiosity about this new ideology was another factor, as idealism or an experimental mindset for a better future for mankind attracted them. In such a context, I found a very interesting piece of material: a lecture by Chunwon Yi Gwang-su titled "Bolshevism," reproduced in *Dongnip Shinmun* and published in Shanghai on March 18, 1920.[37]

Even though Yi later became a pro-Japanese turncoat, he was then a famous patriot and manager of *Dongnip Shinmun*. And, as the paper had a considerable readership in North Gando, this article should be paid special attention. Already by February 1920, the North Gando Korean People's Association, the biggest independence movement organization, forced subscriptions to "*Dongnip Shinmun*, our Provisional Government's official newsletter," on the residents under its jurisdiction, including Myeongdong.[38] Doubtlessly, this article must have been read widely among Myeongdong residents.

Because of its importance, Yi Gwang-su's lecture, though quite long, is reproduced here in its entirety, as reported in the newsletter.

At the beginning of his lecture, Mr. Yi stated, "I will speak about the history of Bolshevism as an introduction." He discussed the causes and kinds of revolution and asserted that Bolshevism is a revolution that will inevitably take place worldwide. His core points are summarized here.

***

Bolshevism is the revolution of the economy. What first came to the awakening of mankind was the revolution of ideas. It supported freedom and equality of ideas, bringing forth the Renaissance and the Reformation. Next came the revolution of politics. It supported freedom and equality in politics, bringing forth the French Revolution and subsequent revolutions. Afterwards came the revolution of the economy. It supported freedom and equality of wealth, bringing forth the socialist movements of contemporary nations.

Generally, a revolution starts from some defects in the social system. When these defects profit a particular class but injure another class, the profiting class strives to preserve them, calling them strong points, while the injured class strives to eliminate them, calling them defects. Thus the two classes collide. The oppressing class naturally has all the power though small in number. The oppressed class, on the other hand, is significant in number though lacking power. The classes continue to fight wretched bloody battles because the oppressing class counts on its power, and the oppressed class counts on its number. History, however, is record of conquests by the revolutionary class.

In this way, when the oppressed class succeeds in revolution and establishes a system, the new system oppresses another class, and the revolution goes through a cycle. Even if defects before one's eyes are eliminated, as life is not omniscient, other defects always exist, and revolution has no end.

After we obtain freedom and equality of ideas, we desire freedom and equality of politics. After obtaining them, we again desire freedom and equality of economy. This produced today's revolution of an economic system. But it is neither that the ideological revolution must come before the political revolution, nor is it that the political revolution must come before the economic revolution. When freedom and equality of ideas reach a certain level, a desire for freedom and equality of politics rises, and also comes a desire for freedom and equality of economy. Thus, these three revolutions can coexist, although economic issues are at the center now.

The model of today's economic revolution is Russia. German and Austrian Empires have imitated it. Even in nations like England and America, whose existing system is on a stable foundation, we hear from reports in *Maeil Shinmun* that the blazing fire of the third revolution is underlying.

"Politically, let us eliminate the distinction between the ruling and the ruled classes, between the privileged and the underprivileged classes." This is a natural conclusion of contemporary ideas. The day the blazing fire of economic revolution rises all over the world is not far away. In Japan, too, countless small signal fires rise at random.

"As socialism is entrusted with the economic revolution, the proletariat, who serve socialism, are its revolutionaries." "Bolshevism is a branch of socialism based on Karl Marx's ideas. Lenin and Trotsky are its representatives. Bolshevism is the most thorough, most representative of socialism. I would like to gain another opportunity to explain and critique Bolshevism." "Our movement is not merely a movement for independence from Japan but, in truth, a movement to construct a new nation and society. Therefore, by examining all thoughts and ideas that move *minjung* (the people—Trans.) of the contemporary world, we strive to build the nation upon a perfect foundation." Thus, the examination of ideological issues is a part of the independence movement.[39]

After his sellout to Japan and return to Korea, Yi Gwang-su never again spoke out about these issues. Circumstances changed his speeches and actions. At any rate, it is important to pay attention to the fact that the best elite and leader of the independence movement had this type of view on Bolshevism and also that he tried to widely disseminate such view to *minjung*, the term used by Yi Gwang-su, through the medium of *Dongnip Shinmun*. This example clearly demonstrates the intellectual curiosity and goodwill toward Marxism that the intellectuals had at the time.

As the five factors discussed above interplayed with and affected one another, all of Manchuria was becoming communized. As a result, a series of events known as the Gando Communist Incidents took place one after the other, the first in October 1927, the second in September 1928, the third in March 1930, and the fourth in May 1930, also called the Gando May 30th Riot.[40]

When seen under these circumstances in North Gando, the meaning of Myeongdong's people's school incident becomes clearer. At the conclusion of the people's school issue, Myeongdong was different. Chinese police officers came and guarded the school with rifles in order to prevent communists' terroristic activities.

Reverend Han Jun-myeong stated:

It became more and more scary. Every night, sixteen- or seventeen-year-olds went around committing terrorist acts. Once, they were riding a kind of old Jeep—already there were things like that. After they drove through, a fire started and burned the stack of grain stalks that we harvested. Somehow, they started the fire. The police could not stop it. The Chinese guards chased after them, though in vain, and made a lot of commotion.

In the end, I left Myeongdong Village for good on December 30, 1930. My name was already on the communists' blacklist for execution, and my parents kept pestering me to leave. So I meant to stay at my elder sister's house in Wonsan for a while and left Myeongdong, carrying only a pair of German-made skates I treasured. But after that, I never got to return to Gando.[41]

He shared another episode. Han was writing an entry in his journal in his room one night when men armed with rifles barged in at both ends of the room through the front and back doors. He stared in shock and realized that they were the Chinese police officers who guarded the school. They also recognized and greeted him, "Ah, teacher," putting their rifles down. They had suspected that terrorists were there because the light was on in the room. This episode reveals the frightening atmosphere in which even keeping a light on at night could cause trouble. Reverend Han added: "I heard that from the following spring after my departure, it got even worse. My aged parents would hide in the sorghum fields at night. What more should be said?"[42]

Mrs. Kim Shin-muk remembered another incident, a murder by communists that took place in the Donggeou section of Myeongdong, where she lived:

> There was a man named Choi Myeong-jin, originally from Hoeryeong. He was an affluent farmer and had a prudent character. They say his wife spoke ill of the communists, and one night those terrorists came to their house. She was a wife by Choi's second marriage and gave birth to two sons. She was trembling in the hallway, holding the young ones. She heard her husband in the room begging to them, "I'll give all I own, just spare our lives." And then it got quiet. The communists came out of the room and said, "We've got him." She went inside and saw her husband dead.[43]

As the situations developed this way, many affluent people or nationalists of Myeongdong began to depart, one by one, for urban areas that had better security. Reverend Mun Ik-hwa's family left in early 1931, and Yun Dong-ju's family followed suit in late autumn of the same year. They both moved to Yongjeong.

In these tumultuous times, in circumstances like standing in a blazing fire that spewed out black smoke, what must have come across the mind of the boy Yun Dong-ju? And how did that influence his life? If a conclusion can be deduced, Yun must have been fed up with Marxism as he witnessed the everyday horror that took place in Myeongdong Village.

This is more clearly evidenced by his friend Song Mong-gyu. Initially, he was enthusiastic about turning the church-owned Myeongdong School into a people's school, to the point of making speeches in front of adults despite his young age. But as Song faced the escalation of the situation, he "graduated" from Marxism. When he entered the military academy in Nakyang (Luoyang—Trans.) in 1935, there were several factions in the academy, including the anarchists' faction. Song joined the party of Kim Gu, which was the most nationalistic group, and never turned toward Marxism again throughout his life.

Likewise, Yun's thorough nationalistic character has its origin in the memory of fear and blood induced by the communists' indiscriminate acts of terrorism.

Back in Myeongdong Village, Myeongdong Church did not immediately close its doors just because affluent or respected nationalists had fled. Those who were not in immediate danger, because they had neither money nor fame, remained there to keep the church going. Sometimes not having can be power in itself.

These situations are not normal in the cultural aspects of a society but are rather transient patterns. Nevertheless, these patterns began the third period of Myeongdong's culture, as noted earlier. In Yun's life, this new Myeongdong was no longer his hometown. More directly put, his "hometown" had disappeared for good.

To Yun Dong-ju the poet, Myeongdong was a place filled with boyhood experiences of purity, abundance, and peace. But now these experiences remained only in memory. Because of that, the memories became even more vivid and dear to Yun.

These days, some Yun Dong-ju researchers place great importance on the direct link between this Myeongdong and the imagery of hometown that appears in his poems. However, because his hometown itself has not been sufficiently identified, this link is not without its empty echoes. Studies on the imagery of his hometown, then, should start again from these considerations: deep insight into the changes that came to Myeongdong and the accompanying social situations, as well as the historical circumstances under which Yun's family gave up their life in Myeongdong and left for Yongjeong.

CHAPTER 3

Yongjeong

The Heart of the Haeran River

Rugged Years, Rugged Dreams

WHAT KIND OF place was Yongjeong (Longjing—Trans.), the city for which Yun's family departed Myeongdong?

By simple geographical descriptions, Yongjeong is located at the center of the lower delta plain formed by the Haeran River. From the viewpoint of Koreans settled in North Gando, and especially those who lived alongside the Haeran River, Yongjeong was the heart of the Haeran River.

Though the green Ilsongjeong pine[1] grew old alone,
For one thousand years River Haeran has flown.
You were galloping a horse by the river then, O Pioneer,
Where are your rugged dreams now growing deeper?

When all night by the *yongdure* well sounds were heard,
The moon shone quietly on Yongmun Bridge undeterred.
You were shooting arrows over foreign skies, O Pioneer,
Where are your rugged dreams now growing deeper?

As the knell from Yongju Temple reached Mount Biam,
Deep down in the heart he engraved his firm will.
You were vowing to save Fatherland, O Pioneer,
Where are your rugged dreams now growing deeper?

This song, titled "The Pioneer," is the embodiment of Yongjeong and captures the joys and sorrows of its painful history. Its original title was "The

Song of Yongjeong," given by the man who penned the lyrics, Yun Hae-yeong, when he approached the composer, Jo Du-nam. After liberation, Jo changed the title to "The Pioneer."

Among the songs that pay tribute to places, few have quality and beauty as praiseworthy as this one, both in music and in words; perhaps no better song will ever be sung about Yongjeong. Before we contemplate the lyrics of this famous song, let us examine the history of the city.

After the law prohibiting the crossing of the Tumen River was repealed, Koreans entered the land and established Yongjeong. At that time, Yongjeong was an uninhabited wilderness dotted by a few vegetable fields owned by Qing people who lived in an area called Toseongbo across a small stream.

In this wilderness was a well, meant to water the nearby vegetable patches. A large column was built next to the well, and a long pole was installed on it. At one end of the pole hung a water-lifting bucket and at the other end a large rock. The bucket was lowered into the well, and when it was submerged in the water, the rope was let go. Because of the weight of the rock, the bucket containing the water would be pulled up of itself. This rope-and-pulley system was called *yongdure* (dragon bucket—Trans.), and from this *yongdure* well came the city's name, Yongjeong (Dragon Well—Trans.).

Now let us look at the lyrics of the song.

It was 1933 when Jo Du-nam (1912–1984) received a poem one evening from a visitor, a stranger named Yun Hae-yeong.[2] This was the year following Yun Dong-ju's enrollment at Yongjeong Eunjin Middle School. Thus, "The Song of Yongjeong"/"The Pioneer" reflects the painful circumstances of Yongjeong in 1933. For those who are familiar with Yongjeong, the lines "You were galloping a horse by the river then, O Pioneer, / Where are your rugged dreams now growing deeper?" tug at the heartstrings. Yongjeong—the land where accomplished and high-spirited freedom fighters like Yi Sang-seol unfolded their lonely, rapturous, and rugged dreams—had become a land lorded over by Japan. Yongjeong's sorrowful history is well reflected in these two lines of plaintive moaning.

Until that time, Jo Du-nam had never been to Yongjeong. A native of Pyeongyang, he had wandered northern Manchuria after running away from home. He was rooming in a cheap inn by the Mudan River when Yun Hae-yeong came to see him upon hearing that Jo was a composer. Jo remembered Yun as a young man, "short and scrawny, wearing an old coat and speaking with a Hamgyeong accent; gaunt but with eyes poised and intense, giving an impression that he might be a freedom fighter."[3]

Jo reminisced that when Yun first told him about Yongjeong, he felt as if he were actually seeing and hearing the land. However, as someone who had neither seen Yongjeong nor understood its history, he had his limitations.

Jo did not alter the first verse written by Yun. In the second and third verses, however, he omitted phrases like "the tear-soaked bundle" and "drifting fate," substituting them with "shooting arrows over foreign skies" and "vowing to save Fatherland." However, those omitted by Jo reflect the true face of Yongjeong. The newly inserted phrases (like "shooting arrows") were nonsensical words supplied by a literary youth, as there never was an arrow-shooting pioneer in Yongjeong. Even traced back to its early settlement period, it was the era of rifles, not arrows.

Nevertheless, the song will continue to be passed down for a thousand years, with the imagery of Yongjeong engraved in the hearts of those who love the land: "green Ilsongjeong pine," "River Haeran," "*yongdure* well," and the moonlight on the Yongmun Bridge. . . . Among these, some explanation is needed for "green Ilsongjeong pine." Strangely, the outskirts of Yongjeong are devoid of pine trees but for one place. As one continues to climb up a low hill past Yongmun Bridge across the Haeran River, a large rock is seen on top of the hill, where an enormous pine stands, alone. This pine was called Ilsongjeong. "Jeong" is the character for the word "jeongjeong," which has two meanings in the dictionary: (1) a towering shape like that of a tree, and (2) a firm and vigorous shape of an old person. The "jeong" in Ilsongjeong, of course, refers to the first meaning. Yongmun Bridge was a big bridge that allowed even large automobiles and horse carriages to pass.

Bearing in mind this scenery of Yongjeong that Yun experienced when he left his hometown of Myeongdong to move there, we now examine its history.

Geographically, the most notable point in the distinct regional characteristics of North Gando was that there were two centers in it. One was Yongjeong, and the other was Yeon'gil (Yanji in Chinese—Trans.), also called Gukjaga.

Yongjeong was a city where Joseon Koreans were concentrated, whereas the Chinese administrative and public buildings were all in Yeon'gil. Taxes were paid and crimes were punished in Yeon'gil. According to the dictates of common sense, North Gando's development should have centered on Yeon'gil. Yet few Joseon Koreans wished to settle there. Consequently, Yeon'gil became a Chinese city, whereas Yongjeong became a city with Korean characteristics.

Under the circumstance in which two pivots, formed by two ethnic groups, coexisted, what did the cunning authorities of imperial Japan do?

They chose to establish their major agencies not in Yeon'gil, where the Chinese administrative bodies were, but in Yongjeong, which was populated by Joseon Koreans. Thus, the Gando Police Office of the Resident-General of Korea (August 1907–November 1, 1909), an instrument of Japan's Gando invasion, was placed in Yongjeong. After it was removed, they set up the Gando Consulate General of Japan (November 2, 1909–August 15, 1945) in Yongjeong. Typically, a foreign nation's diplomatic machinery is established in a city that houses administrative agencies of the country of sojourn. Nevertheless, Japan set a higher value on Yongjeong than on Yeon'gil because Yongjeong had the characteristics of the Joseon Koreans' center.

A point should be made here. While both the Gando Police Office of the Resident-General and the Gando Consulate General of Japan were official organizations of Japan, each signified a clearly different meaning. The Gando Police Office was under the jurisdiction of Japan's Department of Interior, while the Gando Consulate General was under the jurisdiction of its Department of Foreign Affairs. In other words, during the period in which imperial Japan set up the police office in Gando, it regarded the land as that of the Korean Empire. After the Gando Convention of September 1909—an international treaty between Qing and Japan in which Japan rescinded the claim that Gando is the land of the Korean Empire in exchange for the railway rights to rebuild the Anbong Line and other privileges—Japan took down the sign "Police Office" and replaced it with "Consulate." This was an act of international disposal, conceding that Gando was Qing's territory.

Related to this, one of the greatest misunderstandings about North Gando held by the general public is that it was the land of freedom for the independence movement. Many people even have the same impression of Yongjeong, but this cannot be further from the truth.

When the Gando Police Office was in place, imperial Japan posed as the ruler of administration and public order, and indeed, it assumed the role at times. In order to stop that, Qing exacted a concession from Japan that

"Gando is Qing's territory" by giving away enormous rights to Japan. Despite that, Japan continued to exercise the same function and authority, albeit within limits, even in the era of the Gando Consulate General.

Having procured through the Gando Convention a right to establish consulates in four districts of North Gando, Japan set up the Consulate General in Yongjeong as well as three consular offices—in Yeon'gil, Dudogu, and Paekchogu. These four locations were where the North Gando population was concentrated. These districts were designated as "open areas," where freedom of residence by foreigners and free trade were guaranteed. The treaty guaranteed that Japan's public order system would operate as before.

In the Consulate General and the consular offices, Japan made arrangements for a systematic police structure and imprisonment facility under the pretense of public safety, calling them "consular precincts" and "consular jails." As a result, many freedom fighters were arrested, tortured, and penalized there. For anti-Japanese activists, entering one of the four districts meant risking the danger of being arrested by the Japanese police. Thus, freedom fighters had to avoid them, traveling to other parts of North Gando.

In the first verse of "The Pioneer," the lines "You were galloping a horse by the river then, O Pioneer, / Where are your rugged dreams now growing deeper?" grieved these circumstances.

After Japan's power infiltrated North Gando and was coiled up in Yongjeong, the only Koreans who could freely gallop a horse by the Haeran River were either the pro-Japanese or the pioneers of the Japanese' Manchu invasion. During the *Yusin* era,[4] it was reported that "The Pioneer" was one of the favorite songs of then-President Park Chung-hee, who had graduated from a Japanese military academy in Manchuria and been an army officer of Manchukuo, Japan's puppet state in Manchuria. When the report reached the ears of North Gando natives, they were greatly displeased. Their reaction can be understood in that context.

Even in Yongjeong, however, there was a special district untouchable by both Japan and China. This was the area around East Mountain, where the Canadian Presbyterian Mission had settled. This area, on a plateau in a hilly district of eastern Yongjeong, was commonly referred to by the nickname "English Hill" because of Canada being in the Commonwealth. No one could enter the mission district without a special permit. Inside the district were schools, hospitals, and other institutions built and operated by the Canadian mission alongside their dwellings. Eunjin Middle School, which Yun attended; Myeongshin Girls School; and Jechang Hospital (St. Andrews Hospital) were all in the district and operated by the missionaries, enjoying the privilege of extraterritoriality. Eunjin Middle School's special characteristics originate from this.

The extraterritoriality of English Hill was mighty, as it was backed by the strong national power of England during its heyday of imperial ambitions. Additionally, the Canadian missionaries, with great understanding and sympathy for the cause of Korean independence, helped them in earnest. One of the missionaries, Min San-hae (Dr. Stanley H. Martin), even won an official commendation from the North Gando Korean People's Association, the biggest independence movement organization in North Gando.

Because of these distinct characteristics, schools within the mission district could give an ardent nationalistic education without the interference of Japan. Moreover, Jechang Hospital provided not only treatment for Joseon Koreans' illnesses but also meeting and hiding places for freedom fighters. For instance, when Yongjeong's large-scale demonstration for independence on March 13, 1919, resulted in bloodshed after the Chinese military fired at demonstrators, both the wounded and the deceased were quickly moved to Jechang Hospital in English Hill. The bodies of the seventeen who were killed were respectfully laid there until the funeral services, and the wounded were treated and protected by the hospital.

There is an interesting record kept by the Japanese that speaks to the power of extraterritoriality enjoyed in English Hill. The record is dated November 27, 1919, and comes from secret intelligence documents of the Joseon military staff. As the content of the record relates to Mr. Jeong Jae-myeon, who brought Western education to Myeongdong, it is even more interesting.

Jeong, who started his post at Myeongdong School in 1909, resigned in February 1913 and was appointed at a teachers' school in Gukjaga (Yeon'gil). While in Myeongdong, he was arrested by the Japanese police, taken to Korea, and jailed there in the spring of 1911. He had been scheduled to officiate the marriage between two of his students, Mun Jae-rin and Kim Shin-muk, in a Western-style ceremony on March 2, 1911, by the lunar calendar, and in his absence, his colleague Mr. Pak Tae-hwan took his place.

Jeong was not confined for long. Mrs. Kim Shin-muk noted that "Mr. Jeong came back to Myeongdong before long and taught again."[5] Because his absence was not long and without explanation, no one at that time knew that he had been arrested. At first, they thought that he had been called away on an emergency. Later on, Jeong confided that he had been arrested and taken to Korea. According to his son Dr. Jeong Dae-wi (1917–2003—Trans.), the family believed that "Father had a Chinese citizenship, and because the Chinese government's protest was effective, he was released soon."[6]

At that time, freedom fighters in Korea carried forward numerous schemes for independence, such as setting up a military school in West Gando. Many were found out and imprisoned for security violations in an incident known as Security Violations by Yang Gi-tak, Et al. A great many people were arrested, and Jeong's arrest is assumed to have been related to this affair.

So why did Jeong move to Yeon'gil, the Chinese city with few Koreans, in February 1913? No reasons are found in the historical records, and Mrs. Kim Shin-muk had no insight to offer.

In light of the timing and circumstances, however, conjectures can be made. At that time, Ganminhoe (president: Kim Yak-yeon, vice president: Kim Yeong-hak, and manager: Jeong Jae-myeon), the first Joseon Korean autonomous body in North Gando, was working vigorously. As a managing officer of Ganminhoe, Jeong might have moved to Yeon'gil so that he could process negotiations with Chinese authorities and accomplish liaison work more smoothly and quickly.

Jeong started making arrangements for Myeongdong residents soon after arriving in Yeon'gil, including arrangements for some of them to continue their studies in Beijing. Because he first secured an escort to take the students to Beijing before contacting Myeongdong, five young men made a quick decision to go to Beijing. Yun's father, Yun Yeong-seok, was among the five, the first to go abroad to study. The other four were: Mun Jae-rin (Reverend Mun Ik-hwan's father), Kim Seok-gwan (Elder Kim Jeong-gyu's son), Mun Seong-rin (Mun Byeong-gyu's great-grandson), and Kim Jeong-hun (Reverend Kim Yak-yeon's son).

While staying in Yeon'gil, the Jeong family suffered the loss of their only son, who had been born in Myeongdong. While it is not clear when they moved to Yongjeong from Yeon'gil, Kim Shin-muk clearly remembers visiting Jeong's home in Yongjeong in 1915, and the move certainly predates that. At that time, Jeong was still working as a teacher but had some financial difficulties. His mother and his wife made a living by grinding buckwheat. Offspring were rare in the Jeong household, and Kim saw that they had a small jar of liquor in the corner of the kitchen, which was believed to help with conception. Perhaps the liquor was effective, as a baby was born to them in Yongjeong in 1917, Jeong Dae-wi, who is Jeong's only heir.

In consideration of all these circumstances, one can assume that Jeong moved to Yeon'gil for Ganminhoe's work and moved to Yongjeong after Ganminhoe was disbanded by the Chinese government in 1914.

Following the end of World War I in November 1918, new spirits for independence rose in North Gando. This phenomenon was greatly encouraged in the principle of "national self-determination," presented by U.S. President Woodrow Wilson as a measure for handling the end of the war. Jeong dove into the independence movement in earnest. When the representatives of the movement's organizations gathered in Nicholisk, Siberia, in February 1919, Jeong was elected to attend the meeting along with Kim Yak-yeon as two North Gando representatives. After the meeting, Jeong left for Shanghai by himself.

"Special Report No. 78," reproduced here, is a secret intelligence document from Joseon military staff that describes the circumstances of Jeong's return to Yongjeong, North Gando, from Shanghai in October 1919.

Suddenly, on October 28, Jeong Jae-myeon, who had been in Shanghai, Yun Jun-ryeol, who had been in Siberia, and Yi Yik-chan and three others who, as consular policemen, joined the independence party after May, and four or five other comrades came to Yongjeong and entered a house of a Joseon person on the American-operated Christian hospital premises. Soon, Kim Hwa-seok [the misspelled name for Kim Ha-seok, who was a Christian-line freedom fighter close to Yi Dong-hwi and the mastermind behind the Gando 150,000-Won Incident], who seems to be the chief of staff for Yi Dong-hwi, stayed overnight in Myeongdong Village on the 30th and the 31st, in the Yongjeong Christian hospital. After that, he went toward Gukjaga like a comet. Their daring act of staying overnight in front of our Consulate surprised us somewhat, and we endeavored to find out their purpose. From their subsequent action, we suspect that they wanted to force a rich Joseon man to pay for their fighting fund. Jeong's group seems to be staying there still, but *because they are in the area of territoriality, we cannot even budge a finger. Grinding our teeth, we are only on the lookout for an opportunity to arrest them.*[7]

By reading this record alone, we can recognize how powerful the extraterritoriality of the English Hill must have been. The whirlwind circumstances of that time are vividly described in this document: Joseon freedom fighters anxiously working to recover their fatherland, Japanese policemen seeking to arrest them, and Western missionaries assisting the anti-Japanese activists outright. Their endeavors were interconnected like revolving cogwheels; added to that was the involvement of the Chinese administrative authority, which had jurisdiction over the area.

These were the past and the present of Yun Dong-ju's new place of abode (Yongjeong) and new school (English Hill). This place of rugged history, a station of the epoch flickering on and off with rugged dreams, received the future poet in its arms.

Here, a historical fact should be pointed out, relating to my earlier comment that Kim Ha-seok was the mastermind behind the Gando 150,000-Won Incident. In writings about Yun Dong-ju, it is often mentioned that Principal Kim Yak-yeon was involved in the incident, which took place in January 1920. This is incorrect. The patriotic martyrs of the incident have nothing to do with Myeongdong School. It is true that Choi Bong-seol, one of the leaders, was Mr. Kim Ha-gyu's son-in-law and that Pak Ung-se was also related to Kim Ha-gyu, but they were not graduates of Myeongdong School. Moreover, when this incident took place, Kim Yak-yeon had long been imprisoned in China and thus had nothing to do with this important incident.

Another erroneous supposition proposed by researchers is that Kim Yak-yeon procured military funds for General Kim Jwa-jin's army. General Kim joined and served as the commander of North Road Military Station, which, at that time, was called Jeong'uidan (Justice Troop—Trans.) and later became Korean Military Station. After the Battle of Cheongsan-ri in October 1920 and during the massacre by the Japanese army, General Kim fled via Ando (Antu in Chinese—Trans.) Prefecture. He never came back to North Gando and was murdered in 1930 in Northern Manchuria's Yeong'an Prefecture. Principal Kim Yak-yeon was being held in a Chinese prison even before General Kim came to North Gando and was not released until after General Kim's departure. Thus, not only was it impossible for him to procure military funds for General Kim's army, but he never had any contact with General Kim.

EUNJIN MIDDLE SCHOOL

North Gando was swept into a great financial and political whirlwind while facing ideological problems at the same time. The Great Depression began in December 1929 with the American stock market crash, and its aftereffects immediately rushed into North Gando. Grain prices plummeted in the autumn of 1930. North Gando's economic and social prospects were dismal, and the Communist Party was gaining even more power.

Political and militaristic cataclysms followed. The Manchurian Incident broke out in 1931, and Manchukuo was established in 1932. Japan had staged the event in 1931 to invade Manchuria in full force and placed Qing's last emperor, Puyi, as the nominal ruler of Manchukuo, a puppet state consisting of three eastern districts (Fengtian sheng, Jilin sheng, and Heilongjiang sheng—Trans.), Yeolha (Rehe in Chinese—Trans.), and the eastern part of Inner Mongolia. At this time, North Gando became a part of Manchukuo. For the patriotic Joseon Koreans, circumstances became even more difficult than when the place was under China's jurisdiction.

Yet trees grow despite the storms—that is the nature of the living. The same is true for children, who grow without ceasing and reach for the sky. Thus did Yun Dong-ju, a boy who moved to Yongjeong.

As to when the Yun family moved to Yongjeong, according to Professor Yun Il-ju, Yun's brother, "In 1932, he [Yun Dong-ju] enrolled in Eunjin Middle School, a Christian mission school in the small city of Yongjeong which was 30 *ri* north of Myeongdong. With that, and for other reasons, we let out the farm and house and moved to Yongjeong."[8] Thus, Professor Yun states that they moved "around the time when Yun Dong-ju started Eunjin Middle School in April 1932."

However, Kim Jeong-u, the poet's cousin and fellow Myeongdong Grade School graduate, writes that "Dong-ju's short life of less than 30 years [can be marked by] leaving Myeongdong Village for Yongjeong in late autumn when he was fifteen,"[9] fixing the date as "late autumn" of 1931.

While Professor Yun was only five years old in 1932, Kim Jeong-u was fourteen, so his memory may be more reliable. Also, wealthy people were leaving Myeongdong for fear of the Communists at that time. It makes more sense that the family would have left for the safer city as soon as the autumn harvests were done.

Professor Yun probably ruled out 1931 because Yun Dong-ju attended a Chinese grade school then. However, his aunt's family (including his cousin Song Mong-gyu) remained in Myeongdong, and when Song and Yun started Eunjin Middle School together, Song stayed in Yun's home in Yongjeong to attend school. It is not difficult to see that a reverse arrangement was made while Yun attended the Chinese grade school.

At any rate, the Yuns' move to Yongjeong brought about great changes to the family.

First, for the patriarch Yun Ha-hyeon, this move was nothing but a loss. He had been a farmer all his life—and a successful, diligent farmer at that—and for a farmer, not having a farm is as bad a punishment as a teacher with no pupil.

His son Yun Yeong-seok was thirty-six years old. As he entered city life, he attempted a successful transformation by opening a printing shop. As an intellectual starting a business in the city, he probably liked the fact that it was a cultural enterprise. But, like all cultural enterprises, "culture" is something seen externally; it is still a business one has to manage from the inside. Yun Yeong-seok was more of a scholar and proved to be a poor businessman. He failed in the business. Later, he managed a dry goods store but failed again. And the same was the case when he started a poultry business. Time after time, he failed to make a living, remaining a pale-faced intellectual.

He lost his faith, too, and stopped going to church. After moving to Yongjeong, the family began attending Jungang Presbyterian Church, served by Reverend Mun Jae-rin after his return from his studies in Canada in 1932. Yun Yeong-seok alone turned his back on the church. An elder's son losing his faith and not going to church was a very painful wound, but nothing could be done. In later years, after hearing of his son's arrest and imprisonment in Japan, Yun Yeong-seok started going to church again. Facing enormous anxiety and misfortune, he felt helpless and could not help but turn to God. A father's ardent love, compelling him to beseech God for his son's safety, consumed all his doubts.

It was not just the family's lifestyle that changed after the move. Their dwelling conditions saw great changes. Their new home, 36, District 1, Borough 2, Yongjeong, was a twenty-*pyeong* house with a thatched roof.[10]

The house in Myeongdong had vegetable gardens, threshing floors, a deep well, and a small orchard. Featuring a big gate with a roof, it was the biggest tile-roofed house in the village. After having lived comfortably in such a big house for many years, they moved to a small thatched-roof house. And under this small thatched roof lived a family of eight, consisting of grandparents, parents, three children (the fourth child, Gwang-ju, was born later in Yongjeong), and Song Mong-gyu. In this hard-up environment, Yun started Eunjin Middle School.

These circumstances, however, did not have a negative effect on Yun, and he grew like a sapling. The extant records about his years at Eunjin Middle School reveal an untainted, innocent youth. Professor Yun writes:

> During middle school, his hobbies were various. He was a soccer player but also stayed up late to write mimeographs for the school magazine. He'd alter store-bought clothes himself, taking in the waist or making them wide hemmed, all by using the sewing machine without his mother's help. During his second year, he took first place in the school's speech contest with a speech titled "One Drop of Sweat."[11] A framed painting of Jesus that he received as a prize always hung in our house. He'd place an orange crate on a large mortar and practice the speech standing on top. I can still see his face in my mind. But he was not an orator. They said he won the contest because of his composed tone and the content of the speech. He was not interested in oration after that. He was good at math, too. He especially liked geometry.[12]

Picturing Yun according to these statements brings a pleasant smile to one's face: a literary soccer player, a dandy who alters his clothes fashionably using a sewing machine, a book lover who's good at math, and so on.

Reverend Mun Ik-hwan, Yun's childhood friend and classmate from Myeongdong Grade School, Eunjin Middle School, Sungshil Middle School, and Gwangmyeong School, had an interesting anecdote to tell relating to Yun's sewing skills: "Dong-ju was so good at sewing machines. Our school soccer club members had to have their numbers on the uniforms, and Dong-ju brought all the uniforms home and sewed them on." Perhaps his mother's excellent sewing skills were passed on to him.

This episode also provides important information about his character. Good sewing skills speak not only to his dexterity but also to his aesthetic sense. In addition, this story defies the common image of Yun as an introverted and passive person. In the early 1930s, Korean men's ways of thinking were like those of the Middle Ages. It was almost unthinkable that a man would sew, but Yun did so openly. He had a potential, or conscious determination, to actively take action if needed.

Here Reverend Mun provides some insight into their middle school years:

In the spring of 1932, Dong-ju, Mong-gyu, and I met again at Yongjeong's Eunjin Middle School. Eunjin Middle School was a mission school operated by the Canadian Presbyterian Mission. It was on the same hill as Myeongshin Girls School, where the poet Mo Yun-suk taught for a while. The missionary-operated Jechang Hospital, and four houses for the missionary were there. The hill was located on the south-east side of Yongjeong. We called it the English Hill. Until [this should be "Even after"] Manchukuo was set up, it had extraterritoriality, and the Japanese police and the Chinese authorities could not enter without a permit. We could wave our Taegeukgi flag and sing the "Aegukga" anthem all we wanted. It was elating. Whenever there was a school program or even a simple class meeting, we started it with "Aegukga."[13]

There was a teacher who greatly influenced all of us in the school. His name was Myeong Hui-jo. He studied East Asian history at Tokyo Imperial University, but he said he never rode the streetcar while studying there because he did not want to hand in money to the Japanese. During break one year, he rode his bicycle all the way to his hometown Pyeongyang from Yongjeong. He was a crotchety man but also an unbelievably dedicated patriot. His East Asian history and Korean history classes were truly exciting. He opened our eyes to see Korean history in relation to East Asian history, and further to world history. He enlightened us, enabling us to see the liberation of Korea in the long run.

This Mr. Myeong Hui-jo, the legendary veteran teacher at Eunjin Middle School, sent Mong-gyu to China. I think it was when we were in the third year. I never got to ask Mong-gyu on what mission he had gone there. Mong-gyu suffered greatly because of the trip and did not graduate from Eunjin Middle School. Later he graduated from Daeseong Middle School and went to Yonhui College.

The Japanese police must have paid attention to Mong-gyu. In the end, Mong-gyu's sentence was six months longer than Dong-ju's.

Mong-gyu was very talented. During our second year [it should be the third year], his short story was selected at *Donga Ilbo*'s writing contest. Dong-ju used to say, "A great talent matures slowly." He was conscious of Mong-gyu's successes.

During our first and second years at Eunjin Middle School, Dong-ju was absorbed in Yun Seok-jung's children's ditties and songs.[14]

One thing must be clarified here. Waving Taegukgi and singing "Aegukga" are heartwarming elements to Koreans, but, as Reverend Mun added, "All textbooks in Eunjin Middle School were entirely in Japanese."

Surprising as this statement was, we can look at this quote alongside an earlier statement and correctly see that Eunjin Middle School was protected by extraterritoriality in light of the surrounding circumstances: "But the funny thing is that our teachers would open the Japanese textbook and read it aloud in Korean. Of course, the teaching was done in Korean, too. We grew up being taught like that."[15]

These days, the term "simultaneous interpreting" is used commonly, but it seems that the Eunjin Middle School teachers conducted classes by simultaneous translation.

In 1935, there were significant events taking place in Eunjin Middle School. Before the spring semester, Mun Ik-hwan transferred to Pyeongyang Sungshil Middle School, and during the spring, Song Mong-gyu sneaked into China for resistance work. In autumn, Yun left home for the first time to transfer to Pyeongyang Sungshil Middle School.

These changes had a great effect on Yun's life. In particular, Song's career of devoting himself to the independence movement became the decisive factor in Yun's arrest and death while imprisoned.

Among the events that took place in 1935, the most noteworthy was Song Mong-gyu winning *Donga Ilbo*'s annual spring literary contest. Song entered the contest in December 1934, and the newspaper published the winners on January 1, 1935. Song won for the conte genre with his entry titled "The Spoons," which was printed in the January 1 edition of *Donga Ilbo*.

Song was in his third year at Eunjin Middle School at the time and was competing with adults for a spot in the major newspaper contest. His was a splendid feat, as spring literary contests in the 1930s were an authoritative gateway to the literary world, much more so than they are now.

This was also notable because it gave as much of a literary motivation to Yun as it did to Song, who had been keen on literature since he was young and was greatly encouraged by the feat. This "small success" by Song was the background about which Yun commented, according to Rev. Mun Ik-hwan, "A great talent matures slowly."[16]

In terms of the compilation and organization of Yun Dong-ju's literary work, Song's success was an especially significant event, as it marked the moment when Yun started to date and collect his works with care.

Throughout his life, Yun was exemplary when it came to recording the completion date of a work and safeguarding it. Needless to say, this practice was immeasurably valuable to scholars researching his life and work, even though they failed to notice what the starting date of this practice signified.

The first works dated and kept by him are "Life and Death," "A Candle," and "There's No Tomorrow," all dated December 24, 1934. The chronology attached to his poetry collections indicates that these three poems are his very first works.

It cannot be said, however, that all three poems, which are of notable quality, were all written on December 24, 1934. Instead, the date should be regarded as a final completion date of what had been written before.

Of all the drafts that must have been made before Yun reached the level of quality we see in the three poems, few remain. This shows that Yun did not have the precise determination or tenacity to organize and keep his works before December 24, 1934, which was one week prior to Song's work winning the prize and its publication in the national paper. From this we can see that Yun, greatly stimulated by Song's feat, acquired a new awareness and firm determination about his own works and dated the three poems he had completed the week before. From this point on, Yun dated and safeguarded every poem that he wrote.

The three poems thus became a new literary starting point for Yun. Among these, "A Candle" has received much attention from Yun scholars as a symbolic representation of his life as a "pure sacrifice," as is described in the poem.

A CANDLE

A candle—
I breathe in its fragrance in my room.
Before the altar of light collapsed,
I saw a pure sacrifice.

Its body like a goat's rib cage—
Even its will, which is its life—

It burns them to ashes,
Shedding tears of white jade and blood.

It shimmers on the desk,
Dancing like a heavenly maiden.

In my room, where
Darkness fled through the window
Like a pheasant fleeing upon seeing a hawk,
I breathe in the great fragrance of the sacrifice.

(December 24, 1934)

CHAPTER 4

Song Mong-gyu

H ERE, A SPECIAL chapter is devoted to Song Mong-gyu, Yun's cousin and bosom friend. From birth to death, Yun and Song lived their lives intricately intertwined. Thus, Yun Dong-ju's life cannot be thoroughly elucidated without examining Song's as well.

"The Spoons"

We start by examining Song's contest-winning story "The Spoons." Its Korean title, "Sulgarak," has the same meaning as *sutgarak*, the Korean word for spoon. As seen in the proverb "One-*sul* of rice cannot fill one's stomach," the word *sul* was used to mean "spoonful" in the past. Beggars would knock on the gates of houses, yelling, "Please give me a *sul* of rice!"

When "The Spoons" won the contest, Song was using his childhood name, Han-beom. Thus, the author's name was recorded as Song Han-beom.

WINNER IN THE CONTE GENRE[1]

"The Spoons" by Song Han-beom

My wife and I have no choice but to starve now.

All pawnable things are pawned, and nothing is left.

"Ah, husband! Can't you go out and find a way?"

Despite her hunger, my wife can yell as crossly as any other woman.

I keep my seat warm and say nothing. Watching me blinking and sighing there quietly, she turns her head and starts producing tears again. Sure enough, my heart smarts at the sight. But it is what it is.

Silence stays with us again.

"Ah, wife, there's a way!" After some moments, I'm the first one to break the silence suddenly.

"What? A way? What way?"

Perked up by the sound "a way" she turns to look at me and asks in a gentle voice.

"You know, when we got married—those silver spoons, I mean."

"What? You mean to pawn even those?"

No sooner than my answer came, I get her ferocious words and glare.

In fact, the pair of spoons are untouchable. My father-in-law sent them as a wedding present, from a faraway foreign country where he lives. And I think about the letter that came with those spoons.

"Congratulations on your wedding. I wish you good years together till your hair turns gray. I am sending these spoons as a present. Don't skip meals, even if rice gruel is all you can spoon with these. My good wishes will be contradicted if you can't even get rice gruel."

But we don't even have rice gruel to eat. My tears flow ceaselessly as I think about my predicament of having to pawn even these spoons. But we're hungry, and I can't think about such things.

"What can we do, honey?" I open my lead-weight mouth and console her with my faint words. Tears are rolling down her cheeks.

"I'd rather starve than pawn them," she whimpers in a choked voice.

"But what can we do? We will get them back again soon!" I tell her gently, prying about her, who's quiet and droopy now. At this sight, I tell her again with renewed strength, "Honey, let's do that. We will get them back soon, won't we?"

"Well, it's up to you," says my wife as if resigned, but more tears are flowing down her cheeks.

Indeed, it cuts to the heart to part with the spoons, our whole fortune. It's not just because they are silver spoons. It's because they are the only wedding present from my wife's father, who had to go to the country of —— in exile.

"One is for you, and one for your wife—always keep them with you even if the world comes to an end!" My eyes can still clearly see the words in the letter.

On the backside of the spoon, my wife's and my names are engraved in the square style, underneath the Chinese characters for "Congratulations" and "Wedding."

I pawned them and returned home with rice, kindling, meat, and vegetables.

Without words, my wife starts making rice. Rice is boiling loudly in the pot, and its savory fragrance pierces my nose. As I breathe in, my stomach wiggles, and I swallow saliva.

Rice is ready. Steam rises thickly from the rice between us as we sit facing each other.

My wife glares at me suddenly as she is about to eat.

"Let's eat," I offer her apologetically, but she continues to look daggers at me as if she hasn't heard. At last, two streams of tears slowly flow down her cheeks. What's the matter with her now? I wonder. Ah! I turn my face away, only realizing then that we no longer have spoons to eat with. [The End][2]

This is the unedited original text.[3] At any rate, "The Spoons" is a superb story that possesses the charm of flash fiction. Its composition, development, and reversal at the end are woven together to make a unifying theme, creating a deep pathos about life. The story reveals Song's precocious literary accomplishment.

Song's Birth and Development

Song Mong-gyu was born on September 28, 1917. He was the eldest son of Song Chang-hui (1891–1971), a Christian and Joseon (Korean) language teacher at Myeongdong School.

Song Chang-hui's family is a Eunjin Song clan based in Ungsang-dong, Unggi-eup, Gyeongheung-gun, North Hamgyeong Province. At age fifteen, Song Chang-hui's father left his hometown in Chungcheong Province for Vladivostok, Russia, but on his way there he settled in Ungsang, becoming successful. Song Chang-hui was born and raised in Ungsang, but he was sent to Seoul to receive a Western education. Afterward, he went to Myeongdong, married Yun Shin-yeong (Yun's aunt, 1897–1966) and became a member of Myeongdong School's faculty.

The history behind Song Chang-hui's marriage to Yun Shin-yeong reveals an active part taken by Yun Dong-ju's mother.

At first, Myeongdong School had a Joseon-language teacher named Pak Tae-hwan. Pak was a graduate of Cheongnyeon Hakgwan in Seoul and a favorite student of Ju Shi-gyeong, the greatest Korean scholar of the time. Pak even wrote an introduction to Ju's seminal *Urimalbon*. A scholarly family in Myeongdong asked the respected Pak Tae-hwan if he could introduce them to a man suitable to marry their daughter. Pak brought his friend Song Chang-hui to Myeongdong for a meeting with the family. During the visit, Song Chang-hui was staying at the home of Mr. Kim Yak-yeon.

Yun's mother, Kim Yong, who was Kim Yak-yeon's sister, saw Song while she was visiting there. Impressed with his appearance, character, and intellect, Kim Yong thought that he would be a good match for her sister-in-law, who had reached a suitable age for marriage, and she went home to report about him. After her father-in-law, Yun Ha-hyeon, met him, Song Chang-hui was rushed to meet Yun Shin-yeong, after which the two were married. The groom had been snatched up.

Immediately following the marriage, Song Chang-hui became a member of the faculty at Myeongdong School. He taught Joseon language and sericulture, and after Myeongdong Middle School closed down, he taught at Myeongdong Grade School.

According to his relatives, Song Chang-hui attended both Cheongnyeon Hakgwan and Oseong School in Seoul. The late Reverend Kim Jae-jun, who was acquainted with him, stated that Song also attended Boseong School. The late Professor Yun Il-ju, Yun's brother, remembered going to his uncle Song Chang-hui's house and seeing a certificate written in Korean *purossugi* [a linear organization of letters] among diplomas and certificates in a drawer. Ju Shi-gyeong used to bestow on his pupils certificates that he wrote in *puros-*

sugi, which means that Song Chang-hui also completed Ju Shi-gyeong's Korean lectures.

Song Chang-hui's father, Song Shi-eok, was still alive when Song Mong-gyu attended Yonhui College; Song Shi-eok was the head elder of the family and is recorded as so in Song Mong-gyu's Yonhui College registration. He became a Christian early on, and in his later life, he became a leader in the church. A big and tall man, he was masculine and broad-minded and enjoyed drinking liquor. He was even chastised once by the church about his drinking.

Song Chang-hui was the fifth son of Song Shi-eok, who had fathered six sons and one daughter. Among the children, the eldest son, Chang-hang, passed away when he was young, leaving behind a son named Won-gyu. The second and fourth sons moved to Russia via Vladivostok, and the third and fifth sons moved to Myeongdong Village. Only the youngest son remained in his hometown.

The Song clan in Ungsang had contact with Western culture early on because geographically, it was on the road to Vladivostok. The family was progressive in character and embraced Christianity and Western culture without hesitation. They established an elementary educational institution named Bukil School in Unsang-dong to educate the young. Many of them dedicated themselves to the independence movement or went abroad to study. Among Song Chang-hui's second cousins, Chang-bin fought in General Hong Beom-do's independence army and was killed by the Japanese during a battle in 1920, and Chang-geun went first to Japan and then to the United States to study, returning to Korea as a pastor in 1931. He was the first Korean to receive a PhD in theology from an American university.

Song Shi-eok's eldest living grandson, Won-gyu, had a teaching post in Hoeryeong after studying in Japan. Later, however, he became keenly interested in new farming techniques and left his post to go back home to start an apple orchard and a poultry farm. His success defied the popular belief that "you can't grow apples in Hamgyeong Province," and the then-new breed of Leghorn chickens became a popular breed in the area. Many people learned from him and accumulated wealth through poultry farming. The fact that Song Chang-hui taught sericulture in addition to the Korean language demonstrates the family tradition.

In the spring of 1916, Song Chang-hui married Yun Shin-yeong, the eldest daughter of the town leader and elder Yun Ha-hyeon. As both families were

Christian, the ceremony was a Western-style Christian wedding. Mrs. Kim Shin-muk was a bridesmaid. Unlike the usual custom at that time, under which the bride was older than the groom, Song Chang-hui was twenty-five and his bride, nineteen.

After the wedding, the couple lived in the Yun house, as the Yun family was the richest in town and Song Chang-hui had only recently moved there.

The following autumn, on September 28, 1917, Song Mong-gyu was born, and three months later, on December 30, Yun Dong-ju was born in the same household, beginning their lifelong affinity. When Mong-gyu was five years old, his family left the Yun house to live in their own place.

Mong-gyu's childhood name was Han-beom, which he was called both at home and at school, even during Eunjin Middle School. The name Han-beom has the great meaning of "the law of Korea." The "gyu" in "Mong-gyu" is from the generation character *gyu* (star). Because his mother saw a great star in her dream before he was born, his parents chose the character *mong* (dream).

The following testimonies about Song Chang-hui vividly illustrate the family atmosphere in which Song Mong-gyu grew up.

> THE POET KIM JEONG-U: He was strict and had a prominent nose, and students gave him the nicknames "Tiger Song" and "Nose Ridge."
>
> PROFESSOR YUN IL-JU: Uncle was a large-framed man with strong features. When he was smoking his pipe, which he always enjoyed, he didn't look Korean but rather like a German. He was very fond of us and good to us.
>
> YUN HYE-WON (YUN'S SISTER): Uncle had a regal appearance. He was strict but also considerate. When it came to his children's education, he was understanding and supportive. My father was trying to force Dong-ju to go to medical school, even though he wanted to study literature. But Uncle said, "Children's inclination and intention should be respected. We should not try to control them according to our own desire," and respected Mong-gyu's desire to study litera-ture. Uncle was a devoted husband and loving father.

Song Chang-hui later became the principal of the grade school in Chil-dogu (Qidaugou in Chinese—Trans.), and around the time Song Mong-gyu went to Yonhui College, he was the town head of Daerapja Village in Hwaryong (Helong—Trans.) Prefecture. Nevertheless, he never learned Japanese. Song

Ung-gyu (1916–1988), who was Song Mong-gyu's cousin and had lived in Unggi throughout childhood, reminisced, "Toward the end of colonization, Uncle came to our home because of some family affair. I thought it was very strange that he spoke no Japanese even though he was a school teacher and a town head in Manchuria."[4] At that time, not only in public offices but also in all schools, everyone had to use Japanese. Yet Song Chang-hui rebelled against the idea of learning and speaking Japanese.

Yun Hye-won lived with the Songs for a year while Song Chang-hui was the town head of Daerapja. According to Ms. Yun's recollection, Song Chang-hui did not get along with the police chief in town, who was also Korean, while in other towns, town heads and police chiefs had good relationships. Whenever Song came back from a meeting with the police chief, he'd have a drink in a fit of anger and tell his second son U-gyu, "No one from our family should bear a gun or a saber."

Giving vivid descriptions of Song Mong-gyu in childhood, the poet Kim Jeong-u, Song's Myeongdong Grade School friend, reminisced as follows during my interview with him:

> To me, the name Han-beom feels more affectionate than the name Mong-gyu because I always called him Han-beom when we went to school and played.
>
> Han-beom was smart, a good student, and outgoing. Being enthusiastic in everything, he would often come out and say, "Let's do this!" and then we'd follow him.
>
> Han-beom's house was a big tile-roofed house that stood at some distance across the stream from Dong-ju's house. In the front of the house was a small pear orchard and several kinds of fruit trees. He had a little sister [Han-bok, born in 1923] and was the only son [his brother U-gyu was born in 1931, the year they graduated from grade school]. His mother was very considerate and attentive to whatever Han-beom wanted, and I liked going there because I felt free to do things. On Christmas Eve, we'd go to Dong-ju's house, which was next to the church, but usually, we went to Han-beom's house to play. But when his father came home, we felt uncomfortable and returned to our homes.
>
> I remember that in fourth grade, Han-beom developed a tick of blinking his eyes. Our teacher Mr. Han Jun-myeong stood silently facing him and blinked his eyes until Han-beom stopped.
>
> Han-beom was always a leader. He was the leader when Dong-ju and others published a mimeographed magazine called *New Myeongdong* in

fifth grade. When we put on a Christmas play directed by one of the teachers, Han-beom would assign the roles to the classmates. Once, when we put on a play called *The Shoeshine Boy*, Han-beom told me to take the lead role and I did.

He was outgoing and would go to many places. I remember that once, he was called as a witness during a trial. It was when we were in fifth grade. One Sunday, we were in Sunday school service when Han-beom ran into the classroom. He said that a middle-aged man was hanging on a big branch in the willow forest near the stream. So we all went out to see it.

Afterwards, I kept seeing the dead man in dreams and couldn't sleep well for days. A few months passed, and the incident was almost out of our memory. Then, they held a trial in relation to the death of the man in Dae-rapja, the prefecture capital. All the children who had gone to the scene were summoned. Other children stayed with the teacher outside of the courthouse while Han-beom and another boy named Kim Jung-man entered the courthouse and gave testimony.[5]

During Eunjin Middle School, Song Mong-gyu honed his literary skills, as we saw from his winning of the national spring literary contest. Additionally, it is interesting to note that in 1934 he gave himself a literary, or art name: Munhae (Ocean of Writing). This art name, or *ho*, reveals his literary ambition. His use of the *ho* has left physical traces: he had a square seal made for himself that reads "Munhae Jangseo" (Library of Munhae—Trans.), and he used the seal when categorizing and organizing his books. Among Yun's remaining keepsakes is a book titled *The Dictionary of Philosophy* (Japanese edition), which bears the seal.

Nakyang Military School

Song Mong-gyu went to China in March 1935. He had completed the third year at Eunjin Middle School that month but left before the fourth year began. Because North Gando was part of Manchukuo at the time, China was a foreign country. Moreover, since the Manchurian Incident of September 18, 1931, Japan was spreading its evil hand over China with the ambition of continental invasion. Gruesome battles between China and Japan continued.

The armies of the two countries fought fiercely during the First Shanghai Incident, which took place on January 28, 1932. The Shanhaiguan Incident broke out on January 1, 1933,[6] and a ceasefire agreement was not reached until May 31.

Additionally, the Chinese continent was covered with blood and gun smoke as a civil war continued between Kuomintang—led by Chiang Kai-shek, the leader of the Republic of China—and the Communist Party. On October 5, 1933, Chiang Kai-shek's National Revolutionary Army of one million soldiers began its fifth communist cleanup operation, which continued into the following year.

The year 1934 was also a gloomy and hopeless time of worldwide lunacy. The riot of February 6 culminated when far-right leagues created a great disturbance in France. On August 18, Hitler was elected by popular vote as the chancellor of Germany and wielded absolute power. In China, the communist cleanup operation continued for nearly a year. This bloody civil war finally came to a lull when the Red Army retreated and began the Long March toward the west on October 16.

The year 1935 dawned. Political situations were boiling like molten iron in a smelting furnace, and Song Mong-gyu left for China, the country that had been overwhelmed by angry waves of history. This visit to China influenced Song greatly. Moreover, it became the root cause of his and Yun Dong-ju's deaths.

Why did he drop out of school and go to China? What was the truth behind the trip? Its purpose was top secret. Even his bosom friend Reverend Mun Ik-hwan knew little about it: "Mr. Myeong Hui-jo, the legendary veteran teacher at Eunjin Middle School, sent Mong-gyu to China. I think it was when we were in the third year. I never got to ask Mong-gyu on what mission he had gone there. Mong-gyu suffered greatly because of the trip."[7]

Song's cousin Professor Yun Il-ju had understood it simply as studying abroad. "Many Korean students in Manchuria at that time wanted to study abroad, especially in Korea. Song Mong-gyu went to Jilin and then to Beijing; Mun Ik-hwan transferred to Pyeongyang Sungshil Middle School. Dong-ju was so envious of them that he persuaded the elders in the family to let him transfer also to Pyeongyang Sungshil in September 1935."[8]

Until the end of 1977, these were the only pieces of information on Song Mong-gyu's visit to China available to Yun Dong-ju researchers when groundbreaking information was unearthed: interrogation records of Song and Yun by imperial Japan's Special High Police "under strict secrecy." The documents were disclosed to the public in Japan, and *Munhak Sasang* translated and printed them in its December 1977 issue. Song's visit to China received new attention.

According to the interrogation records: "[Song Mong-gyu], while attending Eunjin Middle School, went to Kim Gu's group that had laid dormant in Nanjing in order to join in their work and stayed there until November that year, receiving training. But when he saw that his goal might not be reached because of internal problems in the group, he went to Jinan to join another independence fighter Yi Ung. Pressured by investigating authorities, he did not achieve his goal and returned to his parents in his hometown in March of 1936."[9] Having seen this material, I became intrigued and started collecting other materials on Song Mong-gyu's visit to China. As a result, I gathered a few pieces of quite important information.

First, it was revealed that those who were very close to Song Mong-gyu's parents knew more about the nature of the visit and yet stayed silent. The interrogation records simply state that Song "went to Kim Gu's group . . . in Nanjing . . . [and] receiv[ed] training." However, it was revealed through Mrs. Kim Shin-muk's testimony that he had actually "received training in the military school run by the Provisional Government of Korea." Additionally, Dr. Song Ung-gyu, Song's cousin, confirmed the same. From April 1936, Song was jailed at the police station in his family's hometown of Unggi, North Hamgyeong Province. When he was released in September 1936, Dr. Song went to the police station as the receiver of a released detainee. On the way home, when Dr. Song asked Song, "Why were you arrested?" Song answered, "Because I went to the Provisional Government's military school." Song also told Dr. Song that after the military school was disbanded, he went to Jinan and worked with other independence fighters but was arrested and sent to Korea by the Japanese police that belonged to the Japanese consulate in Jinan.

Second, more concrete evidence remains in the strict security documents of imperial Japan's Special High Police. Until Japan's defeat at the end of World War II, the Ministry of Security in the Department of Interior, in order to assist its Special High Police's operation, put together various kinds of information, issued the records "under strict secrecy," and disseminated them only to the applicable agencies. Included among these documents are records relating to Song's attendance in the military school.

At that time, the Special High Police classified incidents by the year. Thus, the activities of Korean independence fighters in China that took place in 1936 are put together under the subtitle "The Status of Seditious Schemes by Rogue Joseon People in China in 1936." Recording in detail about military schools operated by Joseon Koreans in China at the time, it lists the names of thirty-eight Korean students who were arrested in 1936 under "Table of Arrestees from the So-Called Joseon Military School Incident." Song Mong-gyu's name is found in this table.

The following is the part relevant to Song Mong-gyu.

Agency: Jinan Consular Police
Place of Arrest: Jinan
Date of Arrest: April 10, Showa 11
Aliases: Wang Wi-ji, Song Han-beom, Go Mun-hae
Legal Name and Age: Song Mong-gyu, 21
Place of Origin: North Ham-gyeong
Occupation: None
Military School Type: Nakyang Military School (Kim Gu faction)[10]

This record provides several pieces of information about Song Mong-gyu's activities while staying in China.

First, the official name of the military school that Song referred to as "the Provisional Government's military school" is Nakyang Military School, whose allegiance was to the Kim Gu faction.

Second, Song used three aliases, Wang Wi-ji, Song Han-beom, and Go Mun-hae.

Third, Song was arrested on April 10, 1936 (Showa 11) in Jinan (capital of Shandong Province) by Jinan's Japanese consular police.

Fourth, as a result, he was put on the Special High Police's blacklist for surveillance.

Later on, the continuous surveillance of Song Mong-gyu as a "person under suspicion" from 1936 led to the July 1943 arrest of Song Mong-gyu and Yun Dong-ju in Kyoto, Japan.

Both "the Provisional Government's military school" and Nakyang Military School refer to the Joseon Koreans' section in the Nakyang Campus of the Central Military School in Nanjing, China.

The reasons for and details behind the establishment of this military school are recorded in *Baekbeom Diary*, the autobiography of Baekbeom Kim Gu. The following excerpt gives the full account of the school. After the patriotic martyr Yun Bong-gil's heroic undertaking of bombing Shanghai's Hongkew Park (now Lu Xun Park—Trans.) on April 29, 1932, Kuomintang and its leader Chiang Kai-shek finally took an active interest in the Provisional Government of Korea. Their support became the motivation and background of the Korean military school.

As Pak Nam-pa was a Kuomintang member, he was acquainted with Chen Kuo-fu, head of Kuomintang's Department of Organization and chairman of the government of Jiangsu. With Chen as a go-between, I was notified that Chiang Kai-shek requested a meeting with me. I went to Nanjing, accompanied by An Gong-geun and Eom Hang-seop. Key figures like Gong Pei-cheng and Xiao Zheng came to greet me as representatives of Chen. They took us to the Central Inn.

The next evening, I rode in Chen's automobile to General Chiang's residence located in the Central Military School, taking Pak Nam-pa as interpreter. Mr. Chiang, dressed in Chinese attire, greeted me with a pleasant expression on his face. After the greeting, he spoke to me in a clear, brisk tone, "Each nation in the East should achieve democracy according to the Three People's Principles of Mr. Sun Chung-shan [Sun Yat-sen]." I agreed and added, "As Japan's evil hand of continental invasion is infiltrating China day by day, I will say a few more words to you in private."

After Mr. Chiang said, "Hao, hao [good, good]," Chen and Pak left us.

I took my brush and wrote, "If you provide a million yuan, I will make disturbances in Japan, Joseon, and Manchuria within two years and cut off Japan's route to continental invasion. What do you think?"

He read it and wrote in turn, "Please provide me with a plan." Afterwards, I left him.

The next day, after I made a brief plan and submitted it to Premier Chiang, Chen Kuo-fu invited me to his summer villa and held a party for me. He delivered a message from Premier Chiang: If we kill the emperor, there will be another emperor, and if we kill the leader, there will be another leader. How about training military officers for the future independence war? I replied that even though that was my utmost wish, I had dared not ask.

Thus, it was decided that Luoyang [Nakyang—Trans.] Military School in Henan Sheng would have a branch school for the purpose of training

Korean military officers. Initially, about one hundred young Korean men would be recruited from Beiping [Beijing—Trans.], Tianjin, Shanghai, and Nanjing. They would be enrolled in the school and taught by Yi Cheong-cheon and Yi Beom-seok from Manchuria. (However, the Nanjing government, under pressure from Japanese Consul Suma, shut down the military school after it graduated its first class.)[11]

With these backgrounds, the Korean section of Nakyang Military School was installed, and with utmost secrecy, ninety-two Korean students were recruited from China and Manchukuo and enrolled in the school. Actual military training began in February 1934. Financial support came entirely from the Chiang Kai-shek regime. It was a one-year program, and Song Mong-gyu went there to be in its second graduating class.

At that time, the Chinese government kept the existence of the Korean military school in utmost secrecy, in consideration of China's relationship with Japan. It feared that great complications would develop if Japan found out that the official military training institution of the Chinese government was producing Korean independence fighters. This was prior to the official breakout of the Sino-Japanese War. In order to maintain secrecy, Koreans were disguised as Chinese. Materials related to the military school reveal that all the Korean students made up and used Chinese names. This was why Song Mong-gyu had three aliases, including the Chinese-style name Wang Wi-ji.

How did Song Mong-gyu, who lived in North Gando belonging to Manchukuo, know about the existence of the military school and go there to enroll?

With regard to this issue, there is a definitive witness, Reverend Ra Sa-haeng (born 1914 in Gaecheon, South Pyeongan Province). He was a year ahead of Song at Eunjin Middle School and then became a classmate of Song at Nakyang Military School. In April 1935, Ra went to China to enter the military school. As Song had gone before him, they met again in China. Ra gave a very important testimony to be remembered in the history of the Korean independent movement, as well as the personal history of Song Mong-gyu:

Reverend Ra's Testimony Regarding Nakyang Military School

Q: When and through what route did you hear about Nakyang Military School?

A: While the first class was being trained in 1934, I was in the fourth year, the graduating class, at Eunjin Middle School. Our history teacher

Mr. Myeong Hui-jo told us, "Such a military school was established, and some of our school's graduates went to attend it." That's how I heard about it. Some from Eunjin Middle School were already there.

Q: How did Mr. Myeong receive such information?

A: He was well acquainted with the prominent figures of the anti-Japanese struggles, such as Kim Du-bong and Kim Gu. That's probably how he knew about it.

Q: What was Mr. Myeong like? What kind of influence did he have on the students?

A: He was a great scholar and nationalist. He was a graduate of Tokyo Imperial University and taught history and Chinese writing. He'd teach us "The Ode to the Red Cliffs." He was a great scholar of Chinese classics. He was an open-minded person. In those days, the fabric was of poor quality, and when we had suit pants made, they would not last long because the knee area would wear out quickly. So, he had his slacks made like women's, with no distinction between the front and the back, and rotated them alternately. He was unconventional. He influenced us greatly, awakening the historical consciousness in us.

Q: Could you give specific examples?

A: I will give my case as an example. At that time, I was reading the novel *Earth* by Yi Gwang-su, and I was greatly moved by it. [Note: Serialized in *Donga Ilbo*, from April 12, 1932, to July 10, 1933, *Earth* was Yi Gwang-su's major work in enlightenment literature.] It wasn't just me. So many young people were moved by it. We wanted to devote our life to the "Ideal Village Movement," like the protagonist in the novel. The idea became quite popular. So, I wanted to go to Sungshil Agriculture College after graduating. But Mr. Myeong drove a wedge on the popular idea. He explained, "A nation needs three elements—territory, people, and sovereignty. But right now, without sovereignty, we are slaves. Without sovereignty, nothing can be accomplished. Your Ideal Village Movement is no exception. That can't be done with individual efforts. What is the purpose of the Ideal Village Movement? For human beings to live lives worthy of human dignity. Then, let us think about it. Even if our dwelling or living environment improved somewhat, if our status remains as slaves, with our sovereignty robbed from us, is that a living worthy of human dignity? That is why, if we want to lead the true Ideal Village Movement, we first have to achieve independence before anything." Because of this explanation, I gave up the thought of enrolling in the agricultural college and chose to go to Nakyang Military School.

Q: Which route did you take to go to China? Did you travel with anyone else?

A: It was three of us, Hwang Guk-ju, Yi In-yong, and myself. The Japanese control was extreme on the way. By then, even Tianjin, near Beijing, was filled with Japanese troops. Whenever we encountered a roadblock, we showed our student identification to them, lying that we were going to a Chinese teacher's school in order to become teachers. Our initial destination was Tianjin. At that time, in Jinan, an Eunjin graduate by the name of Yi Ung was engaged in resistance work. We were to have a secret rendezvous with Yi Ung when we arrived in Tianjin.

After we got there, Yi Ung directed us to "go to Nanjing and find Hyeon Cheol-jin, who is attending Nanjing Central University." So, in the end, we chose the route of Tienjin to Jinan to Xuzhou to Nanjing, and met with Hyeon in Nanjing. Hyeon was also an Eunjin graduate. He connected us to Leader Kim Gu. In other words, we followed a kind of relay course from North Gando to Nanjing, where Mr. Kim Gu was. Song Mong-gyu followed the same course.

Q: What was your life like afterwards?

A: Song Mong-gyu had been there before me. Because of the protests and pressure from Japan, China could not directly enroll us in Nakyang Military School at that time. So, all of us in the second graduating class had to lodge together in a large Chinese civilians' house at 32 Dongguantou, inside the city walls of Nanjing. The Chiang Kai-shek government gave each of us twelve won a month, nine won for food and three won for spending money. It was quite a sum at that time, and we had no difficulty living on it. Basically, we had thirty *jeon* for food a day, but actually, fifteen *jeon* was enough to buy decent meals. We'd each order food for delivery.

Q: How many students were there?

A: About thirty.

Q: What was the curriculum like?

A: Military training and language classes, like Chinese.

Q: Who were the teachers?

A: Mr. Kim Gu came sometimes, but mostly we were taught by Mr. Eom Hang-seop and Mr. An Gong-geun. After living at 32 Dongguantou for a couple of months, we transferred to Longchi Temple, which is located in Longchi Mountain in Yixing Prefecture, Jiangsu Province. It was about one hundred *ri* from Nanjing.

Q: Is Longchi Temple a Buddhist temple?

A: Yes. Chinese temples were huge and very rich, too. Longchi Temple was also large in scale with the capacity to house three thousand people. A whole battalion could enter without notice and stay there. We stayed and received training there from June to early October. During that time, Kim In (Kim Gu's eldest son and one of Nakyang Military School's first graduates) taught us as a drill instructor. Mr. Kim Gu and Mr. An Gong-geun visited from time to time as well, and Mr. Eom Hang-seop stayed there with us as general director. After that, we came back to Nanjing in early October.

Q: What do you remember especially from those times?

A: I remember the evening of Korean Thanksgiving Day we had in August [in the lunar calendar] of 1935 while we were living in Longchi Temple. Mr. Kim Gu and several other leaders of the independence movement came to the temple to spend the day with us. We had conversations all night long, sharing Chinese moon cakes. As we talked about the past and what had happened to our nation, we were enraged at first and ended up wailing. It became a sea of tears. Also, we talked about international politics, like Italy's potential invasion of Ethiopia, the signs of another world war, and the chance of Korea's independence as a result of that. Mr. Kim Gu also told us in detail how he had killed a Japanese man in Chihapo and drank his blood to avenge the assassination of Empress Myeongseong.

Q: Did you do anything else besides military training?

A: With Song Mong-gyu taking the lead, we published a booklet when we were in Longchi Temple. He asked all of us to submit essays, and we ended up with quite a thick booklet, about 300 pages. I submitted one, too, starting with, "All for the independence of our Fatherland!

All for the people of Korea! All for Christ!" and it was included in the book.

Song was gifted in literature. He was cheerful in disposition and was a good writer. He bought a mimeograph machine, hand-copied the manuscripts, and produced the book himself. Mr. Kim Gu praised it highly and named the book *New People* because Mr. Kim had once been a member of a group by the same name, and he also wanted all of us to be "new people."[12]

The testimony of Reverend Ra about Nakyang Military School is very valuable to the study of the Korean independence movement, as it illuminates the preparations for anti-Japanese military resistance that the Provisional Government attempted and the circumstances surrounding it.

Historical meanings aside, this testimony is interesting in that, like the full moon rising to the night sky, it shines a light on two individuals.

The first one is Mr. Myeong Hui-jo. The young students were intoxicated with a pseudo-idealism suggested by Yi Gwang-su's enlightenment literature, but Mr. Myeong sternly awakened in them the great cause and correct perspective for history. He retained both strict fairness and dignity, as appeared in the guiding principle of Confucius when he was writing the *Annals*. The figure of the "true teacher" is revealed splendidly here. Yun Dong-ju's poetics, defined by purity, came out of an environment where he was trained strictly under the tutelage of such an excellent teacher.

The second person is Mr. Kim Gu. While we have examined through *Baekbeom Diary* the personal history behind the establishment of Nakyang Military School, Reverend Ra's testimony explicitly reveals all the expectations and endeavors Kim Gu had for the school. In particular is the moving story about the "sea of tears" and wailing under the full moon by Kim Gu and the young students on Korean Thanksgiving Day in 1935. Leader Kim Gu also has his own warm episode relating to the military school, which is also recorded in *Baekbeom Diary*:

In Nanjing, I was told that my mother had arrived at Eom Hang-seop's home in Jiaxing after visiting An Gong-geun in Shanghai. I rushed to Jiaxing to meet her for the first time in nine years.

As soon as she saw me, she told me something unexpected: "From now on, when I address you, I will not use the familiar term 'you,' but use the more formal term instead. I may still rebuke you verbally, but will no longer use a rod to punish you. I heard that you have started a military school to educate young men and now serve as an example to others, and I do not want you to lose face."

I was much obliged and grateful for her instructions.[13]

Baekbeom Kim Gu was born in 1876 (the Year of the Red Rat). When Nakyang Military School started in 1934, he was already fifty-eight years old. Yet only then did he hear from his mother that she would no longer exercise corporal punishment on him and would address him using the formal term.

The first graduation of Nakyang Military School was on April 9, 1935. Out of ninety-two enrollees, sixty-two graduated. The curriculum covered regular military training such as operating and handling various artilleries and machine guns, revolutionary moral education, and equestrian training using forty war horses that had been placed there.

One flaw here was that the students were divided three ways and fiercely opposed to each other. The supporters of the Chinese government were greatly concerned with this issue as well. According to Dr. Song Ung-gyu, who had received Song Mong-gyu after his release from Unggi Police Station, Song had also expressed his fears about the serious "faction struggles" among the independence fighters while telling his cousin about his military school experience.

After the first graduating class, Nakyang Military School did not officially enroll students. Strictly speaking, therefore, it cannot be said that Song Mong-gyu and his class were students of Nakyang Military School. However, in other Japanese intelligence materials, the school was referred to as the Training School for Korean Independence Army Special Reserve or the Korean People's Party Reserve Training School.

Nevertheless, Song and others went to China to enroll in Nakyang Military School, and all the characteristics of their education, such as recruitment, training, and financial support from China, were continuations of it. Viewed that way, they were clearly graduates of Nakyang Military School, and that is why the Japanese intelligence document "Table of Arrestees" listed Nakyang Military School as their affiliation.

The students of the second graduating class were dispersed after they entered Nanjing proper from Longchi Mountain in early October 1935.

A review of related documents shows that they left Longchi Mountain because the financial support from China was discontinued.

Why did Chiang Kai-shek stop the financial support? At that time, Chiang was in the middle of warfare against the Red Army, commanding the army himself in various battles. By early 1932, the Red Army had grown to 200,000 soldiers with 160,000 rifles. A full-scale war with such an enemy was exerting on Chiang, and he did his best.

In the end, the Red Army was pushed off by Chiang's army and began a great retreat from their base in Jiangxi, known as the Long March, and all the while, Chiang continued to fight, chasing after them. Both armies scaled eighteen mountains and crossed seventeen rivers, covering 12,000 kilometers. During the march, chasing and being chased, the bloody, wretched battles continued. In November 1935, with the Red Army's arrival at Yanan in northern Shanxi, the Long March ended.

Chiang's discontinuation of financial support for the Korean military school took place during the Long March and must have been connected to the situation in China. The following excerpt shows the fierceness of the battle between Chiang's army and the Red Army led by Mao Zedong:

> From around that time, the Red Army started to fight with Mao's unique war strategies. They looked as if going north toward Szechuan but would suddenly proceed westward, only to turn around, meandering to Zunyi. At that time, Chiang Kai-shek was staying in Guiyang, the capital of Guizhou and south of Zunyi, as he was flying on planes this way and that way to command his army. Mao's army seemed to go south again to attack Guiyang. While Chiang was mustering troops from Yunnan to protect Guiyang, Mao's army bypassed eastern Guiyang at once and proceeded west toward Yunnan, which now had a weak defense.[14]

At that time, Chiang had enemies both in and outside China. Inside was the fierce civil war with the Red Army; outside, Japan was intensely provoking a war for continental invasion. Unable to fight two enemies at the same time, Chiang asserted the policy of *an nei rang wai*, or "achieve peace inside, then defeat the foreign invasion." Thus, he was fully occupied with subjugating the Red Army while Japan took over Manchuria and threatened Beijing. With patience and caution, Chiang merely tried to avoid an official outbreak of war with Japan.

Thus, the reason for the sudden cut off in the financial support to Nakyang Military School is explained by Chiang's policy of not provoking Japan. Later on, after the infamous Xi'an Incident on December 12, 1936, Chiang changed his policy to *rang wai an nei,* or "first defeat Japan, then achieve peace inside." But by then, Korean independence fighters' plans for producing military forces had suffered a setback.

After coming back to Nanjing, Ra lived with Kim Gu's mother and brother Kim Shin near Nanjing's Central Park. Yi Ji-seong, a fellow trainee, stayed there as well. Ra went by the name Ra Cheol at the time.

Stating that he'd "really like people to know about this person," Ra gave the following account:

Sixteen from the first graduating class of Nakyang Military School transferred to the Central Military School in Nanjing after graduation. Among them was a man named Kim Gap-seong. He was from Onjeong-ri near Geumgang Mountain and a classmate of mine at Eunjin Middle School. Unlike me, who had finished the four years of middle school, Kim had entered the military school after finishing the third year.

Around mid-October of 1935, while attending Central Military School, Kim was gravely injured during grenade-throwing training and died shortly after. A trainee in front of him had delayed throwing a grenade after taking the safety pin out, and the grenade blew up above them. Kim was hit by shrapnel, taken to Central Hospital, but pronounced dead.

The Central Military School honored him by awarding a posthumous commission of second lieutenant of the Chinese army and gave a military funeral. However, concerned with potential issues with Japan regarding Kim's identity, they only wrote his name as "Wang Ui-seong, a Martyr from the Northeast." Wang Ui-seong was his Chinese alias, and "Northeast" referred to Korea, as Korea was north-east of Nanjing.

Ra finished the story with the following words:

Do you know how much we cried and cried at the funeral? Even at death, in the last moment of departure, neither his name nor his country could be revealed. He had to be buried under an alias. The sorrows of not having one's own country felt bitter to the bone marrow.[15]

Have the wounds from the pitiful epoch now been healed? I was choked with emotion while scribing his story.

Arrested, Incarcerated, and Blacklisted

Song Mong-gyu was arrested on April 10, 1936, in Jinan, Shantung, by the Japanese consular police.

When had Song moved from Nanjing to Jinan? According to the case report drawn up by the Kyoto Regional Trial Court on Song Mong-gyu's violation of the Maintenance of the Public Order Act, Song left Nanjing "around November 1935" and "entered a Korean independence movement group under the Yi Ung faction in Jinan." This meant that Song was arrested within six months of his arrival in Jinan. What led to his arrest?

We can infer Song's case from Reverend Ra Sa-haeng's account of his own arrest.

After spending about one month at Kim Gu's mother's house in Nanjing, Ra went back to Shanghai. He, too, left Nanjing around the same time as Song, in November 1935. Shanghai and Nanjing were about 500 *ri* (about 180 miles—Trans.) apart. After Yun Bong-gil's 1932 bombing of Shanghai's Hongkew Park, the leaders of the Provisional Government had fled Shanghai to avoid the Japanese police's sweeping roundup and were wandering all over the continent. In other words, the Provisional Government had moved.

Ra was arrested by the Japanese police soon after arriving in Shanghai. One day he was visited by Japanese officers from the Gaecheon Police Station in South Pyeongyang Province, where he was originally from. They entered his boardinghouse and told him, "Let's go." They took him and locked him up in the Shanghai Consular Police Station. Subsequently, he was transferred to Gaecheon Police Station and then to Pyeongyang Police Station. He spent almost one year in a cell at the Pyeongyang Police Station.

"The Table of Arrestees" in the Japanese police's intelligence document shows that graduates and trainees from Nakyang Military School were being arrested one after the other, dating from October 1935. It seems that as intelligence on these students continued to leak to the Japanese government, the students were rounded up one by one.

The following episode about Yi Ung, a resistance fighter who was the intermediary base for Song and Ra as they traveled southward, clearly shows how threatening these times were.

While Ra was still locked up in Pyeongyang, a man named Hyeon Cheol-jin was transferred from Nanjing. It turned out that Hyeon was arrested for assassinating Yi Ung, who in fact was a traitor and double agent of Japan.

Yi Ung was an independence fighter based in Jinan, who had a very wide circle of acquaintances at all levels of society. He was on familiar terms with not only Korean independence movement leaders but also powerful top officials like Han Fuju, the governor of Shandong. At that time, a governor had enormous power, holding legislative, legal, and administrative powers, and even the authority to issue currency circulated in the province. Yi Ung would greatly show off his acquaintance with such high-level people. When Yi met Ra's company, he told them, laughing, "Han is magnanimous in character but an ignoramus. He asked me once, 'Do your people eat eggs from hens, too?'"

Being acquainted with many influential men, he seems to have collaborated with Japan later, perhaps for money. After Hyeon Cheol-jin discovered that Yi was a double agent, he and Yi Ik-seong, another Eunjin Middle School graduate, killed Yi Ung. It was actually Yi Ik-seong who killed Yi Ung, but only Hyeon was arrested. These Eunjin graduates were interconnected through independence activism, and when a traitor appeared, they made him pay for the price of treachery with his life.

The Japanese police's top-secret records on Hyeon state:

Name: Hyeon Cheol-jin
Date of Arrest: May 1936
Place of Arrest: Tianjin
Age: 27
Place of Origin: South Hamgyeong Province
Uses four aliases, Yang Cheol-saeng, Hyeon Cheol-jin, Choi Seong-ho, and Yang Cheol-san [This record, however, mistakenly classifies him as a member of Uiyeol Faction of Nakyang Military School.][16]

Here is another noteworthy fact. Song, who was with Yi Ung in Jinan, was arrested on April 10, 1936, by the Japanese consular police, while Hyeon Cheol-jin was arrested in May for killing Yi Ung. There is a probability, then, that Song's arrest and Yi Ung's treachery are connected.

Let us now see what happened to Song Mong-gyu after the Japanese police arrested him in Jinan, China.

Following his arrest, Song was transferred to Unggi Police Station in North Hamgyeong Province, where his family was registered. At that time, the Japanese police, after arresting suspects abroad, would often transfer them to the town of their family register to be interrogated. This practice by the Japanese police is clearly confirmed with the arrest of Ra Sa-haeng, who trained with Song at Nanjing and Longchi Mountain.

According to Japanese police records from that time that are still preserved, the so-called Nakyang Military School Cases were well known to them through ongoing investigations as the students were arrested one after the other beginning in October 1935.

In the case of Ra Sa-haeng, he was arrested in Shanghai on November 12, 1935, about a half year before Song. Later, a *Donga Ilbo* article printed a full account by Ra, a summary of which follows.

The police in Gaecheon, South Pyeongan Province, detected that Ra was rooming somewhere in Shanghai. They went to Shanghai to arrest him and brought him back to Korea (reported on November 26, 1935, in *Donga Ilbo*). First, he was brought to Gaecheon and then sent to jail in Pyeongyang. *Donga Ilbo* reported the judicial decision on Ra in its August 26, 1936, issue, stating that the Pyeongyang police closed its nine-month interrogation of the parties concerned with the military school. On August 25, it placed Ra and two others in custody for violating the Maintenance of the Public Order Act and sent them to the Pyeongyang District Prosecutor's Office. The rest were released. Reverend Ra stated that he had been tried and released on probation.

As for Song, there was an eyewitness to his transfer to Unggi Police Station. Dr. Song Ung-gyu, Song's cousin, lived in Ungsang-dong, Unggi, and happened to witness the scene. He stated:

Mong-gyu was taken there by train. As soon as he got off the train, he was taken to Unggi Police Station and locked up. He was alone, with no family member accompanying them. We did not know why he was arrested. He was in jail for a long time. The elders of our clan tried hard to find out, and rumors were that he'd be indicted and sent to a prison in Cheongjin or things like that. But then he wasn't sent to Cheongjin. The police told us to "take away Song Mong-gyu." So I went. I found him emaciated and pale like white paper because he hadn't seen the sunlight for a long time. The police instructed him to remain in Unggi. Despite that, Mong-gyu took off to Manchuria after a few days of rest. But they did not harass me for that, even though I was the one who had taken him away.[17]

Dr. Song thought that Song Mong-gyu had not been taken to Cheongjin, which is incorrect. The documents relating to Song Mong-gyu extant in the Japanese police records confirm that Song was arrested on April 10, 1936, in Jinan, China, taken to the Unggi Police Station on June 27, and sent to the Cheongjin Prosecutor's Office on August 29. He was jailed there for sixteen days and was sent back to Unggi Police Station on September 14. He was then released under the restriction of residence. Dr. Song must have assumed that Song Mong-gyu had stayed in Unggi all this time because he was released there.

As we compare judicial decisions concerning Song and Ra, we see that they were released at around the same time and under similar circumstances. It looks as if the Japanese law enforcement authorities had guidelines on how to treat the parties related to the Korean military school and uniformly executed those guidelines. It can be assumed that they saw legal hurdles in applying the Japanese public order laws to prosecute and sentence Korean students who were under Chinese jurisdiction. Instead, they decided to release them for the time being and to put them under surveillance as blacklisted.

Song ignored the restriction-of-residence order and returned home to North Gando to rest. The following year, in April 1937, he enrolled in his fourth year at Yongjeong Daeseong Middle School. His studies had been interrupted for two years while he was in China and then jailed in the Unggi Police Station and the Cheongjin Prosecutor's Office. When he resumed his studies, he lived in Yun's house in Yongjeong and commuted to school. Even though he wanted to go back to Eunjin Middle School, the school was being watched and investigated often then, and it could not take a problem student.

Yun's sister, Hye-won, vividly remembers the conditions Song was living under at the time. After his release, he often complained that his back was getting slouched over. He tried to straighten his shoulders and chest, and slept without a pillow to help straighten his back.

Song's trip to China became the root cause that would ultimately lead him and Yun to death in prison in the days to come. From this time on, the Japanese police had Song on a blacklist and watched him. Eventually, the police arrested Song and Yun, and they were tried and sent to the same prison, where they died side by side.

CHAPTER 5

Seven Months in Pyeongyang

As 1935 began, the third-year students at Eunjin Middle School were feeling unsettled because they were at a turning point where their paths would diverge.

First was the path of resistance activism, like the one Song Mong-gyu took. Those who chose it would have to leave not only the school but also their home and family behind, preparing themselves for unknown places between life and death.

Second was the path to higher education. In order to be admitted to a higher school, they would have to transfer to a five-year middle school. At that time, the formal middle school curriculum was five years. Thus, graduating from a four-year middle school would be disadvantageous when applying to high school, junior college, or university preparatory courses.

Transfer Examination for Sungshil Middle School

Five-year middle schools accepted transfer students up to the incoming fourth year. It was almost impossible to transfer to a five-year middle school as a fifth-year student after graduating from a four-year middle school. Therefore, if they wanted to transfer, they had to complete their transfer papers between the conclusion of the third year and the beginning of the fourth year.

In Yongjeong, the only five-year middle school was Gwangmyeong Middle School, a pro-Japanese school authorized to receive financial support from Japan's Ministry of Foreign Affairs. Schools outside Japan with such authorization were regarded as being just as prestigious as those in Japan. Because Gwangmyeong was a pro-Japanese school, however, Yongjeong's nationalistic Korean families and Christian Koreans did not wish to send their children there. Instead, they bore the high financial burdens of sending them to Sungshil Middle School, a five-year missionary school in Pyeongyang. Yun Dong-ju's classmates were now at this turning point.

As the new semester began in the spring of 1935, there were many empty seats in the classrooms. Among Yun's friends, Song went to China, and Mun went to Pyeongyang to attend Sungshil. Yun also wanted to transfer to Sungshil, but his family would not allow it, so he had no choice but to start his fourth year at Eunjin. However, after pressing his family constantly, he was permitted to go to Pyeongyang by the fall semester, which began on September 1.

In the process, however, Yun experienced failure for the first time in his life: He did not pass the transfer examination and was told that he could transfer as a third-year student but not a fourth. It would be the same as if he had failed and stayed behind one year.

At that time, all who wished to transfer to Sungshil had to take a rigorous transfer examination. Mun Ik-hwan, of course, took the exam, too. One of Mun's fellow exam takers was a son of a minister who had just become a member of the school's board of trustees; he, too, did not pass and had to start in the grade below. Sungshil had high standards for transferring students, administering a transfer exam that was as rigorous as the entrance examination.

Yun wrote to his sister, Hye-won, sorrowfully notifying her and the rest of the family of the result: "They won't put me in the correct year." Disappointed by the news, the older members of his family sent him a letter rebuking his performance. Yun suffered greatly upon reading the letter. Even those around him noticed it.

But even if they had offered warm words of comfort and encouragement, Yun would have had a hard time. The one who fails is least likely to forgive the failure. And this failure was not only painful in itself but also seemingly ironic in that his friend Mun, who had been his classmate five months ago, would now become his senior in school. This situation seemed to accentuate his failure even more clearly and wretchedly.

In the end, however, Yun endured the situation honorably and became adjusted to his new school and his life in Pyeongyang, a big city that used to be the capital of Goguryeo.

A passage from his poem "Hospital" probably describes how he felt then: "This excessive ordeal . . . I should not get angry."

Professor Yun Il-ju writes, "He arrived there during the semester and had to repeat the fall semester of the third year because of the different system."[1] From the fact that Professor Yun did not disclose his brother's failing the exam even decades later, we can see how much the Yun family, as well as Yun himself, took this situation to heart.

Yet covering up the truth with the inaccurate and ambiguous "different system" is beneficial to no one, as it blocks a passageway to further understanding Yun's poems and life.

From what basis can such an argument be made?

In the analyses of Yun's poetry, the most frequently discussed is the "aesthetics of shame." In fact, truly remarkable are the phrases that mourn and ruminate on the agonies of life in the presence of, and with a keen awareness of, shame. Through these passageways that Yun prepared, we are furnished with a new reading of the limitations of human life and their sorrows.

Let us examine the opening of "Prelude," which is considered his magnum opus:

Looking up at the sky to my dying day
I wished no speck of shame within me,
But even at the breeze between leaves
I suffered.

A journalist once wrote that we might have to wait for one generation, or even two, for a great poem that a whole people can sing together. No Korean poet before Yun Dong-ju had ever confronted with their whole existence the deeply rooted shame that was carried like karma. We had waited countless generations to gain these lines at last.

As we read them, we come to realize at last that shame is not merely an ordinary feeling but rather a pattern of introspection about human existence itself. Shame is a type of repentance by imperfect beings, mourning their imperfection. In order for a person to honestly face shame, his whole existence, his whole weight of being, must be present. Lacking the experience of standing eye to eye with shame, one cannot sing so beautifully, so piercingly.

How and when did Yun come to see this terrifying essence of shame?

We see no other time but when he failed the transfer examination to Sungshil. At that time, his circumstances were miserable. His failing meant a failure in many aspects.

Though he could return to Eunjin and continue with the fourth year, entering a higher school would still be a problem after graduating from Eunjin. Moreover, it would be too shameful to return to Eunjin after he had failed the exam in Pyeongyang. On the other hand, it was just as embarrassing to repeat the third year in Pyeongyang. He was caught between a rock and a hard place.

It was a financial predicament, too. It could not have been for any other reason than a financial one that his family was against his going to Pyeongyang in the first place. Like other parents, his parents must have wanted Yun to get a diploma from a big five-year school in Pyeongyang, even if nobody else could. They had seen some of Yun's friends successfully transfer, but they had to consider the financial situation. They were no longer a small-town rich family. They had left their farm to tenant farmers when they moved to Yongjeong in order to avoid the terrors of communists, and the farm's grain production had gone down by more than half in no time. Each of his father's new businesses took a bad turn. Despite the difficulties, Yun had begged his parents for the transfer to Pyeongyang, but because he had failed the exam, they would end up paying one more year of tuition. Had he not failed, the time and money invested would not have been wasted.

As for failing, he would have accepted it more easily had he been a poor student. On the contrary, however, he was considered a good, even an excellent, student. How could such an unreasonable thing happen? The more unreasonable it seemed, the greater were his feelings of pain and shame.

In the summer of 1987, Omura Matsuo, a professor at Waseda University in Japan and a Yun Dong-ju specialist, visited Seoul. When he went to see Reverend Mun Ik-hwan for an interview, I accompanied him. At that time, Reverend Mun stated:

> Since young, Song Mong-gyu, Yun Dong-ju, Yun Yeong-seon, and I, the four of us were always the top students. Yeong-seon became a medical doctor later on, but he was the type who only studied and was not very noticeable. The other three stood out, and our feelings for each other were like this: I felt inferior to Dong-ju because he was always a step ahead of me, and he felt inferior to Mong-gyu because Mong-gyu was a step ahead of him. Dong-ju used to say to Mong-gyu, "Great talents are slow in

maturing," and what he admitted, in fact, was, "Right now, I'm behind you." Those two were so very extraordinary.

Considering this statement, we can feel Yun's embarrassment and shame surfacing above water. At the core of his shame was the fact that Yun did not pass the exam that Mun, who felt inferior to Yun, had passed.

An episode illustrates Yun's inner psychology, as related by Reverend Mun.

During Sungshil days, Dong-ju, I, and two others took a picture together. I still have the picture, and when I look at it, old memories come to me. We took the picture after Dong-ju and I swapped our hats, and I remember why we did that.

In the picture, I'm wearing Dong-ju's hat and Dong-ju's wearing my hat. Dong-ju had his eyes set on my hat so much that I let him swap the hats. At that time, the school hats weren't bought off the shelf but were custom-made at the hatter's shop. Like going to a tailor for a suit, you'd go to the hatter and he'd measure the circumference of your head and make the hat. My hat came out straight and square, but Dong-ju's hat came out a bit crooked and crushed. He hated his hat and coveted mine. Dong-ju was never greedy about anything and would never covet other people's things. It was so unusual of him to want my hat. So I said, "Alright, then, if you want my hat that much, I'll swap it with yours. Just buy me some *hotteok*." He agreed, so we went to the bakery and I had my fill of the hotcakes there. We swapped the hats, and the picture was taken after that.

As darkness deepens, light is yearned for. The murkier things get, the greater purity is cherished. Why did Yun hate the "crooked and crushed" hat so much? His sense of identity suffered so much from his distorted position that he hated his "crooked and crushed" hat, too. Against his usual character, he truly coveted his friend's hat because it was "straight and square." Yun longed for an image that was straight, flawless, and dignified.

This episode shows how sincerely and honestly he stood before his failure and shame. He would not have suffered so much if he could have let it go and comforted himself by saying, "I feel bad that I failed the exam, but that was just bad luck" or "One can stumble at times in life, but a stumble may prevent a fall." But he did not do that. He was honest and sincere before shame because he was pure in heart, a blessing from God. Not everyone can be pure in heart, as it is an innate character with which one is born.

"Blessed are the pure in heart for they shall see God," says the Bible. What did his pure eyes see when he stood eye to eye with his own shame? He saw the imperfection in human nature. From that place, from that very spot, he penetrated into the human imperfection that cannot be helped, that cannot escape shamefulness. It was not a vague glimpse from afar but a clear recognition as if it were a face-to-face encounter in broad daylight. A soul that had never walked through the purgatory of such recognition cannot emit the deep, reverberating groan of:

> Looking up at the sky to my dying day
> I wished no speck of shame within me,
> But even at the breeze between leaves
> I suffered.

And this deep reverberation is the terrifying force that lifts mankind to take a step forward toward divine perfection. Only with such a groan in front of us can we completely understand that we are powerless beings and must prostrate before the demand of the stern Christ, "Be perfect as your father in heaven is perfect." Only when we desperately suffer from human imperfection can we truly recognize divine perfection.

If the nature of God can be defined as perfection, and if recognition of human imperfection leads to recognition of God's perfection, the promise that "the pure in heart . . . shall see God" can be fulfilled in us.

The Collected Poems of Jeong Ji-yong: Before and After

Pyeongyang is an old capital, the oldest city in Korea. Abutting the Daedong River, it is the hub of the Gwanseo region (the northwestern area of Korea—Trans.) in administration, economy, culture, and transportation. A city of history, it boasts numerous legends and scenic spots of renown and beauty and is famous for its arts and pleasures, as demonstrated by its nickname, Home of Beauties. One popular saying about it is, "Only a fool refuses a high position in Pyeongyang." The city's traditions continued through the end of the Joseon dynasty. Because of its opulence, Western missionaries who arrived in Pyeongyang in the early stages of evangelism called it "the Sodom of Korea."

The missionaries first started coming in 1887. In 1893, the American Northern Presbyterian Mission's station was established in Pyeongyang, and Christianity expanded rapidly except when it became a battleground for the Sino-Japanese War (1894–1895). Eventually, Pyeongyang became a city of Christian culture and was called "the Jerusalem of Korea."

Sungshil Middle School was a splendid achievement for Christian education. It was founded in 1897 by American missionary William M. Baird, who taught thirteen students in his own house. The school grew rapidly, and in 1908 it obtained formal authorization as a "university" from the Korean Empire's education department. It became famous as the best Western educational institution in the Gwanseo region, with a university and a middle school on one campus.

At first, Sungshil's school year started in September, following the American way. In 1912, however, after the annexation, the Japanese school calendar was forced upon it, and its school year now started in April, following the trimester calendar. This system continued until the school was shut down for refusing to follow the ritual of Japanese shrine worship.

Under the trimester calendar, the first semester was April through August, the second semester was September through December, and the third semester was January through March.

Yun attended Sungshil for the duration of the second and third semesters of the third year. This was the first time he had been away from home. Public transportation between North Gando and Pyeongyang was very inconvenient. His train would take him to Seoul, after crossing the Tumen River and stopping at Sangsambong, Hoeryeong, Cheongjin, and Wonsan. From Seoul, he would take the train back north toward Sinuiju and get off in Pyeongyang. Yun stayed in the school dormitory and ate in the school cafeteria, which used the meal ticket system. One of his poems describes this simply:

MEAL TICKETS

Meal tickets give three squares.

The kitchen maid gives young men
Three white bowls.

Soup boiled with water from the Daedong River,
Rice that came from Pyeongan Province,
Paste made from hot peppers of Joseon,

Meal tickets fill our bellies.

(March 20, 1936)

The life at Sungshil became a new turning point in poetry writing for him, as is clearly shown when a chronological list of his works is reviewed.

After "A Candle," "Life and Death," and "There's No Tomorrow," the three poems dated December 24, 1934, he wrote only one poem—"In the Streets" (January 18, 1935)—in the eight months before he left for Sungshil Middle School.

However, after he started at Sungshil, things changed. He was eighteen years old at that time, an impressionable age. As he experienced life away from home for the first time and the conflict and agony of failing the exam, his eyes opened to a new horizon.

During the seven months he spent at Sungshil, he finished fifteen poems, at the rate of two poems a month:

- Ten regular poems: "Daydream," "Azure Sky," "Southern Sky," "Pigeons," "Parting," "Meal Tickets," "At Moranbong," "Twilight," "Heart (I)," and "Skylark"
- Five children's poems (*dongsi*): "Seashells," "Home," "Chicks," "Bedwetter's Map," and "Mr. and Mrs. Rooftile"

Among these, "Daydream" is a monumental work in that it is Yun's first poem to be published. It was printed in the October 1935 issue of *Sungshil Hwalcheon*, a school magazine that was first issued in 1922 and published by Sungshil Middle School's student body:[2]

DAYDREAM

Daydream—
The tower in my heart,
Silently, I am building this tower.
In the sky of fame and vanity,
Not knowing that it will crumble,
Floor by floor I build it.

My limitless daydream—
That is the ocean of my heart.
I spread my arms
To swim freely in my ocean
Toward the horizon of
Knowledge of gold.

Not only did Yun contribute his poem to the magazine, but he also worked as its editor. Reverend Mun Ik-hwan stated:

Dong-ju only attended Sungshil for a semester [two semesters], but during that time, he was in charge of editing the school's literary magazine. I remember that he published a poem in it. Even though Dong-ju was a newly transferred student, Yi Yeong-heon (now a professor at Presbyterian Seminary School), who had known Dong-ju from Eunjin, asked him to take over the editor position when he became the editor-in-chief. At that time, Dong-ju also asked me to submit a poem, so I did. After looking at it, he said, "That's no poem!" and returned it to me.

Ever since then, I had nothing to do with poems. Had Dong-ju lived and helped me with Bible translations (I'm sure he would have), I would not have written any poems.[3]

Mun's statement is interesting in light of the changes in Yun's own poetry around the time he published "Daydream." The fact that he rejected Mun's poem with a blunt comment, "That's no poem!" tells us that he had his own clear view of poetry. What was his view? We can only deduce it from "Daydream," a work that he considered to be worthy.

Let us reexamine "Daydream." Perhaps he thought a poem should elegantly catch a metaphysical concept with a net woven by fancy and mature rhetoric? Such an impression cannot be denied in the poem. Besides "Daydream," his poems written through October 1935 give similar impressions:

On that summer day
To caress the azure breasts of the sky
The passionate poplar
Opened its arms and shook.
On that narrow spot under the boiling sun.
. . . .
The tender young heart burns with the ideal

On the day of longing,
Scoffing at the tears of decay in fall.
                —Excerpted from "Azure Sky" (October 20, 1935, in Pyeongyang)

As I am walking
In the street of distress,
In the grey street of nighttime,
A whirlwind starts in my heart.
Lonely shadows of the heart
Blooming layer by layer
Azure daydreams move
Up and down, up and down.
                        —Excerpted from "In the Street" (January 18, 1935)

Today, too, life sang a prelude to death
When will this song end?

People—
They dance to the song of life
Of bone-dissolving pain
They had no time to think
Before the sunset
Of the horror at the song's end.
                        —Excerpted from "Life and Death" (December 24, 1934)

The poetic trend consistently revealed in these poems written up to October 1935 enables us to grasp what Yun Dong-ju considered a poem. Yun did not consider Mun's submission a poem because it did not reach the standard and structure that Yun held at that time.

But these "difficult" poems, with the conceptual or pedantic tendencies of a young aspiring poet, disappear at once after October 1935. What happened afterward? Surprisingly, he wrote a *dongsi* (poem for children—Trans.), titled "Seashells," in December 1935:

SEASHELLS

Shimmering glimmering seashells
My brother brought the seashells
From the seashore.

A precious present are seashells
In our country in the north,
Toy seashells

Rolling and rumbling seashells
One lost its mate
It misses its mate

Shimmering glimmering seashells
Like me, they miss it—
Sound of water, sound of waves
(December 1935)

This is the first *dongsi* among Yun's extant works. From this moment, like a dam had burst open, Yun produced one *dongsi* after another. A great transformation also came about in that the poetry of Yun Dong-ju that we now know began to appear—that is, poems with distinct features and flavors and a way of expressing emotions fully and sincerely with simple words. "Pigeons," the next *dongsi* he wrote, is also unique:

PIGEONS

Huggable lovable
Seven wood-pigeons,
In the smooth
Harvested rice field
On a holiday morning
Clear as can be.
They hurriedly
Peck at kernels
Talking seriously.

Shapely wings shaking quiet air,
Two of them fly away
Remembering their babies at home.
(February 10, 1936)

How did this sudden transformation, this fast-forward advancement, come about? Many Yun Dong-ju researchers have had difficulty explaining Yun's sudden abandonment of writing the fancy, conceptual words of a novice poet and move toward producing *dongsi* composed of simple, straightforward words. A critic went so far as saying that Yun went through infantile regression at that time.

The key, however, is elsewhere. It is *The Collected Poems of Jeong Ji-yong*, published on October 27, 1935, by Simunhaksa in Seoul. A collection of eighty-nine poems, this was the first poetry book by Jeong, one of the most renowned poets of the time. Jeong was Yun's lifetime favorite poet. Among the belongings left by Yun is a copy of *The Collected Poems of Jeong Ji-yong*, filled with underlining in red ink and comments in the margins, showing how much Yun had pored over it. While comparative analyses of the influence Jeong's poems had on Yun Dong-ju's poems are for literary scholars to make, the status that the genre of *dongsi* held in *The Collected Poems* should be evaluated. Only by doing so can one explain the transformation of Yun's poems after *The Collected Poems* was published—that is, why Yun suddenly started writing *dongsi* with confidence.

First, the structure of Jeong's collection should be noted. "Apcheon," "Homesickness," and "Café France" are regarded as Jeong's masterpieces as well as some of the finest poems in the history of Korean literature, and they appear in part 2 of the collection. Surprisingly, twenty-three *dongsi* and folk-song-style poems—including "Sunflower Seeds," "A Shooting Star," and "The Third of March"—are collected in part 3, an independent section of the collection.

Let us look at two of Jeong's *dongsi*:

THE THIRD OF MARCH

Monk, monk, colorful monk
Our baby is a bald-head
On the Third of March
Wings go flitter flutter
Baby swallows go flitter flutter

We plucked mugwort,
Made half-moon rice cakes.
Zizz, zizz, put him to sleep
Yum, yum, we ate them all.
Monk, monk, colorful monk
Buy our baby to make him a monk

A SHOOTING STAR

Where a shooting star landed,
I stored the place in my heart
To go there the next day.
I kept meaning to go—
Now I've all grown up.

These innocent, naïve sounding *dongsi* were placed next to famous verses like the following:

Neither a viscount's son nor a somebody I am.
My hands lament for they are unusually white!

Neither a country nor a home I have.
My cheeks lament as they touch the marble table!

O you foreign-breed puppy
Suck on my feet
Suck on my feet
                    —Excerpted from "Café France"

Seeing that Jeong gave his *dongsi* equal treatment as his famous poems, what did Yun feel? Just as a tree is known by its fruit, we guess at the process by looking at the result: Yun reevaluated *dongsi* as a genre and challenged himself with it.

Once started, his *dongsi* writing continued through 1938, his first year at Yonhui College. The result was the birth of outstanding *dongsi*, such as "What Do They Eat?," "Mandol-i," "Sunlight, Wind," "The Sunflower Face," "A Baby's Dawn," and "The Rumbling of a Mountain."

In Yun's copy of *The Collected Poems of Jeong Ji-yong* is an inscription, "1936.3.19." This is probably the date Yun bought the copy. It is my understanding that Yun read the book immediately after its publication even though he purchased it at a later date. This is likely so because the book was the talk of the town from the date it was published. Baek Seok's poetry collection is another example. When Baek Seok's *Deer* was published, Yun borrowed the school library's copy in order to read it, then hand-copied the entire book from the library's copy. Most of all, though, the clearest evidence of the influence of Jeong Ji-yong is Yun's *dongsi* "Seashells," which was written in December 1935.

Recently, however, a very different interpretation from mine was introduced. In an article titled "The Formation of Yun Dong-ju's Symmetrical Ideas: Centering on the Poems from Early Summer of 1936," Professor Pak Eun-hui (Bukkyo University, Kyoto, Japan) claims that Yun started writing *dongsi* after he met "Kang So-cheon, poet of children's songs, in Yongjeong."[4] She goes on to say, "After Yun came back to Yongjeong from Pyeongyang, he was introduced to Kang So-cheon (1915–1963), who was staying with Yun's maternal grandparents in Yongjeong. Kang was a famous, leading figure in children's literature, who had already published numerous *dongsi* since 1930 in major children's literary magazines like *Kids' Life* and *Shin Sonyeon*. This meeting became the driving force for Yun to start writing *dongsi* again in September."[5]

When taken literally, the two met after Yun came back following his withdrawal from Sungshil Middle School, which does not make sense chronologically.

In order to determine the validity of Professor Pak's claim, the following should be examined in order: (1) the time period when Yun and Kang met in Yongjeong; (2) analyses of their respective works during that time period; and (3) the time period when Yun first started writing *dongsi*.

First, when did Kang go to Yongjeong and stay there? "So-cheon returned to his hometown at the start of the winter recess during his fourth year in 1933 and never returned to school. [Instead,] he went to Yongjeong in North Gando, where his paternal aunt lived. There, he stayed for nearly two years. During this period, he befriended Yun Dong-ju, who was two years younger. According to Jeon Taek-bu, Yun's early *dongsi* was greatly influenced by Kang. Jeon stated, 'So-cheon told me that Dong-ju's [poems] were still rough but very good.'"[6]

Kang was from Midun-ri, Sudong-myeon, Kowon-gun, South Hangyeong Province. In late December 1933, during his fourth year at Hamheung Yeong-saeng High School, Kang returned home at the start of the winter recess. When the recess ended in January 1934, however, he headed to his aunt's house in Yongjeong instead of going back to school and stayed there for "nearly two years." At the end of his chapter on Kang So-cheon, author Kim Yong-seong lists the chronology of Kang's life as follows:

1934 (age 19): Stayed briefly in hometown during winter recess; went to North Gando to live in Yongjeong for one and a half years.

1936 (age 21): Returned to hometown; according to Jeon Taek-bu, around this time, Kang got married to Ms. Jeon from Yeongheung.[7]

Jeon Taek-bu is the only person who testified to Kang's stay in North Gando. However, Jeon claimed that Kang stayed there "for about one year."[8] Here is the relevant statement: "He [Kang So-cheon] returned to his hometown at the start of the winter recess during his fourth year in 1933 and never went back to school. Subsequently, he wandered in North Gando for about one year and returned to his hometown. Meanwhile, *Donga Ilbo* and *Joseon Ilbo*, the two papers [that] often published his poems, were forced to cease publication, and even *Kids' Life* was no longer there. So-cheon reached the point of despair."[9]

Thus, the duration of Kang's stay in Yongjeong has three versions: (1) "nearly two years" between 1934 and 1935 (Kim Yong-seong); (2) "one and a half years" (Kim Yong-seong's chronology of Kang's life); and (3) "about one year" (Jeon Taek-bu). In this chapter, the first version will be examined, as this version is most advantageous for the validity of Professor Pak's claim, it being the longest duration of the three.

As for Yun's whereabouts, it was March 1936 when he returned to Yongjeong from Pyeongyang. He had gone back to Pyeongyang before the new semester that would start in April but came back home after deciding to quit school as a protest against the shrine worship forced on students. By then, Kang had already left Yongjeong. Therefore, it does not make sense to state, as Professor Pak did, that they befriended each other after Yun left Sungshil and returned to Yongjeong. So when did they meet? The duration of Kang's stay in Yongjeong has been discussed, so let us examine Yun's case.

Yun moved to Yongjeong from Myeongdong Village in late 1931 and lived there until August 1935. In late August, he went to Pyeongyang, took the exam, and started at Sungshil. At the end of the year, he visited Yongjeong during the winter break. In March 1936, he went back to Pyeongyang for the new school year, only to return shortly after dropping out of Sungshil. In early April, he transferred to Gwangmyeong School as a fourth-year student. When Yun was in Yongjeong at the end of December, he could not have met Kang, since the latter had already left Yongjeong by then.

Therefore, the time period in which Yun and Kang could have exchanged their literary views extends from the spring of 1934 until August 1935, almost "one and a half years."[10] Afterward, they never met again. During this possible time period, however, what did their literary activity entail?

As for Kang, he started publishing *dongsi* in 1930 (or 1931, as some sources say), when he was fifteen. However, according to the list of his published works, nothing was published in 1934 and 1935.[11] This time period coincides with the duration of his stay in Yongjeong, and it is assumed that he was in a slump at the time.

In Yun's case, he published nothing during the time period when the two could have met. On December 24, 1934, he finished three poems for the first time: "A Candle," "Life and Death," and "There's No Tomorrow," the first three of the poems he started dating and storing. Besides these, only one more poem, "In the Street," was written before he left Yongjeong in late August 1935 to start at Sungshil Middle School.[12]

What Yun had written up to this point were poems, not *dongsi*. Moreover, they were long conceptual poems made up of pedantic words. Thus, during the long period of "one and a half years" of friendship, Yun's poems clearly show the absence of any literary influence from Kang.

The same is the case with the poems that Yun wrote after he left for Sungshil, leaving behind Kang in Yongjeong. "Daydream" (October 1935), "Azure Sky" (October 20, 1935), and "Southern Sky" (October 1935) are also pedantic, conceptual, and difficult, completely different from Kang's *dongsi*, which guilelessly express the innocence of children with simple, short, and genuine words. The three poems show that Yun continued to pursue his own poetry with no influence from Kang after they parted. Between the spring of 1934, when Yun supposedly became acquainted with Kang, and October 1935, when *The Collected Poems of Jeong Ji-yong* was published, he never wrote *dongsi*.

However, after *The Collected Poems* was published in October 1935, Yun's poems suddenly changed. One poem that was written between then and his actual purchase of the book was a *dongsi* ("Seashells," December 1935)—the first *dongsi* he ever wrote. It is reasonable to conclude, then, that Yun's *dongsi* writing was inspired by the literary stimulation of *The Collected Poems*.

From a commonsense point of view, it is unreasonable to conclude that a young, aspiring literary poet who had a strong conviction that long, conceptual, pedantic poems constituted true poetry would be so strongly taken by a two-year-older contemporary *dongsi* poet (who was in a literary slump and could not write at all) that he suddenly discovered the *dongsi* genre and started writing it. In fact, Yun never wrote a *dongsi* the whole time he was around Kang. Therefore, the "Kang influence" theory is difficult to accept. Instead, Yun was likely to have marveled at both the outstanding *dongsi* in the collection by Jeong Ji-yong, a renowned poet whom Yun admired, and the status those *dongsi* enjoyed in that collection, providing him with a new awareness of the genre and inspiring him to start writing them.

Further, the literary status that Professor Pak claims for Kang So-cheon is problematic.

She referred to Kang, at the time of his meeting with Yun, as "a famous, leading figure in children's literature, who had already published numerous *dongsi* since 1930 in major children's literary magazines like *Kids' Life* and *Shin Sonyeon*," but this is an exaggeration. Kang was a student at Yeongsaeng High School at the time, and during the four (or five) years between 1931 (or 1930), when his first poem was published, and the spring of 1934, when he first met Yun, he had published a total of nine poems.[13] Kang was still a teenager and had not yet published many poems. Overestimating Kang's influence, regarding him as "a famous, leading figure in children's literature, who had already published numerous *dongsi*" at that stage, is inappropriate. Kang's literary recognition and fame did not begin until 1941, when his first *dongsi* collection, *Pumpkin Flower Lantern*, was self-published.

Not much else is noteworthy from Yun's life at Sungshil except that he had a school trip in the fall to the Dongnyong Cave at Yongmun Mountain in Yeongbyeon, North Pyeongan Province.

In many ways, the time spent at Sungshil was meaningful to Yun's life in terms of his rediscovery of, and devotion to, poetry, even though it lasted only seven months. Its end came with his decision to quit school in protest of imperial Japan's shrine worship policy, which became a painful scar in the modern history of Korea.

Various writings relating to the chronology of Yun's life state that Yun returned to his hometown Yongjeong after Sungshil School was shut down at the end of March 1936 for refusing the shrine worship, and transferred to the five-year Gwangmyeong School as a fourth-year student.

However, that chronology is inaccurate. Yun did not return to Yongjeong after Sungshil was shut down but rather dropped out of Sungshil before it was shut down. Sungshil Middle School was officially shut down on March 19, 1938.[14]

So what is the truth behind Yun's "dropping out"?

The governor-general of Korea began the construction of Joseon Shrine on Nam Mountain in Seoul, which was completed in 1925. Afterward, it was renamed the Joseon Shrine Palace, and shrines started being built all over the country, even in small towns. After starting the Manchurian Incident in 1931, Japan started to force all Koreans to worship shrines under the pretense of "spiritual mobilization."

It was in Pyeongyang that the Japanese started to force shrine worship even in Christian schools operated by Western missionaries. On November 14, 1935, Anmu (Yasutake in Japanese—Trans.), the governor of South Pyeongan Province, mustered all public and private secondary school principals and ordered them to worship the Pyeongyang shrine. Everyone complied except three who operated Christian schools:

- Yun San-on (George McCune's Korean name), an American missionary, principal of Sungshil Middle School, and president of Sungshil Junior College; both schools were established by the American Northern Presbyterian Mission[15]
- Jeong Ik-seong, deputy principal of Sungui Girls Middle School, operated by the same mission
- Yi Hui-man, a missionary and principal of Uimyeong Middle School in Sunan, established by the Seventh Adventist Church Mission

These three principals refused to participate in shrine worship, expressing that their religious doctrine did not allow it.

After this congress of principals, Governor Yasutake sent them letters, notifying them that as shrine worship was a citizen's duty, refusal to do so would be dealt with through firm measures.[16] Thus began the struggles of Christian missionaries against imperial Japan to defend their doctrines.

On January 16, 1936, Governor Yasutake summoned Yun San-on, the principal of Sungshil, along with Mapo Samyeol (Samuel A. Moffett's Korean Name—Trans.), its former principal, to the provincial government building. Yasutake demanded that Yun San-on submit a letter of resignation by the 18th of the month in the case of disobedience.

During the process of struggle, the Seventh Adventists' Uimyeong Middle School surrendered, agreeing to shrine worship. Sungshil and Sungui, however, resisted vehemently. Principal Yun San-on submitted a reply to the governor on January 18 at two o'clock in the afternoon: "I refuse shrine worship and also refuse to resign."

Immediately, the governor revoked Yun San-on's principal license for Sungshil Middle School, and on January 20, the governor-general of Korea revoked Yun San-on's president license for Sungshil Junior College. On that same day, the governor-general also revoked the license of Velma L. Snook, principal of Sungui Girls Middle School.[17] Yun San-on returned to America on March 21, 1936, leaving words of comfort and encouragement for Korean churches in this time of adversity.

Principal Yun San-on was succeeded by Jeong Du-hyeon, a professor at Sungshil Junior College. When the school year started in April, Sungshil Middle School students started creating disturbances. In order to show their respect for Principal Yun San-on, who had sacrificed his position by refusing shrine worship and resisting imperial Japan's unjust pressure and tyranny, they had one demonstration after another. To show their strong and clear opposition against imperial Japan, some students quit school. Yun Dong-ju and Mun Ik-hwan also quit around this time.

Sungshil, adrift in the midst of acute pains, was finally shut down on March 19, 1938, when imperial Japan accepted the petition to close down the school submitted on October 29, 1937.[18] Facing imperial Japan's base coercion to choose either shrine worship or shut down, the Northern Presbyterian Mission chose the latter to sustain its doctrinal purity.

Testimony by Kim Du-chan (b. 1920), a classmate of Yun, clearly attests to the hardship suffered by Sungshil and its students. Later, while attending Meiji University in Japan, Kim was arrested and imprisoned for the bombing of Kyeomipo Ironworks in 1943. After liberation, he enlisted in the military and became commander of the Korean Marines. While serving as a consultant for Gwangbokhoe in 1982,[19] Kim wrote the following article in *Donga Ilbo*:

Brutality and Its Truth: Imperial Japan's Aggression That I Went Through

I was in the third year at Sungshil Middle School in late 1935 when imperial Japan's coercion of shrine worship was at its climax. It was a December morning. Because of the birth of Emperor Hirohito's second son, all students in Pyeongyang were ordered to attend the so-called lantern light worship at Wakamasu Seminary. Sungshil School, which had refused shrine worship, made an exception on that day.

Pyeongyang Shrine Palace was the second grandest shrine in Korea after Joseon Shrine Palace on Nam Mountain in Seoul. It was near the summit of Moranbong hill and required a long climb on steep stone steps to reach. While climbing, we saw other school students' frowning faces as they returned from their turn at the shrine. Sungshil was at the end of the shrine worship file. We were about halfway. Pak In-shik, a fifth-year and president of the student body, suddenly shouted, "Stop! Turn around!" As if a current of electricity touched us, we yelled out and ran down the steps. Terrifying solidarity united us in communion.

As a consequence of this, Principal George S. McCune (Yun San-on) was fired the next month, on January 20, 1936.

In early February, after hearing about Mr. McCune, students started to gather at the school in twos and threes, even though we were still in winter recess. Led by the new student president Yu Seong-bok, we started a demonstration, demanding the restoration of our principal.

Japanese policemen were immediately dispatched, surrounding the school, including those on horseback. When students got louder, the police entered the school. The atmosphere at that time, however, was quite spirited. We outnumbered them by far, and we weren't afraid. We charged at them, and a hand-to-hand combat ensued. We took their caps and coats and threw them on the ground. We took their sabers and broke them. It had snowed quite a bit before, and the memory of throwing down the Japanese policemen on the snow-covered school grounds is still a thrilling and gratifying one even now.

Because of this incident, Sungshil was closed indefinitely, and leading demonstrators, including myself, were arrested. Our classmate and patriotic poet Yun Dong-ju had to transfer to Gwangmyeong School, and Jang Jun-ha (former publisher of *Sasanggye*) had to transfer to Sinseong School in Seoncheon.

Sungshil School, Sungshil Junior College, and Sungui Girls School were located in Shinyang-ri, in the outskirts of Pyeongyang. They were built by the American Northern Presbyterian Church and were known for their spirit of resistance and criticism.

Even before this, in 1932, Japan had built a memorial tower for the "loyal dead" at the foot of Seogi Mountain in Pyeongyang and sent students to the so-called "emperor's spirit memorial" worship.

The emperor's spirit memorial, which the Japanese called the "citizens' rite," was the forerunner of shrine worship. They ordered people to bend their backs deeply and bow before the guardian spirits of Japan and the ashes of Japanese soldiers in the cinerarium. Koreans hated this like death, and Sungshil students refused to obey. Persecution of Sungshil School had already started then, but it never joined in shrine worship.

In September 1936, Sungshil reopened but kept repeating the cycle of "shrine worship refusal—school closure—reopening" until it was shut down for good on March 18, 1938, along with Sungshil Junior College and Sungui Girls School. We called it the Three-Sung Closure.

Professor Kim Seong-shik was a 28-year-old Western history scholar who sowed the patriotic spirit in us. Kim Geon (Professor Emeritus at Konkuk University), Kim Sun-yang (Professor at Yonsei University), Jo Yeong-shik (former President of Kyung Hee University), and Jeong Hui-seop (former head of the Ministry of Health) were some of those who refused shrine worship.

Students who resisted shrine worship at Sungshil Junior College and Sungui Girls School, such as Reverend Kang Shin-myeong (of Saemunan Church) and An Seong-gil (An Chang-ho's niece) are surviving witnesses to this.

It is interesting to point out that Kim Ok-gil, the former president of Ewha Womans University, still claims to be a Sungui alumnus, although she had to transfer to Seomun Girls School after Sungui was shut down.

Many mission schools, in order to stay open, grudgingly used an expedient by sending to shrine worship their school principals and representatives of teachers and students.

Besides shrine worship refusal, one thing I cannot forget is the moving scene on every March first. It is the March First Movement day, but the Japanese made it the "patriots day" of shrine worship. On the first of March, Sungshil students sat all day at their desks with their heads bowed, holding a silent demonstration. Even the Japanese teachers, as well as Korean teachers, were overwhelmed by this solemn scene and walked out without a word.

I also remember Mr. Bae Chi-ryeop, who was the dean of student affairs, would walk amongst us when we were protesting or demonstrating, encouraging us, "Be careful not to get hurt, not to get caught!"

Reverend Jeong Jae-ho, the school's chaplain, and Mr. Byeon Eung-ho, the dormitory superintendent, taught us the Korean language and Korean history whenever they could. Because of that, they were taken and suffered at the hands of the Japanese police.

Imperial Japan worked itself into a frenzy persecuting Koreans, ordering a one-month suspension for using Korean during a Japanese class and expulsion from school if it happened again.

Our classmate Kim Yeong-gil, who refused shrine worship, was taken to the police in 1937 and died after severe torture. That the renowned Reverend Ju Gi-cheol was martyred for refusing shrine worship, everyone knows.

Even among the current leaders of Korea are those who suffered greatly because of their refusal of shrine worship, but the Japanese still claim that there was no coercion but "encouragement" for shrine worship!

Perhaps it is too much to expect the small-minded people of an island country to restore their conscience. It is so lamentable.[20]

Reproduced below is "Skylark," written toward the end of Yun's stay at Sungshil. Through unaffected language, Yun expresses a nineteen-year-old's yearning and envy for a bright, cheerful world, as well as frustrations about the suffocating reality, summarizing the seven months in Pyeongyang as if in a self-portrait.

SKYLARK

Early spring day,
Skylark dislikes
Back alleys of muddy streets.
Reaching his two light wings
Toward a cheery spring sky,
He adores
Bewitching spring songs.
But today,
Dragging hole-ridden shoes
Nimbly toward the back streets,
I roam about like a baby fish.
Is it because I have no
Wings nor songs?
My heart is stifled.
   (March 1936, Pyeong · Sang[21])

Elder Yun Ha-hyeon, Yun Dong-ju's grandfather.

Yun Dong-ju's father, Yun Yeong-seok.

Yun Dong-ju (top right) while he attended Eunjin Middle School and Mun Ik-hwan (top middle).

Yun Dong-ju's mother, Kim Yong.

Yun Dong-ju (seco[nd] from left, standing) during his Yonhui Junior College day[s] and Professor Yi Yang-ha (third fro[m] left, standing).

Jeong Ji-yong (left), the poet Yun Dong-ju admired throughout his life. Influenced by *The Collected Poems of Jeong Ji-yong* (right), Yun turned away from conceptual, abstract poems, expressing his true feelings with everyday words.

Song Mong-gyu, while a student at Yonhui Junior College.

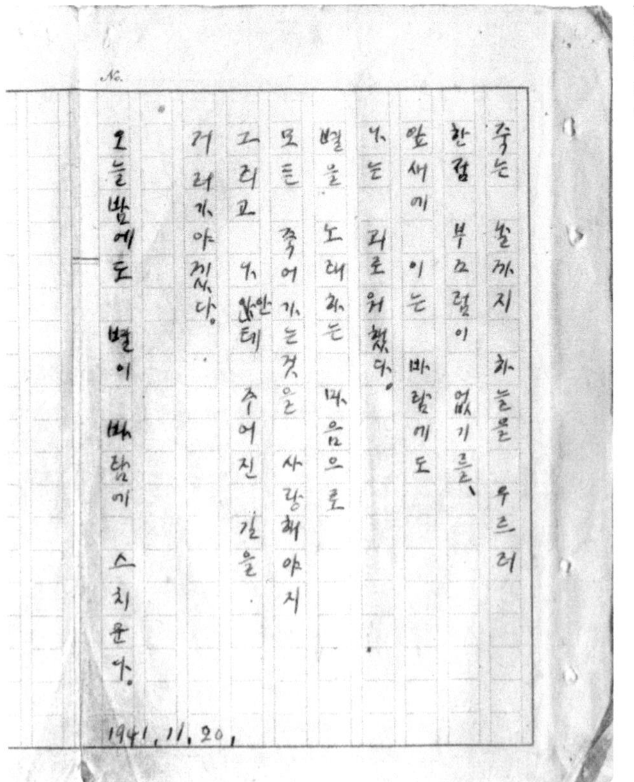

Yun Dong-ju's handwritten manuscript of the poem "Prelude."

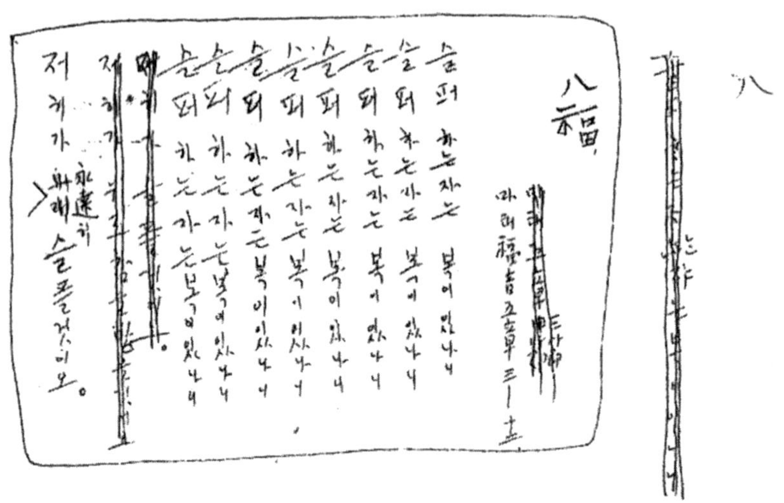

Yun Dong-ju's handwritten manuscript of the poem "Eight Beatitudes." One can see his thought process and feelings from the crossed-out phrases and added words.

The poem "Daydream," published in Sungshil Middle School's student periodical *Sungshil Hwalcheon*. It was Yun's first poem to be printed.

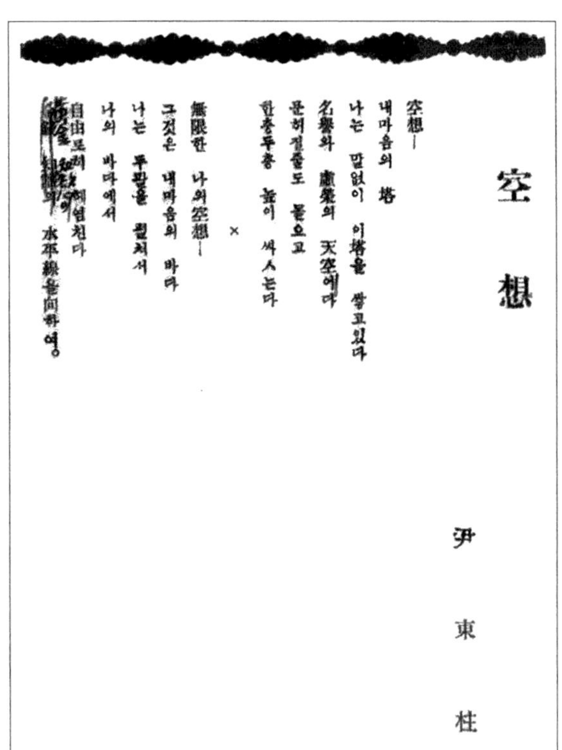

Covers of *Munu*, published by Yonhui Junior College's Munuhoe, archived at Yonsei University Central Library. The first issue (left) was published in 1932, and the 1941 issue (right) was edited by Song Mong-gyu.

Yun Dong-ju's graduation yearbook picture taken in 1941. The yearbook was published after his departure to Japan, and his friend Kang Cheo-jung kept it for him and delivered it to Yun's family after liberation.

Yun Dong-ju (top right) during his return home from Japan in the summer of 1942. Counterclockwise, Yun Gil-hyeon (distant relative), Yun Yeong-seon (Yun Yeong-chun's brother), Song Mong-gyu, and Kim Chu-hyeong (Yun Yeong-seon's niece's husband).

Yun Dong-ju (left) and Jeong Bye uk (right) during Yun's senior yea Yonhui Junior College. Jeong kep Yun's handwritten manuscript of *and Wind and Star and Poem* unti Korea's liberation and delivered i Yun's family.

Kang Cheo-jung's graduation yearbook picture. Kang safeguarded some of Yun's poems, which would otherwise have been lost, and played a crucial role in publishing Yun's poetry in 1948.

The last known photograph of Yun Dong-ju (front right) taken in May 1943 when he went on a picnic with his Doshisha University friends in Uji-shi, Kyoto Prefecture.

The funeral of Yun Dong-ju held at his home in Yongjeong. It was officiated by Reverend Mun Jae-rin (left of Yun's displayed portrait).

Song Mong-gyu's tomb and tombstone, after they were moved closer to Yun Dong-ju's tomb. Song's father added an inscription, "Cheongnyeon Munsa" (Young Man of Letters).

Yun Dong-ju's tomb, shown from the backside.

CHAPTER 6

Return to Yongjeong

AFTER QUITTING SUNGSHIL MIDDLE SCHOOL, Yun Dong-ju and Mun Ik-hwan returned to Yongjeong and transferred to Gwangmyeong School in early April 1936. Yun started the fourth year, and Mun started the fifth year. Yun's student record at Gwangmyeong indicates April 6 as the exact start date.

Gwangmyeong School

Yun's transfer into the fourth year was nothing unusual, but Mun's transfer into the fifth year was exceptional. Mr. Jang Rae-won (later secretary-general of UNESCO Korea), who taught English at Gwangmyeong, volunteered to sponsor them. With that as a condition, their transfer was allowed.

Taking a closer look at Gwangmyeong School, it becomes clear that the school had had a continuing influence in the Third Republic of South Korea.

In Yongjeong, there were four middle schools for boys: Eunjin (Christian), Daeseong (nationalistic), Dongheung (socialist, its students used "comrades" among themselves), and Gwangmyeong (pro-Japanese). The first three were anti-Japanese but four-year schools, whereas Gwangmyeong was pro-Japanese but the only five-year school in the city.

Gwangmyeong, however, had not always been pro-Japanese. It began as Gwangdong Uisuk in 1910 and became a Christian school in 1912 under the new name Yeongshin. Unlike other Christian schools like Eunjin, which was operated by Western missionaries, Yeongshin belonged to the Gando branch of the Joseon Presbyterian Church and was managed by Korean Christians. It was the only school that started out as a five-year secondary school. In 1924, however, after a year of bad harvests, it fell into financial difficulties and was sold to the Japanese businessman Hidaka Heishiro, who had been living in North Gando.

The transaction raised a great social scandal. Legal proceedings ensued after a Yeongshin schoolteacher was accused of and arrested for swindling. Moreover, those who opposed the sale distributed copies of a public accusation signed by influential Koreans in Gando expressing their belief that a Korean-built school, a Christian institution at that, should not be handed over to the Japanese. Gando society boiled with excitement.[1] Nevertheless, the transaction was completed and the school was renamed Gwangmyeong. Hidaka Heishiro did not teach at the school, but he served as its financial director.

Hidaka Heishiro was an eccentric, a "continental wanderer." His acquisition of the Korean school had a more significant meaning than what appeared.

Who were continental wanderers? According to *The Dictionary of Modern Japanese History*, published by the Office of National History at Kyoto University School of Letters, they were "patriotic civilians who, with a sense of duty to support the nation, were actively engaged in furthering the goal of continental advancement in China." They were revered by other Japanese because "they neither pursued political power or high offices nor tried to gain personal wealth or fame. Their supreme goal was Japan's glory and prosperity, making it a great nation. Such patriotic ideology became the impetus for Japan's modernization since the Meiji Era and making Japan a great nation."[2]

Tohoyama Mitsuru and Uchida Ryohei, the most legendary characters in modern Japanese history, were considered continental wanderers. They created such organizations as Hyeonyangsa ("Hyeonyang" refers to the Genkai Sea, connoting the goal of invading Korea) and Heukryonghoe ("Heukryong" refers to the Amur River, connoting the goal of invading Manchuria), instruments for invading the Korean Peninsula and continental China. Surrounding Japan's Asian invasion, which resulted in the Russo-Japanese War, the annexation of Korea, and the establishment of Manchukuo, these so-called patriotic civilians and chivalrous fighters were always in the background. To achieve their goals, they would not even hesitate to commit murder.

Their power was enormous. Politically, they were the government inside the government. Tohoyama, who was their de facto chief, was so powerful that he could control the prime minister of Japan. Socially, they were beyond the law. Opposing their will was suicidal. If Tohoyama demanded, wealthy Japanese businessmen would remit payments. The following story was well-known even to Koreans.

Tohoyama once visited a CEO who was said to have the greatest amount of ready cash in Japan. The amount Tohoyama requested for a loan was almost as much cash as the CEO had. The CEO handed over the cash, knowing that he had no choice. As Tohoyama turned away to leave with the money, the CEO supplicated with a trembling voice, "Um, c-could you wr-write, um, an IOU?"

Tohoyama turned to stare at the man who dared ask him for an IOU.

"An 'IOU'?" he asked, and drawing the saber from his waist, cut off a finger from his hand.

"Is that enough?" said Tohoyama, throwing the finger at the CEO. He left without glancing at the shaking CEO, who realized that Tohoyama's word should have been enough and that his audacity to ask for an IOU had displeased and insulted Tohoyama.

Whether true or not, stories like this veiled the continental wanderers mysteriously. Moreover, these men did not use the collected money for their private purposes. It is said that they financially supported revolutionaries in several countries, making large-scale strategic moves for the benefit of Japan.

Tohoyama sent money to Subhas Chandra Bose for India's independence. Lenin also took money from Uchida Ryohei before the Russian Revolution. In China, reformist revolutionaries like Sun Wen, Liang Qichao, and Kang Youwei benefited from the continental wanderers' money. According to Dr. Jeong Dae-wi, rare material about Tohoyama and others like him are collected at Anthony College, Oxford University, including evidence of Uchida's payment to Lenin. So, these people had spread their invisible hands out to numerous countries in the continent to fulfill the ambition of imperial Japan's "continental advancement." From Japan's perspective, they were true patriots.

Hidaka Heishiro, who was residing in North Gando, was a continental wanderer. Like Tohoyama, he was born in Kumamoto, Kyushu. Dr. Jeong, who had personally met him, said that he was heavyset and bucktoothed, with a face of Russian bread (flat, round, and homely). It is not exactly clear when he went to North Gando; it might have been when Japanese power first infiltrated North Gando. He spoke quite good Korean.

He won the hearts of North Gando Koreans, being kindly, mild, and down-to-earth, even criticizing Japanese policies. He made gestures of goodwill, building facilities for the welfare of Koreans. Strangely, the powerful consulate general of Japan and military officers would get flustered in front of him. Nevertheless, he did not seem to notice. North Gando Koreans would ask him for a favor when they encountered difficulties with Japanese officials. If he wanted to, he could even make the Japanese Consular Police release those who were locked up for independence-related crimes. When Myeong-dong School was burned down by the Japanese army during the Great Gando Liquidation in 1920, Principal Kim Yak-yeon contacted him, and at his arrangement, the Japanese government built an identical building. It is easy to see how great his influence was.

When he went to Japan, he would meet with the prime minister. When he was in China, he socialized with the highest Chinese officials. There was a rumor that he was well acquainted with notorious bandits. In other words, he was a typical continental wanderer.

Hidaka Heishiro took over Yeongshin and changed its name to Gwangmyeong. He brought many Tokyo Imperial University (TIU) graduates from Japan as teachers. Abe, a TIU graduate regarded as an excellent principal in Japan, invited Kudo Shigeo to teach there. Kudo Shigeo was also a TIU graduate and a professor at an exclusive commerce college in Japan. The translator of *Joseon: Thirty Years Ago* and *The Last Days of the Romanovs*, he was a well-learned and capable teacher. Hidaka Heishiro also established a girls' school within Gwangmyeong. In the end, Gwangmyeong School had four schools within it: a middle school, a girls' school, a grade school, and a kindergarten. He contacted the Ministry of Foreign Affairs to make Gwangmyeong School Japan's "designated school abroad" under the Ministry of Education. Approved as a designated school abroad, the school would have the same status as schools in Japan, and its graduates would have an added advantage when advancing to higher schools in Japan.

Reverend Mun Ik-hwan described the school as follows: "The middle school that we transferred to in Yongjeong after [quitting Sungshil for the reason of] refusing shrine worship was Gwangmyeong, which was operated by Japan to 'Japanize' Koreans. It was like jumping from the pot to the frying pan. The Japanese teachers were trying frantically to send any able-bodied students to become police officers for the Ministry of Foreign Affairs or to the Manchukuo Military Officers School."[3]

Manchukuo Military Officers School was also called Manchu Military School or Manchurian Officers School. Because it was in Shingyeong (current name in Chinese: Changchun), it was also called Shingyeong Military School. Graduates of the Manchu Military School became officers of the Manchukuo army, which was the instrument of imperial Japan's continental invasion. What magnificent fruit was borne by Hidaka Heishiro's hidden ambition! Graduates of Eunjin, Daeseong, and Dongheung Schools did not go to Manchu Military School, but many Gwangmyeong graduates, including Jeong Il-gwon, went there and became Manchukuo army officers. Later, these people became the leading faction, known as "the Manchu officer connection." *Wolgan Joseon*'s staff writer Seo Byeong-uk wrote the following article titled "Park Chung-Hee's Manchu Officer Connection":

There were 49 graduates from Shingyeong Military School, a.k.a. Dongdeokdae. . . . The majority of them were from Hamgyeong Province. The first graduates Kim Dong-ha, Kim Yeong-taek, Yun Tae-il, Yi Ju-il, and Choi Chang-eon were all from Gwangmyeong Middle School in Yongjeong, Gando.

Most of the Dongdeokdae graduates enlisted in the Korean army after liberation and became high-ranking officers of the military during [South Korea's—Trans.] First Republic era,[4] except those executed during the Great Purge in the military, such as An Yeong-gil, Yi Byeong-ju, Yi Sang-jin, and Hwang Taek-lim. Jang Eun-san was also executed in Busan during the early stages of the Korean War for desertion while being suspected of string-pulling for the assassination of Kim Gu.[5]

Many of the same high-ranking officers, however, appeared as the main actors of the Third Republic.[6] It was because they joined the May 16 military coup (5.16 Coup) carried out by Park Chung-Hee, also a former Manchukuo officer. Many of the 5.16 Coup actors were Gwangmyeong graduates. One of them was Yi Hak-su, the owner of Gwangmyeong Printing Company, a civilian who contributed to the coup by printing the Pledge of the Revolution and propaganda bills. Later on, many of them were purged by Park Chung-Hee. However, it is historical truth known to all that the 5.16 Coup could not have succeeded had it not been for these ex-Manchukuo officers. In the end, a "continental wanderer" in North Gando persistently cast a long shadow in contemporary Korean history. The importance of education cannot be emphasized more.

Gwangmyeong was a school of such history. Thus, Reverend Mun's "jumping from the pot to the frying pan" was such a fitting satiric expression. Needless to say, the school's goal and management policy were completely different. However, the greatest difference between Sungshil and Gwangmyeong was the language. At Sungshil, Korean was used; at Gwangmeyong, only Japanese was used.

Yun Dong-ju's student records start to appear from the year he started at Gwangmyeong. His report cards at Gwangmyeong were brought to light by Professor Omura Morio of Waseda University, a Yun Dong-ju scholar. In 1985, he visited North Gando to investigate the sites related to Yun and collected relevant materials.

During the fourth year, Yun took sixteen subjects, as recorded here (the number in parentheses is the grade): Self-Improvement (78), Civic Virtues (66), Japanese (Reading 40, Grammar 48, Composition 52), Korean and Chinese Characters (Reading 80), Manchu (86), English (Part I 80, Part II 60), Geography (83), History (77), Algebra (69), Geometry (82), Physics (85), Chemistry (60), Business (60), Drawing (82), Gym (78), Bookkeeping (78).

During the fifth year, he also took sixteen subjects, with some changes: Self-Improvement (83), Civic Virtues (75), Japanese (Reading 50, Grammar 62, Composition 52), Korean and Chinese Characters (Reading 88), English (Part I 81, Part II 67), Geography (76), Algebra (81), Trigonometry (59), Physics (78), Chemistry (65), Business (72), Drawing (78), Gym (68), Bookkeeping (91).[7]

Throughout the fourth and fifth years, Yun's worst grade was in Japanese. His Japanese was probably weak because he had taken classes only in Korean at the anti-Japanese schools, Eunjin and Sungshil, while other students had studied in Japanese from the time they entered Gwangmyeong.

Notable in the curriculum was that there were many language subjects he had to take, as Yongjeong was somewhat of an international city. Yun had to take four language classes during the fourth year: (1) Japanese, (2) English, (3) Korean and Chinese characters, and (4) Manchu.

Of course, the Japanese course was given the greatest weight. It had three separate graded components: reading, grammar, and composition. Next in weight was the English course with two components: reading (part 1) and conversation/composition/grammar (part 2). The subjects of Korean language and Chinese characters were combined into one category, and Manchu was taught because Yongjeong was a territory in Manchukuo. However, the latter two languages were not divided into multiple components and were probably dealt with carelessly.

In the fifth year, language courses changed somewhat. Given a choice between English and Manchu, Yun chose English. This extra English class was called English Part III and consisted of extra reading practice.

At Gwangmyeong, each grade was made up of one class, typically of fifty to sixty students, and the entire middle school had about three hundred students. There were some Japanese students, but most students were Korean.

When Yun finished the fourth year, he was ranked eighteenth out of thirty-eight in the student record, indicating that his class had thirty-eight students. At the end of the fifth year, he was ranked sixth out of eight. The "eight," however, must have been an error, as the number of students could not have reduced from thirty-eight to eight in one year.

An Exam-Preparing Poet

How did Yun spend his days at Gwangmyeong after "jumping from the pot to the frying pan"? We may examine what was going on in his heart by looking at the poem "A Day Like This," written two months after his transfer from Sungshil to Gwangmyeong:

A DAY LIKE THIS

When the Five-Colors and the Rising Sun dance[8]
Above the twin columns of the front gate,
Happy are the children of the lined territory.

A day of dull studies brought
Innocent languor in them;
They've become too simple
To know the meaning of "paradox."

> On a day like this,
> I want to call on the brother I lost,
> My obstinate elder brother.
>
> (June 10, 1936)

The "twin columns of the front gate" refer to Gwangmyeong School's gate frame. Above it dance the Five-Color flag of Manchukuo and the Rising Sun flag of Japan; it is the festival of the aggressors. Yet their victims, "the children of the lined territory," are "happy," too, and it troubles him. He moans that "they've become too simple / To know the meaning of 'paradox,'" and lets out his pent-up anger, saying "I want to call on the brother I lost, / My obstinate elder brother."

Who did he mean by "the brother [he] lost," his "obstinate elder brother"? Was it simply poetic rhetoric, or did he mean his cousin Song Mong-gyu?

It was on April 6, 1936, that Yun started Gwangmyeong School after returning to Yongjeong. On April 10, 1936, Song Mong-gyu was arrested by the Japanese police in China, where he had gone for resistance activism. On June 10, when this poem was written, Song was suffering at the hands of the Japanese police while locked up in the Japanese consular police station in Jinan. Of course, no one knew of this back home.

However we interpret the "lost . . . obstinate elder brother," this poem vividly portrays the pent-up anger of someone who had "jumped into the frying pan." But was his anger directed only at the "happy" children? What about at Yun himself?

Yun had left Sungshil in a protest against imperial Japan, which had fired and deported the school's principal for refusing to participate in the shrine worship. Yet now he was in a place where students were "simple" and "happy" under the national flag of Japan. He had voluntarily entered the "lined territory" where shrine worship would be performed reverently as sacred duty. Truly, this was paradoxical. His own paradox was too painful to even acknowledge. He only represented his anguish through the bitter ending, "On a day like this, / I want to call on the brother I lost, / My obstinate elder brother."

If "the brother I lost, / My obstinate elder brother" meant Song Mong-gyu, then we may interpret that Yun admired Song's "obstinacy"—that is, Song's impetus with which he boldly propelled his belief into action regardless of the dangers and accompanying hardship. And this was Yun's ideal during his Gwangmyeong days.

In such paradoxical circumstances, Yun continued with his studies under the tutelage of Japanese-speaking teachers, learning English, Japanese, and the Manchu language. At the same time, he was laying the foundation for his poetic prowess in the Korean language.

During the two years he attended Gwangmyeong, Yun produced a large body of work. During the first nine months of 1936 following his transfer in April, he wrote twelve poems and sixteen *dongsi.* (The total for 1936 was nineteen poems and twenty *dongsi.*) Thus, we can say that Yun focused more on *dongsi* after he transferred to Gwangmyeong. In 1937, however, *dongsi* was given less weight: six *dongsi,* compared to fifteen poems.

What is special about the two-year Gwangmyeong period is that he published five *dongsi* to the world. In Yanji, there was a children's monthly named *Catholic Boys* at the time, and Yun's submissions were selected for publication. He even came up with a pen name.[9] He was not paid for the poems:

1. "Lies" (October 1936 issue)
2. "Chicks" (November 1936 issue)
3. "The Broom" (December 1936 issue)
4. "Bed-Wetter's Map" (January 1937 issue)
5. "What Do They Eat?" (March 1937 issue)

Among these, "What Do They Eat?" stands out:

WHAT DO THEY EAT?

People living by the sea
They catch fish to eat.

People living on the hills
They roast potatoes to eat.

People living in stars
What do they eat?
        (October 1936)

Though unpublished, "Mandol-i" is an amusing *dongsi*:

MANDOL-I

On the way back from school,
Mandol-i picked up five rocks
By the utility pole.

Aiming at the pole,
He threw the first rock.
—Snap!
He threw the second rock.
—Oops!
He threw the third rock.
—Snap!
He threw the fourth rock.
—Oops!
He threw the fifth rock.
—Snap!

Three out of five—
That's enough.
Tomorrow's test,
I'll get three out of five—
Count by fingers and multiply,
Sixty points, no problem.
Let's go kick the ball!

The next day,
Did Mandol-i turn in a blank sheet
To teacher, or,
Did he really get sixty?

(1937?)

Let us now examine the poems from this period. Of all of them, "The
Sunny Side" is the most widely read. Yun was nineteen when he wrote this,
but the poem shows precocious maturity in both perspective and quality.
Through the two children portrayed, who are playing the "take-the-land"

game, the poem superbly hints at the stormy situation that surrounded them as imperial Japan was plotting the continental invasion against China:

THE SUNNY SIDE

Spring breezes bearing yellow dust undulate
Like a Manchurian's waterwheel.

The hand of the variegated April sun touches
Every strand of an unfamiliar heart against the wall.

Two children playing take-the-land lament
Their short fingers
Not knowing whose land it belongs to.

Stop that! Peace, already thin,
May be shattered.

(June 26, 1936)

The "peace, already thin," described by Yun in this poem, did get shattered during his last year at Gwangmyeong, when the Lugou Bridge Incident (or the Marco Polo Bridge Incident—Trans.) broke out on July 7, 1937. Engineered by the Japanese army stationed near Lugou Bridge, about six miles southwest of Beijing, this incident triggered the start of the second Sino-Japanese War, and the Chinese continent was engulfed in war. A great crisis was oncoming.

At the time, Yun had two important goals: first, literary studies; second, higher education.

How serious and diligent he was in his literary studies is evidenced by his possessions that survived. The best example is his copy of Baek Seok's poetry collection *Deer*. *Deer* was published on January 20, 1936, with only a limited printing of a hundred copies. Because Yun could not obtain a copy, he made his own by scribing each poem from the copy in the school library. He also bought many literary books. His brother Yun Il-ju said:

Of those that were in his bookcase during middle school days, I remember *The Collected Poems of Jeong Ji-yong* (acquired in Pyeongyang on March 10, 1936), *The Heart of Joseon* by Byeon Yeong-ro, *A Beautiful Dawn* by Ju Yo-han, *The Night at the Border* by Kim Dong-hwan, *The Silence of My Beloved* by Han Yong-un, *The Poetry and Songs of Three Poets* by Yi Gwang-su, Ju Yo-han, and

Kim Dong-hwan, *The Pulsation of Joseon* by Yang Ju-dong, *The Collected Sijo of Nosan* by Yi Eun-sang, *The Lost Ribbon*, Yun Seok-jung's children's song collection, *Loud Singing* by Hwang Sun-won, *The Collected Poems of Yeonglang*, and *Eulhae Anthology of Poetry*. Among these, I still have *The Deer*, *The Collected Poems of Jeong Ji-yong*, *The Collected Poems of Yeonglang*, and *Eulhae Anthology*, because he had brought them with him to Seoul. They must have been special to him.[10]

Yun Hye-won's story about her brother's book purchases is also interesting: "I remember my father scolding him severely once when he was in middle school. Yongjeong was so cold in winter that students would go to the tailor and have lining put on inside the uniform. But Dong-ju had spent the money elsewhere instead of lining the uniform. Later, he confessed to Mother that he had bought books with the money."[11] She then added, "We weren't so poor that he'd have to spend the lining money for books. Why did he do that?" Yun was already an avid reader then. He had his own room and would stay up until two or three o'clock in the morning reading books. When his siblings woke in the middle of the night, they'd find him reading in his room.

Professor Yun Il-ju's chronology of Yun Dong-ju's life states: "During Gwangmyeong days, Yun pores over the Japanese edition of *The Complete Anthology of World Literature* and Korean novels and poetry. . . . He scrapbooks Korean literary works from magazines and daily papers. He scrapbooks works of Yi Sang."[12] We can guess at the kind of books he read until two or three o'clock every night.

However, literary studies were an ongoing proposition and completely personal to him. The urgent issue that faced him, especially for his family, was moving on to a higher school after graduation.

As Yun started the fifth year at Gwangmyeong, this issue created turmoil within his family. Yun wanted to enroll in the liberal arts program at Yonhui Junior College, whereas his father pressured him to study medicine to become a doctor.

It is well known that Yun's character was gentle and mild. Yet once his mind was made up, he would not hold back. His family was surprised to see the rebellious and tenacious side of Yun as he confronted his father. Professor Yun Il-ju stated that "the father and son's months-long confrontation was so serious that we younger siblings became scared," and that Yun "would go out before his father came home and wander around, only to come home in the middle of the night." Yun would "sigh often and beat his chest."[13]

In contrast to Yun's household, Song Mong-gyu's family was supportive of Song's decision. After his release from Unggi Police Station, Song took a few months off at home to recuperate. In April of that year (1937), he transferred to Daeseong Middle School (a four-year program) and was also in the graduating class. When Song expressed his wishes to enroll in Yonhui's liberal arts program, his parents gave their consent. His father, Song Chang-hui, even criticized Yun's father, saying that parents should respect their child's wishes instead of forcing their own desires upon him.

Nevertheless, Yun's father was unbending. According to Yun Hye-won, their father kept repeating to Yun: "I've also studied literature before. It's useless. How will you make your living by studying literature, especially nowadays? You need to figure out how to make a living. The most you can become afterwards is a journalist. Only a journalist. You mustn't study literature. Study medicine. That's how you'd make a living, free of worries."[14]

In fact, Mr. Yun Yeong-seok had gone all the way to Beijing and to Tokyo to study, learning English and literature. He taught briefly at Myeongdong School and was known for his oratory and writing. Yet he had never been fully independent financially, though he tried at many things. At the time of this argument with his son, he ran a drapery shop (per Yun's student record at Gwangmyeong), but even the drapery shop was not doing well. Consequently, he was still financially dependent on his own father, Yun Ha-hyeon. As his life turned out so, he was determined that his son would not take the same steps.

When Yun insisted, even fasting to protest, that he must study literature and "would rather die than to study medicine," his father was enraged. He would throw bowls outside and have an uproar. Yun Hye-won laughed out loud, remembering that time: "I was in Myeongshin Girls' School at that time. I didn't know what 'literature' or 'journalist' meant. From what Father was saying to my brother, I just thought, 'Oh, "journalist" must be someone who can't even feed himself.'"

As the confrontation continued, the situation became worse. One night, for the first time, Yun did not even return home. The tense conflict between father and son was eventually resolved by the grandfather, who brought a victory to

Yun. "What can we do if the student says he cannot study medicine?" was his opinion. The fact that Yun Ha-hyeon had waited all that time to give his own opinion tells us that he had agreed implicitly with the father.

Meanwhile, Yun's Gwangmyeong days passed. He played on the school's basketball team, and in September, he went to Geumgang Mountain and Songdowon Beach in Wonsan on a school trip. Two poems, "The Sea" and "Biro Peak," were written from this experience.

On February 17, 1938, Yun graduated Gwangmyeong Middle School. Afterward, he was to leave for Seoul to take the entrance examination for Yonhui. Yun Ha-hyeon's income came from the harvest that the tenant farmers reaped each year. When the harvest grain was sent to him, it was stored in a very large grain chest. Elder Yun took the grain out of the chest in order to fund his grandson's studies in Seoul. Witnessing that, Yun Hye-won thought to herself, "Grandfather is such a great person!" But, as she saw later, Yun Ha-hyeon had his own preconceived plan: "When it was time for Dong-ju to leave, Grandfather told him firmly, 'You must study hard and take the high civil service exam. Pass the exam and be successful. Also, if you get married, it will be hard to study, so don't think about getting married early. Just work hard to pass the high civil service exam and be successful.' That's what Grandfather said."

He must have heard that aside from being a doctor, one could establish himself by passing a thing called the high civil service exam. Yun carefully listened to his grandfather. However, right before his departure, he said to his sister, "Even though Grandfather tells me to take the high civil service exam, that's for law students. Studying liberal arts is a different matter."

Side by side, Yun Dong-ju and Song Mong-gyu left for Seoul, where side by side, they took and passed the entrance examination for the liberal arts program at Yonhui Junior College. It was early spring of 1938. These two were the only ones from North Gando who enrolled in the literature program at Yonhui that year.

CHAPTER 7

Yonhui Junior College

A Station for Youths

IN THE TWENTY-SEVEN YEARS and two months of Yun's life, what did the four years at Yonhui mean to him? They could perhaps be defined as the richest, the freest, period in his life.

Yonhui Campus and the *Taegeuk* Mark

Yun's regard for and pride in Yonhui is revealed in the statement by Professor Jang Deok-sun (former professor of Korean literature at Seoul National University), Yun's schoolmate at Gwangmyeong. During the summer break after his first year, Yun returned home and spoke about Yonhui to Jang, who was in his fourth year at Gwangmyeong:

Dong-ju and I took a walk around the Haeran River, which had a pretty name but was bleak looking. He emphasized the need to study literature and stressed that his school was the best one for it.

Literature must be based on the foundation of national ideology, he said, and Yonhui's tradition, its professors, and its atmosphere were the most fitting ground for promoting national sentiments.

Roses of Sharon [Korea's national flower], which did not grow in Manchuria, were in full bloom on the campus. *Taegeuk* marks, symbolic of the Korean national flag, were engraved everywhere. Students did not speak Japanese, and they even had a course on Korean literature, whose lecture was given in Korean. Dong-ju told me these compelling stories in a calm but firm voice.

My decision to study Korean literature was influenced by my grandfather, an enlightened thinker, and my brother Yohan. Still, I enrolled in Yonhui Junior College's liberal arts program because of what Dong-ju said. I wished to escape the Japanese-managed middle school in a foreign land and be embraced in the arms of my homeland. As a Christian, a missionary school also felt like a home to me. I was satisfied and happy at Yonhui.[1]

Jang's and Yun's families, both Christian, had a long-standing friendship between them. Jang's elder brother Yohan was in the same grade as Yun at Eunjin Middle School, and the three of them had been friends since childhood. They grew up in the same environment, in the same atmosphere. Jang felt more at home in Yonhui than in his hometown Yongjeong. Yun shared this feeling as well.

This should be understood in the context of the late 1930s, when imperial Japan was acting at its worst. Even in grade schools and secondary schools, Koreans had to learn in Japanese, and schools would be shut down if they refused shrine worship. While the circumstances were oppressive for Korean schools, missionary schools had a more relaxed atmosphere and learning environment.

Such an environment was possible because, politically, the missionaries who owned and ran the schools were Westerners, and ideologically, their mottoes were based on Christian ideas of equality and liberty. Thus, Yonhui school could afford to have *Taegeuk* marks in the buildings and cultivate roses of Sharon, both of which symbolized Korea. Professor Yu Yeong (a poet and classmate of Yun at Yonhui and then a professor at Yonsei University) described that because of such a spiritual climate at Yonsei, the college was an object of hatred by the Japanese during the period of brutal tyranny.[2]

Yonhui Junior College was established in April 1915. Under the management of the joint commission of the Northern Presbyterian Church of America, the Southern and Northern Methodist Churches of America, and the Canadian Presbyterian Mission, it became the headquarters of Christian education in Korea. Its first superintendent was Reverend Horace Grant Underwood, succeeded by Dr. Oliver R. Avison, who was head of Severance Medical School at the same time. When Yun started at Yonhui, the school was under the management of the third superintendent, Dr. Horace Horton Underwood, whose Korean name was Won Han-gyeong. (Dr. Underwood was born to Reverend Underwood in 1890 in Seoul and died in 1951 in Busan during the Korean War.)

The greatest peril that Yonhui faced since its establishment was also the shrine worship issue. While Sungshil Schools in Pyeongyang were shut down because of their flat refusal, Dr. Underwood, to keep the school open, reached a compromise with the Japanese by agreeing to shrine attendance.

At that time, the faculty included renowned Korean scholars like Yu Eok-gyeom, Yi Yang-ha, Yi Myo-muk, Hyeon Je-myeong, Choe Hyeon-bae, Choe Gyu-nam, Kim Seon-gi, Baek Nak-jun, Shin Tae-hwan, and Jeong In-seop. Besides Dr. Underwood, others included several Western missionary-scholars.

The school had only three departments, without further distinctions for major: liberal arts, commerce, and natural sciences. Each department taught general subjects under the discipline. Interestingly, while liberal arts and natural sciences had a four-year curriculum, the commerce curriculum was three years. The Confucian Joseon custom of revering "pure" studies and looking down on commerce must have remained even then.

The entrance examination for Yonhui was very stringent. At that time, there were not enough schools; in fact, Yonhui and Boseong were the only men's junior colleges for liberal arts in Korea.

Taking the exam would be Yun's first trip to Seoul. Having no relatives there, Yun had written to Ra Sa-haeng for help, who was attending Methodist Theological School in Seoul at the time. As mentioned earlier, Ra was an upperclassman at Eunjin Middle School who went to Nakyang Military School with Song Mong-gyu in 1935. After his arrest in China and imprisonment in Pyeongyang, he was released in 1936. Having decided to study theology, he took the entrance exam and started a five-year program at Methodist Theological School in April 1937.

When Yun and Song arrived in Seoul, Ra was living in his school's dormitory. The seminary, now Methodist Theological University (since 1959— Trans.), was at 31 Naengcheon-dong, Seodaemun-gu. Ra went to the Seoul station on the appointed day to meet Yun and Song. They went to his dorm room and stayed there for about ten days. Yun and Song took the exam and passed it. At the time, the seminary's dormitory housed sixty students (forty men and twenty women) in thirty rooms. Each room had two single beds, and by placing long benches between them, a couple more people could sleep there.

Through his connection with Ra, Yun was able to procure a personal reference needed for admission to Yonhui. Yun's student registration record at Yonhui states, "Reference: Mun Jang-uk / Relationship: Relative." A lecturer at the seminary at the time, Dr. Mun was from Dangjin, South Chungcheong Province. After graduating from Yonhui in 1925, he went to America, received a master's degree at Columbia University and a doctorate in philosophy at the University of Southern California, and taught history at the seminary upon his return. After liberation, he served as the vice minister of foreign affairs during the American occupation and then the vice minister of education when the Republic of Korea was established.[3] (It should be noted that Song's student registration does not contain a reference. Song might have been concerned that his status as a blacklisted person would harm any reference he might procure, so he left it blank.)

By the time Yun and Song entered Yonhui, the signs of imperial Japan's desperation were everywhere.

After the Sino-Japanese war broke out on the Chinese mainland in July 1937, the governor-general of Korea promoted a threatening warlike atmosphere in Korea, ordering blackouts in Seoul the following month even though it was not even remotely close to the battlefields. The governor-general became even more impatient in 1938, promulgating the Joseon Army Recruitment Order in February, followed by the National Full Mobilization Order in May. The entirety of Korea was driven into taking a war footing. It was in March of the same year that An Chang-ho, who had been imprisoned for the Suyang Tonguhoe (Cultivation Fellowship—Trans.) Incident, died in Gyeongseong Imperial University Hospital. In July, the Japanese force clashed with the Russian force in Changkufeng in China. The same year, Hitler annexed Austria.

Within and without, dark and cruel slaughter and lunacy of oppression were weltering about. Naturally, an ordeal of Korean intellectuals took place in succession. In June 1937, over 150 intellectual leaders were arrested for violation of the Maintenance of the Public Order Act as part of the Suyang Tonguhoe Incident. In February 1938, Pyeongyang Seminary professors and students were arrested for refusing shrine worship, and many patriots were arrested in the Heungeop Gurakbu (Industry Promotion Fraternity—Trans.)

Incident. Yun Yeong-seok's reluctance to allow his son to enroll in liberal arts was completely understandable.

Even under such circumstances, however, Yonhui's climate and spirit were not daunted. A good example is the case of Oesol Choe Hyeon-bae, who taught the Korean language at Yonhui. Having been implicated in the Heun-geop Gurakbu Incident, he was forced by the governor-general to resign from the post. Immediately, Yonhui appointed him as librarian, enabling him to continue teaching as a school employee. It was a bold protest.

Professor Yu Yeong, Yun's classmate, gave the following descriptions of Yun at Yonhui:

You can say those who came to Yonhui, the base for the nationalist movement at the time, all had their ambitions. It goes without saying that professors, too, were the most renowned leaders of the Korean people both academically and spiritually. Moreover, the school's foundation spirit expressed by the Underwood family as well as the missionaries' spiritual support and international interest became the bases for its growth and academic research. . . .

Thus, Dong-ju, with his great aspirations, arrived at the ideal school. And not alone, but with his cousin Song Mong-gyu. They were related, yes, but they seemed more like twins, with similar height and faces. Having come from the same place to the same school, they naturally took the same path together in school. First, they lived in the dormitory, in front of which now is Yun's memorial. Their personalities, however, were completely opposite. Dong-ju was gentle, quiet, and reserved whereas Mong-gyu was rough, talkative, and extroverted. But they both studied poetry and wrote poems. Their personalities were revealed in their poems, making contrasts. But their differences in personality never seemed to create a discord or distance between them.

Dong-ju seemed like an iron hand in a velvet glove. He interacted with others in gentle, sweet, and humorous ways, but his integrity and will were firmer than anybody's. [. . .] Our class, many of whom eventually became leaders in many areas, took classes and studied together. Eom Dal-ho wrote many children's songs and stories; Kim Sam-bul was a pioneer in *pansori*; Kim Mun-ung was a wanderer and person of taste; Han Hyeok-dong and Gang Cheo-jung were geniuses at English; Heo Ung became a great scholar of Korean; Yi Sun-bok currently teaches English literature at Hanyang University. Where Yonsei Science Center is now used to be rice fields, and next to it was a grass lawn. Whenever we had time, we'd gather there and engage in small talk and debate. [...]

When we took the Urimalbon (Patterns of the Korean Language—Trans.) course by Professor Oesol [Choe Hyeon-bae—Transl.], we felt incredibly excited and honored. We were also grateful to our school for the opportunity. I can still see Dong-ju sitting always in the front seat, engrossed in the lecture.

Professor Ha Gyeong-deok's English grammar class often put us in a spot with homework presentations, and Dong-ju, too, was afflicted by them. But later on, we told each other even though we had hated Professor Ha then, how grateful to him we were for his class.

[...] I think Professor Yi Yang-ha's class influenced him greatly in many aspects. Professor Yi was an essayist and was also interested in poetry. Some of us would show our criticisms and poems to him for feedback. Dong-ju met with him frequently for advice, too. Professor Yi was not an eloquent speaker but his lectures were profound and meaningful. We all respected him. Soon after we started at Yonhui, we took a picture with him in front of the statue of Dr. Underwood. [...]

And Professor Son Jin-tae made all of us cry with the anecdote about Marie Curie. When she was little, her country was under the rule of Russia, but she and her classmates secretly studied Polish. A Russian official made an unannounced visit to the classroom, and they had to hide their Polish textbook. [...] Telling us this story, Professor Son could not help crying. As he took out his handkerchief, we all broke out in tears and wailed. [...] Other classes were Professor Kim Seon-gi's phonetics class, Professor Min Tae-shik's Chinese writing and classics class, and Professor Yi Myo-muk's English speech class. Professor Gang Nak-won subtly inspired nationalism in us in his gym class. All these greatly influenced our way of thinking. Dr. Won Han-gyeong's down-to-earth sermons, Professor Yu Eok-gyeom's character, and the teachings of Professors Yi Chun-ho, Choe Gyu-nam, and Kim Du-heon were also the source of our intellectual wealth.[4]

Freshman Year at Yonhui and a Splendid Homecoming

The first poem Yun wrote after starting college was "A New Road." Both the title and the rhythm speak to the healthy and refreshing vigor of a young man starting a new life in a new place.

A NEW ROAD

Across the stream to the woods,
Over the hill to town.

Yesterday and also today
I walk on my road, a new road.

Dandelions bloom and magpies fly;
A maiden passes by and wind rises.
My road is always a new road,
Today and also tomorrow.

Across the stream to the woods,
Over the hill to town.

(May 10, 1938)

The stone building in which Yun took classes are still a part of Yonsei University's liberal arts school. The three-story building "in the midst of thick pine grove fit for Master Monk Seosan,"[5] which was used as the dormitory, still remains.

From the first day of school, Yun started living in the dormitory, with roommates Song Mong-gyu and Gang Cheo-jung. They were given a room on the top floor. The third-floor room had a slanted ceiling that paralleled the slope of the roof like an attic room. One moonlit autumn night, Yun looked out the window and described the scenery: "Autumnal sky looks crystalline and the thick pine grove paints a *mukhwa*. As the moonbeam is pouring upon pine trees, branch after branch, I almost hear it as if it's a wind" (excerpted from Yun's essay "Shooting the Moon," written in October 1938).

In 1938, Yun wrote eight poems, including "A New Road"; five *dongsi*, such as "Mountain Echoes"; and the essay "Shooting the Moon." The latter was written as an assignment for Professor Jeong In-seop's class. Everyone in class had to write an essay under the given title. Perhaps because of the rigidity of the assignment, Yun's essay is mediocre.

However, as for his *dongsi*, he seems to have attained the skills of a master artisan:

MOUNTAIN ECHOES

Because the magpie caws
Mountain echoes.

Nobody hears
Mountain echoes.

The magpie hears
Mountain echoes.
He hears alone
Mountain echoes.
         (May 1938)

Among the other four *dongsi*, "Baby's Dawn," "Sunflower Face," and "Sunshine-Wind" are also remarkable. After these five, however, he never wrote *dongsi* again, as if he had graduated from this form of writing. It is interesting to consider why he would have stopped writing them after having honed his *dongsi* skills. Perhaps it was something internal, and he no longer had the presence of mind for children's poems.

Children can always write *dongsi*. Even when nothing is put down on paper, their laughter, their eye movements, their gestures, all these are their poems. With adults, it's different. They can write *dongsi* only when they are happy, because only when they are happy can they return to the hearts of children. Perhaps the only year of happiness for Yun during his Yonhui days was the initial year.

Turning now to his poems, we will focus on "The Hall of Love," "Miracle," and "A Mournful Clan," all written in 1938:

THE HALL OF LOVE

Sun-a, when have you entered my hall?
And when have I entered yours?

Our halls are the Hall of Love
Tinged with antique customs.

Sun-a, close your crystal eyes like a doe.
I will smooth my hair tangled like the mane of a lion.

Our love was merely mute.

Youth!
Before the light goes out on the holy candlesticks,
Sun-a, run out through the front door.

Before darkness and wind hit upon our window
I will cradle eternal love and disappear
Through the backdoor, far, far away.

Now,
A cozy lake in the forest greets you,
And steep mountains face me.

(June 19, 1938)

This poem is interesting in various ways. First of all, this is the first poem in which Yun writes about unrequited love using a specific woman's name, "Sun" (which later becomes "Suni").[6] Imagery from this poem is repeated later in "The Boy" (1939) and "Snowy Map" (March 12, 1941), where it is amplified and intensified. Of course, the name Sun (or Suni) may have been used as a generic girl's name rather than a specific proper name. Still, it is peculiar that the same name always appears in his poems about unrequited love. This makes one wonder about his romantic life. A biographical examination regarding this will follow in chapter 8.

Second, the last stanza, "Now, / A cozy lake in the forest greets you, / And steep mountains face me," reveals for the first time Yun's humanitarian willingness to bear sacrifices and suffering, which climaxes in "The Cross," discussed later.

"Miracle," bearing the same composition date as "The Hall of Love," also provides a milestone in Yun's poetry:

MIRACLE

Like twilight descending upon the lake,
Shall I shake off the dirt from my feet
And walk with soft steps?

Truly a miracle it is,
That I am brought here
To this lake
Though no one invited me.

Today of all days,
I keep caressing like gold medals
Romantic feelings, narcissism, and jealousy.

But, with no other thought,
I will let all these wash away in the current.
So invite me, thou, to the surface of the lake.

(June 18, 1938)

Some people label Yun Dong-ju as a Christian poet. In fact, he wrote some poems of a Christian nature beginning with this one. The context of this poem is the miracle of Jesus and Peter walking on water, found in Matthew 14:25–33: The disciples were on a boat against a high wind when Jesus walked upon the water to them. They became frightened, thinking it was a ghost. When Jesus revealed that it was he, Peter asked Jesus to tell him to walk on the water, too. Jesus did so, and Peter got off the boat and walked on water.

Why did this story suddenly pull on his heartstrings? Some might say it is the mystery of faith. At any rate, this poem became a turning point for him. Both a poet and a Christian from birth, his poetry and faith converged in this poem, opening the door to a new path.

Let us now examine "A Mournful Clan":

A MOURNFUL CLAN

White kerchief covers black hair
White rubber slippers deck rough feet
White skirt and jacket hide the mournful body
White sash tightens the small waist

(September 2, 1938)

It is merely a simple and sympathetic sketch of a woman. She is not very old, as guessed from "black hair," but "rough feet" tells us of a hard life. "Mournful body" attests to the current hardship, and "small waist" reveals a gaunt body. Notice, however, that Yun gives this woman a "white kerchief," "white rubber slippers," a "white skirt and jacket," and a "white sash."[7] With the title "A Mournful Clan," the Korean people are personified through this woman. When the circumstances Korea faced in 1938 are considered, Yun's identification of the Korean people as "a mournful clan" can be understood.

Thus far, we have examined Yun's school life and poems. Let us now turn to his return home during school vacation, as the mosaic of his Yonhui school days will not be completed without looking at his homecoming.

The journey from Seoul to North Gando consisted of a series of train rides. From Seoul, one took the Gyeongwon Line, which stopped in Uijeongbu, Cheolwon, and then Wonsan in South Hamgyeong, a beautiful port city on the eastern coast. The distance was 233.7 kilometers, or 580 *ri*. The Wongeyong Line, a single-track railroad, started in Wonsan and went past Gowon, Hamheung, Gilju, Cheongjin, and Hoeryeong. Its final stop was Sangsambong, by the Tumen River at the tip of North Hamgyeong. The distance was 666.9 kilometers, or 1,669 *ri*. After traveling 2,249 *ri* to arrive at Sangsambong station by the border, one had to take yet another train to Yongjeong, across Tumen.

After starting at Yonhui, Yun took these trains back and forth between Seoul and North Gando during summer and winter recesses. Yun's sister, Hye-won, told me: "You know the poem 'Portrait of a Younger Brother,' dated September 15, 1938? He wrote that poem while staying home during his first summer recess. I heard from Il-ju that the conversation took place just like that. Dong-ju asked the questions, and Il-ju answered them like that. How overjoyed Il-ju and I were whenever Dong-ju came home on vacation!"[8]

In his sister's memory, Yun Dong-ju as a young man is gentle and warm-hearted man with an almost maternal warmth: "Now I think of it, Dong-ju was an adult and must have had his own things to do. We younger siblings must have been a nuisance, but he never seemed bothered by us and did things for us as we bid. He told us about Seoul, taught us songs. . . . I learned the Negro spiritual 'Carry Me Back to Old Virginny' from him."[9]

She also provided an example of Yun Dong-ju's considerate and attentive character. When Yun stayed in Seoul, it was Hye-won who usually wrote to him for the family. When Yun replied to her, he would return her letter, with spelling and other mistakes corrected in red ink. He did not treat his young siblings carelessly or indifferently. His poem "Portrait of a Younger Brother" reveals his generous and down-to-earth character:

PORTRAIT OF A YOUNGER BROTHER

With a frigid moon upon the red forehead,
My brother's face is like a sad picture.

I stop to hold his young hand
Furtively and ask,

"What will you become when you grow up?"
"I will be a person,"
Is his naive, truly naive reply.

Gently, I let the hand go.
I look into his face again.
With the red forehead dampened by a frigid moon,
My brother's face is like a sad picture.

(September 15, 1938)

People often say, "The writing reveals the writer." If the reverse is also true, testimony regarding Yun's character, as remembered by his family members, offers a great interpretation of his writing. Yun Hye-won continued:

He wasn't considerate just to us. Even though he was a college student, when he came home during recess, he'd dress in Grandfather's hemp jacket and help Grandfather make feed for the ox and chickens. He tended to the ox, taking it to the hills to graze. The ox was not raised by us. We bought the calf, it was raised by someone else, and we bought it back. But the people who raised the ox worked it too hard. When it became too emaciated, Grandfather brought it back to rest and get fat. Moreover, when our grandmother and mother made tofu, he'd grind the beans in the grinding stone because he couldn't stand watching the elderly in the family doing strenuous work. His character was so indescribably kind and gentle.[10]

During the Japanese rule, junior college or university students wore mortarboards, the "university caps." When the students came back during recess wearing them, people were envious and respectful. They were the object of envy. But always disdainful of showing off, Yun would take off the uniform and cap as soon as he arrived: "Father was at first displeased that Dong-ju refused to study medicine. But when he came back home for summer recess, our father was very proud of him and would tell him, 'Put the cap on!' whether [he was] going to church or paying a visit to the elders in town. Ha ha! Dong-ju had no choice but to wear it, but then, once outside, threw it back into the house over the wall or stuck it in the back pocket of his pants. Ha ha."[11]

However, not every memory was a pleasant one. While in Seoul, Yun would buy the children's monthly literary magazine *The Boys*, published by

Joseon Ilbo, and mail it to Il-ju. Whenever the issue arrived, both younger siblings rushed to be the first one to read it.

However, Song Mong-gyu, who returned with Yun during recess, told Hye-won an unexpected story. Their father, seeing that Yun was sending the magazine and other literary books, had written to Dong-ju, scolding him severely. "Don't send those books. Do you want even your brother to study literature?" Yun had shown the letter to Song in the dormitory. Song told Hye-won, "Please make sure that your father doesn't send letters like that. Do you know how much that letter pained and disappointed Dong-ju?"

This story made her heart ache for a long time. Professor Yun Il-ju also reminisced about the books sent by his brother:

> In 1938, during his first summer recess, he gave me a gift of a thick historical novel by Kim Dong-in titled *Agi-ne*. While in Seoul, he mailed the magazine *The Boys*, published by *Joseon Ilbo*, every month. Kim Nae-seong's *The White Mask* was being serialized in it, and I waited for it with pleasure each month. He also sent me *The Complete Children's Literature*, published by *Joseon Ilbo*, Ogawa Mimei's *Children's Stories*, Gang So-cheon's *Pumpkin Flower Lantern*, and others. Especially in the first book, he made annotations for me in pencil: A story by Yi Gwang-su (I forget the title, but it was about a child waiting for his mother in the train station), Pak Yeong-jong's "The Ferry," and Jeong Ji-yong's "Words," commenting that they were good stories because they were portraying real life rather than fantasy.[12]

Such literary exchanges between brothers must have alarmed their father.

Professor Yun Il-ju's memory of his brother back at home during recess gives various portraits of Yun. Being the testimony of a family member, it speaks of Yun Dong-ju in everyday life:

> We learned much from him while he was home for recess. He helped me with summer assignments, and we played ball and marbles together. Even though he didn't have enough time for his reading, he doted on us and spent time playing with us.
>
> During his first- and second-year recesses, he told Hye-won and me, in a quiet voice, about the meaning of the *Taegeuk* mark, roses of Sharon, and Aegukga, as well as the March First Movement and the Gwangju Student Movement. I also can't forget when he taught me about the constellations. I think I was in fourth grade. He'd take me out to the courtyard and point

at the Big Dipper and the North Star I only saw in textbooks. I miss that time, the cool breeze in summer evenings, his familiar scent when he held me, the way he pointed at the stars with his finger, and so on.

…He'd bring with him a lot of books home, thinking he would get much reading done. But it wasn't that easy. We were the head family of the clan, and the house was always in commotion with some family visitors.

He went out to hills and fields for long walks every day. He often did so without me and Hye-won knowing, but sometimes he took me out with him. I loved walking with him, holding his hand. I think the conversation in his poem "The Portrait of a Younger Brother," written in September 1938 after his first recess, took place in the way he described. Aside from this specific example, I think most ideas for his poems were brewed and refined in his heart during his walks while contemplating nature. When he took a walk, he was usually in a hanbok made of hemp or calico, and at no time was he seen without a book in hand. He usually wore a hanbok, which became him. But when he wore the dark blue school uniform with the university cap or an American-style low straw hat popular among Yonhui students, he looked very good, too. In subtle ways, he took care of how he looked and was stylish with whatever he put on him. His anti-Japanese sentiments were so strong that he turned away disgusted when seeing Koreans wearing yukata or haori kimonos. When his friends spoke to him in Japanese, he'd try to reply in Korean.[13]

These were the portraits of Yun Dong-ju during his first year of college.

The following is the first-year transcript of Yun at Yonhui (the number in parentheses in each subject is the grade): Self-Improvement (80), Bible (89), Japanese (81), Korean (100), Chinese characters and writing (85), Introduction to Literature (70), English Grammar (80), English Reading (81), English Writing (74), English Conversation (79), Phonetics (78), Asian History (85), Natural History (75), Music (95), Gymnastics (79), Korean History (74).[14]

The Second Year at Yonhui: Study of Poetry and Jeong Ji-yong

Yun became a sophomore in 1939.

From the beginning of the year, Yun concentrated on publishing his poems, usually submitting to *Joseon Ilbo*. According to Professor Yu Yeong, the paper allotted a special section for student submissions. The paper selected some from mailed-in submissions and gave one- or two-month subscriptions to the paper as payment. Professor Yu said that he once received such a subscription after his writing was selected. Another classmate, Eom Dal-ho, who wrote children's stories and songs, had already been accepted as an established writer and was often asked to contribute to *Joseon Ilbo*'s *The Boys* rather than the paper's student section.

Three of Yun's writings—"Shooting the Moon" (essay), "The Last Will" (poem written at Gwangmyeong), and "The Portrait of a Younger Brother" (poem from the year before)—were printed under his real name or "Yun Ju" in the student section of *Joseon Ilbo* in January, on February 16, and on an unknown date, respectively. Moreover, "Mountain Echo" was published in *The Boys* (date unknown) under Yun Dong-ju (written in different Chinese characters). After its acceptance, he met Yun Seok-jung, the children's poet and editor for *The Boys*, and received payment for his poem for the first time.

Strangely, while he concentrated on publishing his previously written poems, he composed only six in 1939: "Like the Moon," "A Sick Rose," "The Ravine Water," "Self-Portrait," "The Boy," and "Turgenev's Hill." "The Ravine Water" and "The Boy" are undated, and the other four were not written until September.

We will now examine Yun's sophomore year, many elements of which were unknown until now. The first is his dwelling.

The chronology of Yun's life compiled by Professor Yun Il-ju states that Yun lived in the dormitory for the first three years at Yonhui. Only in his last year was he supposed to have lived outside the campus with Jeong Byeong-uk. The facts seem different, however, in that Yun moved out of the dorms during his second year, went back to the dorms in his junior year, and moved out again with Jeong in the last year.

That he did not live in the dormitory in 1939 is clear from the statements of Yu Yeong and Ra Sa-haeng.

Yu Yeong took time off from school in November 1939 for personal reasons and returned to school two years later, after Yun graduated. Yu remembered that before leaving school, he had visited Yun to discuss poetry in Yun's boardinghouses in Ahyeon-dong and Seosomun-dong: "Dong-ju first got a place in Ahyeon-dong and then moved to Seosomun. I think he had his own room then. The Seosomun place was near the old Seodaemun District Office and looked like the countryside then. There was a small stream in front and a well was nearby. The well appears in his poem 'Self-Portrait.'"

Between Shinchon, where Yonhui was, and Seoul station were three stations, Yonhui, Ahyeon, and Seosomun. It seems that Yun moved to areas near stations for an easy commute. The poem "Self-Portrait" and the well mentioned by Yu are examined here:

SELF-PORTRAIT

Visiting a lonely well by the field around the hill,
Quietly and alone, I look into it.

In the well, the moon is shining, the clouds flowing, the sky
Sprawled. Azure breezes blow and autumn is there.

And there is a man.
I turn away, hating him for some reason.

Thinking again, I take pity on him.
When I return and look in, he's still there.

Again, I turn away, hating him.
Thinking again, I miss him.

In the well, the moon is shining, the clouds flowing, the sky
Sprawled. Azure breezes blow and autumn is there.
And, like a memory, there is a man.

(September 1939)

Many Yun Dong-ju scholars have assumed that the well in "Self-Portrait" (original title: "Self-Portrait inside a Well") is the deep well by his Myeongdong home, known for its excellent-tasting water. Professor Yu Yeong, however, concludes that the well is the one by Yun's boardinghouse in Seosomun.

The author agrees with Professor Yu for a couple of reasons. First, "Self-Portrait" was written in September 1939, while he lived in the boardinghouse in Seosomun. If we were to look at the Myeongdong-well theory, it does not seem plausible that Yun, now a young man, would suddenly remember the well from his childhood and internalize it.

Second, the well in Myeongdong is supposed to have been many feet deep, and the well would echo if one shouted into it. Structurally speaking, one cannot see one's face reflected in such a deep well. So the idea of a "self-portrait" is inconceivable.

However, such discussion regarding the design of the well itself may be meaningless. Yun writes that the moon is shining in the well. Even a shallow well may not reflect a face under the moonlight. If one looks into the well at night, the very act itself will block the moonlight, precluding the reflection on the surface of water. The well that shows a bright moon, clouds, sky, azure breezes, and even a man's face—this might as well be the well within one's own heart. Thus, it may not benefit us greatly to quibble over which well became the poem's background. Instead, the meaningful question should be why Yun wanted to see his reflection on the water, and to see that reflection in the well at nighttime.

Nevertheless, a thin string of attachment remains with the well in Seosomun. It seems that Yun was inspired to look for ways of self-introspection through the meager medium of a well. What caused such soul searching? Thus, it is important to examine the period he lived in Seosomun.

Reverend Ra's statements piece together Yun's life in 1939. He not only remembered Yun's North Ahyeon-dong place but also had the critical experience of visiting the poet Jeong Ji-yong with Yun: "When Dong-ju started Yonhui and lived in the dormitory, I would visit him there, or he'd see me in my dormitory on Sundays. But he left the dormitory the following year to live in North Ahyeon-dong. So I went there to meet him, too. And once, Dong-ju took me to visit the poet Jeong Ji-yong, who also lived in the neighborhood. I remember we talked about poetry with him there."

Yun's posthumous poetry collection *Sky and Wind and Star and Poem* was published in January 1948. Upon the request of Gang Cheo-jung, Jeong Ji-yong wrote an introduction in the first edition, stating that he had not personally known Yun. Thus, it had been assumed that they had never met. Yet while Jeong did not remember, Yun had visited Jeong at his home. Aspiring poets frequently visited Jeong, and it is plausible that Jeong did not remember Yun, a college student.

Reverend Ra stated that affluent people's houses lined the lower, flat area of North Ahyeon-dong, and that houses became smaller as one went up the hill. Jeong's house was in the upper part of the neighborhood, a medium-sized Korean-style house with a tile roof.

I was intrigued by this statement and interviewed Jeong Gu-gwan (b. 1928), the poet's son. He confirmed that his father had lived in a tile-roofed house in North Ahyeon-dong in 1939; his address was 1–64 North Ahyeon-dong. Jeong Gu-gwan stated that he was eleven in 1939 and remembered numerous guests coming ceaselessly to the house: the poet's friends, students, and aspiring writers.[15]

Around the same time, Song Mong-gyu also left the dormitory and roomed in North Ahyeon-dong. Dr. Song Ung-gyu, Song's cousin, stated that the two of them moved to 240 North Ahyeon-dong but that after a year, for financial reasons, he had to find a tutoring job that provided room and board. Song went back to living in the dormitory.

In an essay, Yun humorously wrote about why he had left the dormitory and found a place in a boardinghouse:

Events are often caused by not great but small motivations.

It was a snowy day. A friend of my roommate's came to spend an hour or so before the street car arrived to take him inside the Gates [referring to the downtown area within the four gates of Seoul—Author's note]. The following was their conversation:

"Hey, are you going to become the fixture in this house?" [the dormitory—Author's note]

"Isn't it a perfect, quiet place for studying?"

"Flipping pages of books, is that the only way to learn? Scenes from the street cars, what you experience in the train station, and all the things you encounter on the train—these are all part of living. Submerged in the life struggles, seeing and thinking and analyzing—Isn't that the true meaning of learning? Hey, learning only from books to discuss what life is and how society should be—that's for the Middle Ages. You should shake it off and go live within the Gates."

This wasn't directed toward me, but I couldn't help thinking it was indeed so. It wasn't only about the dormitory. Cultivating one's mind away from people is merely a game. A game cannot be "living," and without "living," learning is no longer alive. Learning should be part of living, I thought, and my mind was made up to go and live within the Gates soon.[16]

Here, I pay special attention to Yun's proclamation, "Cultivating one's mind away from people [or where they live, the world—Author's note] is merely a game." This idea becomes a lever when studying and understanding his poems. He instinctually understood that a person's work and efforts must be rooted in the world, in the actual place of living itself. That understanding became his power, his vitality, and was reflected in his poems.

But what was the state of the world that surrounded him?

In order to assist in the Sino-Chinese War started by Japan in 1937, the governor-general of Korea proclaimed the Protective Order for Military Resources and other ordinances, restricting the lives of Koreans. The office of the governor-general instituted naval military training in middle schools and forced the nation into a wartime emergency system. At the same time, it carried out the people's conscription system.

As the war intensified, the United States openly endorsed China. The Roosevelt administration clarified its position through the famous Quarantine speech, implying that it did not condone Japan's invasion of China. In the summer of 1938, it banned the shipping of airplanes, weaponry, and other war supplies to Japan. In July 1939, it terminated its commercial treaty with Japan.[17]

As the U.S.-Japan relationship deteriorated, so did the relationship between Yonhui, run by American missionaries, and the governor-general. Various pressures and persecutions were unleashed on the school. Won Il-han (Horace Grant Underwood)—the then superintendent of Yonhui and the son of Dr. Won Han-gyeong—gave the following description of the times:

> My first job as English lecturer was at Yonhui in which the statue of my grandfather (Reverend Underwood) stood and where my father (Dr. Underwood) was its superintendent.
>
> On return to Korea [he graduated from high school and college in America and returned to Korea in the summer of 1939], the colonial policy of Imperial Japan became conspicuous. The curriculum emphasized Self-Improvement and Japanese, and Korean classes were on the verge of eradication.
>
> Across the nation, the use of Korean was banned in school, and Japanese was forced upon Koreans. At Yonhui, however, Korean lectures were being held.
>
> Three hours of Korean language class per week were mandated for freshmen and sophomores, and two for juniors and seniors. The school strove to maintain them as long as it could, despite Japan's so-called "Imperial Citizens' Education" policies.
>
> Korean classes, however, were replaced by "Japanese studies" in the following spring.
>
> We were forced to lecture only in Japanese. The professors who were not fluent in Japanese made many mistakes during lectures, which made students laugh.
>
> Even the English education came to a halt. The government limited importing of English-language books that went against Japan's national

policy. We could teach neither Bertrand Russell, who criticized Japan after the Sino-Japanese War, nor John Stuart Mill, the author of *On Liberty.* [...] My father, as the superintendent of the school, faced great distress and hardship.

The Education and Management Bureau of the Governor-General ordered the school to take down all signage and posting of school banners and songs, as well as notices written in English, to replace them with propaganda posters that supported the position of Imperial Japan.

After the Sino-Japanese War, even small groups were disbanded by illegal roundups, and many professors at Yonhui were arrested as well.

It is a well-known fact that "The Song of Joseon," printed on the first page of Professor Hyeon Je-myeong's collection, was banned.

I heard that a year before my return to Korea, the high-level detectives of Seodaemun Police Station searched university and college libraries and confiscated hundreds of rare books as "seditious books." Among the confiscated books were historical records written in English regarding the annexation of Korea.[18]

As imperial Japan was crushing Korea's unique culture, resistance against it grew. Here, let us examine the literary resistance.

In July 1938, the Korean linguist Mun Se-yeong published *Urimal Sajeon,* the first Korean dictionary, and the poet Kim Gwang-seop published a poetry collection titled *Longing.* In February 1939, the first issue of the Korean literary magazine *Munjang* was published, followed by numerous poetry collections in Korean one after another: Kim Sang-yong's *Homesickness,* Pak Yong-cheol's *Poems,* Kim Gwang-gyun's *Gas Lamp,* Kim Gi-rim's *Customs of the Sun,* Shin Seok-jeong's *Candlelight,* Jang Man-yeong's *The Festival,* and Yu Chi-hwan's *Poems of Cheongma.* All of them were published in 1939, as if a flickering candle was trying its best to emit the last glimmer of light.

Yun seems to have read these books diligently. Among his possessions preserved by the family members are Pak Yong-cheol's *Poems* and Jang Man-yeong's *The Festival,* among other poetry books. One may appreciate this fact in connection with some critics' view that Yun's poems reflect the poetic influence of Jang Man-yeong and Shin Seok-jeong.

On the other hand, the pro-Japanese Joseon Literary Association was formed, and other activities of pro-Japanese forces spread like wildfire. In short, it was a turbulent age.

Among the six poems written in 1939, aside from "Self-Portrait" (previously discussed), "Turgenev's Hill" stands out. When it was included in the posthumous collection, it was categorized as an essay, and it has been treated since as such. However, I regard it as a prose poem:

TURGENEV'S HILL

As I walked over a hill, three beggar boys passed me.
The first boy carried a basket on his back. The basket was filled with
    refuse: soda bottles, tin cans, iron scraps, and old socks.
The second boy, too.
The third boy, too.
Overgrown hair, tearful and bloodshot eyes in blackened faces,
    lusterless bluish lips, rags in tatters, torn bare feet.
Oh what horrific poverty has swallowed up these young boys?
I was moved with compassion.
I dug into my pocket. A fat wallet, a watch, a handkerchief . . . all these
    things were there.
But I had no courage to give them blindly away. I kept fingering them.
I'd just have a nice talk with them, I thought, and said, "Boys . . ."
The first boy only looked back askance with bloodshot eyes.
The second boy, too.
The third boy, too.
And they walked over the hill, whispering among themselves as if
    saying, you have nothing to do with us.
No one remained on the hill.
Only twilight was surging in—

(September 1939)

This is a piercingly satirical poem, which has not been appropriately interpreted or evaluated. One reviewer even said that the poem "has a theme of compassion for 'neighbors'" and suggests a "symbolic event" in a matter-of-fact way, elaborating on the "practical resolution as a humanist the poet has shown in 'Prelude.'"[19] But this interpretation misses the mark. The poem was in fact derived from one of Turgenev's prose poems, reprinted here:

THE BEGGAR

I was walking along the street . . . I was stopped by a decrepit old beggar.
Bloodshot, tearful eyes, blue lips, coarse rags, festering wounds. . . . Oh,
    how hideously poverty had eaten into this miserable creature!

He held out to me a red, swollen, filthy hand. He groaned and mum-
    bled for help.
I began feeling in all my pockets. . . . No purse, no watch, not even a
    handkerchief. . . . I had taken nothing with me. And the beggar was
    still waiting . . . and his outstretched hand feebly shook and
    trembled.
Confused and abashed, I warmly clasped the filthy, shaking hand . . .
    "Don't be angry, brother; I have nothing, brother."
The beggar stared at me with his bloodshot eyes, his blue lips smiled,
    and he, in his turn, gripped my chilly fingers.
"What of it, brother?" he mumbled; "thanks for this, too. That is a gift
    too, brother."
I knew that I, too, had received a gift from my brother.

(December 1878)[20]

This prose poem, written by the great Russian novelist Ivan Sergeyevich
Turgenev, was introduced to Koreans in February 1919, translated by the poet
Anseo Kim Eok. After it was published in *Taeseo Munye Shinbo*, the poem was
embraced wholeheartedly by Koreans. The September 20, 1922, issue of Shanghai's *Tongnip Shinmun* published a plagiarized version of it under the Korean
name "Gyeong Jae." As it was completely plagiarized, its content, core theme,
and conclusion are, of course, the same as the original: The narrator met a beggar in rags, but when he searched his pockets, he found "no purse, no watch,
not even a handkerchief. . . . I had taken nothing with me." When he grabbed
the beggar's filthy hand and asked for forgiveness, the beggar, in turn, was
humbly obliged and grateful.

Perhaps it was because no one had enough in those days that Koreans liked
the story. Getting the beggar's gratitude and heart without giving anything to
him—Turgenev could not have been aiming at that conclusion, yet the result
at the end of the poem is just that. Why did this prose poem attract people so
much? If we were to infiltrate the unconscious of their hearts, could we not
say that the balance sheet of receiving gratitude after giving away nothing
satisfied them?

Jesus pointed out bitingly, "Where your treasure is, there will your heart
be also" (Matt. 6:21). This is true. But compassion with only words and ges-

tures, no treasure—how valuable is it? Even if it was genuinely earnest, how would that help the beggar in rags?

Facing a fundamental question like this, if one were to close one's eyes and be satisfied that he had spoken nicely while offering an empty hand to a beggar asking for alms, it would be a type of deception, a cheap self-absorption. That is why the sentiments one feels from "The Beggar" are perfidious.

Yun revolted against the fake fraternal love, the cheap compassion. He exposed the self-deceit and dishonesty behind the charity of Turgenev's "The Beggar"—getting one's gratitude and heart without giving away anything— and that is why he titled his poem "Turgenev's Hill." The external condition of the hill may symbolize the hurdle one must get over to be free from the cheap sentiment or self-absorption created by Turgenev.

For this purpose, Yun paid attention to the composition of the poem. Instead of the circumstantial setting of "no purse, no watch, not even a handkerchief," fortunate for the ease of conscience, he set the unfortunate circumstance of "a fat wallet, a watch, a handkerchief . . . all these things," mocking and satirizing the pretense and cheap compassion that are rooted deeply within us.

A satire is a kind of mental exercise that becomes possible in the presence of a highly critical faculty that can sneer at everything and everyone, including oneself, while maintaining an objective perspective. Yun instinctually had the ability, and this was not his first satirical poem. Before "Turgenev's Hill," he wrote a satirical poem of the same pattern titled "Woman":

WOMAN

The first apple ripened with its flowers
Fell first.

An autumnal breeze just passes by today.

The red apple fallen by the street
Is picked up by a passerby.

(July 26, 1937)

This poem was written two years before "Turgenev's Hill" during Yun's summer recess in his last (fifth) year at Gwangmyeong Middle School in Yongjeong.

What is this poem about? On the surface, it is about a red apple that ripened first and fell, making it a descriptive poem. However, with the title "Woman," its meaning changes. Under the premise that a "red apple" is a woman, the poem becomes a cynical, almost heartless satire. A girl who has fully bloomed before any other girl has fallen; that her virtue is violated meaninglessly by an undeserving man is satirized coldly through the medium of fruit.

Yet one quickly realizes that such a reading is not altogether correct. For "Woman" is derived from Sappho's "One Girl." I chanced upon the poem while reading the poet Kim Gwang-seop's memoir *My Prison Diary*. Kim commented on the Greek poetess's fragment as follows:

> At that time [while Kim was enrolled at Waseda University (1929–1932)] I also read Sappho's "One Girl":
>
> ONE GIRL
> Like the sweet apple which reddens upon the topmost bough,
> Atop on the topmost twig,—which the pluckers forgot, somehow,—
> Forget it not, nay; but got it not, for none could get it till now.[21]
>
> What is remarkable about this poem is not the melancholy sentiment but its intellectual charm. What is essential in a poem is not melancholy but poesy.[22]

When compared side by side, Sappho's "One Girl" and Yun's "Woman" are similar in terms of titles and basic composition. But Yun's perspective on the girl/woman is opposite to that of Sappho's.

Sappho sang about the existence of a lofty, highly dignified, and beautiful virgin, who is like a red apple hanging at the end of a high branch, not reachable by men. But Yun's critical senses felt dissatisfied with the poem. He must have felt, if Kim Gwang-seop's expression can be borrowed, that it lacked poesy. Using the same figure of speech and technique, he challenged Sappho's poem. Even if one cannot be "reached" by men's hands, a ripened fruit is bound to fall, and that is the fate of a woman. An extraordinary girl, who has bloomed before other girls, is caught futilely by an unexpected man, a mere "passerby." Yun has sharply expressed that this is the reality of life.

Yun was twenty years old when he wrote "Woman," and his perspective on women at that young age is acutely revealed in the poem.

What do his satirical poems signify? Yun used the genre of satire as a means to discern and understand the world and to express his insight poetically. His approach to poetry was a fierce one.

After writing "Turgenev's Hill" in September 1939, however, he stopped writing for a long period. (Of six poems from 1939, four were dated September, and the two undated poems—"The Boy" and "The Ravine Water"—also seem to have been written by September.) The next poem he wrote was from December 1940. Although his fourteen months of silence have caught little attention from scholars and researchers, they should be carefully examined so that the entire body of his poetry can be understood organically.

What happened during those fourteen months?

Domestically, what created the greatest stir was the proclamation of the ordinance regarding the change of family names of Koreans (*changssi gaemyeong*) on November 10, 1939. Effective February 11, 1940, it mandated that Koreans change their surnames to Japanese names.

Changssi gaemyeong was the brainchild of Minami Jiro, who was appointed the seventh governor-general of Korea on August 26, 1936. Of all his cruel work in Korea, this was the worst one. From the outset, he paid special attention to destroying the very essence of "Koreanness." He enacted the Pledge of the Imperial Subjects, forcing all Koreans to recite it, and banned all Korean language classes in school. These cruel rules delivered a heavy blow to the spiritual realm of Koreans. The success of his measures was shown when over one thousand well-known leaders of Korea, such as Choe Rin, Yi Gwang-su, and Yun Deok-yeong, were gathered in Bakmun (Hirobumi) Temple, a place in Seoul for shrine worship to Ito Hirobumi, to hold a memorial service for Ito Hirobumi and others who were instrumental in the annexation of Korea.

Internationally, World War II broke out in Europe. In August 1939, Germany declared war on England and France and invaded Poland, Norway, the Netherlands, and Belgium.

In that year, Yun's sophomore-year transcript was as follows: Self-Improvement (80), Bible (94), Korean (86), Chinese characters and writing (90), English Grammar (50), English Reading (87), English Composition (90), English Conversation (72), Western History (90), Sociology (65), Economics (75), Logic (85), Gymnastics (82), Military Training (88).[23]

Junior Year: Period of Religious Skepticism and Meeting Jeong Byeong-uk

The year 1940 came. To Koreans under the powerful oppression and wretched control of imperial Japan, the new year brought neither hope nor joy. Instead, choking pressures increased.

It was a doubly special and monumental year for the Japanese in Korea: It was the 2,600th anniversary of Japan as a nation and the 30th anniversary of the annexation of Korea, Japan's first colony abroad. According to Mr. Won Il-han's memoir, "In that year, various types of oppression were perpetrated under the pretense of 'academic reform.' No one could know how great my father's distress must have been."[24]

Yet comparatively speaking, the oppression of education was a collateral problem. Japan's goal of making perfect *Kōkoku Shinmin* (imperial subjects—Trans.) out of Koreans was being pushed ahead fiercely. A notorious example was the execution of *changssi gaemyeong*. Going into effect on February 11, it forced the registration of new names, and following its fierce enforcement, 79.3 percent of Koreans had registered new Japanese surnames by September 20, just seven months since its start. Traditional Korean culture was profoundly rooted in ancestor worship and heritage. The worst possible epithet anyone could be given was *seong eul gal nom*—one who should change one's family name. Yet the colonial government forced 79.3 percent of the people to change their family names and officially register them. The statistical number reflects imperial Japan's viciousness, atrocity, and dreadful violence.

Other measures were employed to eradicate the spirit of Koreans. *Donga Ilbo* and *Joseon Ilbo*, the two biggest Korean-language daily newspapers, were shut down on August 10. The numbers of political prisoners were multiplying, and in September, numerous Christians were arrested nationwide during an anti-Christian operation. Various ordinances systemized the rationing of daily necessities, excluding blacklisted individuals from the rations lists. Survival itself was at stake. A nationwide network called the National Mobilization League controlled not only the daily life of Koreans but also their mental activities.

Yun was in his third year in college. How did he bear the dark, wretched days?

The following three events, listed chronologically, mark the year 1940 in Yun's life:

1. Meeting Jeong Byeong-uk, his lifetime friend
2. Becoming skeptical of the Christian faith
3. Writing only three poems in December, after more than a year of not writing

First, let us examine his friendship with Jeong.

In the spring of 1940, Yun moved back to the dormitory as his junior year began. In early spring, Jang Deok-sun from Gwangmyeong, two years Yun's junior, arrived in Seoul from North Gando to take the entrance examination for Yonhui Junior College. Yun helped Jang find a room near Yonhui at 51 Changcheon-dong. Yun had already moved into the dormitory before the term started.

Jeong Byeong-uk was Jang's classmate at Yonhui. Jeong became friends with Yun soon after starting at Yonhui, and their friendship lasted throughout Yun's stay. Moreover, Jeong kept the only handwritten copy of Yun's manuscript safe until liberation, and took an important role in having it published.

In the absence of the friends who safeguarded and published the manuscript, the poet Yun Dong-ju and his poems, however great, would have been forgotten. Thus, Yun's friendship with Jeong was a fortunate event in his personal history. Jeong described their friendship as follows:

I got to know Dong-ju in the Yonhui dormitory. [. . .] He was two years ahead of me in grade but five years older. He cared for me like a younger brother, and I regarded him as an older brother. At mealtime, he'd come to my room and take me to the dining room to sit together. So I'd always wait until he knocked on my door. I was a freshman, and he helped me shape my college life. A country bumpkin I was, but gradually I got adjusted to city life. When we went to the bookstore, I didn't buy a book until I consulted him, and when I bought gifts for my younger siblings at home, he picked them out for me. [. . .]

On moonlit nights, he'd knock on my door and get me up from the bed to take a walk through the Yonhui woods and Seogang fields for a couple of hours. He seldom talked during those hours. When he opened his mouth, it was something like, "Jeong, did you like the book you were reading before?"[25]

Second, the fact that Yun felt skeptical about faith is important.

Yun was born into a Christian household, a grandson of an elder, and received infant baptism. Growing up, he always went to church and participated in church events. In Eunjin Middle School, he started teaching children in Sunday school. There are photographs taken from that period. It was likewise during his time at Gwangmyeong. After he went to Yonhui, he still taught summer Bible school in Yongjeong during his recesses.

Yet during his third year at Yonhui, he became skeptical of the Christian faith and had little interest in church. However, he did not stop going to church, according to Jeong Byeong-uk: "I was from the hilly area by Jiri Mountain in the South and had never seen a church growing up. I never went to church in middle school, either. Somehow, I ended up following Dong-ju to church on Sundays. [. . .] We attended Hyeopseong Church, whose members were Yonhui and Ehwa students. It used the smaller auditorium in Ehwa's music building as its sanctuary. After the service, we'd go to the English language Bible study led by Mrs. Cable, Pastor Cable's wife."

On the surface, Yun seemed to be a devout Christian. But people around him noticed his religious skepticism. His friend Mun Ik-hwan and his brother did, too:

> MUN: He, too, had a period of religious skepticism. It was when he was at Yonhui. Even though it must have shaken up his innermost being, on the surface, he seemed like a calm lake.
>
> YUN IL-JU: In late 1939, that is, during the second semester of his second year at Yonhui, our family bought a bigger house, 1–20 Jechang-ro, Jeongan-gu in Yongjeong. After we fixed it, we moved there. It was under Yongjeong's most scenic hill, which was a Canadian concession, which was perfect for Dong-ju's walks. When he was a Gwangmyeong student, he taught Sunday school, and even during his first and second years in college, he helped out with the summer Bible school. When he was in his third year, I received the impression that he was less interested in church. Perhaps he had a period of doubt as his perspective widened. It must have been

during his third year, as it happened in the new house: we had a family worship at home for a special occasion, and Grandfather said, "Dong-ju, you say a prayer today." Dong-ju knelt and said a prayer, but his prayer was quite awkward unlike other times. After the worship, he flashed a smile at us and said, "One's prayer resembles one's faith."[26]

Yun Il-ju's testimony that "Dong-ju knelt and said a prayer, but his prayer was quite awkward unlike other times" is very suggestive. Even though he had lost much of his faith to the point that his prayer became awkward, he still knelt in order to pray.

He had had religious training and been devout up to this point, so what made his faith waver?

We can quickly identify the answer if we look at the circumstances he was under. What shook his faith in 1940 could not be anything else but the circumstances at that time. There were no personal events that would cause despair or loss of faith in him. It is clear from testimony that his private life was pious, and his relationships with others were harmonious and friendly.

Yun must have despaired at the appalling and humiliating conditions he was experiencing. He was a cultured man who had set a lifetime goal of studying and writing in Korean, and he had devoted his soul to it. But now, his people's language had been taken away and even the empty shell of his family name, as well as given names, had been stolen. Like a lamb kneeling under a whip, he and his people had no choice but to succumb to violence, cruelty, and evil. We may conjecture what must have gone through his heart.

First of all, he despaired at the circumstances. Further, he despaired over the fact that while men were violating other men so wickedly and appallingly, God seemed to condone it in silence. This feeling of despair shook his faith from its roots. That is why, even though his knees were humbly bent before God, his lips could not form the words to God.

But then, how is his despair, or his doubt, connected to his literary silence at the time? Exploring the third notable event of that year may provide an answer.

Yun ended the year 1940 with three poems he composed after a silence of over fourteen months. During the long period of silence he endured, events were continuously transpiring, increasing his agony over the situation, including those involving his relative Ra Sa-haeng and others. In May that year, Ra was arrested and imprisoned for one month. In October, the Methodist Theological School was shut down. "October 30, 1940, is the day the Methodist Theological School had to close its doors.[27] Its sixty students lost their teachers, and the teachers lost their students. None knew where to go. As a prelude to the school shutdown, the Japanese disseminated a written declaration on the campus in May, and many students were taken to Seodaemun Police Station, including Yi Gyeom-mok, Yu Jeung-seo, Ra Sa-haeng, Jeon Jong-ok, Jang Shi-hwa, Pak Geon-ik, and Pak Ok-nae. They were detained there for a month."[28]

The Methodist Theological School is where Yun stayed when he first went to Seoul to take the entrance exam for Yonhui. Watching his relative Ra's ordeal and the bitter fate of the school must have pained him too.

Moreover, the relationship between the United States and Japan was worsening. To retaliate against Japan's military actions, the United States was putting diplomatic and economic pressures on Japan. Japanese leaders were infuriated, and the United States felt apprehensive about its citizens in Japanese territories. In the autumn of 1940, the U.S. government sent SS *Mariposa* to the Incheon port to evacuate all Americans staying in Korea. About three-quarters of them, including missionaries and professors, got on the *Mariposa* and returned to America. The Underwood family, however, remained in Korea. "My father said, 'I will never leave Korea unless Korea deports me,'" reminisced Mr. Won Il-han.

At that point, the oppressor's outrageous violence went without hindrance. The poems "Eight Beatitudes," "Consolation," and "Hospital" were written under such circumstances, and they must be read with this background in mind:

EIGHT BEATITUDES

Matthew 5:3–12
Blessed are they that mourn
Blessed are they that mourn
Blessed are they that mourn
Blessed are they that mourn
Blessed are they that mourn

Blessed are they that mourn
Blessed are they that mourn
Blessed are they that mourn
They shall mourn forever.
   (ca. December 1940)

The poem is based on the famous Beatitudes of Jesus recorded in the Gospel of Matthew. Yun, therefore, titled it "Eight Beatitudes" and cited the source as Matthew 5:3–12. (Actually, the Beatitudes are listed from verses 3–10; verses 11–12 state other blessings.)

This poem vividly expresses Yun's psychological state and his despair, like the dripping of blood. Let us first read the Bible verses:

Blessed are the poor in spirit: for theirs is the kingdom of heaven.
Blessed are they that mourn: for they shall be comforted.
Blessed are the meek: for they shall inherit the earth.
Blessed are they which do hunger and thirst after righteousness: for
 they shall be filled.
Blessed are the merciful: for they shall obtain mercy.
Blessed are the pure in heart: for they shall see God.
Blessed are the peacemakers: for they shall be called the children of God.
Blessed are they which are persecuted for righteousness' sake: for
 theirs is the kingdom of heaven.[29]

These are the original eight beatitudes.

Yun was familiar with the English Bible. The second beatitude is translated into Korean as those who are *aetong-hanun* (bewailing) in Chinese characters, but Yun used the expression *seulpeo-hanun* instead, using the Korean word that means "sorrowful, grieving, mournful."

The reader may have noticed that "Eight Beatitudes" is a satirical poem like "Woman" and "Turgenev's Hill." It is a twig that grew out of the same roots.

Earlier, Yun had challenged Sappho concerning the theme of the fate of a woman. In contrast to Sappho's praise of the haughty grace and beauty of a woman who is like a red apple hanging on a high branch unreachable by a hand, Yun challenged that even a high-hanging fruit falls when ripened, after which a "passerby" picks it up.

He also challenged Turgenev with the issue of true neighborly love. He protested against Turgenev's pseudo-compassion and faux satisfaction that the beggar was grateful when the narrator, who did not have anything in his pockets at the moment, expressed his compassion with words. With "Turgenev's Hill," he challenged the reader to climb this hill, and mocked, Will your feeling of satisfaction stay on this hill?

Now he revolts against God about the beatitude of a mourner. What is the true nature of the revolt?

First of all, who is "they that mourn"? Of course, they are the Korean people. In "A Mournful Clan," he had already established the equation that the Korean people = the mournful clan.

"Eight Beatitudes" was a poem of revolt against the silent God while his people suffered and were persecuted. What did he intend to say by repeating "Blessed are they that mourn" eight times under the title "Eight Beatitudes"?

To him, categorizing the eight types of people God would bless—the poor in spirit, those who mourn, the meek, those who hunger and thirst for righteousness, the merciful, the pure in heart, the peacemakers, and those persecuted for righteousness' sake—would be meaningless as long as one was born a Korean. Even if all the virtues were in the person, that Korean person would remain as "they that mourn." That was what he saw, felt, and experienced in life. That is why the eight types of people were substituted with only one, repeated eight times: "They that mourn."

Thus, the eight kinds of blessings promised to the eight types of people—heaven, comfort, the earth, fulfillment of righteousness, mercy, seeing God, being called the children of God, the kingdom of heaven—one could not believe in such rewards. The only certainty was that one would "mourn forever."

This was an expression of such tremendous despair and unbelief. The inability to believe in God's promise meant the inability to believe in God. And if one could not believe in God, one could not believe in anything in the world.

Yet here we see a great paradox. Yun despairing so much at the inability to believe in God's promise reveals his yearning to believe in the promise and his supplication for the fulfillment of the promise. His unbelief, then, like his belief, was another kind of prayer revering God. That is why he, even with the hell of despair and unbelief in his heart, quietly knelt before God.

Let us now examine "Consolation" and "Hospital," written around the same time as "Eight Beatitudes." Yun was in a dual agony of despair at the world and unbelief in God. What was his way out while groping in that darkness, in that deep mire? The answer is in these poems, as if surfacing above water.

CONSOLATION

With wicked intention, the spider built a web between the railing behind the hospital and the flowerbed unfrequented by people. It is in the right spot for the young man convalescing outside to observe from his bed.

A butterfly was caught in the web on her way to the flowerbed. Yellow wings flutter and flutter while she gets entangled more and more. The spider moves to it like a bullet and wraps her with his endless, endless silk. The man exhaled a long sigh.

Countless toils robbed him of youth and health—how do I console him? No words of consolation but to rip the spider web.

(December 3, 1940)

HOSPITAL

Face shaded by an apricot tree, a young woman sunbathes in the garden of the hospital. Her ochre legs are revealed under her white gown. She has pains in her chest. All through the afternoon, no one, not even a butterfly, visits her. The apricot branches are not sad, and no wind stirs them.

I, too, long endured mysterious pains before coming here. But my old doctor knows not a young man's sickness. He says I am not sick.
This excessive ordeal, this excessive fatigue—I should not get angry.

The woman gets up, adjusts her gown, and picks a marigold from the flowerbed. She pins it on her chest and walks off the ward. Wishing for her speedy recovery and mine, I lie down where she was.

(December 1940)

These two poems have been discussed exhaustively by scholars. Yun's view that the world is a hospital is revealed in them. But in this place called society, filled with sick people, what does he suggest that we do for this hospital?

An attempt to console another, persevering and enduring, and compassion for others: these humanistic efforts are suggested.

Can we be healed through these acts? Healing is probably near impossible. Yet if we are to look for things that we can do without the power of God, that is all we can do, like small pups curled up together to share body temperature with each other on a cold winter morning.

In 1941, after these sufferings, challenges, and exploration, Yun found the path that was for him. He regained his faith too. "The Cross" and "Prelude" were written after this period, and his reverence for life and willingness to sacrifice are crystallized in these poems, meekly but immaculately.

And he no longer wrote satirical poems based on well-known poems that shared the title, content, and structure but with an unexpected twist. In the end, the genre of satire was one of the big hills that his character and poesy had to go through and then put behind him.

***

While writing this biography, I received priceless assistance from the poet's family. They provided me with many precious anecdotes about Yun that are private in nature. They also offered for my review a handwritten selection of Yun's poems, his Yonhui Junior College yearbook, and books he had possessed and read. They allowed me to sift through these sources, and I was the first person outside the immediate family who was able to study them in person.

I remember vividly how deeply moved I was—so moving that it was almost painful—while holding Yun's handwritten manuscripts in my own hands. Reading the manuscripts felt clearly different from reading a printed book. I felt a sense of his presence, and seeing the poems in their original form was inspirational.

Yun followed the spelling custom of his time. But after his poetry collection was published posthumously, it went through numerous editions, and in that process the spelling was edited according to the contemporary spelling rules. When compared with the originals, current versions contain some discrepancies.

Of course, those spelling discrepancies are peripheral issues that do not affect the essence of the poems. What impressed me was his own edits on the manuscripts and the scribblings that reflect what went on in his mind while writing the poems. These were all preserved in the manuscripts. Evidence of his inner conflicts, his thought processes and emotive changes, seemed alive on those pages.

When the first draft of this biography was completed, his handwritten manuscripts had not been officially made available to the world. His family had requested that descriptions or comments regarding the manuscripts themselves not be included. Thus, the first edition did not mention any details regarding the manuscripts.

On March 1, 1999, however, a facsimile of Yun's collected handwritten manuscripts was published by the family. As the original restriction by the family is now moot, a handwritten manuscript of one of his poems is examined here.

The manuscript of "Eight Beatitudes" impressed me the most. It was not a neat final version but a messy one with corrections. Thus, it was a rare example that showed the poet's thought process. With this manuscript as an example, let us trace the essence of his poetry and the stream of his thoughts.

"Eight Beatitudes" is a unique poem. In the body of this chapter I categorized it as a satirical poem. Just as its structure is unique, its development is peculiar. Analyzing the handwritten manuscript, we can imagine the inner conflict and anguish that tormented him when he wrote it.

"Blessed are they that mourn" is repeated eight times. What was going on in his mind? It was a deep groan. The price of mourning was only mourning. That was the reality, and he understood it sharply. So he wrote, "They shall mourn."

Even if poetry is a means of satire, a means to look at reality straight in the eye, the despair and hopelessness of reality can be too painful.

He thinks of escaping this, takes the pen, crosses out the line with two strokes, and writes: "They shall be comforted."

But this sentence causes him to feel an even greater pain. Those who mourn will not be comforted, he knows. He is sure of it through his daily experience. The promise of "they shall be comforted" is so unreal that it pains him even more. It feels desolate, like a wind that whirls inside an empty jar. He cannot stand it.

He takes the pen again. The empty, meaningless promise, with its deceit, will add more pain to the mournful. So he again erases the line with two streaks of black. And then he moves one step back. With a distance between him and the line, he contemplates the types of "the mournful." He reconfirms it. Yes. More mourning will come. He takes the pen and writes: "They shall mourn for long."

Yet this does not satisfy him. He is keenly aware that this sentence does not express his sorrow and despair. So he picks up the pen again and crosses out the phrase "for long." He replaces that with: "forever."

Thus, the very last, and the best, part of this poem ends with the famous line containing self-torment, agony, resignation, pain, curse, blame, and endless sorrow: "They shall mourn forever."

The poet's outlook on the world and future was summarized, rising and falling, in this sentence.

There is a curious part: Two scribblings are outside the lines enclosing the poem. One is the Chinese character for the number eight, and the other is equivalent to "Blessed are they who mourn," written with the obsolete Korean vowel "ˑ"—What did he mean by them?

***

The following is Yun's transcript from his third year at Yonhui: Self-improvement (87), Japanese Studies (70), Bible (85), Japanese (87), Chinese characters and writing (90), Chinese (98), History of English literature (80), Western history (90), Psychology (73), Gymnastics (83), Military training (88), French (74), Law (78).[30]

The Senior Year at Yonhui: *Sky and Wind and Star and Poem*

Yun moved many times during his senior year. When the spring semester started, he left the dormitory to room with Jang Deok-sun in Shinchon, but he moved back to the dormitory after two months. In early May, he moved out again with Jeong Byeong-uk to live in Nusang-dong, and he never moved back to the dormitory. Jeong stated that they moved from the dormitory because the meals there had become poor due to Japan's harsh food policies.

In 1941, Yun and Jeong moved to a boardinghouse in Maruteogi, Nusang-dong, then to novelist Kim Song's house at 9 Nusang-dong (from the end of May until the end of summer recess), then to a boardinghouse in North Ahyeon-dong (from early September until graduation at the end of December).

Jeong stated that they had spent the most fruitful, meaningful days when lodging at Kim Song's house:

Our daily schedule around that time was like this: Before breakfast, we took a walk to the middle of Inwang Mountain behind Nusang-dong. We could wash our faces anywhere in the streams there. After returning, we tidied up the room, had breakfast, and went to school. After classes, we took the streetcar to the Bank of Korea and walked around Chungmu-ro to visit bookshops such as Jiseongdang, Ilhan Bookshop, Maruzen, and Gunseodang. After the excursion to these new and used bookstores, we might stop at a "music café" and inspect the books we purchased. On the way home, we sometimes went to Myeongchijwa (now Myeongdong Art Theater) to see a movie if they put on anything of interest.

If we did not go to the movie theater, we walked from Myeongdong, past Cheonggye-cheon, to browse used bookshops in Gwanhun-dong. We walked again to Yugil Bookshop in Jeokseon-dong. By then, lights would be on in the streets. When we went back to Nusang-dong, Mrs. Kim had dinner ready. After dinner, Mr. Kim would invite us to the hall and we talked for an hour or so. Then we came back to our room and read books until we fell asleep near midnight. It may seem monotonous, but now I think, these were fruitful days. Because neither Dong-ju nor I had friends who drank, we hardly had occasion to drink. If we were out late to see a movie, we might eat at a Chinese restaurant with a shot of kaoliang liquor. Even when he had some alcohol, Dong-ju did not act differently. He might talk a bit more than usual but would not speak uncharacteristically. There were many aspects of his character that I admired, but the greatest was that he never put others down.

Their living arrangements at Mr. Kim's, however, had to end because of a Japanese detective. Kim Song, blacklisted by the Japanese police, had been under surveillance, and almost daily the detective came by and searched their room, copying down the titles of the books, probing their belongings, and confiscating their letters. Based on the fact that lodgers at a blacklisted person's house suffered such afflictions, we can imagine the afflictions perpetrated on the blacklisted person himself as well as the sufferings of Korean intellectuals in general during Japan's rule. It was a "hospital," as Yun appropriately identified: All were sick and wounded.

Persecution by Japan, which was anxious over the prolonged war, worsened with each passing day. Changes followed at Yonhui Junior College too. With the pressure from Japan, a new superintendent was appointed. Won Il-han wrote:

My father, who had gone through so much trouble not to hand over Yonhui Junior College to the hands of the Japanese, had to resign from the superintendent position on February 25, 1941, coerced by the Japanese government.

The governor-general was further persecuting the Americans who had refused to leave Korea on the *Mariposa*. On top of that, the relationship between America and Japan worsened, and my father could no longer bear the pressure.

His successor was Yun Chi-ho, who had studied in America and sympathized with the situation at Yonhui. The governor-general favored him as well, and the school board felt that he would be the right person for the future of the school.[31]

Yun Chi-ho was considered pro-Japanese, and many recognized that he was being used by the governor-general as a means to take over Yonhui Junior College. (As expected, on August 17, 1942, the governor-general took over Yonhui, replacing Yun Chi-ho with Takahashi Hamakichi, a Japanese superintendent.) By March 1941, Yonhui was promulgating the Reserve Detention Order for Korean Political Offenders and the National Defense Security Law. Under the name Student Volunteers, it mobilized students for forced labor. By April, it forced the cessation of the Korean-language literary magazines *Munjang* and *Inmun Pyeongron*. By this time, the war in Europe was spreading, and major forces all over the world were being swept into it. The German army had a bloodless victory over Paris the previous year, and the German air force were operating air raids. In June 1941, Germany declared war on the Soviet Union.

Japan, too, was deep in war. It expanded its battlefields under its southern advancement policy, stationing itself in French Indochina. On December 8, 1941, it attacked Pearl Harbor in Hawaii, starting the Pacific War between Japan and America.

In the meantime, how was Yun's life as a senior at Yonhui Junior College?

Yun was a beloved grandson, a precious son, an affectionate brother, a hardworking student, a good friend, and a considerate classmate and roommate. Yet behind that person was another being: a poet who trained himself like a monk practicing asceticism in the wilderness and a reverential rebel against God at the sight of his people's suffering. To understand how he tried to overcome the reality of his time and his agony, let us examine the poems that burst forth from him during 1941.

He wrote seventeen pieces of work that year (sixteen poems and one essay). The earliest of them is the poem "Terrifying Hours." It is indeed a terrifying poem. Like a still photograph, with its intense contrast of light and darkness, it reveals the poet's response, from his body and soul, to the challenges of his time:

TERRIFYING HOURS

Who is it that summons me?

Under the shade where oak leaves sprout new greens,
My breath still remains here.

I, who has never raised his hands,
I, who has no sky to point with his raised hands.

Is there a sky that can house this body of mine,
That I am being summoned?

On the morning of my death after all is done,
Remorseless oak leaves may fall. . . .

Do not summon me.

(February 7, 1941)

The poem's scale and attitude are sharply contrasted with the mournful despair contained in "Eight Beatitudes" and the dismal feeling of suffocation and his efforts to fight it through the simple and heartrending sharing of body warmth, expressed in "Consolation" and "Hospital."

Yun Dong-ju recognized that the present was "terrifying" and reacted sensitively. By doing so, the aspiring poet emerged as a full-fledged poet. His poems acquired his own voice, his own color, and his own character, beginning with this poem.

How did this leap come about? How did he overcome the agony, pain, and unbelief expressed in "Eight Beatitudes," "Consolation," and "Hospital" and come to discern the voice of history?

Another poem, "Street without Signs," dated only with the year, may be key to the answer:

STREET WITHOUT SIGNS

No one was on the platform
When I got off,

I saw only guests,
Those who are like guests,

With no sign on each house,
There are no worries about looking for a house,

There are no burning letters
In red,
In blue,

In each corner,
Lighting up a tender,
Old gas lamp,

When I hold their wrists,
All are—virtuous people
All are—virtuous people

Spring, summer, fall, and winter
Take turns.

(1941)

The poem seems rather ordinary at first glance but contains a significant message when read metaphorically. What is its message if we are to interpret a "street without signs" as a metaphor for Korea? Annexed by Japan, it is a country without a name, a street without signs.

The street without signs is crowded with "guests" and "those who are like guests." There are no owners. Even though there's "no sign on each house," when one goes, with "no worries about looking for a house," and "hold[s] their wrists, he finds that "All are—virtuous people" who live there.

With this interpretation, we see at last the meaning contained in "Terrifying Hours" dazzlingly clear. When Yun, having moved away from the perspective that his people are destined to "mourn" and "mourn forever," can view them anew as "virtuous people," he becomes renewed as well. With his whole being, he feels the sound that summoned him and the sense of duty to answer the summons.

The hour that he realized it—it was a truly terrifying hour, a fearful hour. To the point of crying out, "Do not summon me" his realization was horrifying. It was reminiscent of the prayer of Jesus on the night before crucifixion: "Father, if thou be willing, remove this cup from me." Just as the premise of the prayer was the acceptance of the cup, Yun's cry of "Do not summon me" was premised on his having to answer to the summons. Had his untimely death in the prison been prepared already during these "terrifying hours"?

It may be that with the crying out, he recovered his faith. After writing "Terrifying Hours," the five consecutive poems that followed—except "Snowy Map," written on March 12—are based on the Bible, written in reverential, Christian words:

"The First Morning": Genesis
"Again, the First Morning": Genesis
"Until Dawn Comes": the morning of the Resurrection in Revelation
"The Cross": Passion of the Christ in the New Testament
"Walk with Your Eyes Closed": the parable of the sower in Matthew 13

All five poems express the poet's tenacious mindset and conviction to cope actively with life.

With the premise of the "first morning," whose preparations were completed the night before, Yun described the new morning that he would face:

AGAIN, THE FIRST MORNING

Covered white with snow,
Electric poles vibrate,
Sounding the word of God.

What revelation is this?
Quickly,
When spring comes,
When sins are committed,
My eyes
Will open.

When Eve's labor is complete,
Covering the shame with fig leaves,
I will shed sweat on my forehead.

(May 31, 1941)

Those who think about the first day would also think about the last day.
"Until Dawn Comes" describes the trumpet sound of judgment day, at the
dawn of the second coming when the living and the dead stand before God.
He also contemplated the cross:

THE CROSS

The sunlight that chased me
Was now caught on the cross
Above the church steeple.

How did it climb up
The high steeple?

I hear no bells ringing
As I pace about whistling.
If the cross is allowed to me
Like the happy Jesus Christ
Who suffered,

I will drape my neck,
Quietly shedding Blood blooming like flowers
Under the darkening sky.

(May 31, 1941)

What kind of calling did he have in mind as he was resolved in a martyr's
death? A poem written around the same time containing the parable of the
sower answers the question:

WALK WITH YOUR EYES CLOSED

Little ones that adore the sun,
Little ones that love the stars,

Walk with your eyes closed
As the night has come.

Scatter the seeds that you have
As you walk.

If you stumble on rocks,
Open your eyes wide.
                    (May 31, 1941)

According to the parable, the sower is the son of man, and the field is the world. Who are those that "scatter the seeds that [they] have / As [they] walk," with their eyes closed in the world enwrapped in darkness? They are the pioneers of Korea, those who "drape [their] neck[s], / Quietly shedding / Blood blooming like flowers / Under the darkening sky." Such was the life Yun pursued.

His poetry and life had come so far; he was able to trust himself. The poem "Wind, Blowing," dated two days after "Walk with Your Eyes Closed," reveals his confidence with both humility and firmness:

WIND, BLOWING

Where does wind
Come from and go to?
The wind is blowing, and
My suffering has no reason.

Does my suffering have a reason?

I have never loved a woman.
I have never lamented the time I am in.

The wind keeps blowing, and
My feet stand on the rock.

Water keeps flowing, and
My feet stand on the hill.
                    (June 2, 1941)

In this poem, Yun thoroughly denies everything that belongs to him.

He had been in love. He had written a prose poem about lost love ("Snowy Map"): " I cannot follow you, for the snow keeps covering your tiny footprints. When snow melts, flowers will bloom from each footprint. When I set out to search your footprints among the flowers, it will keep snowing in my heart for the twelve months of the year." He mourned for the time he was in, lamenting that he would "mourn forever" ("Eight Beatitudes").

Despite that, or perhaps because of that, he reproaches himself for not loving more thoroughly and not mourning more thoroughly. So great and deep was his self-reproach that he torments himself, stating, "I have never loved a woman. / I have never lamented the time I am in."

At the same time, his confidence in himself and his life survived the reproach and remained with him like a diamond. Thus, he feels his feet "on the rock" and "on the hill."

This phenomenon can be seen again in "The Night I Returned to My Room": "Unable to wash away the pent-up anger, I quietly close my eyes. Then, there's a sound running through my heart. Now, thoughts are ripening like apples" (last stanza of "The Night I Returned to My Room," June 1941).

A significant event occurred for Yonhui liberal arts students while Yun was writing these poems. The college's liberal arts student group Munuhoe issued its last literary magazine, *Munu*, on June 5. Two of Yun's poems, "A New Road" and "Self-Portrait in the Well" (later retitled "Self-Portrait"), were included in it.

Munu was first issued by Munuhoe in 1932 and did not publish continuously. According to Yun's classmate Professor Yu Yeong, the 1941 issue, published during Yun's senior year, was the only issue that he had seen. Its editor in chief was Kang Cheo-jung, who was the president of Munuhoe. Song Mong-gyu was the managing editor, who handled the day-to-day operation and wrote the editor's afterword.

The "Japanese only" policy was strictly enforced at the time. Thus, articles, stories, and essays, as well as the afterword, were all supposed to be written in Japanese.

One notable fact was that "A Message from the Superintendent Emeritus" and a long article on William Wordsworth, both written by Dr. Underwood, were included in English. Seven poems and four pieces of *dongsi* written by the students, and two translated Rilke's poems—a total of thirteen pieces—were published in Korean. It is not clear how these pieces passed the censorship.

Another noteworthy fact is that the editors published the writing of Dr. Underwood (Won Han-gyeong), the superintendent emeritus, but not that of the current superintendent, Yun Chi-ho. It was their way of expressing their distrust and rejection of the pro-Japanese Yun Chi-ho.

Song's afterword states, "Munuhoe will be dissolved to establish the school's new system because of the mobilization campaign. . . . Thus, this will be the last issue of the magazine."

It is apparent that, as imperial Japan's coercion caused the dissolution of Munuhoe, the editors of *Munu* intended to honor and preserve the name in history by publishing the discontinued magazine once more.

It seems that Song Mong-gyu, who became the managing editor in his senior year, put great effort into publishing the new issue in time though he lacked much-needed editing help. Song wrote in the afterword, "I realized for the first time how difficult it is to publish a magazine. Articles, advertisements, censorship, and proofreading—all these things could not be done well by two or three people."

Despite this statement, we see that he was quite experienced in magazine work. When he was in his fifth year in Myeongdong Grade School in North Gando, he started a monthly magazine, *New Myeongdong*, which continued for a few months. Also, during his Nakyang Military Academy period, he produced a magazine called *Shinmin*. Compared to his classmates with no experience, he was more familiar and efficient with the work. That is probably how *Munu* was successfully published that year.

Munu, at the time of its first issue, was a Korean-language magazine. But now, the Korean language was being taken away from them, and it became a Japanese-language magazine. With the 1941 issue as its last one, the magazine was discontinued until 1960, when Yonsei University students revived it.

In the 1941 issue, Song printed his own poem "Together with the Sky" under the pen name "Dream Star" (Kkum Byeol). This was the time when Koreans could not use Korean and were coerced to change their names to Japanese, and Song translated his Chinese-character name into pure Korean words (*mong* means "dream," and *gyu* means "star"). His defiant spirit is felt in the poem:

"TOGETHER WITH THE SKY" BY DREAM STAR

Sky—
A fractured sky that mourns with me
Still, I discover the whole sky from you—

Blue shades covering,
The sun crossing,

Clouds passing,
The moon peeking,
Stars smiling,

With you, and with you only,
I'd love to repeat the long-gone stories

O Sky—
All things have gone past us,
Emptier than the dreams,
Scattering painful ideas,
Without regrets, quietly, quietly—

In my heart remains only a vestige of desire
And rumination of bitter memories
I weep, brooding over the hills

Yet,
Though I am not lonely, with no lover,
Though I am not homesick, with no home,

Because now I only
Want to lock my heart in the sky,
Want to keep the sky in my heart

I wish for a morning when gentle breezes smile

I quietly wish to sing with you
On that morning.

Song regards "sky" as a conversation partner with whom to talk about the ugly reality he faces. But it is a "fractured sky," not the "whole sky." What he shares with that fractured sky is the "long-gone" stories, "emptier than the dreams." Still, he does not stop there. He wishes quietly "to sing" with the sky on a "morning when gentle breezes smile."

Though deeply mourning the fractured sky, an embodiment of the fatherland lost to the aggressor Japan, he indirectly expresses the hope of liberation kept in the depth of his heart. It was a poem of willpower.

In July, following the June publication of *Munu*, summer recess started. Yun and Song returned home to North Gando, carrying a copy of *Munu*. It seems that they left it there when they went back to school.

Three years and eight months after the publication of *Munu*, when Yun died in prison in Japan on February 16, 1945, his family brought his remains to North Gando to give him a Christian burial. At the funeral, Yun's family read "A New Road" and "Self-Portrait in the Well," published in *Munu*. One can imagine that "Together with the Sky" was read at the funeral of Song, who died in prison several days after Yun.

We have already examined Yun's poems that had been written before the summer recess. Let us now turn to the poems written after the summer. During the last semester at Yonhui, genuinely great poems poured out of him.

One of the merits of Yun's poems is their comprehensibility. Yet there are two difficult poems: One is "Another Home," written soon after the summer recess, and the other is "Liver," the last one written that year. Incomprehensibility can be both a shortcoming and a merit. Since no interpretation can be deemed wrong, readers can relax and read the poem in whatever way they choose. There lies its attraction. At the same time, it can be unsettling. It is like a beautiful woman whose identity is unknown. While attracted to it, one hesitates to approach it. Despite that, one must take up the challenge:

ANOTHER HOME

The night I returned home,
My skeleton followed me to the room and lay with me.

The dark room connects to the universe;
The wind blows like a sound from heaven.

Observing the skeleton, weathering finely
In the darkness, who is weeping?
Is it I?
Is it the skeleton?
Is it the beauteous soul?

The dog with an unyielding principle
Barks the darkness away all night long.

The dog that barks the darkness away
Must be pursuing me.

Let us go, go,
Go like a fugitive.
Let us go to another beautiful home,
Hiding from the skeleton.

(September 1941)

In this poem, the poet's self is divided into three: "I," "skeleton," and "beauteous soul." What does this split mean? Numerous critics have tried various interpretations on this point. What is the truth? From the perspective of a biographer examining the close relationship between the poet's life and his poetry, I feel obligated to review the biographical circumstances under which this poem was written.

In September 1941, when this poem was written, the summer recess had just ended. Chronologically, what had transpired during the summer may have inspired the poem, as is the case with September 1938's "The Portrait of the Younger Brother." If so, Professor Yun Il-ju's following anecdote is significant: "It was when Dong-ju's graduation from Yonhui was around the corner. In our home in Yongjeong, our elders, including grandfather (Elder Yun Ha-hyeon), talked with Dong-ju and Mong-gyu about their careers after graduation. When grandfather expressed his simple expectations for them to get a job, get settled, and support the family, Mong-gyu immediately refuted, 'Do you think we have studied to live like that?' He was saying that they had greater ideals. Next to him, Dong-ju hushed him, stealthily dissuading him from talking back to the elders." From this anecdote, we can guess at the circumstances that divided Yun's self into three:

1. The present self ("I")
2. The self that meets the expectation of the family—that is, getting a
   job, making money, supporting the family ("skeleton")
3. The self that pursues the ideals ("beauteous soul")

Clearly, Yun was aware of the conflict among his three selves. What distinguishes this analysis from that of other critics is the interpretation of the meaning of "skeleton."

The following context is what led this author to conclude that through the skeleton, Yun was describing his having to make a living to support his family. What kind of person was he? In his copy of *The Selected Poems of Jeong Ji-yong*, he underlined in red the verse from the poem "The *Taegeuk* Fan": "I suddenly remember rice, money counting, and a roof leak." Yun commented in clear, red letters, "This is the blackmail from livelihood." As much as his father, concerned with his son's livelihood, tried to dissuade him from studying literature, Yun knew what "livelihood" demanded of him. It was toward the end of 1941, the times of darkness, when only the Japanese language could be used. Moreover, even if he could find a job, it would be as "a newspaper reporter at best," as his father had said. The life of a salaried man to support his family meant giving up all his ideals and principles. He felt that such a life fit the empty frame of a skeleton, not that of a human being. We can now understand why he used the metaphor of "skeleton."

The family finances were worse than ever, and his younger siblings were growing fast. It was a given that he should make enough money to support them. He must have thought seriously of living as a skeleton. It had been an ongoing issue that he could not help thinking about, but especially when he was back at home with his family, the pressure became even more unbearable. In fact, it became so real that he had to write, "The night I returned home, / My skeleton followed me to the room and lay with me."

Once the conflict structure among the three selves is understood concretely, the poem is no longer incomprehensible. We can easily grasp not only the meaning of the mysterious skeleton but also the part about "Observing the skeleton, weathering finely / In the darkness, who is weeping?" We quickly recognize that tears flow as the poet pictures the "skeletal" life, weathering away over time in the rain and wind.

However, he feels that because of his principles, he cannot live a life of "darkness." That is why he cries out, "Let us go, go, / Go like a fugitive. / ... / Hiding from the skeleton." He is desperately yearning to go to "another beautiful home" where he need not weep over a skeleton's life, where it is not the home that pressures him to live like a skeleton.

"Another Home" is a scream that burst out in the poetic form: the scream of conflict and anguish between "ideal" and "reality," between "great cause" and "familial love."

This analysis is strongly supported by the following testimony by Jeong Byeong-uk: "After summer recess, we moved to North Ahyeon-dong for the fall semester. It was a boarding house crowded with seven or eight boarders. Having moved from the previous small, family-like place, we found the new place sloppy, inconvenient, and noisy. Moreover, Dong-ju became quite busy as he was about to graduate. He seemed to be suffering greatly from worries about going to university, what was going on in the country, the family, and so on."

Under the desperate, confusing circumstances of not knowing where he should be headed, he wrote the important poems for which he is now most famous. Besides "Another Home," these are "Counting Stars at Night," "Prelude," and "Liver."[32]

Following "Another Home," "The Road" was written on September 31. The effusion that "I live, only to look for what I have lost" at the end of the poem reaffirms his choice of the "unyielding principle."

What comes afterward is the untainted, beautiful poem "Counting Stars at Night."

COUNTING STARS AT NIGHT

The season-passing sky
Is filled with autumn.

Without a care in the world, I could count
All the autumnal stars.

I cannot count now one by one
All the stars that are engraved in my heart
Because morning comes easily,
Because tomorrow's night remains,
Because my youth is not yet over.

A star for a memory
A star for a love
A star for loneliness
A star for a longing
A star for a poem
A star for Mother, Mother,

Mother, I give each star a beautiful word. The names of the children who
shared the desk with me in grade school, the names of the foreign girls
like Pae, Gyeong, and Ok, the names of the girls who've already become
mothers, the names of poor neighbors, dove, puppy, bunny, mule, roe
deer, and names of poets like Francis Jamme and Rainer Maria Rilke,

They are too far away.
Just as the stars are so far and high.

And Mother,
You are far away in North Gando.

Longing for something,
I wrote my name on the hill
Covered in light from so many stars.
Then I covered it with earth.

The insects chirp the night away
Mourning their shameful names.

But when spring comes to my star after winter
Grass will thicken the hill
Where my name is buried,
Just as green grass appears on a tomb.

(November 5, 1941)

The title in Korean is "별 헤는 밤," or "Byeol-Heneun-Bam" (star-counting-
night—Trans.). According to the dictionary, *heneun* is a North Hamgyeong
dialect for *seneun* (counting). Here, North Hamgyeong refers to the Yukjin
dialect.[33] The sound of *heneun* is much softer and prettier than *seneun*. In all
other parts of Korea, the sound changed to the harsher one due to glottaliza-
tion, but it was preserved in the Yukjin region.

The standard Korean spelling dictates *seneun*, but many Koreans now use the word *heneun* rather than *seneun* because of this poem. Although the original Korean sound had been preserved only in the Yukjin area, it was resurrected and became familiar following Yun's use of it in the beloved poem, reminding us of the correlation between language and literature.

The poem is filled with luminous stars on a clear autumn sky. The poet's pure, noble character, as well as his remarkably exquisite lyricism, is revealed within its stanzas. Having seen his pain and struggles, his agony from endless introspection and resolution, we feel a smarting pain in our hearts when we hear his soliloquy, "Without a care in the world, I could count / All the autumnal stars" while standing "on the hill / Covered in light from so many stars." Had he finally arrived at the state of perfect serenity?

After finishing the beautiful poem, he began to compile his poems for a poetry book. He selected eighteen poems from what he had previously written and completed "Prelude" on November 20, 1941, to be the first poem in the collection. Naturally, "Prelude" became a vessel in which he, after deep reflection, placed the resolution for his life to come:

PRELUDE

Looking up at the sky to my dying day
I wished no speck of shame within me,
But even at the breeze between leaves
I suffered.

With a heart that sings the stars
I shall love all those dying
And walk the way
Entrusted to me.

Tonight, too, the wind brushes against the stars.

(November 20, 1941)

It is extremely rare to see the weight of one's life, the weight of one's truth in life, expressed in such purity and depth. With this poem, we can declare, "There is a true poet!"

Besides "Prelude," the following titles were selected by the poet for his first poetry collection:

1. "Self-Portrait"
2. "The Boy"
3. "Snowy Map"
4. "The Night I Returned to My Room"
5. "Hospital"
6. "A New Road"
7. "Streets without Signs"
8. "First Morning"
9. "Again, First Morning"
10. "Until Dawn Comes"
11. "Fearful Hours"
12. "The Cross"
13. "Wind, Blowing"
14. "A Mournful People"
15. "Go with Eyes Closed"
16. "Another Home"
17. "The Road"
18. "Counting Stars at Night"

Yun tried to publish the nineteen-poem collection in a seventy-seven-copy limited edition. This might sound strange, but at the time, poetry books were often published in small-number printings. Baek Seok's *Deer* was a two-hundred-copy printing. The famous collection *Striped Snake* by Seo Jeong-ju, published on February 10, 1941, printed only one hundred copies.

Yun bound the nineteen poems and titled it *Sky and Wind and Star and Poem*. By transcribing by hand, he made two more copies. He kept the original and gave a copy to Professor Yi Yang-ha, whom he revered, and a copy to his beloved friend Jeong Byeong-uk. Professor Jang Deok-sun said that Yun only showed the collection to him.

The collection, however, could not be published. About this, Jeong Byeong-uk stated:

After completing "Counting Stars at Night," Dong-ju wanted to publish a collection of hand-picked poems for graduation. He transcribed the manuscript, added "Prelude," and bound them. He brought me a copy of it and explained the book's long title, showing me "Prelude." Penciling the word "Hospital" on the front page, he said that, at first (before "Prelude" was written), he had planned to give the title "Hospital" because the world was currently filled with patients. Since the hospital is a place that heals patients, perhaps this collection would help those who were ailing, he added modestly.

Upon receiving a copy of the collection, Professor Yi Yang-ha advised on delaying the publication. He probably thought that, not only the poems such as "The Cross," "A Mournful People" and "Another Home" could not survive Japan's censorship, but Dong-ju's safety would be threatened.... After giving up the idea of publishing, Dong-ju wrote "Liver" by November 29, 1941. As an intellectual whose freedom to present and publish his work was taken away, he expressed his erupting anger and at the same time, tried to console himself.[34]

According to Jeong's statement, Yun took Professor Yi's advice and gave up the idea of publishing it. However, that was not the case. Professor Yi was consulted, as he was well-known in the media and the press, but Yun did not simply give up there. Yun returned home immediately after graduation and discussed its publication with his father. Yun Hye-won remembered that Yun was deeply disappointed, muttering, "It can be done only if I had 300 won ... just 300 won." Yun Il-ju also stated, "Father was inclined to publish it as well, but the circumstances did not allow it."[35]

Considering these statements, we can assume that Yun tried to publish the collection in Yongjeong, after it seemed unfeasible in Seoul, but there was no money for him to self-publish the book.

On the morning of December 8, 1941, eighteen days after "Prelude" was written and nine days after "Liver" was written, what is known as the Pacific War erupted. Without warning, Japan attacked Pearl Harbor in Hawaii, and war broke out between America and Japan. Dr. Won Han-gyeong (Underwood II), who remained superintendent emeritus at Yonhui, and Professor Won Il-han (Underwood III) were arrested that afternoon by the Japanese police. Along with other American missionaries and civilians, they were locked up in the Methodist Theological School building that had been shut down. They were imprisoned there for six months until May 31, 1942, and on the following day were deported to America.

Japan, having begun a campaign against the United States on top of the ongoing Sino-Japanese War, reorganized everything on a war footing. Even the school system changed. Instead of the customary March graduation, Yonhui

Junior College had to graduate its students three months earlier, on December 27, 1941. Yun had a new navy-blue double-breasted suit made for graduation. The Underwoods, Yonhui's founder and superintendent, were still locked up in the Methodist Theological School building, and the commencement took place under the direction of the new superintendent, the pro-Japanese Yun Chi-ho.

The graduates were twenty-one students from the Liberal Arts Department, fifty from the Commerce Department, and eighteen from the Math and Sciences Department.

Reverend Kim Jae-jun remembers the commencement vividly. Together with Reverend Song Chang-geun, he went there to congratulate Song Mong-gyu. Song had the second highest GPA and received an academic award from the superintendent. The prize was a large box of books. After the ceremony, Song opened the box and found propaganda justifying Japan's militarism, such as *The Greater East Asia Co-Prosperity Sphere*. Song became angry and threw out the books, saying, "Gee, that old codger, he calls this trash a prize?"

The claim of a "Greater East Asia co-prosperity sphere" was propaganda to glorify Japan's invasion of Asian countries, claiming that "Asian countries cooperate and prosper together to eradicate Western colonialism." In reality, Japan was using this claim to accelerate its aggression toward other Asian countries. And Yun Chi-ho had given the hateful propaganda books as the academic prize at graduation. This was the suffocating reality at Yonhui, wrought by the hands of imperial Japan.

The four years at Yonhui were behind Yun Dong-ju and Song Mong-gyu now. Jang Deok-sun, who had spent a lot of time with them at Yonhui, reflected as follows:

Their personalities were like night and day. Dong-ju was reserved and introverted, whereas Mong-gyu was active, masculine, and talkative. Dong-ju was quiet but enjoyed sports, while Mong-gyu was extroverted but not athletic. Dong-ju wrote poems, and Mong-gyu wrote stories, many of which I've read.

While being so different, they were also very close. Of course, they were cousins, but they shared a refined culture. Their friends at Yonhui were of the same stock.

Yonhui had become Yun's second home for four years, and now he was leaving it behind. Without his days at Yonhui, would he have been the same Yun Dong-ju we know today? While at Yonhui, he was his most productive, and his work was of high quality. The climate of Yonhui provided Yun with the ideal environment for his talent, and Yun was one of the greatest fruits of Yonhui.

The Period of "Confessions"

Both Yun and Song planned to study at universities in Japan after graduating from Yonhui Junior College, and their families were supportive. Unlike four years before, Yun's father wholeheartedly approved of the plan.

In 1942, however, they faced a serious problem, a prerequisite for going to Japan. Namely, it was the issue of *changssi gaemyeong*. Not only was it impossible to study in Japan without the name change, but they could not even obtain their pass-port certificate, which was vital for boarding the ferry to cross the Hyeonhaetan to Japan.

The nature of this so-called pass-port certificate is not clearly understood by present readers. However, I found one source that explicitly addresses its true nature: Chunwon Yi Gwang-su's article published in the May 1939 issue of *Jogwang* under the title, "Pass-Port Certificate." Yi had gone to Japan in May 1936 to visit his wife, Heo Yeong-sook, who had been studying in Japan. Yi recorded his experience with the pass-port certificate:

I left Seoul in early May to see my family in Tokyo. A Korean must obtain a pass-port certificate in order to take the ferry to Shimonoseki. Even a government official, if he is Korean, had better obtain this, which is not an easy task. One has to go to the photography studio to take a picture and get two copies. Then go to Gyeongseong and obtain a copy of the family registry. Then go to a transcription office to apply for the pass-port certificate. When it is prepared, [one must] bring it to the police station under the jurisdiction. While submitting that, one has to explain in detail what business he's doing, to which house in what region and for how long he's traveling, when he's leaving, and so on. Moreover, one must plead repeatedly why he must go. If the head of the High Police accepts the pleading, one must again appear at the police station on the day of departure. Finally, his joy cannot be explained when one gets the certificate. One cannot help but bow repeatedly to them to express sincere gratitude.

The certificate is merely a copy of one's family registry submitted with two photographs glued onto it, upon which is some writing in red ink. This is only an introduction to leaving the port; it is not a passport. It is the word "introduction" in which the authority's worries and agony lie.[36]

Yi Gwang-su writes this short essay in his signature style with black humor. Like heavy steam arising from a boiling pot are the pent-up anger and humiliation felt by Koreans, colonial subjects of Japan, when applying for the pass-port certificate necessary for a trip to Japan.

The Busan Marine Police was a special police force that regulated and oversaw all boats and people that entered the Busan port, including the Kampu ferries that operated between Korea's Busan and Japan's Shimonoseki ports. A Korean had to present the pass-port certificate before being permitted to board the ferry.

Yi's pass-port certificate reads: "This introduces [Name]'s travel to the Native Country [Japan]. The destination is Tokyo, and the purpose of travel is to visit his wife." By commenting "It is the word 'introduction' in which the authority's worries and agony lie," Yi is being sarcastic, sneering at Japan's lip service of its *Naeseon Ilche* policy (Japan and Korea Are One). While stating that "both Koreans and Japanese are legitimate children of the Emperor," Japan required only Koreans to submit the pass-port certificate. Since that would be a clear contradiction of its so-called policy, Japan cunningly employed the rhetorical expediency of using the words, "This introduces..." The necessity for pass-port certificates showed the true status of the Korean people. Thus, Yun and Song, in order to study in Japan, first had to obtain a certificate.

Moreover, to enroll in a Japanese university, they had to satisfy the requirement that the name on the Yonhui student registry be the same as the name on the family registry. With regard to this, Professor Mizuno Naoki of Kyoto University pointed out: "By 1940, the Yun family changed their surname to Hiranuma and the Song family changed theirs to Somura. However, Yun and Song did not submit the change of names to Yonhui, using their Korean names. Both Yun and Song's diplomas bore their Korean names. To go to Japan, they needed pass-port certificates, while their university application required certified copies of the family registry. Their names on the family registry were Hiranuma and Somura. With different names on the Yonhui diploma and the family registry, they could not prove each person was the same person."[37]

Consequently, they had to request to Yonhui Junior College that the names on the diploma be changed to the new Japanese names.

Yun and Song returned to Seoul after their visit to North Gando immediately following graduation and applied for a name change. On the student registry archived at Yonsei University, their name change records clearly show the new names and the dates of change:

Yun Dong-ju: Hiranuma Doojyu, January 29, 1942
Song Mong-gyu: Somura Mugei, February 12, 1942

Under the *changssi* (create surnames) *gaemyeong* (change given names) law, Yun's Japanese surname was chosen randomly by his family. Song's family added another Chinese character, "Chon," to "Song" to make up a Japanese-sounding name, which reads "Somura" in Japanese.

Changssi gaemyeong was an unspeakable humiliation. Yun became Hiranuma Doojyu, and Song became Somura Mugei, to which they had to answer when called on in class. *Changssi gaemyeong* directly proved the cruel reality of the times.[38]

When Yonhui's pro-Japanese superintendent, Yun Chi-ho, changed his name to Idong Chiho (pronounced in Japanese "Ito Jiko"), the nationalistic students at Yonhui and Ehwa ridiculed the name by pronouncing it "Ittong Chiwo" (Take the poop away). What must Yun and Song have felt when submitting name change requests to their alma mater?

The dates they submitted the requests show that they waited until the last possible minute to change their names.

Song started Kyoto Imperial University on April 1, 1942, and Yun started at Rikkyo University on April 2, 1942. Estimating the time it took to mail application papers and process them, to travel to Japan to take the entrance examinations, and to receive admission and registration information, we can conclude that February 12, the date Song submitted his name change request, was the latest date he could have done it. Clearly Song wanted to delay the name change as long as he could.

On the other hand, Yun submitted his name change request on January 29, two weeks earlier than Song. The January 29 date, however, must be connected to his poem "Confessions," written on January 24, 1942.

Yun submitted the request five days after the poem was written. Considering the poem's title, content, and circumstances, I posit that Yun collected his thoughts and arrived at a resolution by writing "Confessions" before submitting his request. That is, he wrote "Confessions" as the result of feeling excruciating shame once he concluded he could not avoid *changssi gaemyeong* if he was going to carry out his plan of studying at a university in Japan:

CONFESSIONS

My face remains in
The copper mirror corroded green;
Which dynasty's artifact is it that
It is so shameful.

I abridged my confessions into one line.
    —Twenty-four years and one month:
    What kind of joy did I hope for?

Tomorrow or the day after, on a happy day,
I have to write another line of confessions.
    —At that young age,
    Why did I make such shameful confessions?

Night after night, let me wipe the mirror
With the palms of my hands and soles of my feet.
Then appears in the mirror
The backside of a sorrowful man
Walking alone under a meteor.

(January 24, 1942)

For a long time, this poem has generally been regarded as a self-reflective poem with historical consciousness. Some even regarded the word "confessions" as an excess or exaggerated expression of emotion.

Among Yun's poems, however, "Confessions" is his most powerful poem of resistance based on concrete reality. At the very moment of giving in to imperial Japan's *changssi gaemyeong*, Yun, as a descendant of the ruined Korean Empire, confessed that his "face" is the "dynasty's artifact" that is "so shameful." The shame and humiliation were so wretched that he became skeptical of the meaning of his whole life of "twenty-four years and one month." Born in December 1917, he was precisely twenty-four years and one month old in January 1942.

His "confessions" were holistic, but their true meaning went beyond looking squarely at the shame. He was also resolved to see "Tomorrow or the day after, on a happy day."[39]

Here is a curious question: Why did Yun and Song have to study in Japan despite the agony and humiliation? What are the reasons or motivations behind that choice? Eighteen months later, they were arrested by the Japanese police, and during interrogation, they had to state their reasons for studying in Japan. They responded that, to study their own national culture, for the independence of Korea, it was not sufficient to have studied in junior college.

In the space on the paper on which he wrote "Confessions," Yun scribbled the following words: "Confessions of a poet," "pass-port certificate," "advancement," "power," "life," "survival," "living," "literature," "what is poetry?" "not knowing the way," "old mirror," and "sorrows prohibited." The layers of torment he experienced are clearly expressed in these words.

When Yun and Song decided to study in Japan, they both aimed to go to Kyoto Imperial University. Jang Deok-sun, their Yonhui underclassman, remembered Yun and Song expressing their desire to study there.

Kyoto Imperial University is a national university in Kyoto. Kyoto was the royal capital of the Heian period for over a thousand years, from 794 until Tokyo became the new capital in the Meiji era. With its historical sites and attractions, it was, according to Professor Yi Yang-ha, "reminiscent of the Shilla era."

Those whom Yun revered and respected went to school in Kyoto. The poet Jeong Ji-yong, whom Yun had worshiped in his adolescence, spent six years in Kyoto and graduated from Doshisha University. Professor Yi Yang-ha, whom he respected the most at Yonhui Junior College, went to Kyoto's most prestigious Third High School and, after receiving his degree in English literature from Tokyo Imperial University, went to graduate school at Kyoto Imperial University. These personal connections must have given Yun feelings of affinity toward the city.

Kyoto Imperial University was an attractive place. While almost as prestigious as Tokyo Imperial University, it boasted a more liberal atmosphere and excellent humanities and natural sciences education. Tokyo Imperial University, on the other hand, was more bureaucratic and known for its strong law and business schools. Even to this date, Kyoto University has produced more Nobel Prize recipients than any other school in Japan, and it is believed to be the result of its liberal approaches that allow free and creative thinking. Thus, it is not surprising that both Yun and Song wanted to study at Kyoto Imperial University.

It is not clear when Song and Yun left for Japan. It is only assumed that they went to Japan in early March because Yun's trial document indicates that he "arrived in Japan in March of Showa 17 (1942)."

Yun left his low portable desk, books, and manuscripts with his friend from Yonhui, Kang Cheo-jung, who must have been his closest friend who remained in Seoul. According to Jeong Byeong-uk, when they were rooming together, Yun seemed like Song's and Gang's "bank." Whenever they needed money or other necessities, they would come and ask Yun for them, and Yun would give whatever he had.

After Korea's liberation, Gang worked as a reporter for *Kyunghyang Sinmun* and endeavored to publish Yun's poems in the paper. When Yun's brother Yun Il-ju moved south from North Gando, Gang handed over to him, among other things, Yun's manuscripts, desk, and Yonhui Junior College yearbook, which came out after Yun's departure to Japan. These are the majority of Yun's possessions that remain now. Among these, Yun's book collection shows his in-depth interest in reading and studying:

- Korean poetry: *The Carnival* (Jang Man-yeong), *Complete Works of Pak Yong-cheol I* (Pak Yong-cheol), *A Tribute* (O Jang-hwan), *Candlelight* (Shin Seok-jeong), *Baekrokdam* (Jeong Ji-yong), *Poems of Jeong Ji-yong* (Jeong Ji-yong), *Poems of Yeonglang* (Kim Yeong-lang), *Striped Serpent* (Seo Jeong-ju), *Selected Poems from the Year of the Blue Pig*.
- Japanese poetry: *Poems* (Kusa Senri), *Poems of Yamauchi Yoshio* (Yamauchi Yoshio), *Modern Poems* (Japanese Poets' Association), *The Flag Bearer, Cape in Spring* (Miyoshi Tatsuji), *Symbolic Squid* (Ikuta Shungetsu), *Modern Poems* (I, II, and III), *Poems of Joyce, Songs of Night* (Francis Jamme, trans. Miyoshi Tatsuji)
- English books: *Selected Poems of Walter de la Mare, Bitter Sweet and the Vortex*, the Bible, *Memoirs of a Fox-Hunting Man*
- Criticisms (in Japanese): *Science of Arts, The Logic of Planning Ability, Poetics, Students and History, The Art of Poetry* (Paul Valery, trans. Kawamori Kozo), *Aesthetics of Fiction, Modern History of Aesthetics, The Fate of Ideology, On Literature* (Paul Valery, trans. Horigachi Daigaku), *Writing Poetry, Poetry and Experience* (Wilhelm Dilthey), *Fables* (Paul Claudel, trans. Hasegawa Yoshio)

Yun's brother Yun Il-ju spoke about Yun's books:

Among the books he had in middle school years, I remember *Poems of Jeong Ji-yong* (purchased in Pyeongyang on March 10, 1936), *The Heart of Joseon* (Byeon Yeong-ro), *Beautiful Dawn* (Ju Yo-han), *Night at the Border* (Kim Dong-hwan), *Silence of the Beloved* (Han Yong-un), *Poems of Three Poets* (Yi Gwang-su, Ju Yo-han, Kim Dong-hwan), *Heartbeats of Joseon* (Yang Ju-dong), *Nosan's Sijo* (Yi Eun-sang), *Lost Ribbon* (Yun Seok-jung), *Loud Singing* (Hwang Sun-won), *Poems of Yeonglang,* and *Selected Poems from the Year of the Blue Pig.* Dong-ju must have had a special affection for those books.[40]

He brought a bag of books home during each recess, and about 800 volumes were collected. These books became good nutrients for us, his siblings. During Yonhui years, he read many literary magazines, too: Korean magazines like *Munjang* and *Inmun Pyeongron* as well as Japanese magazines such as *Le Serpent, Poetry, Four Seasons, Poems and Poetics,* and *Black and White* (an essays and prints periodical). There were more, but I can only remember those.

One side of his room was lined with books: *The Complete Modern Joseon Literature* (8 volumes published by *Joseon Ilbo*), *The Complete Classical Joseon Literature* (published by Samjungdang), *The Complete Works of Hoam* (3 volumes), *Jindan Hakpo, Urimalbon* (Choe Hyeon-bae), complete issues of *Munjang* and *Inmun Pyeongron,* and Korean poetry books. Books in Japanese translations included complete works by Andre Gide, complete poems by Paul Valery, studies on Dostoyevsky, poems by Rilke, and other French poetry books. Dong-ju loved them. He also had Japanese books on English literature and other books in English.[41]

Yun's friend Mun Ik-hwan also remembered: "He was a voracious reader. During the school recess, he brought home many books he had bought, and I was envious of the collection that he piled up on his shelves. I remember that he had many philosophy books as well as literature. Once, we discussed Kierkegaard, and I was amazed that his understanding of Kierkegaard was much deeper than my own, even though I had been studying theology. He ceaselessly studied and read such a wide range of books, but now I wonder how his poems read so 'easy.'"[42]

***

The following are the classes Yun took (with marks he received) during his last year at Yonhui Junior College in 1941: Self-Improvement (85), Japan Studies (65), Bible (71), History of Korean Literature (86), Chinese Writing (90), Chinese (96), English Reading (81), English Composition (60), English Conversation (80), English Literature (74), History (85), Philosophy (85), Pedagogy (75), Gymnastics (85), Military Training (79), French (84), Martial Arts (84).[43]

CHAPTER 8

Japan

The Place of a Six-Tatami Room

SONG MONG-GYU STARTED Kyoto Imperial University on April 1, 1942, as a Western history major in the university's preparatory division. Likewise, Yun started the next day at Rikkyo University in Tokyo as an English literature major in its preparatory division.

Matriculation at Rikkyo University in Tokyo

At the time, Japan's university entrance examination was not given on the same date. Rather, universities were divided into two groups, and each university in the first group would give its exam on a date it chose, followed by those in the second group. Mrs. Kim Shin-muk, a Yun family relative by marriage (her brother being married to Yun Dong-ju's aunt), explained Yun's matriculation at Rikkyo as follows: "Actually, Dong-ju and Mong-gyu took the Kyoto University examination together. Mong-gyu passed it, but Dong-ju didn't. Afterwards, Dong-ju took the Rikkyo University examination and got in."[1]

A Kampu ferry from Busan took them to Shimonoseki, a port in Japan. There, they took the train that ran east along the Seto Inland Sea to Kyoto, which was halfway between Shimonoseki and Tokyo. As Rikkyo was in Tokyo, Yun parted with Song after four years of being together.

Rikkyo is a private university run by an Episcopalian mission. Japan being a country of the Shinto religion mixed in with Buddhism, which worshiped the shrines and the emperor, its Christian population, despite its long mission history, was scarce. Nevertheless, the Christian missionaries were very active, and there were several missionary-run universities.

Particularly, the younger brother of then-emperor Showa became an Episcopalian while studying in England, and after he came back to Japan, the sect received the support of some royal family members. Consequently, the Episcopal Church became more influential than other Christian denominations, and Rikkyo University had a good reputation.

Yun was an English literature major in the preparatory division rather than in the main university program because he had graduated from a Korean junior college, which was considered inferior to a Japanese high school. At the time, Japan's regular education system was as follows: elementary school (6 years), middle school (5 years), high school (3 years) or university preparatory program (3 years), university (3 years).

In Japan, there were eight national high schools (named First High School through Eighth High School) and about a dozen others. The high school curriculum was equivalent to that of the university preparatory program. The cream of the crop in Japan gathered at Tokyo's First High School and Kyoto's Third High School, the two best schools. The seven national imperial universities did not have a preparatory program because all students were supposed to have completed the preparatory program in high school. On the other hand, Gyeongseong Imperial University in Seoul had a preparatory program, as Japan did not build high schools in Korea.

Preparatory programs were only available at private universities. Upon completing the program, students could proceed to the regular university program.

Junior college graduates had disadvantages when applying to universities because junior colleges were deemed inferior. Even those who went through the identical curriculum were placed in the preparatory division, to be differentiated from high school graduates. Only after they graduated from the university did the distinction cease. For these reasons, Yun and Song had the preparatory division label attached to their university records.

Such discrimination based on the previous school attended was present in other levels of school as well. At Yonhui, for instance, even though Yun and Song were taking the same classes together, their statuses were different. Yun's was "regular" because he had graduated from the five-year program at Gwangmyeong Middle School, whereas Song's was "special" because he was a four-year Daeseong Middle School graduate.

Yonhui's student records show a notable fact: The starting dates for Yun and Song are different.

Song Mong-gyu: began the special program on April 6, 1938
Yun Dong-ju: began the regular program on April 9, 1938

This record shows that the entrance examination and acceptance dates for four-year-school graduates and five-year-school graduates were different. First, Yonhui College gave the entrance examination to four-year-school graduates earlier so as to select the best students. After that, a regular entrance exam was given to five-year-school graduates. Thus, in order to pass the special program examination, applicants had to prove themselves at a higher standard. That is why, knowing these issues, Yun and Mun Ik-hwan transferred to the five-year Gwangmyeong School, even though it was a pro-Japanese school.

Similar phenomena existed in Japan. In order to go to university as a "regular" student in Japan, one had to complete high school or the preparatory program. Junior college graduates who passed the examination were labeled "preparatory division" students. Here, too, they were subjected to a much higher standard than "regular" students. That is why Reverend Mun Ik-hwan described Song's acceptance into Kyoto Imperial University, one of the best schools in Japan, as a near miracle. Some researchers now regard the preparatory division status as that of auditors; this is far from the truth.

The extant Rikkyo University student records for Yun list his first semester courses and grades:

Survey of English Literature (Professor Sugimoto): 85
History of East Asian Philosophy (Professor Uno): 80

Rikkyo's records also show Yun's address as c/o Hiranuma Nagaharu. Hiranuma here refers to his uncle Yun Yeong-chun, who was also recorded as a reference. The address was actually that of the Korean Hall at Tokyo YMCA, where Yun Yeong-chun was staying. The address was recorded only as a formality, however, and Yun lived on the outskirts of Tokyo. Reverend Mun visited Yun in the boardinghouse before Yun's move to Kyoto and remembered that "it was a two-story house and his room was on the second floor. I think it was a six-tatami room [the size of six sheets of tatami, or about 100 square feet—Trans.]. He was packing to move to Kyoto when I visited him."

Yun's stay in Tokyo was not long, lasting about five months: from March, when the examination was given, until the end of July. We have little information about Yun during this period. Only Yun Yeong-chun and Kim Jeong-u had some memories from the period:

> YUN YEONG-CHUN: I was teaching in Tokyo when Dong-ju and his cousin Mong-gyu came to visit me not long after Dong-ju started studying English literature at Doshisha University [he confused it with Rikkyo] and Mong-gyu started studying philosophy [he confused it with history].
>
> I took their arms and took aimless walks in the Ueno Park and Nihonbashi areas. While talking about literature and life, Dong-ju seemed to have arrived at a philosophical stage where he became more spiritual, beyond material desires. He kept mentioning poetry and Joseon, like a refrain. It's not safe anywhere, I warned him, so make sure to be careful and just focus on studying.[2]
>
> KIM JEONG-U: I was in Tokyo, going to school, in the spring of 1942. As soon as Dong-ju's uncle Mr. Yun Yeong-chun gave me the news of Dong-ju and Mong-gyu staying in his room at the YMCA, I ran over there to see them. Dong-ju was planning to start at Rikkyo, and Mong-gyu was to go to Kyoto. I remember him telling me to read the Psalms of King David, as I was also an English lit major.[3]

Both statements seem to have taken place around the same period. Yun and Song first went to stay with Yun Yeong-chun for a few days after their respective university admissions in spring 1942. With his uncle as a guide, they toured the downtown areas of Tokyo and met their childhood friend Kim Jeong-u. A few days of happy moments are described like a picture in their statements. The fact that Yun told Kim to read the Psalms tells us that Yun had been reading the Book of Psalms and was impressed with it.

Biographically, Tokyo became a very meaningful place for Yun as a poet. During the course of three years, from the early spring of 1942 until he died in prison in February 1945, only five of his extant poems were written in Japan, all of which were written in Tokyo:

"White Shadows" (April 14, 1942)
"Flowing Streets" (May 12, 1942)
"Lovely Memories" (May 13, 1942)

"An Easily Written Poem" (June 3, 1942)
"Spring" (Date unknown)

All five poems were inserted in letters to his Yonhui friend Gang Cheo-jung. Even though Japan was enforcing its strict Japanese-language policy, Yun had written poems in Korean and mailed them to his friend in Korea.

Yun's letters to Gang no longer exist. Gang, for his safety, destroyed the letters and kept only the poems. The last of the five poems, "Spring," is missing the conclusion and the completion date.

Yun also included his poems in letters to others. Reverend Ra Sa-haeng stated that he had received a letter and poem from Yun but lost the letter.

Only Gang Cheo-jung kept the poems until liberation and handed them to Yun's brother Yun Il-ju. One wishes that Gang had at least transcribed the last part of "Spring" before destroying the letter, yet Gang was the only person who preserved Yun's poems written in Japan, and no one can dispute Gang's contribution to the study of Yun's poems and life during that period. The five poems are not only mature works of art but also a primary source that speaks to Yun's Tokyo period in the poet's own voice.

Among the five, the earliest one, "White Shadows," provides a crucial piece of information about the poet, namely his inner psychological state:

WHITE SHADOWS

In the street corner of darkening twilight,
My wilted ears, abused all day long,
Hear the traces of my life at dusk.

Have I been smart enough
To hear the traces of my life?

Foolishly, now I've understood all,
I send to their homes one by one
My numerous aching selves
That had long settled deep inside me;
White shadows disappear soundlessly
Into the darkness of the street corner.

White shadows—
White shadows that I loved ardently.

After sending back all that was me,
I walk along the backstreets with emptiness
To my room imbued with twilight.

Like a mature sheep with a deep conviction,
Let me graze absent-mindedly all day long.
                              (April 14, 1942)

Upon graduation from Yonhui, Yun had conflicting emotions and thoughts about his responsibility as a family member, about his ideals and principles, and ultimately about his future path. Now, these issues were to be postponed until the completion of university. The tension that had built up had now eased itself. So now, "send[ing] to their homes one by one / [His] numerous aching selves / That had long settled deep inside [him]," he senses "White shadows disappear[ing] soundlessly / Into the darkness of the street corner." When his conflicts and tension were at their climax, he suffered desperately from obsessive thoughts as if being chased by a dog "with an unyielding principle / Bark[ing] the darkness away all night long" ("Another Home"). Now, the tension had eased, and he could "graze absent-mindedly all day long" like "a mature sheep with a deep conviction."

But such a state of psychological relaxation can be dangerous. Like a fort without watchmen, unknown forces can creep into it. For Yun, it was homesickness. The two poems from May 1942 reveal his severe homesickness:

As I stand holding the red post box in the street corner, everything
    flows. The vague light of the streetlamp does not go out; what does
    it symbolize? My loving friend Pak, my loving friend Kim, where are
    you now? Fog flows in endlessly.
                    (Excerpted from a prose poem "Flowing Streets," May 12, 1942)

The train took me far
Without any new tidings.

Spring is gone—In a quiet rented room
In the outskirts of Tokyo, I long for

The me that remained in the old streets,
Like hope and love.

Today too the trains keep passing by meaninglessly,

Today too I'd be hovering on the hill near the station
Waiting for someone.

—O youth, stay there as long as you can.
(Excerpted from "Lovely Memories," May 13, 1942)

As we read these poems, a question strikes us. Are these poems really by the poet who, less than four months ago, wrote the acutely tragic poem "Confessions"? Is this the same poet who, less than a half year ago, screamed out grim, heroic cries like coagulating fresh blood in "Liver"?

Naturally, we ask these questions because we recognize in these poems a young man who feels lost and homesick in a foreign land. But when we move closer to the young man, we see beneath the hovering, wandering surface a distressed heart looming larger. His homesickness signifies that his pains for the loss were deep. His eyes were only on himself and what he had left behind, despite the new customs and environs of the foreign country. Nothing in Japan moved him or penetrated his heart.

Earlier, the poet Jeong Ji-yong wrote about the Seto Inland Sea as he saw it from the inside of the Sanyo Main Line train:

From far hills gallop toward me like war horses,
Nearby the woods tumble away like winds
Like a spread-out glass floor is the boundless water
Of the Seto Inland Sea. Water, water, water.

Dip the finger and it becomes wine;
Wet the lips and they fizzle like soda water.
(Excerpted from "The Sad Train" by Jeong Ji-yong)

The Sanyo Main Line runs from Shimonoseki, the port for Kambu ferries, to Kyoto, bypassing the Seto Inland Sea, famous for its beautiful scenery. Yun also traveled on the train, but the beauty of the sea that so moved Jeong did nothing for Yun. He could neither see nor hear it. He was still "hovering" on the place where he wrote "Liver" and "Confessions."

With this, we ask the next question, with concern: Would he overcome his homesickness? If so, would he regain his voice?

He did not "hover" for long. Only twenty days after he wrote, "Today too I'd be hovering on the hill near the station / Waiting for someone. //—O youth, stay there as long as you can," the poet gave the answer:

AN EASILY WRITTEN POEM

As night rain whispers outside the window,
The six-tatami room is a foreign country.

Though I know it is a sad calling to be a poet,
I write another line of a poem.

Tuition money that carries the fragrance of sweat and love
I receive in an envelope;

Carrying a notebook in the crook of my arm,
I go to the lecture of an old professor.

Looking back, I have lost
All my childhood friends one by one.

For what desire,
Am I sinking alone?
That a poem is written so easily
Is a shameful thing.

The six-tatami room is a foreign country,
As night rain whispers outside the window.

I light the lamp to chase away the darkness a little,
And await the morning that will come like an epoch.

I offer myself a small hand
For a first handshake of tears and consolation.

(June 3, 1942)

When he overcame the homesickness that was devouring his heart, what realization did he have? It was the cold distance between himself and the country called Japan. He did not hesitate to sing: "The six-tatami room is a foreign country."[4]

A young man from an annexed country in the capital city of the colonial ruler, the enemy state, declared that he was not its subject, and the declaration sufficed. Here is the wondrous power of poetry.

Reversely, this declaration also meant, whether intended by the poet or not, that Japan is a country of merely six tatami mats.

"An Easily Written Poem" was the starting point for Yun's literary life in Japan. Asking himself, "Looking back, I have lost / All my childhood friends one by one // For what desire, / Am I sinking alone?" he coldly defines his "hovering" life since his arrival in Japan as "sinking" and engages in deep self-introspection: "That a poem is written so easily / Is a shameful thing."

At last, he "light[s] the lamp to chase away the darkness a little, / And await[s] the morning that will come like an epoch." Like a warrior before a battle, he exchanges a "first handshake of tears and consolation" with himself.

At this point, as we examine the poetic depth and determination he has arrived at, we cannot help but regret the disappearance of the rest of his poems, which were confiscated when he was arrested, and lament their fate.

At the end of July 1942, Yun returned to his Yongjeong home in North Gando after finishing his first semester at Rikkyo University. Unlike previous years, his stay there was short. According to his sister, Yun Hye-won, it was only for a fortnight.

It would be his last visit to his home. During his stay, he reminded his brother and sister, "Everything printed in Korean will be gone, so collect anything in Korean, even songbooks." These were the last words he spoke to them.

Song Mong-gyu came home with Yun too. There remains a photograph from that visit, which they took with three other relatives, dated August 4. What is odd about it is Yun's hair. Song had longer hair, what they called "gentleman's hair," but Yun had nearly shorn hair. Yun's hair had been longer at the time of his Yonhui graduation picture, meaning he must have shaved his head after starting at Rikkyo. Was it required by the school?

While he was visiting, his mother was bedridden with an illness. He was spending much of every day with his mother when he received a telegram from Japan. A friend of his who went to Tohoku Imperial University sent it, informing him of a transfer opportunity to Tohoku. Yun must have asked his friends for information about transferring, wishing not to continue at Rikkyo University.

It seems that the transfer examination dates and application deadlines were imminent. As soon as he saw the telegram, he departed for Japan without time to bid goodbye to his brother, who was at the playground.

Tohoku University is located in Sendai, the capital city of Miyagi Prefecture. It is north-east of Tokyo, about the same distance from Tokyo as Kyoto is south of Tokyo. However, the school that Yun actually transferred to was not Tohoku Imperial University but Doshisha University in Kyoto.

During the time of the Japanese Empire, all imperial universities were public universities. It is said that Yun's father became quite upset when he heard that Yun had transferred to Doshisha University, a private mission school, instead of Tohoku Imperial University.

Yun's father's wish that Yun transfer to an imperial university must have been instigated by his worldly desire for prestige. Japan was known for its discrimination between public and private institutions. Yun's father had only studied briefly at a private institute (not a university) and must have felt inferior about his education, wishing Yun to do better.

At the time in Japan, the value judgment of each university was directly connected to the salary one received after graduation. Imperial university graduates received the highest, followed by the graduates of Keio Gijuku, Waseda University, and Tokyo Higher Commerce School (five to ten won lower). Other higher commerce public school graduates received another five won less, and private university graduates received even less.[5]

Yun's transfer from the private Rikkyo University to Tohoku Imperial University might have been nearly impossible to begin with. Yun had first aimed for Kyoto Imperial University and then tried to transfer to Tohoku Imperial University. Just as his grandfather supported Yun's decision to study liberal arts at Yonhui, thinking that Yun would become successful by passing the higher civil service examination, Yun's father must have hoped that Yun would graduate from an imperial university and make a good living. Yun Il-ju also wrote that Yun's "studying in Japan was suggested by our father." Further, Yun's father must have been impressed by his nephew Song's decision to go to Kyoto Imperial University.

These anecdotes reveal Yun's position and circumstances, causing him to feel agonized and conflicted by a sense of duty. Knowing such context greatly adds to our understanding of his poems.

In any case, Yun's life in Tokyo came to a close when he transferred from Rikkyo University in Tokyo to Doshisha University in Kyoto.

Behind-the-Scene Stories from Rikkyo University, Discovered by Yanagihara Yasuko

In 2002, Ms. Yanagihara Yasuko found important information relating to Yun's Rikkyo University period. Yanagihara is a graduate of Rikkyo University and a member of the Yun Dong-ju Homecoming Society, a group that was started by Japanese readers in Tokyo to read Yun's poetry and discuss his life. Several years back, she had read the Japanese translation of the earlier edition of this biography published by Tsukuma Shobo and began to search for materials relating to Yun's life during his stay at Rikkyo University, her alma mater. After reading about Yun's hair being nearly shaven, she decided to visit Rikkyo University to confirm the school's rules regarding that.

While going through old issues of Rikkyo University newspapers, she found an article dated April 10, 1942 (eight days after Yun started school), stating that the university had executed a school-wide "haircut ordinance," subjecting all its students to a buzz cut. The headline of the article stated that "starting in mid-April," all students were to have a buzz cut "in order to promote the simple and robust spirit appropriate for the mobilization of Japan."[6] That was precisely why Yun's hair was shaven like a monk's in the photograph.

Encouraged by this discovery, Yanagihara pored over the university documents from the period and unearthed many precious pieces of information. Her research of the school records and interviews with Rikkyo graduates from the period reveal important and fascinating facts about what Yun's days at Rikkyo must have been like. The following are her findings.

ARMY MAJOR IIJIMA NOBUYUKI

Major Iijima Nobuyuki of the Eastern Command taught military training at Rikkyo University from the fall of 1941. His post was a tangible representation of the situations and hardships that Rikkyo, a Christian university, faced.

All the male students had to receive one hour of weekly military training in the training field (now occupied by Rikkyo Elementary School).

Attendance was strictly enforced. The training included running with rifles and practice-stabbing of each other with bayonets under an assigned officer's watch. Once a year, they had to go to a four-day training camp in Narashino, where the Army Officers' School training ground was, or to a place on Fuji Mountain.

A militarist to the core, Major Iijima Nobuyuki was extremely strict and feared by the students during this military period when uniformed soldiers were seen everywhere, even on campus. Rikkyo graduates never failed to mention his name when they spoke about their university days. It is said that when he left his post at Meiji University to teach at Rikkyo, Meiji students were raising their glasses and toasting in joy.

A few months after Major Iijima came to Rikkyo, Japan started its war against the United States, mobilizing the country even further. Naturally, his militaristic character and tyranny worsened. For instance, one Japanese student, who happened to fall into disfavor with his assigned officer, was placed under Special Police surveillance and faced numerous persecutions until the demise of imperial Japan, despite the fact that his father was an aristocratic congressman.

Major Iijima despised Christianity, publicly announcing, "I hate this Jesus." Likewise, he was suspicious of Rikkyo University, claiming that the missionary school "must be completely reformed because there is a great possibility of spies working for America." As a militarist, he looked down on the literature department, calling it the "wimperature department," and was said to have chased after students with a pair of scissors when he saw their unshaven heads.

University students feared assigned officers because of draft issues. Officers had the prerogative to issue a suspension of attendance to military training to whomever they wished. University students had the privilege of draft deferment at the time. Once they were suspended from military training, however, their privilege was revoked, and they had to enlist.

The second Sino-Japanese War had continued since July 1937 after the Marco Polo Bridge Incident, and the Pacific War against the United States had begun in December 1941 after Japan's attack on Pearl Harbor. Fighting both wars, the demand for young men to be sent to the battlefields greatly increased. For university students, suspension of attendance meant leaving the university to be sent to the frontier to die like flies. Consequently, they were extremely cautious when dealing with the military training officers.

In fact, a good number of Rikkyo students had to enlist because Major Iijima suspended their military training attendance. Some of those students even volunteered for the navy, fearing the army major's influence should they be enlisted in the army.

He was particularly harsh on Korean students in the school, making them stay behind after training sessions because they "were not fully one with Japan" and "useless for the Empire."

The following excerpt is from a commemorative publication titled *Oh! Rikkyo of Our Youth*, written by those who had started the preparatory program at Rikkyo in 1941.

> Sometimes, the major mustered us in the classroom and asked each of us questions like these, demanding answers.
>
> "Who is greater, Jesus Christ or Amaterasu Omikami [the sun goddess—Trans.]?"
>
> "Which do you follow? Totalitarianism or individualism?"
>
> Even though you want to oppose him, you will harm the school and yourself after enlisting if the major's wrath is kindled. So you say, "Amaterasu Omikami is greater," or "Totalitarianism is better."
>
> But Isobe Yozo, who was from Dalian, Manchuria, calmly replied, "I worship Jesus Christ, and individualism leads to the advancement of mankind." As soon as we heard it, we anticipated the major's angry roar, but he only muttered, "Is that so?" and became silent. We thought that the courage of a helpless man, who nevertheless did not conceal his beliefs, touched even the major's heart.

At the time, the leaders of Japan deified their emperor as the descendant of Amaterasu Omikami, the omnipotent goddess. The Ise Grand Shrine, the shrine of the emperor's ancestor god, is the home of Amaterasu Omikami and the Suzerain Shinto of Japan. Thus, the question "Who is greater, Jesus Christ or Amaterasu Omikami?" meant "Which is greater, Christianity or Shinto?"[7]

HARDSHIPS SUFFERED BY RIKKYO UNIVERSITY DURING MOBILIZATION

Presumably, the placement of extreme militarists like Major Iijima Nobuyuki in mission schools such as Meiji University and Rikkyo University was quite purposeful. Those in charge of education in Japan placed such individuals in Christian schools and pressured them excessively to firmly instill among Christian students imperial supremacy, which prioritized the Japanese emperor above all.

The buzz-cut regulation is one example. While the students at Rikkyo, a private Christian school, were forced to shave their heads in the name of wartime necessity, students at Kyoto Imperial University were not. Thus, as shown in the photograph taken in the summer of 1942, Yun, a Rikkyo student, had a buzz cut, while Song, a Kyoto student, kept a "gentleman's hairstyle," as in his Yonhui days.

Rikkyo University's hardships continued until the surrender of Japan. Professor Paul Frederick Rusch, an American teaching at Rikkyo, was arrested on December 9, 1941, the day after the Pearl Harbor attack. He was held in custody until early June 1942, when he was finally deported.

Further, the Japanese government continued to pressure the university with the slogan of "mobilization" until its board of trustees amended its articles of incorporation on September 29, 1942. In Article 1, its fundamental educational policy of "advancement of character based on Christian principles" was replaced with the clause, "Rikkyo University and Rikkyo Middle School offer education to realize Imperial Supremacy and are managed accordingly." Thus, the goal of education and management at Rikkyo University changed from Christian character development to producing imperial subjects.

In October 1942, the university chapel was annexed and became an armory for weapons used in military training. Christian services were banned, and Shinto ceremonies were held to commemorate the spirits of fallen soldiers. Its traditional cheering song before baseball games, "St. Paul's Will Shine," was banned as "enemy language." The following year, even its official school song, "The School of Liberty," was banned and replaced with a military song.

As the military coercion intensified, some of the professors began to curry favor with the military. According to Yanagihara Yasuko, "Unusually few documents from this period exist at Rikkyo University, perhaps because the administrators disposed of them, fearing the military coercion."

Right after Japan's unconditional surrender on August 15, 1945, certain individuals were punished for their misdeeds and crimes during the war. The American occupation forces limited those individuals' civil rights and banished them from their positions. Among university professors who were subject to this, Rikkyo had eleven professors banished from their posts, the greatest number among all universities. Ironically, this tells us how immense the pressure and coercion to cooperate with the military must have been for Rikkyo.

Yun only attended one term at Rikkyo before transferring to Doshisha University in Kyoto. From the circumstances just described, we can imagine why he did so.

PROFESSOR TAKAMATSU KOJI AT RIKKYO UNIVERSITY

Yanagihara Yasuko discovered the following facts from someone who had interviewed a "Mr. I," a classmate of Yun's at Rikkyo. (She gathered this information after the death of Mr. I.)

On a Thursday afternoon in April 1942, after a lecture on Asian philosophy, Yun asked Mr. I in a quiet voice, "I am from Joseon. Would you happen to know professors who can be helpful to my studies here?" Mr. I recommended Professor Paul Rusch and Chaplain Takamatsu Koji.

Professor Takamatsu Koji taught the history of Christianity, Old and New Testaments, and Greek in the Religious Studies Department while also serving as the school's chaplain, overseeing the worship services at school.

Mr. I took Yun to Professor Takamatsu Koji's campus residence and introduced him. Later, Yun thanked him for "introducing him to a good teacher." Mr. I replied, "You will benefit from knowing him," to which Yun said, "Let us please visit him together." Professor Rusch was detained by the government at the time and was unavailable.

Professor Takamatsu was an outstanding chaplain with great knowledge and a broad perspective. He studied at Rikkyo University and the Episcopalian Seminary School and was regarded as a genius at languages. He went to America to study theology at Harvard University. He also worked as an interpreter for top political officials. Some Rikkyo graduates would even say that the best thing about the school was meeting with Professor Takamatsu because of his great character. Together with Professor Kurose, who taught at the nearby Episcopalian Seminary, he took Korean foreign students and Korean Japanese students under his wing, caring for them in their hardship. It is said that Yun went to consult with him several times more during his studies there.

Professor Tajisaki Kenichi, a Rikkyo graduate who later became a professor there, wrote about Professor Takamatsu in *Rikkyo Literature*, published after the war.

The Sino-Japanese War began in Showa 12 (1937). I was in the late Professor Takamatsu Koji's class. He lectured on Ruskin, his pale face wearing the same expression as usual and his eyeglasses reflecting light. The noiseless classroom was heavy with the fatigue that came with the afternoon.

"A fearful day has arrived at last," said Professor [Takamatsu], pausing briefly after each word. I saw his cheeks trembling slightly and sensed that he was trying to control his emotions. "From today begins a time of darkness. It is a fearful thing." His voice was trembling so much that I felt anxious he might soon cry and collapse. He spoke more, but I can't remember anything else. Only the first things he said above remained. And even now, I think of the consequences. There could not have been many who discerned the predicament of imperial Japan just by hearing about the war that started across the Pacific Ocean. From the coercion he suffered during the war, he became very ill and was bedridden when the war ended. Later on, I heard of his tragic death.

There are many stories about his life and death. As the war reached its final hours, the atmosphere became even more hostile. Professor Takamatsu Koji continued to be critical of the military regime and was eventually fired from the university. Having suffered from illnesses and malnutrition, he passed away on February 19, 1946, one year after the death of Yun Dong-ju. During his career at Rikkyo, many students, like Yun, visited him at his home and enjoyed his wife's homemade cookies and tea as well as dinner.

One of the students had a heartrending story. He was drafted as a student soldier in 1943 and visited the professor with a friend for a farewell before his departure. They were served dinner, which was very special because of the quantity of white rice on the table. At that time, white rice was very precious, but the professor had some that had been sent to him by his family in the countryside. The two students ate their fill very happily. Eventually, the student returned from the war unscathed. When he heard of the professor's death and that it had been caused by malnutrition, among other things, he was deeply aggrieved. A tablet commemorating Professor Takamatsu Koji now hangs in Rikkyo University's chapel, and the university library houses his private library: the Takamatsu Collection.

WHO IS THE "OLD PROFESSOR"?

In Yun's "An Easily Written Poem," written during his Rikkyo days, there appears "an old professor":

Carrying a notebook in the crook of my arm,
I go to the lecture of an old professor.

Yanagihara Yasuko supposes that the "old professor" was Uno Tetsuhito, a great scholar of Asian philosophy and professor emeritus at Tokyo Imperial University, because one of the classes Yun took was his Asian philosophy at Rikkyo, and he was indeed very old. His son Uno Yoshikata examined the material that Yanagihara Yasuko brought to him and confirmed that the poem refers to his father, who was then sixty-eight years old and had snow-white hair, whereas all the other professors were much younger. Others who studied around the same time agreed that the "old professor" must be Uno Tetsuhito.

Professor Uno Tetsuhito was the first scholar to apply the methodology used in Western philosophy to Chinese philosophy, establishing a modern research method. Until he died in 1974 at the age of one hundred, he wrote numerous books and was also the dean at Jissen Women's University for a time.

RUMORS ABOUT YUN DONG-JU'S REFUSAL TO PARTICIPATE IN MILITARY TRAINING

According to Yanagihara Yasuko's sources, one of the reasons Yun transferred from Rikkyo to Doshisha might have been because he had refused to participate in the school's military training.

During Yun's matriculation at Rikkyo, there was a rumor that a Korean student had refused military training. In order to verify that rumor, Yanagihara interviewed Im Yeong-bu, professor emeritus at Rikkyo at the time of the interview, who had been a history student and one year senior to Yun at Rikkyo. Im himself had tried to sabotage the training but was found out by his assigned officer. With five others who were suspended from military training, he enlisted in the navy, because if they were to be drafted into the army, they might be blacklisted and mistreated as a result of the officer's adverse report. Im stated that refusing military training was a very courageous act at that time and that "there were rumors about literature students objectively criticizing the system and expressing displeasure at the actions of the military authorities. However, such opinions were cautiously shared with a few trusted persons so that nothing would leak out to reach the assigned officer's ears." Since he could not know all the events, he suggested that as many people be interviewed as possible.

As Yanagihara Yasuko was interviewing more people, she was told by Mr. I of Yun's refusal to participate in military training. It was a crucial piece of information, which came out while she was asking him about the military training uniform.

"Did Mr. Hiranuma [Yun's Japanese name] also wear the military uniform?" she asked. As if remembering something suddenly, Mr. I said, "I don't think so. Because the assigned officer gave him special treatment," and added that Yun had consulted Professor Takamatsu about sabotaging military training. Professor Takamatsu told Yun, "I don't know what will happen tomorrow, but I am praying to God." Later, he asked Mr. I, "Did you know Hiranuma planned to refuse military training?" and that was how Mr. I learned of it. Surprised, Yanagihara Yasuko reconfirmed with Mr. I three times. "Was it Hiranuma who tried to refuse military training, and did he consult Professor Takamatsu about that?" Mr. I answered "Yes" each time.

All the preceding information is from the sources that Yanagihara Yasuko compiled with dedication and zeal. I express my sincerest gratitude and respect for her endeavors in tracing down minute details and reconstructing Yun's life in Tokyo. Thanks to her research, it seems as if we have in person those who surrounded Yun Dong-ju: Professor Takamatsu Koji, a revered and beloved intellectual of pious character and sincere love; Major Iijima Nobuyuki, a reincarnate of militarism, who tormented so many young students; an old white-haired Asian philosophy professor; and the assigned officers, despots who had conflicts with students over military training—all these people appear so real before us that we are deeply affected.

With what has been examined, we seem to have taken a great step into the period in which Yun Dong-ju lived, lifting the thick gray curtain of time from his Tokyo days.

Clearly, it was a period of madness, of war and blood, and those in it were facing new adversity each and every day.

Pak Chun-hye, a Woman Yun Encountered in Tokyo

What was Yun's love life like?

Many of his readers are greatly interested in it partly because they are intrigued by the fact that Yun was never married and died in prison while studying in Japan. Most of all, he was a poet who wrote about ardent love.

Only a few months after he entered Yonhui College, he wrote "The Hall of Love" (June 19, 1938), a heartrending poem about unrequited love that begins with "Sun-a, when have you entered my hall? / And when have I entered yours?" The poem is far from being abstract and resonates acutely with the reader. The prose poem "The Boy," which he wrote the following year, takes us further into this inquiry:

THE BOY

Here and there sorrowful autumn is dropping like falling leaves. The spots
   from which leaves fall prepare room for spring. The sky is spread over the
   branches. Peering into the sky quietly, his eyebrows are imbued blue.
   Running over the warm cheeks, his hands are also covered in blue paint.
   Looking into the palm again, he sees a clear stream in the lines. A clear
   stream flows, and in the stream is a face sorrowful like love—the beautiful face of Sun-i. The boy closes his eyes, enraptured. Still, the clear
   stream flows, bearing the beautiful face of Sun-i, sorrowful like love.

(1939)

The girl called "Sun-i," his beloved, appears again in "Snowy Map," written two years later, leaving a deep impression:

SNOWY MAP

On the morning when Sun-i is to depart, big snowflakes come down tongue-
   tied and cover the map spread outside the window as if sorrowful. Looking
   around the room, I see no one. The wall and the ceiling are white. Is it also
   snowing inside the room? Are you really leaving lightly like lost history?
   Though I write in letters what must be said before departure, do you remain
   only in my heart because I don't know where you are going, which street,
   which town, under which roof. I cannot follow you, for the snow keeps
   covering your tiny footprints. When snow melts, flowers will bloom from
   each footprint. When I set out to search your footprints among the flowers,
   it will keep snowing in my heart for the twelve months of the year.

(March 12, 1941)

"Sun" or "Sun-i"—who was she? Was she a real person? Even if she was a real person, we already know that their love was not consummated, for those poems are all about unrequited love. At least, that is what the readers imagine.

Yun never had a girlfriend while living in his hometown. His uncle Yun Yeong-chun was clear about it: "[Yun] was handsome, and sometimes girls gave furtive glances. They even initiated conversation. But he was very shy and did not pursue anyone."[8]

After Yun left for Seoul to study, his mother used to joke with him, "If you meet a nice girl in Seoul, I will welcome her as a daughter-in-law." In other words, she encouraged a "free-love" marriage.

Nevertheless, he was never married, and little is known about his relationships with women. In volume 23 of *Nara Sarang*, issued in 1976, Professor Jeong Byeong-uk mentioned something about it for the first time: "Here, I give an account of Yun Dong-ju's love life for the first time because it might be helpful for the readers to understand the poems from the period at issue," he began.

In 1941, when Yun was a senior and Jeong was a sophomore at Yonhui, they left the dormitory and took a room together. Jeong stated that the reason they moved from the novelist Kim Song's place in Nusang-dong to a place in North Ahyeon-dong was due to some disturbing actions by police detectives:

I should reveal here why we moved to North Ahyeon-dong, which was neither in the city like the previous place nor in Shinchon where the dormitory was. Actually, in North Ahyeon-dong lived an acquaintance of Dong-ju's father, who used to be a teacher and later became a businessman. Dong-ju looked up to him very much and visited him sometimes. He had a daughter who was a senior in the literature department of Ehwa Womans Junior College. She also attended the Hyeopseong Church as well as Bible study classes led by Mrs. Reverend Cable. Dong-ju never confided with me about her, for I was younger in age. But I could tell that his feelings for her were not ordinary. [...] As far as I know, however, Dong-ju and she never got together by themselves. They waited for the trains in the same train station, rode the same bus to school, and attended the same church and Bible study. That was it. But perhaps he felt a connection between them.[9]

Hearing this story, we can feel the poet's pure heart in the poem "The Hall of Love," which says, "Our love was merely mute." This was the only account of Yun's love life of which we were aware.

However, there was another woman with whom he had even thought about marriage, from when he was in Tokyo. Yun Hye-won, his only sister six years his junior, knows the story, and her account is summarized here.

When Yun came back home after the first semester at Rikkyo, he showed Yun Hye-won a photograph, about half the size of a postcard. It was a photograph of three people. A girl was sitting in front, and two men, university students, were standing behind her.

"What do you think of her?"

Yun Hye-won saw a face that looked more intelligent than pretty. The girl made a nice impression on her.

"She seems nice. Who's that?"

He told her that she was the youngest daughter of a Reverend Pak in Onseong, North Hamgyeong-do. She shared a place with her older brother in Tokyo and was studying voice. She had several older brothers who were all well-educated.

The two men behind her in the photograph were her brothers' friends, who were also friends with Yun. Yun said he'd visit their place sometimes when he craved kimchi, and they were often invited to dinner. Her name was Pak Chun-hye. Her brother would tell him, "I'd get married today if there's someone like my sister!" Yun also thought that she had a good disposition and was very nice. Yun said that the brother gave him the photograph. It seems that the brother hoped that Yun would become his future brother-in-law.

Sensing that Yun was considering marriage, Yun Hye-won talked to the elders of the family. Onseong was not far from Yongjeong, and the two families probably had friends in common. They were all happy about it and encouraged him to push ahead.

When he returned to Japan, Yun left the photograph at home. When the new term began, a disappointing letter from Yun arrived, stating that the girl had become engaged during the summer recess at home. Years later, after the liberation, Yun Hye-won and her husband lived in Cheongjin for a time. They attended church there, and she saw a woman in the church choir who sang beautifully and looked familiar. She realized that it was the woman in the photograph. She learned that Pak Chun-hye had married a law school graduate and moved to Cheongjin, where her husband had gotten a post in the courthouse. Yun Hye-won talked with her for a bit and found her to be cheerful and genial. She thought, "No wonder my brother really liked her."

With this story in the background, we look at the poem "Spring," the last of the poems Yun mailed to Kang before the summer of 1942. Of all his poems, "Spring" stands out as uncharacteristically bright and gay in tone. I had been quite curious as to how such a "happy" poem could be written all of a sudden, but the story of the girl in Tokyo provided the answer:

SPRING

Spring flows through blood vessels like a stream;
Blooming on the hills near the city are
Forsythias, azaleas, and yellow napa cabbage flowers.

Having borne three months of winter,
I sprout like a patch of grass.

Happy lark, soar joyously
From whatever furrows.

For the azure sky is so high
Glimmering above. . . .

For Yun as a young man, Tokyo became an unforgettable city. His guileless, happy days and sorrowful, shadowy days were interwoven in that tragic city.

Transfer to Doshisha University in Kyoto

Before the fall term began in 1942, Yun moved to Kyoto. Kyoto was the capital of Japan for over a thousand years, beginning in 794 and lasting until 1868, when the capital was changed to Tokyo during the Meiji Restoration. It was known for its beautiful scenery, good water, and excellent schools. Kyoto Imperial University has a long history and was the second-greatest university in Japan after Tokyo Imperial University. Among private schools, Doshisha University boasted the highest distinction in Kyoto.

Yun must have heard much about the city from Professor Yi Yang-ha at Yonhui. Professor Yi, for whom Yun held the highest respect, had graduated from Third High School, studied English literature at Tokyo Imperial University, and then returned to Kyoto to get a master's degree from Kyoto Imperial University. Having spent a total of six years in Kyoto during his high school and graduate studies, Professor Yi always held a special regard for the city. For him, Kyoto meant "longing," "familiarity," and even "heartache." His essay "A Journey to Kyoto" is filled with feelings of affection that border on heartache. Professor Yi described Kyoto as a city nuanced with a subtle color of yellowish green that "is shown after sea-green waves hit the rocks and recede from them." When driving to Kyoto, he felt the sky "becoming infinitely high only after reaching Kyoto" because of the beauty of its sky and water.

What did Kyoto mean to Yun Dong-ju?

Earlier, Yun had written these lines in Tokyo: "Looking back, I have lost / All my childhood friends one by one // For what desire, / Am I sinking alone?"

In Kyoto lived Song Mong-gyu, one of his lost "childhood friends." Now, they met again in Kyoto.

However, this was during the horrifying time of war. In March 1941, the Japanese Security Bureau amended and promulgated the Public Order Maintenance, now even more strict and with severe consequences. In December of the same year, it also promulgated cruel and harsh laws, like Temporary Regulations on the Press, Publication, Assembly, and Association. It desperately sought to prevent and uncover so-called political crimes.

Under such circumstances, it was as if Yun had voluntarily entered the radar of the Special Police's surveillance when he joined the blacklisted Song and spent time with him, for Song had been under the watchful eyes of the Special Police ever since his trip to China to attend Nakyang Military School in 1935. In Yun's life, Kyoto was an ominous place.

Yun's transfer to Doshisha University's English Department in the preparatory division was effective as of October 1, 1942. His transfer examination was probably in August or September. The student records of Rikkyo University, on the other hand, state that Yun "withdrew for personal reasons on December 19, 1942," which must be an incorrect date.

Doshisha University was established in 1875. Like Rikkyo, it was a mission school but of a different denomination. It belonged to the Congregational Church and had a seminary department that produced many Christian leaders. The university's chapel was a magnificently beautiful building constructed in the early Meiji era, which is now designated as a national treasure. In the 1930s, one of the two pipe organs that existed in Japan was in that chapel.

The Congregational Church was a result of John Calvin's Reformation. In terms of denominational character, Yun was probably more at home with the

Episcopalian Rikkyo University than the Congregational Doshisha University, since he himself was brought up in the Presbyterian Church.

Doshisha University's structure and system differed greatly from those of Rikkyo University. Rikkyo had an academic year system. Student records were organized by each academic year, such as the first year, the second year, and the third year, and the courses taken and the grades were entered accordingly. At Doshisha University, however, students took requirements according to their majors, electives, and cores, but without the distinction between the first, second, and third years.

Dr. Jeong Dae-wi, who graduated from Doshisha University after spending two years in the preparatory division and three years in the theology department, explained the system at Doshisha:

> The preparatory division focused on foreign language education. On a day with five hours of lecture, all five hours might be English. We'd call each class after its professor's name, such as "Shibada English" or "Minamiishi English." [...]
>
> In terms of major studies, there was no concept of each grade year. One might say that he had an X number of years there, but regardless of that, anyone could choose a class to take and set his schedule. There was no distinction between upper- and lower-classmen. As long as one was taking required classes, he was free to choose whichever electives and audit as well. It seemed even freer and looser than American or European college curriculums. I benefited from the system. I even took classical Greek which was offered jointly by the philosophy and English literature departments. [...] Not only that, but I was able to audit all three journalism classes offered by the English literature department.[10]

Yun's address in Kyoto was Sakyo-ku (Kyoto) Tanaka Takahara-cho 27, Dakeda Apartments, and Song's was Sakyo-ku (Kyoto) Kitashiragawa Higashihirai-cho 60, House of Shimizu Eiichi. They were five minutes' walk from each other.

Ibuki Gou visited the site of Yun's apartment and retraced Yun's commute to and from the school. She recorded:

> The apartment was located in the north-east side of Kyoto, a residential area consisting of old houses. What happened to the apartment building? I asked an old lady I saw in the shopping area in the neighborhood.
> "Dakeda Apartments? Oh, yes. It burned down one year."

I asked where the building used to be, but it was not clear. After asking several people, I was told that the daughter (who now was an old woman) of the building owner Mr. Daketa lived nearby and went to see her.

Dakeda Apartment building was built in 1936, I was told. It was a large apartment building that housed 70 students from Kyoto University and Doshisha University. Brick walls alongside the front gate and the garden in the center were unique. They raised birds and cultivated flowerbeds in the garden, which was surrounded by two-story wooden buildings. It was a rather "modern" apartment building. When the war reached a climax, the building was sold to a company as its dormitory. A fire destroyed it in 1944 or 1945. [. . .]

On the site now stands Kyoto Arts and Crafts University. Judging from the footprint of the area, I could tell it was quite a large building. [. . .] Yun probably walked to Doshisha University located in Mimadegawa in Jyok-ouku. If so, he probably crossed the Mono-o-o Bridge. From this bridge, one could clearly see Hiei Mountain in good weather.[11]

Yun's apartment was a little over two miles from Doshisha, a somewhat long distance to cover every day. Streams like Kitashitakawa, and Kamogawa River intersected the area, and depending on the route, one would have to cross two or three bridges. Yun enjoyed taking walks, and the streets to Doshisha were lined with Buddhist temples, Shinto shrines, and palaces. Doshisha University itself was sandwiched between the old imperial palace in front and the large Shokoku-ji temple in back.

Above all, there was Kamogawa River, which cross-sectioned Kyoto from north to south. Yun crossed the stream every day. This is the same one that appears in Jeong Ji-yong's famous poem, which Yun loved in his teen years:

KAMOGAWA RIVER

Over the ten-*ri* field by the Kamogawa
The sun sets—the sun sets—

Letting the loved one go each day
The throat is dry—the sound of shallow water—

The cold heart that wrings the cold grains of sand—
Wring them. Crush them. Not even satisfying.

In the nest of water-pepper leaves
A widowed crake cries.

A pair of swallows above
Dance the dance of welcoming rain
Over the watermelon-scented evening breeze.
The young wanderer chews on the orange peel in sorrow.

Over the ten-*ri* field by the Kamogawa
The sun sets—the sun sets—

On his own copy of *The Poems of Jeong Ji-Yong*, Yun wrote in the margins next to this poem in red pencil, "Masterpiece." Not only was he captivated by the poem, but he imitated Jeong's technique and imagery in his "Twilight Becomes the Ocean" (January 1937), which opens with "In the blue-black waters limply / The day sinks—the day sinks—." The Kamogawa of the poem now became a part of his life in Kyoto.

Yun started attending Doshisha University on October 1 and stayed there through the winter instead of returning home for the break. Perhaps he stayed on to be better acclimated to the city and the school, which were both new to him. However, he had been home back in July even though he had only started school in Japan in April. Perhaps he felt uneasy about seeing his father, who was very upset about his transfer to Doshisha University rather than to Tohoku Imperial University. Further, the prospect of marriage that he had mentioned to his family during the summer vacation was gone, and this might have been an additional reason why he stayed in his lonely rooming house in Japan.

December 30 was Yun's birthday. His grandfather was a fervent Christian and elder of his church, and between Christmas and New Year's celebrations, his birthday would have been filled with holiday provisions and spirit. His uncle Yun Yeong-chun in Tokyo, during his return home, stopped by Kyoto to spend New Year's Eve and Day with Yun. It was the first and last winter that Yun would enjoy in Japan as a free man. Yun Yeong-chun reminisced as follows:

On New Year's Eve that year [1942], I stopped in Kyoto on the way home. [With Dong-ju] I went out to the night markets and ate street foods to heart's content—oden, boiled pork, tofu, sparrow meat.... After coming back to the room, we talked about poetry deep into the night. I was worried because he had become too pale, reading all the time. In his cold six-tatami room, he'd read and write and brainstorm until two in the morning;

that was his daily life. He said he was fond of French poems: Francis Jammes' poems were earthy and likable, and Jean Cocteau's poems were too neurotic but attractive because of their sensitivity. He said that he admired [Sarojini] Naidu's poems for their ardent patriotism. He became animated, clapping on his knees.

The following day, the New Year's Day, we took a walk around Lake Biwa. We rode a cable car over the peak and arrived at Lake Biwa. The scenery was so amazing that I was exclaiming and commenting loudly, but Dong-ju was slow in response. I realized that he was still concentrating on the poem he was writing.[12]

In the chronology printed in the 1983 edition of Yun's poetry, it incorrectly records that Yun Yeong-chun, Yun, and Song went to see Lake Biwa. At that time, Song was not in Kyoto, having gone home to North Gando. Yun must have been very lonely during his first winter in Kyoto.

The year 1943 dawned. The spring semester at Doshisha University became his last school term. He spent two semesters at Doshisha, the fall semester (October–December 1942) and the spring semester (April–July 1943). As the concept of "school year" did not exist there, only the courses taken are the indicators of academic progress. Yun took a total of five subjects, four of which were mandatory and one elective (names in parentheses are the professors' last names, and the number next to each is his course grade):

History of English Literature (Katsuda): 65
Practice of English Literature (Takiyama): 85
English Composition (Takiyama): 80
English Composition (Minamiishi): 73
Journalism [elective]: 75

Ibuki Gou, a Japanese researcher of Korean literature, has contributed significantly to the study of Yun's poetry and the discovery of sources relating to Yun's life in Japan. From her research, we can get a glimpse of the mandatory courses that Yun took. Ibuki interviewed a classmate of Yun's, who became a professor at Doshisha University. Professor O. did not remember Yun, unfortunately, but gave descriptions of the professors who taught the courses: "Professor Katsuda taught Shakespeare and Keats, among others, in the History of English Literature class, with comments on each poet's character and personality. He retired in March 1944, and [Professor O.] did not know of his whereabouts. Professor Takiyama's specialty was 18th-century English literature (Defoe), and was a scholar of great learning. He passed away. Professor Minamiishi, who also passed away, was a faithful Christian and elder at Doshisha Church."[13] Yun's mandatory courses were all English classes because his major was English literature. Yun's interest in mass media is shown in the fact that he took journalism as his only elective.

Arrest, Trial, Imprisonment, and Death

J ULY 1943. JULY IN JAPAN is stiflingly hot. Universities start their spring term in early April and end it in mid-July. Having spent the winter recess alone in Kyoto, Yun had decided to return to North Gando and spend the summer there.

Arrest

CHARGED AS A POLITICAL OFFENDER

On July 14, however, while busying himself with his end-of-term work and getting ready for the return home, Yun was arrested by a Special Police detective. After the arrest, he was jailed at Shimogamo Police Station. It was later revealed that Song Mong-gyu had been arrested four days prior, on July 10.

How was his family in North Gando fairing around this time? Before summer recess began, Yun had sent a letter to his father requesting money for the return home and adding that he'd "depart as soon as the money arrived." Yun Hye-won provided the following narrative:

YUN HYE-WON: Of course, father wired money as soon as he received the letter. But he must have had a premonition. After sending the money, he kept going in and out of the house, waiting for Dong-ju's arrival nervously.

AUTHOR: Were there any reasons for such anxiety?

YUN HYE-WON: Well, I wouldn't know. I only saw father being
nervous. It was probably that the state of affairs at that time was
unsettling. Father read a lot from newspapers, and he was aware of
those circumstances. I don't think there were any particular reasons.[1]

Indeed, it was a perilous time. Situations in Korea had worsened significantly since the year before. Mainly, events leading to Christians' arrests
took place one after the other, such as shrine worship enforcement and the
Seongseo Joseon incident.[2] In May, the Japanese cabinet counsel was resolved
to enforce conscription in Joseon. That same month, Koiso Kuniaki, with the
mission of strengthening militarism in Joseon, succeeded Minami Jiro as the
eighth governor-general. In June, Severance Medical School was renamed
Asahi Medical School, and in August, the governor-general requisitioned
Yonhui School outright. The Joseon Language Society Affair took place in
October. Great Korean language scholars such as Choi Hyeon-bae, Yun's former teacher at Yonhui, along with Yi Hui-seung, Yi Yoon-jae and Han Jing,
were arrested and detained. (During interrogation, the latter two died from
torture.)

The great war between the Allied powers and the Axis powers spread from
Europe to North Africa; Germany's Rommel and England's Montgomery
battled their desert warfare; and Soviet land became a battleground for Sta-
lingrad battles. In the Pacific, the United States and Japan were still fighting,
and in China, Chiang Kai-shek's government continued to fight against the
Japanese after moving its capital to the remote Chungking. The Provisionary
Government of Korea also followed Chiang's government to Chungking,
maintaining and training small-scale resistance forces to prepare for the
independence war with the support of the Chinese government.

On March 1, 1943, Japan promulgated a law forcing the conscription of
Koreans, who had been until then exempt from it. The enforcement date was
set to be August 1.

Because of these circumstances, Yun's father must have been anxious for
the return of his son from Japan. He had estimated an arrival date based on
the time it would take for the money to arrive in Japan and the travel time
from Kyoto to North Gando. Yun Hye-won stated: "And that was not enough
to set his mind at ease. He told me to cross the Tuman River to Sangsambong
station and wait for Dong-ju as the expected date approached."

Sangsambong station was like the gateway to North Gando, as everyone had to switch trains there in order to cross the border. At that time, Yun Hye-won lived at home, having graduated from Myeongsin Girls' High School in Yongjeong. Each day, she took the train to Sangsambong and craned her neck for the trains from Seoul. But her brother did not come. One day, as she was leaving for the station from her second cousin's house, where she had been staying for its proximity to the station, she received a message from home: "Return home as soon as possible."

She came back, wondering what had happened. The house was in turmoil, as the news of the arrests of Yun and Song in Japan had reached them. Soon they discovered that Yun had bought his ticket and sent his luggage when he was arrested.

Yun's father was greatly shocked by the news of his son's arrest by Japanese police. While switching between different jobs, from haberdashery owner to office worker to poultry farmer, he had stopped attending church, but from that moment on, he started going to church again.

Why did the Japanese police arrest Yun Dong-ju in July 1943?

After liberation in 1945, Yun's family members stated that it was for his "independence movement activities." This claim was taken for truth until the late 1970s, when opposing opinions began to come out.

Was he really arrested for his independence movement activities, as his family claimed? He was merely a student, a quiet and introverted one at that. Would it be possible for him to have been involved in the kind of resistance work that warranted an arrest by the Japanese police?

Such opinions emerged in the literary scene as a dominant force. Notably, it was the opinion of most contributors to the special issue on Yun Dong-ju in *Munhak Sasang* published in April 1976.[3] They opined that Yun, a young poet of "pure literature," had been unfortunately caught in the excessive zeal of imperial Japan. This came about more than thirty years after Yun's death in prison, who had written, "Looking up at the sky to my dying day / I wished no speck of shame within me, / But even at the breeze between leaves / I suffered."

Yun's family had insisted that Yun was arrested for the crime of Joseon's independence movement, tried, imprisoned, and killed there, but they were helpless against the skepticism and mistrust that mushroomed like dark cumulus clouds. They had no concrete evidence other than the words of the family elders who went to Fukuoka Prison to collect the remains of Yun after his death.

About a year and a half later, however, such evidence was brought to light, proving the family's claim and providing a full account of the incident. Imperial Japan's top-secret documents were finally made public: the December 1943 issue of *Special Police Report Monthly* (containing records of imperial Japan's Special Police, issued by the Security Division of the Department of Interior) and issue no. 109 (covering April, May, and June 1944) of *Ideology Monthly* (containing court records issued by the Criminal Division of Japan's Judiciary). These documents contain records relating to Yun's case.

Interrogation documents contained in the *Special Police Report Monthly* reveal that Yun was charged with resistance activities for independence. The complete account of the case and the conclusion of the police investigation indicate that "the central figure is Song Mong-gyu, who was aided by Yun Dong-ju" and that "Song Mong-gyu, Yun Dong-ju, and Ko Hui-uk, the three suspects, were sent to the prosecution as a result."

Ironically, it is the Japanese government documents that vividly capture both Yun's life in Kyoto and his laments about, and confrontation against, the appalling situation facing Korean culture. Both the interrogation records by the Special Police and the official trial records plainly state what Yun's life in Kyoto was like. From the records, one can see that besides his relationship to Song, which became the central issue, Yun engaged his other friends in "ideological training," as we would say now.

According to the Japanese government documents, Yun, "endeavoring to induce nationalistic feelings," "criticized the ban on Korean language courses in schools in Korea, encouraged the study of the Korean language, and emphasized the need for Korean independence" with a Matsubara Terutada (Japanese name; his Korean name and identity is unknown). Further, after befriending Jang Seong-eon (an upperclassman English major and sophomore at Doshisha University), Yun, "lamenting keenly over the 'Joseon Language Society Affair' over which general arrests began on October 1, 1942, tried to maintain and elevate the Korean nationalism and culture by lending [Jang] a copy of *Introduction to the History of Joseon* so that Jang's nationalism would strengthen." From these descriptions, one can see an upright nationalist in Yun.

So what happened to "the three suspects" handed over to the prosecution after the Special Police's interrogation? Of the three, Song and Yun died in Japan's Fukuoka Prison before liberation. The third, Ko Hui-uk, became known only after the disclosure of *Special Police Report Monthly*. At the time of the arrest, Ko was in his third year at the Third High School in Tokyo. What happened to Ko afterward?

If he was alive, he would be the only one who could tell us about the circumstances regarding their arrest and interrogation, and I spent a whole summer tracking down his identity and whereabouts.

First, I requested assistance from Aiya Akihisa, a Kyoto University researcher, who obtained a copy of Ko's high school student record. (The Third High School was merged into Kyoto University's liberal arts program after Japan's defeat.) From the student record, Ko's father's name was found, which led to the family registry in Korea.

Ko Hui-uk was alive. At last, standing in front of his house in Hong'eun-dong, Seoul, and reading his name on the doorplate, I felt enraptured. As the only survivor, he could tell me about the circumstances leading to the arrest and the subsequent incarceration. The hardship suffered by the national poet Yun could be retraced, though vicariously.

KO HUI-UK'S TESTIMONY

Ko was born in 1921 and thus was twenty-two years of age at the time of the arrest in 1943.[4]

With the following statement, Ko began his testimony:

The whole thing came about because Song Mong-gyu was a "blacklisted person." Not knowing that the Japanese police had him under constant surveillance, we shared our thoughts about "the future of the Korean people" and "the independence movement." I only realized afterwards that the police eavesdropped and recorded all those things to make the case.

So, that's how it started. Song and Yun both died in prison; I survived but also suffered hardship and damage. I was imprisoned over six months and consequently failed school. Afterwards, I was "blacklisted" and constantly under the surveillance of the Japanese police until liberation. I felt as if [I were being] asphyxiated.

It was early 1941 when Ko arrived in Kyoto, having graduated from Gyeonggi Middle School in Seoul the previous year: "After graduating [from middle school], I applied for the preparation program at Gyeongseong Imperial University. I passed the exam but somehow failed at the interview. At that time, those who failed were called 'ronins,' what they would now call 'repeaters.' So I set my heart to study even harder and go to a better school. The following February, I traveled to Japan for the first time and took the exam for the Third High School. This time, I made it."

During the Meiji Reformation, Japan created the high school system. As the pursuit of study without the foundation of knowledge about life in general could only be biased, one was to take core subjects in high school that would form the foundation of the student's character before acquiring more professional, in-depth knowledge at a university.

Thus, eight national high schools, whose names bore numbers, were established in eight different areas throughout Japan. The First was in Tokyo, the Second was in Sendai, the Third was in Kyoto, and so on. Aside from these eight public schools, there were private high schools named after the cities they were in, such as Yamaguchi, Kumamoto, Himeji, and Fukuoka. Competition to get into these schools was always fierce. Private universities were more accessible, but in order to get into one of the "imperial" universities, one had to rigorously follow the steps of six years of elementary school, five years of middle school, and three years of high school.

Among the high schools, the First in Tokyo and the Third in Kyoto were regarded as best of the best. In their characters and atmosphere, the First High School was bureaucratic and authoritarian, like Tokyo Imperial University, while the Third High School was liberal and humanistic, like Kyoto Imperial University, maintaining a likewise reputation. They even had a saying, "One will take a Third High School student as a son-in-law even if he only has one eye." As much reputation as these schools enjoyed, great were their students' pride and elitism. Ko stated: "Looking back, it seems that the happiest moment in the purest sense that I had in life was when I heard that I got accepted to the Third. It was a period of glory. If you graduated from the Third, your entire life would be guaranteed success, and we studied so hard."

He continued, smiling brightly.

The Third was an outstanding school. The students were bright, and their families were impressive, too. Even in the midst of the terrible militarism, the school had a free, liberal atmosphere, prioritizing learning itself as the supreme task. The school's motto was only one word, "Liberty." Even the school's dormitory was called "Liberty Hall." The school song reflects such spirit. It is called Shyoyoka, which means "a song to sing when strolling and wandering about":

The flowers on the hill burning in red
The light over the hill rapturous in blue
As we sing in the flowering season of Kyoto
The moon shines subtly upon Yoshidayama

Yoshidayama is a mountain near the school, and the surrounding area is also called Yoshida. Students had a powerful sense of identity as Japan's greatest elites and respected one another. Even Koreans, once they were accepted, were not treated differently in the Third High School.

Ko was born the first son of a wealthy landowner in Cheolwon in 1921. In the early era of the port opening and "enlightenment," his grandfather Ko Un-ha went to Japan and graduated from Meiji University, majoring in law, then returned to Korea and practiced law after serving a governorship in Gaeseong and a judgeship. Ko's father, Ko Hong-gwon, went to Gyeongseong Medical School and established his medical practice. It was an affluent, intellectual family.

Ko attended Cheolwon Public Elementary School, went to Gyeonggi Middle School, and then went on to study at the Third High School, the highest elite school. He studied night and day for the Tokyo Imperial University examination, was a member of the yacht club in school, and had even traveled to Harbin via Xinjing in Manchuria and to the Diamond Mountains the previous summer. However, meeting Song Mong-gyu and forming a friendship changed the path of his life.

It began with Song moving into his boardinghouse, a two-story building in Kitasirakawa, Sakyoku. The house was only 1,500 meters from the Third High School, across from which stood Kyoto Imperial University.

Japanese boardinghouses rented out rooms but did not provide meals. In their boardinghouse, each room had steam heating, a gas line to boil water for tea, and a wash basin. Thus, the boarders would not see each other for days unless they looked for and visited each other.

On July 14, 1943, Ko Hui-uk was arrested the same day as Yun, as the Japanese documents revealed. From Ko's recollection of the day, circumstances surrounding Yun's arrest can be inferred: "It was after the Pacific War had begun, and we were in the wartime system. The Third's term was shortened from three years to two years and six months. So, we were to take the graduation exam in July. The day of arrest was one day before the last exam, which had lasted the whole week. I was getting ready for school when the detectives rushed in without warning."

Hauling him, the detectives said, "Take your toiletry and come with us." Ko asked why, but no explanation was given. As only two days of final exams remained, Ko pleaded, "I will go, just wait until tomorrow. I just have two more days of exams. Without finishing them, I cannot graduate." They denied his request and took him to the station.

After they arrived, he was locked up for a few days without action. Ko was going crazy with anxiety, thinking about the possible reasons for the arrest and the missed exams. When called to interrogation at last, he was asked, "Do you know Song Mong-gyu?" A lightbulb went off in his head. Song had not been seen for the past few days, but Ko had not paid attention because of his preoccupation with his exams. Song had been arrested earlier, and Ko himself was entangled in the "ideology" problems with Song (the case records indicate Song's arrest date was July 10).

All this time, Song and Ko had shared opinions on the issues of independence for Korea and the cultural movement to awaken the Korean nationalism. Ko remembered telling Song about his ambition to start a nationalist cultural movement through the theater.

At first, Ko tried to exercise his right to remain silent. The interrogator then showed him a series of records. To his surprise, they were records of almost a year of surveillance. They were filled with details: On such-and-such dates, the lights were turned off at certain hours; on another date, Song and Yun and Ko met at such-and-such restaurant; on a specific date, they talked in Song's room until a particular hour, talking about this and that; and so on.

Here, let us pause momentarily and read Ko's remembrance of Yun Dong-ju:

Song introduced Yun to me, but we were not very close. We were all busy with our studies, our dwellings were apart, and our schools were different, too. When Song went to see Yun, I sometimes accompanied him to a restaurant downtown and talked with them. Even though that was the extent of our acquaintanceship, because of our friendships with Song, we were both entangled in the case.

At that time, not only did I not know he was a poet, but I never imagined that he would become such a prominent figure. I still remember his young face. He was quiet, handsome, and coming across well. He was a bit shorter than me or Song, who was 175 cm.

About Song, he stated: "He was thin, with a pale face and a somewhat hoarse voice. He was temperate and calm but also passionate. He was very learned; in one word, he gave the impression of a 'pale-faced intellectual.' He always had the Korean people in his mind and had very strong nationalistic views."

Going back to the time of arrest: The interrogator showed Ko the records of Song and told him, "Song is blacklisted, and we have been constantly watching him." Seeing the records, Ko no longer dared to exercise his right to remain silent and answered the questions. He was not tortured much. Once, his hands were tied together behind his back and he was hung by the rope and tortured. But it did not happen again because he answered questions after he saw all the records.

In Song's and Yun's interrogation records and decision papers, many other names appear: Baek In-jun, Matsubara Terutada (Japanese name; Korean name and identity unknown), Matsuyama Ryukan (same), Jang Seong-eon, and so on. In light of the custom of Japanese police investigations at the time, we can presume that they were all arraigned and interrogated by the police. But after five months of interrogation by the Special Police, it was these three—Song, Yun, and Ko—who were sent over to prosecution.

During interrogation, Ko was in the same jail room as other petty criminals. Of course, those involved in the same case were separated and did not know who was being held where. Ko only knew, from the way the interrogator talked, that both Song and Yun were there as well.

Once sent to prosecution, he was locked up in solitary confinement. The prosecution's prison cells were different from the police jail cells, which had one side open to the hallway with iron bars. Instead, each cell was surrounded by walls once the door was shut. His cell had a tiny window at the top corner of a wall facing outside, which let some sunlight in, and on the ceiling hung a lightbulb. A wooden pail in a corner served as the toilet.

On the middle and lower parts of the door were two small holes, the top one for watching from outside and the bottom one for sliding in a bowl. It was like the solitary cell depicted in the film *Papillon*; in the movie, the cell had a bed made of a wooden board, but Ko's cell had no bed.

Three times a day, he received some boiled barley with pickles and thin miso. He saw no one all day, and the only human contact was when he said "Thank you" to the person who slid the meal to him. They let him borrow some religious books from the library there.

Whether in the police station or in the prosecution's prison, Ko never saw Yun but came across Song in the hallway once. Ko was being taken to the prosecutor's office nearly two months after being sent there. Song was on his way back from the office. Upon seeing Ko, Song gave a smile, a simple, unmistakable smile. After the arrest, Ko was fearful of punishment and had at first blamed Song for not having revealed that he was blacklisted. Later, however, Ko gave up the blame and, feeling lighter, was able to smile back at Song.

Ko remembered the clear, smiling face of Song vividly. Each of them was accompanied by a guard and could not talk to the other. This was the last time Ko saw Song.

The prosecutor did not ask many questions, just confirmed previous answers about his address and name and statement. The prosecutor even told Ko that he was a Third High School alum. The next day, the prosecutor summoned him again to announce his release. Until that moment, Ko could not imagine being released like that. He was released on probation, but he did not know what had happened to the others. His release date was January 19, 1944, six months and six days from his arrest.

Ko returned to his boardinghouse after his arrest in July, seasons having changed twice. He saw that his room and possessions were preserved the way they were when he left; during his long absence, the landlord had not rented out the room.

The landlady profusely apologized to Ko: "We knew the special police was watching you and eavesdropping, but we could not tell you as they threatened us never to let it out."

However, from that moment, he found himself under constant surveillance. If he moved to another house, a detective showed up first. This continued until liberation. Ko had also become blacklisted.

Because he had not finished his graduation exams, he was failed and had to attend the remainder of the third year again after his visit home. After graduation, he was accepted to Tokyo Imperial University as an English literature major. One of his professors at the Third High School praised him, saying, "The only student who received A's for three straight years in this subject is Ko." Even though he excelled in English, he had to leave the school and return to Korea as the American air raid on Japan became fierce toward the end of the war.

At last, Korea was liberated in August 1945. After suffering so long from the stress of the Japanese detectives' watchful eyes, Ko felt as if he had sprouted a pair of wings to fly off anywhere freely.

He transferred to Seoul National University and continued with his studies. His senior thesis supervisor was Professor Yi Yang-ha, also a Third High School and Tokyo Imperial University alum. Ko's thesis, written in English, was titled "Wordsworth: A Nature Poet."

This again shows the great impact his involvement with Song had on Ko. Wordsworth is a great English nature poet, who wrote the famous line, "The child is father of the man." Ko became interested in Wordsworth while locked up in the solitary cell. Because the only books he could borrow were religious books, he spent the whole day reading them. He read the New Testament several times and also read many Buddhist books written by Suzuki Daisetsu. Wordsworth was the writer Suzuki quoted most in his books, inspiring Ko's interest in Wordsworth.

Wordsworth was a pantheist who praised nature and respected providence. His ideas shared roots with the Eastern philosophy. Young people at that time did not find him attractive, and the historical materialists particularly sneered at him. But Ko felt moved by Wordsworth and wrote his senior thesis on him as a result of his days spent in prison.

THE DOCUMENTS OF THE SPECIAL POLICE

It was special detectives of the Kyoto Police in Shimogamo who arrested and interrogated Yun, Shimogamo being the district where Yun lived.

"Special detectives" referred to detectives under the supervision of the Police Department of the Ministry of Internal Affairs and Communications. They were called Special Police, shortened from Special High-Level Police, and they dealt with political crimes.

The Special Police division was established in 1911 in Japan. On June 29, 1928, however, the Japanese government amended the Maintenance of the Public Order Act of 1925, fortifying it with more drastic measures. On July 3, it greatly expanded the jurisdiction of the Special Police to deal with violations of public order, establishing the force even at county-level police stations nationwide. The Maintenance of the Public Order Act and the Special Police were twin entities.

Special Police agents were not supervised by any local police officials, even if they were stationed in a particular local precinct. They operated under the centralized unique interior organization. Each agent's appointment, removal, compensation, and special funding were managed directly by the Special Police's central office.[5] Even their *Special Police Report Monthly* was a classified internal publication. Each month, they edited and published the summary, substance, and disposal of serious cases that would alert the organization. Its purpose was to assist the activities of the Special Police, and only its insiders had access to it.

In other words, structurally, the Special Police was completely separate from the regular police force. Its function and structure were similar to those of the Central Intelligence Agency during President Park Chung-hee's regime in South Korea. They carried out brutal tortures, and their prowess was said to make the flying birds drop from the sky. Due to their special structure, they even had a privileged sense of elitism, feeling superior to the local police.

Thirty years after Korea's liberation, the accounts of Yun's arrest and trial were illuminated for the first time due to the publication of *Special Police Report Monthly*, along with the release of other top-secret documents of imperial Japan. Documents pertaining to Yun's case were discovered by Ujigo Tsuyoshi, librarian at Japan's National Diet Library. The Special Police had named it Case concerning Joseon Nationalist Students Group in Kyoto.

Mr. Ujigo is a Doshisha University graduate deeply interested in Korean writers who studied there. He handed in a copy of the report to Professor Yun Il-ju. In turn, Professor Yun published it in the December 1977 issue of *Munhak Sasang*[6] with the following notes:

Newly Discovered Sources:

Japan's "Special Police" Confidential Records Regarding Poet Yun Dong-ju

About the Translation of December 1943 Issue of Special Police Report Monthly: The Showa-era years were converted to the Western calendar years. The Japanese names of Koreans were changed to their true names. (Toward the end of colonization, Yun Dong-ju and Song Mong-gyu's families had changed their names to Japanese, partly because of the pressure from the Japanese government and partly to obtain their pass-port certificates for their study abroad.) The translation is faithful to the original text, except for correcting apparent misprints.

Professor Jeong Byeong-uk translated the text, and Professor Yun Il-ju, the younger brother of the poet Yun, supplied commentary.

Special Police Report Monthly (December 1943)

Issued by the Police Department of the Ministry of Internal Affairs and Communications

Case Concerning Joseon Nationalist Students Group in Kyoto

Summary of the Scheme

(Paragraph 3 of Joseon People's Movement)

(1) Schemes in Manchuria and Joseon

The central figure Song Mong-gyu[7] was born in Myeongdong, Zhixin, Yanji Prefecture, Gando, Manchukuo. He completed his secondary education at Eunjin Middle School and People's High School[8] in Manchuria. Afterwards, he graduated from Yonhui Junior College and in 1942 entered Kyoto Imperial University, where he is currently enrolled. From his days in Manchuria, he had strong nationalistic ideas and was in contact with subversive Joseon organizations in China. While attending Eunjin Middle School in Manchuria, Song received nationalism training from the school's teacher Myeong Hui-jo.[9] In April 1935, when he was only 19 and attending the third year at Eunjin, he sought out the Kim Gu faction, a Korean resistance group that was on hiatus in Nanjing, with the purpose of joining in the resistance activities. He was trained there until November of the same year. When he realized that it would be difficult to achieve his goal there because of the problems within Kim's group, he went to another freedom fighter Yi Ung in Jinan to engage in resistance work. With the pressure from investigating agencies, however, he had to go back to his parents' home in March 1936 without achieving his goal.

Afterwards, upon his father and uncle's advice, Song turned himself in at the Consulate Police in Dailazi.[10] He was released after further questioning at Unggi Police Station. As such, he has a career of struggles and never denounced his subversive idea of Korean independence. Having witnessed the conflict between the Kim Gu faction and the Kim Won-bong faction during his stay in Nanjing and Jinan, he concluded that the Korean people's worst shortcomings were their local prejudices and factionalism, as well as their low level of culture. He also viewed that the independence movement of the past had failed because it stayed merely as impulsive, emotional outbursts. Thus he was convinced that the first step in Korean independence was to correct these shortcomings by raising Joseon people's cultural level and promoting their unique cultures. Therefore:

Around May 1937, in the family house of Yun Dong-ju in Yongjoeng, Gando, and other places, Song convened with Yun, who had been not only in complete agreement with him but also just as nationalistic as he was since their days at Eunjin Middle School;

They discussed that they should devote their life to the nationalistic enlightenment of the Joseon people as literary scholars and leaders because Joseon's independence hinges on maintaining and advancing its culture as well as correcting shortcomings of the people;

Believing that Yonhui Junior College in Seoul would be the best place to study Joseon literature in order to be Joseon literature scholars, they enrolled in Yonhui together in April 1938. Due to our government's reinforcement of assimilation policy, Joseon language classes were banned at all levels of school in Joseon, and the use of Japanese was recommended. They believed that such policies would inevitably annihilate Joseon literature, that such annihilation of Joseon's unique culture would lead to the demise of Joseon people, and that they must maintain and advance the Joseon culture at all costs;

Around February 1939, with Yun Dong-ju, Baek In-jun, and Kang Cheojung, Song decided to publish a Joseon language literary periodical. Until August of the same year, they met numerously in their dormitory rooms or tea houses in order to critique their nationalistic writings, promoting each other's nationalism and Joseon culture;

When the publication of the periodical became impossible, Song came on the editorial board of Yonhui Junior College's alumni publication

Munu[11] and encouraged Yun Dong-ju to write for the magazine, promoting the Joseon culture and nationalism.

One month after graduating from Yonhui Junior College in March 1942, Song enrolled in the History Department at Kyoto Imperial University to study literature and history because he believed that it was not sufficient to end his studies at a junior college when he wanted to promote the Joseon culture for Joseon's independence. He believed that, in order to clarify Joseon's historical status and maintain the nationalistic characteristics of Joseon by researching Joseon literature, he must continue his studies in university. Since then, he has studied world history and literature with the ultimate goal of Joseon's independence, at the same time endeavoring to promote the Joseon culture.

At the same time, Yun Dong-ju went to Tokyo after he graduated from Yonhui Junior College, studied as an auditor[12] at Hosei University, and then in September 1942, entered the preparatory department[13] for literature at Doshisha University in Kyoto. All this time, Yun was in a close relationship with Song, instigating other Joseon students in Kyoto.

(2) Schemes After Moving to Kyoto

After the start of the Pacific War on December 8, 1941, the above two individuals concluded recklessly that Japan would surely lose the war eventually. Taking advantage of Japan's temporary exhaustion during the war, they intended to achieve Joseon's independence immediately by stirring up public opinion. They spotted and instigated several Joseon students in Kyoto in order to gain comrades; they gained the support of Ko Hui-uk,[14] and from October 1942 until July of this year (1943), the three of them occasionally convened in various places in downtown Kyoto to discuss promotion of nationalism and specific resistance plans. The major points they discussed are as follows:

(a) Under the current situation, Joseon people cannot speak and write their own language and are about to be annihilated. We must not forget that we are Joseon people, that we study the unique Joseon culture, and that we endeavor to maintain and promote it. This is the mission of nationalistic intellectuals. Joseon people are by no means inferior and will be an advanced people of culture once culturally enlightened. When awakened culturally and nationalistically, Joseon's independence is possible.

(b) Nationalistic enlightenment depends on the power of its culture. Theater and moving pictures are effective but restricted by a lack of venues.

Therefore, literature for the masses, which is not limited by space and has a significant influence, should be the direction we take.

(c) Joseon should be liberated as a people of a small and weak power in the "Greater East Asia Co-prosperity Sphere." However, the Joseon people's shortcomings as a whole must be corrected.

(d) It is Japan's historical inevitability that Joseon, as a member of the "Greater East Asia Co-prosperity Spear," must become independent. To do so, the Joseon people must actively demand independence with cultural awareness. A precondition to Joseon's independence is promoting its cultural standards, and its burden is on us.

(e) To achieve Joseon's independence, we must guard the Joseon culture with our lives.

(f) When a peace treaty from the Pacific War is discussed, Joseon's independence must be raised as a condition. Even if not, we should deploy our independence movement when Japan's power wanes or it loses the war, and all of the Joseon people will rise against it. The Joseon soldiers in the force will take a great role, and we must give our lives to rise.

(g) Once the revolt for independence starts, all Joseon people will unite nationwide. Therefore, we need not be hasty in gaining comrades. We must be extremely careful when gaining comrades.

(h) The issue of who should be the political leader after independence can rest for a while during military dictatorship.

(i) From time to time, we worked on enlightening Baek In-jun and Matsuyama Ryukan,[15] Joseon students in Kyoto.

(j) Abolishing Joseon language classes in schools and banning Korean language newspapers and magazines are designed to annihilate the Joseon culture, i.e., its unique characteristics, and destroy Joseon people. Therefore, we must devote ourselves to guarding the Joseon culture.

(k) The propaganda of "naisen ittai" (Japan and Korea are one) is the Japanese government's fake conciliation policy which attempts to deceive Joseon people and destroy Joseon people by annihilating its national spirit.

(l) To guard the Joseon culture and promote the national spirit, Joseon's native culture must be systemized by historical research. In Germany, university professor Fichte's "Addresses to the German Nation" stirred up a national spirit in its people; in Italy, Mazzini's *Young Italy* awakened a national consciousness. For Joseon's independence, we must study the path our people should take and correct our shortcomings.

(m) Because the "Greater East Asia Co-prosperity Spear" theory purports to let each people of East Asia gain its own place, the potential for Joseon's independence is excellent. However, the Joseon people must demonstrate their will for independence and their intention to achieve an autonomous political system.

(3) Suspects to Be Transferred to the Prosecution[16]

Name, Age: Somura Mukei, 27

Occupation: Student, History, Kyoto Imperial University

Permanent Address / Current Address: Hamgyeong-bukdo Gyeongheung-gun Unggi-eup, Ungsang-dong 422 / Kyoto, Sakyo-ku Kitashiragawa Higashihirai-cho 60

Date of Arrest: July 14

Date of Transfer: December 6

Name, Age: Hiranuma Tooju, 26

Occupation: Student, Literature, Doshisha University

Permanent Address / Current Address: Hamgyeong-bukdo Cheon-gjin-bu Pohang-jeong 67 / Kyoto, Sakyo-ku, Tanaka Takahara-cho 27, Dakeda Apartments Date of Arrest: July 14

Date of Transfer: December 6

Name, Age: Takashima Shokyoku

Occupation: Student, The Third High School

Permanent Address / Current Address: Gyeonggi-do Gyeong-seong-bu Gyedong-jeong 14–18 / Kyoto, Sakyo-ku Kitashi-ragawa Higashihirai-cho 60

Date of Arrest: July 14

Date of Transfer: December 6

The publication of the Special Police's interrogation document brought about tremendous responses from the public. Not only did it clearly bear the whole picture surrounding the arrest and trial of the national poet Yun Dong-ju, but it also stood out among the interrogation records of Korean freedom fighters, revealing their proud and unwavering spirit for independence. Against these records, the following should be reexamined.

First, the date of arrest needs to be addressed. The list in *Special Police Report Monthly* says Song, Yun, and Ko were all arrested on July 14, 1943. However, the court's written decision, as reproduced in *Ideology Monthly* (which appears after this section), states that Song was arrested on July 10, while Yun and Ko were arrested on July 14. *Ideology Monthly* is correct, as it reproduces the official record after the trial and is thus definitive. It is further supported by Ko's statement that Song had been arrested a few days before he was.

IS IT TRUE THAT SONG MONG-GYU TURNED HIMSELF IN?

Another point must be clarified here. *Special Police Report Monthly* notes that Song had turned himself in to the Japanese Police in March 1936. Is it true?

As seen earlier, the interrogation record reprinted in *Special Police Report Monthly* describes the circumstances of Song's return to North Gando from the Nakyang Military School:

> In April 1935, when he was only 19 and attending the third year at Eunjin, he sought out the Kim Gu faction, a Korean resistance group that was on hiatus in Nanjing, with the purpose of joining in the resistance activities. He was trained there until November of the same year. When he realized that it would be difficult to achieve his goal there because of the problems within Kim's group, he went to another freedom fighter, Yi Ung in Jinan, to engage in resistance work. With the pressure from investigating agencies, however, he had to go back to his parents' home in March 1936 without achieving his goal. Afterwards, upon his father and uncle's advice, Song turned himself in at the Consulate Police in Dailazi. He was released after further questioning at Unggi Police Station.

The report states that after Song returned from China, he turned himself in at the Japanese Consulate Police.

A strict examination of related documents, however, speaks to the contrary for the following reasons:

> 1. While *Special Police Report Monthly* records that Song returned home in "March 1936," his arrest record from the "List of Arrestees Relating to Joseon Military School Case" clearly states that Song was arrested

by the Japanese Police in "Jinan on April 10, 1936."[17] In March 1936, then, Song was a free man residing in Jinan.

2. The court's trial decision document is an official Japanese government record that clearly tells us that Song had not turned himself in back in 1936. The decision states that because Song "was engaged in independence work again by devoting himself to the activities of the Yi Ung faction, a Joseon resistance group in Jinan, he was questioned while under police custody in his ancestral hometown of Unggi." Clearly, Song was arrested in Jinan on April 10, 1936, and jailed at the Unggi Police Station in the same month. It was customary for the Japanese police to transport Joseon freedom fighters arrested overseas to their ancestral hometown police stations to be interrogated. Thus, Song's trial decision record perfectly corresponds to the "List of Arrestees Relating to Joseon Military School Case" regarding the time and circumstances of his arrest.

3. Song Ung-gyu stated that he witnessed the Japanese police taking Song Mong-gyu to Unggi. This statement also supports the fact that Song did not turn himself in. Had Song turned himself in at North Gando and been taken there, Song's father would have notified his family in Unggi so that they could help Song. This was not the case. Song's relatives in Unggi only found out about Song's arrest after Song Ung-gyu witnessed the police taking him, and they all had to figure out why Song was arrested.

So why did the Special Police state in the interrogation document that Song had "turned himself in"? One possibility is that Song, who had suffered greatly from the Japanese Special Police's surveillance over the years because of his arrest record in Jinan, initially gave false testimony that he had turned himself in earlier to avoid an aggravated punishment as a repeat offender. Later in the trial, however, his false statement may have been exposed, resulting in the trial court's stating the truth.

The following is a reconstruction of the circumstances as revealed by the extant sources:

The Special Police constantly watched Song, a blacklisted individual. As circumstances worsened for Japan, the Special Police's surveillance must have intensified. In fact, the Japanese Department of Interior sent out the following directives to the Special Police in January 1943: "On top of strengthening the surveillance of the blacklisted Koreans, you must pay special attention to the activities of the student intelligentsia, putting efforts into discovering additional suspects. Particularly, look for their scheming activities."[18]

Amid heightened surveillance, Yun moved to Kyoto. From Yun and Song's frequent meetings, the Special Police often heard the mention of "independence of Joseon," which alerted them further. Additionally, Ko Hui-uk joined Yun and Song, followed by other Korean students such as Baek In-jun, a student at Rikkyo University in Tokyo (who had started at Yonhui with Yun and Song and gone to Japan after the second year), and Matsuyama Ryukan (Korean name unknown). Surveillance of their meetings revealed seditious conversations, leading the police to conclude that a seditious group was being formed against the security and safety laws. These views were reflected in the name given the case by the Special Police, the "Joseon Nationalist Students Group in Kyoto." For sure, the Special Police was acting under the directives: "On top of strengthening the surveillance of the blacklisted Koreans, you must pay special attention to the activities of the student intelligentsia, putting efforts to discover additional suspects . . . [and looking] for their scheming activities."

It was inevitable that the Special Police would pay attention to the "student intelligentsia." In 1919, right after World War I, Japan experienced a lot of trouble from the Korean foreign students in Tokyo. The commonly known February 8 Declaration of Independence became the direct catalyst for the March First Movement of the same year. Thus, the Special Police could not help paying attention to the activities of the Korean foreign students, a potentially dangerous group. Some sort of "scheming activity" was expected from them at any moment. Consequently, these students were assumed to be criminals.

As summer recess approached, the Special Police decided to act on their suspicions and they arrested Song on July 10, which was done so discreetly that even Ko, who lived in the same boardinghouse, did not notice it.

It is assumed that the police searched Song's room, finding a sufficient amount of evidence to support a violation of security laws and also implicate others.

On July 14, they arrested Yun and Ko. It is not clear whether additional arrests were made on that day because *Special Police Report Monthly* only lists arrests of those who were eventually transferred to the prosecution.

A total of seven Korean foreign students appear in the Special Police's interrogation documents relating to the case and Song's and Yun's trial records. Aside from Song, Yun, and Ko, it is certain the other four—Baek In-jun, Jang Seong-eon, Matsubara Terutada (Korean name unknown), and Matsuyama Ryukan (Korean name unknown)—were taken into custody and then released after questioning, which was the Special Police's usual procedure.

How was Yun taken into custody? It seems that Yun was arrested at around the same time and in a similar way as Ko. However, an interesting account of Yun's arrest is found in Ibuki Gou's article, mentioned earlier:

> (Having finished writing thus far, I learned of Kim Il-ryong through Professor Yun Il-ju's letter. There was an eyewitness to Yun's arrest. It was Kim Il-ryong, who was a student at Doshisha University and a fellow boarder next to Yun's apartment at the boarding house.)
>
> On the day of arrest, Kim returned home late when he heard cursing in Yun's room and then saw two detectives. Yun was tying up a few books. Kim avoided them by going into the shared bathroom. After the party left, Kim contacted Jang Seong-eon [recorded in the court document as "Shirano Kiyohiko"]. The detectives were about thirty-five or forty years of age, and one of them was short. Later, Kim witnessed Yun walking with the detectives at the corner of Hyakumanben in Kyoto. Yun was wearing zori [Japanese straw sandals].[19]

Kim's statement seems odd at best. The Special Police must have considered Yun a more serious case than Ko and taken greater precautions. Yet according to Kim's statement, Yun was arrested late in the evening, whereas Ko was arrested while getting ready for school early in the morning. It does not make sense and is contrary to the Special Police's usual practice of arresting suspects discreetly, either very late at night or very early in the morning. Moreover, the statement that Yun was wearing zori is also curious. Why would Yun wear slippers when being taken to the police station? Did Kim mistake another person for Yun? Kim's statement is mentioned here merely to show that such testimony exists.

The news of Yun's arrest must have been telegraphed to his parents. Yun Hye-won, who was waiting for Yun at the Sangsambong station, was notified to come back home as soon as the news of Yun's arrest reached the family. Yun had bought the tickets in Kyoto and sent his luggage ahead of his planned departure. After the news of the arrest, the Yongjeong train station notified the family that the luggage had arrived. However, the family could not claim the luggage as they had no luggage ticket. The bags were stored in the station for over a month and recovered afterward with late fees paid when a friend of Yun's mailed Yun's ticket in a letter.

Professor Yun Il-ju stated, "We were waiting at the station day after day, but he never arrived.... A friend [of Yun's] sent us a letter and the ticket, and we learned of his arrest right before departure. We picked up the luggage then with the ticket."[20] Yun Hye-won, who was four years older, had a clearer and more detailed memory.

For a long time, it was said that Yun was taken to Kamogawa Police Station; later on, however, when researchers visited the area, they found out that it was actually Shimogamo Police Station.

During Yun's stay at Shimogamo, two people were able to visit him: his uncle Yun Yeong-chun from Tokyo and his cousin and grade school friend Kim Jeong-u. Only relatives were allowed visitation, and even though Song was related to them as well, they were not allowed to see Song, perhaps because of concerns about corroboration through them.

Yun Yeong-chun remembered the visit as follows:

In July 1943, I heard the shocking news of Dong-ju's and Mong-gyu's arrest by the Kyoto police. As soon as I heard the news, I took the express train to Kyoto. At that time, there was a food shortage in Japan, and rice was rationed in small amounts. I expected that I would not be able to get rice to send to him, so I looked everywhere to get extra rice in Tokyo. Mrs. Jeong Gi-ryeon, who was a general administrator at the Korean students' YWCA, was understanding of the situation after I explained it. She gave me a half gallon of rice saved for emergency. I hid it in my bag so the police would not find it. When I arrived in Kyoto, it was the middle of the night. I went to Dong-ju's boarding house, but they told me nothing. I also visited the dean of student affairs at Doshisha University, who explained nothing. I made two lunches with the rice I brought there and went straight to Sugamo [sic] Police Station. When I requested a visit, they first denied it, but eventually allowed me to see Dong-ju because I'm a relative. The detective in charge directed that I should not communicate anything besides the news from home.

When I entered the interrogation room, Dong-ju was seated at the desk facing a detective and was in the process of translating his Korean poems and essays into Japanese. It seemed that he had translated some of his best poems among the ones he showed me a few months before. A detective named Goroke [a mispronunciation of Koorogi] inquired into these and then sent them with other documents to Fukuoka Prison. The manuscript Dong-ju was translating was quite thick. It contained much more than what he had shown me a few months ago. His smiling face was pale. When I took out the lunch for him, the detective put it on the desk and told me to leave as time was up.

Dong-ju told me, "Uncle, don't worry. Go home and tell Grandfather, Father, and Mother that I will be released soon." This was the last time I met him. I thought to myself, perhaps he will have to stay in prison for a year, but they won't kill him. I left with the detective some change of linens that I brought from Tokyo. As I left the room, my feet dragged on. I felt as if something had hit my head, and I was burning with anger. I wanted to cry out loud.[21]

Kim Jeong-u described his visit as follows:

Upon hearing the news of Dong-ju's arrest in Kyoto from Mr. Yun Yeong-chun, I went to visit him in Kyoto around the spring of 1944 [the year is incorrect; Yun was arrested in July of 1943 and by December was transferred from Shimogamo to the Kyoto District Prosecution Prison, where he was in solitary confinement]. I entered the four-and-a-half tatami room in the Kamogawa Police Station [he meant Shimogamo Police Station] and met Dong-ju, who was accompanied by a detective. His face was pale, but he did his best to smile. He looked at me and repeatedly asked me to give his regards to his grandfather and parents. His pale face and sincere voice were the last memories of him that I have.[22]

During our interview, Mr. Kim Jeong-u stated that the detective in the room, pointing at a high pile of papers, muttered, "You are doing this out of useless heroism! These are the proof!"[23] Among the documents must have been Yun's translated manuscript, which his uncle had seen earlier.

The Trial

DECISION RECORDS OF THE KYOTO DISTRICT TRIAL COURT

Song, Yun, and Ko were transferred to the prosecutor's jail on December 6, 1943. After the transfer, each was locked up in solitary confinement. Each room was windowless, with only two holes on the door, one on top for peeping in and one on the bottom for meals. The trial record shows that their cases were assigned to Prosecutor Eto Takashi, who had indicated to Ko Hui-uk that he was also a graduate of the Third High School.

The Special Police had anticipated that all three would be prosecuted. After reviewing the documents, however, the prosecutor seemed to have wanted to spare Ko from the outset because he was a student at his alma mater, as evidenced by the fact that Ko had hardly been interrogated during his confinement and that he alone was released soon afterward.

On January 19, 1944, the prosecutor decided not to prosecute Ko and released him. Note that Ko was not found innocent; instead, his indictment was suspended. It seems that the prosecutor was letting him slide this time as a fellow Third High alum but warning him to behave.

On February 22, 1944, Song and Yun were finally indicted. Song's case was assigned to the First Criminal Division of the Kyoto District Trial Court, and Yun's was assigned to its Second Criminal Division. The trial of each case proceeded separately from the other. Yun was tried on March 31, 1944, and Song was tried on April 13, 1944.

In 1982, Japanese researcher Ibuki Gou sought to meet all seven people (six judges and one prosecutor) involved in Song's and Yun's cases. Five of them were still alive (four judges and the prosecutor). She questioned them with a copy of the decision papers, but none of them could remember either Song or Yun.

Song's and Yun's trial records were finally unearthed when *Ideology Monthly* was released to the public.

Like *Special Police Report Monthly*, *Ideology Monthly* was a classified document. While *Special Police Report Monthly* was published by the Security Agency of the Department of the Interior's Safety and Intelligence Division, *Ideology Monthly* was published by the Department of Justice's Criminal Division. Every month, the court's decisions involving political crimes were reviewed and selected for publication. Its purpose was to provide reference materials to help so-called political case prosecutors in their duties. Each decision was accompanied by lists disclosing the personal information of other defendants in the case and their trial outcomes.

Included in this specialized classified document was the court's decision on Song (*Ideology Monthly* 109 [April–June 1944]), discovered by Ujigo Tsuyoshi, the same librarian who found the Special Police's interrogation documents relating to Song's and Yun's cases published in *Special Police Report Monthly*.

Ideology Monthly did not publish the court's decision on Yun's case, but the "List of the Disposal of Those Relating to [Song's] Case" contains core information, such as Yun's sentence term and the date of judgment. Additionally, it gives Song's case the official name of Criminal Case in Violation of the Public Order Maintenance Law (Joseon's Independence Movement).

Yun's trial decision was discovered a few years after Song's. Ibuki Gou went to the Kyoto District Trial Court and successfully requested a viewing of Yun's trial records in the annex. However, the court's rules prohibited photocopying or transcribing decisions, and she discreetly hired a photographer to take pictures of the record. These photographs were handed to Professor Yun Il-ju, and their contents were translated and published for the first time in the October 1982 issue of *Munhak Sasang*.[24]

Through these documents, the trials of Song and Yun were wholly disclosed. The following summary is extracted from them:

Song and Yun were indicted on February 22, 1944. Yun was tried first, followed by Song. The prosecutor pursued three years' imprisonment for both Yun and Song.

March 31, 1944: In violation of Article 5 of the Public Order Maintenance Law, Yun was sentenced to two years' imprisonment, including 120 days of detention pending trial, by the Second Criminal Division of the Kyoto District Trial Court (Judges Ishii Hirao, Watanabe Tsunehiro, and Kawaraya Sueo).

April 13, 1944: In violation of Article 5 of the Public Order Maintenance Law, Song was sentenced to two years' imprisonment, including zero days of detention pending trial, by the First Criminal Division of the Kyoto District Trial Court (Judges Konishi Nobuharu, Fukushima Noboru, and Hoshi Tomotaka).

The inclusion of days of detention pending trial needs to be explained here. If included in the sentence, the number of days a defendant spent in jail before trial would shorten the actual term he serves. In Yun's case, 120 days were included, while none were included in Song's. Why was that so?

Upon inquiry to a Korean legal professional, the following was explained. In contemporary South Korea, the Constitution mandates that a defendant's pre-trial detention time be subtracted from the sentence term. The Japanese penal code, however, is different. Such subtraction (inclusion) of the pretrial detention time from the sentence term is up to the trial judge. Article 21 of Japan's Penal Code states that pretrial detention time, in part or in its entirety, "may be" subtracted from the main sentence term. Thus, it is entirely in the judge's discretion to do so. In other words, by excluding the days served in pretrial detention, the judge can add to the punishment.

In Yun's case, the trial took place 260 days after his arrest. It seems that the court only considered the 120 days he served after his transfer to the prosecution.

Yun's and Song's terms were the same, but because of the difference in the calculation of pretrial detention time and the different trial dates, Yun was to be released on November 30, 1945, and Song was to be released on April 12, 1946. Because their families in North Gando could not be present at trial and never received the trial record, they concluded that Yun was sentenced to two years and Song to two-and-a-half years.

Following are the court's judgments on Song and Yun in their entirety:

(1) Song Mong-gyu's judgment (as reproduced in *Special Police Report Monthly* and translated by Ko Hui-uk; the translation is faithful to the source except that the Japanese Showa years were changed to corresponding years in A.D. and the names in Japanese were corrected to their original Korean names)

Judgment on Song Mong-gyu in Violation of the Public Order Maintenance Law ("Joseon Independence Movement")
Rendered by the Kyoto District Trial Court
Name, Age: Song Mong-gyu, 28
Education: Enrolled in Kyoto University
Occupation: Student
Course of Action: Arrested: 7/10/1943, Trial Requested: 2/22/1944
Trial: 4/13/1944—4/17/1944
Ordered: 2 years' imprisonment (3 years requested)

Name, Age: Yun Dong-ju, 27
Education: Enrolled in Doshisha University
Occupation: Student
Course of Action: Arrested: 7/14/1943, Trial Requested: 2/22/1944

Trial: 3/31/1944—4/1/1944

Ordered: 2 years' imprisonment (3 years requested), including 120 days

One Other: Acquitted

JUDGMENT

Name: Song Mong-gyu (D.O.B. 9/28/1917)

Student at Kyoto Imperial University, Preparatory Division, History Department

Place of Origin: Hamgyong-bukdo Gyeongheung-gun Unggi-eup, Ungsang-dong 422

Address: Kyoto, Sakyo-ku Kitashiragawa Higashihirai-cho 60, House of Shimizu Eiichi

Judgment on the above person in the case of Violation of the Public Order Maintenance Law, prosecuted by Eto Takashi, Prosecutor, and heard by the court, is as below.

ORDERED: Defendant is sentenced to two years' imprisonment

REASONS:

Defendant was born to a Joseon school teacher residing in Gando, Manchukuo, and educated there. Since childhood, he felt aggrieved, having experienced discrimination by Chinese people, and grew up to hold fierce national consciousness, aided by the nationalistic education he received. In or about April 1935, taking a school alum's advice, he left school to join the Kim Gu faction, a Joseon resistance group, in Nanjing. While participating in its activities, his nationalistic feelings were heightened. However, as he learned of the group's ugly factious struggles, in or about November of the same year, he moved to Jinan to join the Yi Ung faction, another Joseon resistance group. Because of these activities, he was taken to the police station in Unggi, his place of origin, at or about April 1936, to be questioned. He was released in or about the end of August of the same year. Afterwards, he graduated People's High School in Yongjeong, Gando, and went to Yonhui Junior College in Gyeongseong. In April 1942, he entered the preparatory division of Kyoto Imperial University as a history major, where he is still enrolled. Maintaining his nationalistic bias, he misjudged that the Imperial Government's colonial policy of banning the Joseon language classes, ceasing Joseon-language periodicals, etc., would cause all individualities of Joseon people to sink and annihilate the Joseon culture, leading to its demise. Consequently, he concluded that there was no choice but to separate Joseon from the Imperial rule as an independent nation. In order to do so, he concluded, the culture of the Joseon people must be promoted, and Joseon's nationalistic awareness must be awakened, so that the spirit of independence would grow. To achieve that end:

First, in or about early December of 1942, he told Ko Hui-uk, a Third High School student who had the same nationalistic awareness and who also resides in Kyoto, Sakyo-ku Kitashi-ragawa Higashihirai-cho 60, House of Shimizu Eiichi, that the previous attempts at Joseon independence movement failed because they merely imitated foreign ideology without a firm basis and that they should start a new independence movement with learned systematic methods. By criticizing the past independence movements and suggesting future directions, he promoted the spirit of independence.

Second, in or about April of 1943, in the same residence, he told Yun Dong-ju, a Doshisha University literature student who had the same nationalistic awareness and who was the defendant's close friend from childhood, that during his visits to Manchukuo and Joseon during his four-month convalescence at home, he saw that elementary and middle school students there only use Japanese because of the pressure from the Government General and that the Joseon language is about to be annihilated; that Joseon people are disadvantaged compared to Japanese in food ration and distribution in Manchukuo; that conscription of Joseon men will actually empower them to achieve Joseon's independence. By discussing and arguing these points, he promoted the spirit of independence.

Third, in or about late April of the same year, he convened in Yase Park with Yun Dong-ju and Baek In-jun, a Rikkyo University student with the same nationalistic awareness, to discuss the conscription policy. He applauded the conscription policy, arguing that Joseon people, who previously were ignorant of weaponry, would acquire military knowledge when they were conscripted and that if Japan were about to be defeated in the Greater East Asian War, they would achieve independence by armed national uprising under new leadership. As for the political system after independence, he said that because Joseon people are factious and jealous, a strong military dictatorship might be inevitable and emphasized that they all needed to develop their strengths to contribute to independence. By arguing so, he promoted the spirit of independence.

Fourth, in or about late June of the same year, in the same residence, he told Ko Hui-uk that military might would not be likely to resolve the Greater East Asian War, resulting in cessation by peace treaty, which would include Burma and the Philippines as independent nations, and that meanwhile Joseon should appeal to other countries of the world for its independence. By arguing so, he tried to promote the spirit of independence.

Fifth, in or about late June of the same year, in Kyoto, Sakyo-ku, Tanaka Takahara-cho 27, Dakeda Apartments, he conferred with Yun Dong-ju, after discussing India's independence movement under the leadership of Chandrabose, that because Joseon's annexation to Japan is not yet long in history and Japan's power is great, such a great leader may not appear yet in Joseon; however, because Joseon's nationalistic awareness is abundant, they should rise against Japan when the time comes and a great leader appears. In so encouraging each other, he acted on the completion of his goal.

Based on the evidence, the facts of the case are admitted by the testimony in the trial court.

Pursuant to Article 5 of the Public Order Maintenance Law, defendant's actions fall under its scope, and defendant is sentenced to two years' imprisonment, which is within the prison term of the law.

So ordered.

April 13, 1944

First Criminal Division

Kyoto District Court

Trial Court Judges: Konishi Nobuharu, Fukushima Noboru, Hoshi
Tomotaka

(2) Yun Dong-ju's judgment (Archived in Kyoto Court in Japan and
translated by Professor Yun Il-ju).

Place of Origin: Hamgyeong-bukdo Cheongjin-bu Pohang-
jeong 67[25]

Address: Kyoto, Sakyo-ku, Tanaka Takahara-cho 27, Dakeda
Apartments

Yun Dong-ju (D.O.B. 12/30/1918),[26] Student at Doshisha University,
Preparatory Division, Literature Department

Judgment on the above person in the case of Violation of the Public
Order Maintenance Law, prosecuted by Eto Takashi, Prosecutor, and heard by the court, is as below.

ORDERED: Defendant is sentenced to two years' imprisonment,
including 120 days of pre-trial detention.

REASONS:

Defendant was born to a middle-class farmer residing in
Gando, Manchukuo, and received a middle school education
there. After graduating from Yonhui Junior College in Gyeongseong, he came to Japan in March 1942 to attend Rikkyo
University's preparatory division in Tokyo. In October of the
same year, he transferred to Doshisha University's preparatory
division in Kyoto. From childhood, he held fierce nationalistic
awareness, having received a nationalistic education, pored over
ideological literature, and been influenced by his friends. He felt
deep resentment over the so-called discrimination by Japan.
Thinking that our methods of governing Joseon would annihilate Joseon's unique culture and destroy Joseon people, he
concluded that Joseon must be separated from the Imperial rule
and become independent in order to be liberated and prosper.
To do that, he concluded that Joseon's current merits and past

failures in independence movements must be reevaluated and that Joseon's culture and nationalistic awareness must be promoted so that their ability and national spirit would increase. Especially, after the Greater East Asian War started, he dreamed of Japan's defeat due to inferior science and technology, foolishly thinking that the ambition of Joseon's independence would be achieved. With conviction, he transferred to Doshisha University in order to achieve his goal. He convened with Song Mong-gyu, who had the same ambition, to encourage each other and to promote the spirit of independence in other students such as Matsubara Terutada and Jang Seong-eon. In particular:

First, with Song Mong-gyu:

a) In or about mid-April of 1943, in Song's residence in Kyoto, Sakyo-ku Kitashiragawa Higashihirai-cho 60, House of Shimizu Eiichi, he convened with Song, who informed him that Joseon people are discriminated against in Joseon and Manchukuo, which they criticized together; he also discussed that conscription of Joseon men would actually empower them to achieve Joseon's independence.

b) In or about late April of the same year, in Yase Park outside of Kyoto, he convened with Song and Baek In-jun, a Rikkyo University student with the same nationalistic awareness, to discuss the conscription policy. He applauded the conscription policy, arguing that Joseon people, who previously were ignorant of weaponry, would acquire military knowledge when they were conscripted and that if Japan were about to be defeated in the Greater East Asian War, they would achieve independence by armed national uprising under new leadership. As for the political system after independence, he said that because Joseon people are factitious and jealous, a strong military dictatorship might be inevitable and emphasized that they all needed to develop their strengths to contribute to independence.

c)   In or about late June of the same year, in his residence in
Kyoto, Sakyo-ku, Tanaka Takahara-cho 27, Dakeda
Apartments, he conferred with Song, after discussing
India's independence movement under the leadership of
Chandrabose, that because Joseon's annexation to Japan
is not yet long in history and Japan's power is great, such a
great leader may not appear yet in Joseon; however,
because Joseon's nationalistic awareness is abundant,
they should rise up against Japan when the time comes
and a great leader appears. In so encouraging each other,
he promoted the spirit of independence.

Second, with Matsubara Terutada:

a)   In or about early February of the same year, in Dakeda
Apartments, he criticized abolishing of Joseon language
classes in schools in Joseon and encouraged the above to
study the Joseon language; he also criticized the *naeseon
ilche* policy and emphasized Joseon's independence as the
prerequisite for Joseon people's advancement.

b)   In or about mid-February of the same year, in the same
place, he discussed the employment situation of the
graduates of Joseon schools, pointing out systematic
discrimination against Joseon people and concluding that
independence is the priority for the happiness of Joseon
people.

c)   In late May of the same year, in the same place, he argued
that the Greater East Asian War must be examined
alongside the issue of Joseon's independence, that if they
missed a chance, Joseon would become assimilated into
Japan and not be able to achieve independence, and
that Joseon people must wish for Japan's defeat in war for
Joseon to prosper.

d)   In or about mid-July of the same year, he promoted
nationalistic awareness by emphasizing nationalistic
views on literature that literature must pursue its people's
happiness.

Third, with Jang Seong-eon:

a) In or about late November of 1942, in the same place, he criticized the Government General's arrest of Joseon Linguistic Society members. Asserting that the annihilation of a nation's culture results in its demise, he pointed out that Joseon culture must be promoted.

b) In or about early December of the same year, in the street near Ginkakuji Temple in Sakyo-ku, he condemned individualism, emphasizing that a Joseon person must think beyond his interest and promote Joseon people's collective prosperity.

c) In or about early May of 1943, in the said Dakeda Apartments, he asserted that, despite the superiority of Joseon's classic arts, Joseon culture is currently stagnant and that independence is the only way to enhance Joseon's unique culture.

d) In or about late June of the same year, in the same place, he lent his book *New History of Joseon* to Jang to intensify his nationalistic awareness, encouraging him to study Joseon history.

Thereby, purporting a revolution against the state, the defendant engaged in activities for the goal. Based on the evidence, the facts of the case are admitted by the testimony in the trial court. Pursuant to Article 5 of the Public Order Maintenance Law, the defendant's actions fall under its scope, and the defendant is sentenced to two years' imprisonment, which is within the prison term of the law, and 120 pre-trial detention days are included, allowable by Article 21 of the Criminal Code.

So ordered.

March 31, 1944

Second Criminal Division

Kyoto District Court

Trial Court Judges: Ishii Hirao, Watanabe Tsunehiro, Kawaraya Sueo

EXAMINATION OF THE SENTENCING

Article 5 of the Public Order Maintenance Law applied to the cases sets forth that "a person who organizes a gathering for the purpose of changing the political system of Japan or carries out activities in support of or preparation for the same purpose shall be subject to imprisonment of a minimum of 1 year and a maximum of 10 years."

The statute prescribed that a crime is constituted under the law when activities are accompanied by either of two intentions: (1) to change the political system of Japan, or (2) to deny the private property system. Denying the private property system (communism) was made as serious a crime as conspiracy to overthrow the government. Until Japan's defeat in World War II, this was the will and vision firmly held by imperial Japan's Bureau of Public Order.

The Public Order Maintenance Law, promulgated in 1925 by the Imperial Diet and amended in 1928 and 1941, was applied to various political cases, including Joseon's independence movement cases. Its terms becoming stricter and crueler with each amendment. It was a notoriously bad law, unparalleled by any other Japanese criminal law. Greatly concerned about the use of such expansive and vague terms as "discussion," "instigation," and "propagation" as elements of the crime, some conscientious scholars of criminal law in Japan repeatedly warned that "if the spirit of the law gets lost in its application because of the wording, its mission will fail; thus, it must be interpreted and applied as fairly as other statutes."[27]

Even if "interpreted and applied as fairly as other statutes," the Public Order Maintenance Law was inherently problematic because mere discussion, instigation, and propagation could constitute a crime.

What were the definitions of "discussion" and "instigation"? Case law and common views of the courts defined them as follows:

> "Discussion: Action of two or more persons expressing their opinion with an intent to reach a particular conclusion about an agenda.
> Instigation: Expression of an opinion to stimulate a specified or unspecified group of people so that they would lose the power to judge rationally and make a resolution and/or promote a preexisting resolution."[28]

If such definitions were supported by case law and a common view of the courts, a great question would arise.

Discussion alone could have been sufficient to prosecute not only Song and Yun, who were found guilty and sentenced, but also the other five who appeared in court decisions and Special Police documents. Why were they not prosecuted?

We must first understand Japan's legal culture and customs at the time before trying to answer this question.

Before the Special Police's official record about the arrests was published, some researchers of Yun Dong-ju had expressly doubted whether Yun died in prison because of his Korean independence activities, as his family had attested. This was partly because the official charges against him had not been disclosed, but also because his sentence term was two years of imprisonment. There was a tendency to believe that Yun had been unluckily caught in imperial Japan's excessive regulations and became a passive sacrifice under cliché charges.

This belief may have been the natural result of skepticism prevalent among South Koreans who had been used to the past regime of President Park Chung-hee, which would casually sentence student protesters for democracy to capital punishment, life sentences, or fifteen or twenty years' imprisonment.

However, imperial Japan's judicial system differed from South Korea's. This is clear from the terms of the sentence imposed on various cases for the Korean independence movement. The Japanese judiciary did not impose severe penalties as long as the crime was purely ideological and did not involve physical force. Even in well-known large-scale cases, surprisingly light terms of imprisonment were imposed. This may be rooted in the tradition under the security laws that the maximum term in such cases was limited to two years' imprisonment.

Following are examples of sentences imposed on Korean political prisoners during the thirty-five years of annexation (chronologically recorded):

(1) The Yang Gi-tak Case under the Breach of the Security Law: Applying the Public Order Maintenance Law, the main actors of the case, such as Yang Gi-tak, An Tae-guk, Kim Gu, and Kim Hong-lyang, were each given a maximum of two years' imprisonment.

     Note: During police interrogation, Han Pil-ho was killed as a result of torture. At the same time, Kim Gu and Kim Hong-lyang were falsely found guilty in the so-called An Myeong-geun [brother of Martyr An Jung-geun] Robbery Case (an attempted armed robbery of wealthy Koreans in Anak, Hwanghae-do, to raise money for independence activities). Both Kims were sentenced to fifteen years, resulting in a total sentence of seventeen years.[29]

(2) The Trial of 48 in 1919 (involving the thirty-three representatives of the March First Movement): Applying the Public Order Maintenance Law and Publication Law, a maximum of three years' imprisonment was imposed.

Note: The Gyeongseong District Court, at the first trial, transferred the case to the High Court, stating that "the case belongs to the High Court's jurisdiction because it involves a rebellion." The High Court, however, ruled: "This case is not a rebellion but merely a disturbance of peace under the Public Order Maintenance Law or sedition under the Penal Code; therefore, we do not have jurisdiction and will send it back to the Gyeongseong District Court." Consequently, the Gyeongseong Court of Review tried the case.[30]

(3) The Suyang Association Case (1937): Arrestees of this case were tried for violation of the Public Order Maintenance Law and found not guilty.

Note: During police interrogation, Choe Yun-ho and Yi Gi-yun were killed, and Kim Seon-eop was disabled as the result of torture.[31]

(4) The Joseon Linguistic Society Case (1942): Applying the Public Order Maintenance Law, they sentenced Yi Geuk-ro to six years' imprisonment, Choe Hyeon-bae to four years, and Yi Hui-seung to thirty months. Jang Hyeon-sik was found not guilty.

Note: While waiting for trial, Yi Yun-jae and Han Jing died in jail.[32]

The Japanese judiciary's treatment of "pure" ideological political crimes is clearly different from that of cases involving physical armed forces, as seen in the Yang Gi-tak Case under the breach of the Public Order Maintenance Law. In the case of Kim Gu and Kim Hong-lyang, the main actors of the case, their activities constituted a large-scale independence movement. They planned to establish a command center equivalent to the Japanese governor-general in Seoul, an inspector general to govern the country, and a base in Manchuria to run a military school and produce soldiers for independence war. They selected each province's representative and were in the process of raising the funds when they were arrested. Moreover, they admitted to these facts during the trial. Yet they were sentenced to only two years' imprisonment. On the other hand, both Kims were convicted of armed robbery and sentenced to fifteen years' imprisonment even though they had nothing to do with it.

The same holds true in the cases of the March First Movement leaders. It was a nationwide demonstration with a long-term impact, resulting in public disturbance and countless casualties. Its leaders were deemed to be "agitators of conspiracy and its execution," but their maximum sentence was three years' imprisonment. High-ranking leaders such as Song Jin-u and Hyeon Sang-yun as well as Gil Seon-ju, one of the thirty-three representatives, were found not guilty due to "insufficient evidence." These sentences show that the Japanese courts had stringent standards for the acceptance of evidence.

In light of the countless patriots and innocent Koreans who were killed or disabled as a result of cruel interrogations and torture by the Japanese police and the military police during the thirty-five years of annexation, it is quite surprising that the Japanese judiciary maintained such fairness.

It is said that in the history of Japanese jurisprudence, "Japan established the 'Meiji legal culture' after the Meiji Reformation, having adopted the German legal system in its entirety, especially the Pruisen legal system,"[33] which provides the background of Japan's legal culture. Moreover, it speaks to the level of autonomy and authority the Japanese judiciary had, even under the desperate militaristic system at the time.

In consideration of these facts, it is quite inconceivable that the Japanese court found Song and Yun guilty of political crimes and sentenced them to two years' imprisonment without credible evidence. Ko Hui-uk's stay of prosecution supports this.

Mr. Ko, though literate in Korean, was not proficient in Korean composition, as he had been educated in Japanese-run public schools all his life (his schooling was at Cheolwon Public Elementary School, Gyeonggi Middle School, and Kyoto's Third High School). He stated that during his friendship with Song, he had been very impressed with Song's ability to compose poetry and essays in Korean. Naturally, Ko had written nothing in Korean. Neither did he record anything about their conversations, even though he did express his opinions regarding Korea's independence to Song.

If the letter- of the law were to be followed, Ko's statements could have been sufficient to prove a violation of Article 5 of the Public Order Maintenance Law. However, the prosecutor decided not to prosecute him. While it may be that the prosecutor was lenient because Ko was a student at his alma mater, a better explanation is that he did not have solid evidence against Ko. Even though Ko was released without indictment, he stated that he had suffered so much emotional strain during the Special Police's interrogation that he begged them to release him "even if he had to enlist as a student soldier and go to the battlefield."

The point here is that the sentence of two years' imprisonment that Song and Yun received shows that in light of the Japanese legal culture and climate at the time, there must have been substantial evidence against them to support the charge of a political crime. Mr. Kim Jeong-u stated that when he visited Yun in the police jail, the detective pointed at a high pile of papers and said, "You are doing this out of useless heroism! These are the proof!" Yun's writing must have been used against him at the trial.

Presumably, Song and Yun kept their writing in their possession despite the great danger of keeping "written evidence of pursuing Joseon's independence" because they believed that Japan's defeat in the war was imminent and were preparing for a turning point in history. Both the Special Police's interrogation document and the Kyoto court's decision record mention Song's and Yun's analysis of the failure of the March First Movement and research on the independence movements in Germany, Italy, and India, which further supports this presumption.

Here, special attention should be given to the following: Why did the Criminal Division of the judiciary publish Song's decision in *Ideology Monthly*, and why did the Special Police include their interrogation record in *Special Police Record Monthly*?

It may be because the security bureau found Song's unique views on conscription very dangerous. All other points in Song's decision, such as the nationalistic feelings against imperial Japan's persecution and oppression, the preservation of Korean culture, and the need to promote talent and work power among Koreans, also appear in Yun's decision. Yet Song's decision was selected for the classified publication, while Yun's was not. The only difference between the two documents is Song's views on conscription. Let us now examine this conscription issue.

On May 9, 1942, Japan's Cabinet Council decided that "Japan will enforce a conscription system to our Joseon brethren, effective in the 19th year of Showa (1944)." Under this decision, Directive 24 set forth the governor-general's Committee Rules for the Conscription System, followed by promotion and development work beginning on May 11, 1942. As the work progressed faster than expected, in March 1943 they announced that "Joseon men will be conscripted from August 10, 1943." Most Koreans (aside from the pro-Japanese) were enraged, thinking that conscription would result in Koreans becoming human shields for Japan.

Song's and Yun's thoughts, according to the court's opinion, differed significantly. They welcomed the conscription of Koreans because "Joseon men are not familiar with weapons; by being conscripted, we will gain first-hand knowledge of the military operation, equipped with new weaponry. When Japan is defeated in the Great Asian War, we will have a nationwide military uprising under new leadership. From the nationalistic perspective, we praise the new conscription system because it will enable and empower us to achieve independence." They also encouraged each other to "promote and foster their ability" so that they might contribute to the realization of Joseon's independence.

In the Special Police's interrogation, the same is expressed: "Taking advantage of Japan's weakening power or defeat in war . . . Joseon soldiers must take a great part, and we should be ready to give our life to the cause."

With the conscription of Koreans in the imminent future, this must have sounded like a ridiculous, threatening idea. Against the plan of using Korean men as human shields in Japan's war, viewing it as an opportunity to fight against Japan in an armed uprising must have been a rebellious idea.

It was an idea of Song Mong-gyu, who had left his studies and hometown to enroll in the Korean Provisional Government's military school. And such an idea was not a mere daydream. For instance, General Yi Cheong-cheon, an instructor at Nakyang Military School, was a graduate of the Japanese Army Officers' School and an officer of the Japanese army. During his career as first lieutenant, he defected and joined a military resistance group in China using the knowledge gained from his education and career.

Both the interrogation record and the court decision state that Song Mong-gyu expressed such opinions to Yun Dong-ju and Baek In-jun. Baek, a Rikkyo University student, had only visited Song and Yun once in Kyoto in late April 1943 when they had an outing to Yase Park, and he was not prosecuted. Also, among the seven students who were arrested in this case, the other four who did not discuss conscription but only expressed nationalistic views were not indicted. This also shows that it was Song's opinions about the conscription system that the Japanese government intended to punish as a perilous idea.

The idea of using conscription as a means to achieve Joseon independence was seen as "grave conspiratorial activity by Joseon student intelligentsia" by the Special Police and punished by the court as such, resulting in the none-too-light sentence for a so-called thought offender.

For these reasons, the prosecutor in the case seems to have endeavored to prosecute Song and Yun successfully from the outset while not paying much attention to Ko. For instance, Matsubara Terutada and Jang Seong-eon do not appear in the Special Police's records but are discussed in Yun's decision, the evidence of which must have been produced from the prosecutor's investigation for the sole purpose of providing evidence against Yun. (Both individuals were not legally implicated.)

As such, the issue of conscription of Koreans was at the root of the case, which led both Song and Yun to their death.

Because of his arrest and involvement in the case, Ko Hui-uk failed his senior year in Third High School. What happened with Song's and Yun's matriculation after their arrest, trial, and imprisonment?

Let us examine Song's case. Kyoto Imperial University had meticulous recordkeeping. On March 23, 1944, one month and one day after Song's indictment on February 22, 1944, the school suspended him indefinitely. On May 18, 1944—again, one month and one day after the April 17 sentencing—the school ordered expulsion. As both decisions were effective exactly one month and one day after each event, it seems that the university had paid close attention to the cases.

Doshisha University, on the other hand, was not only lax about it but also inaccurate. Yun's student record there shows that he continued to attend school, even after his arrest. For instance, he was supposed to have "completed again one year of literature classes in September 1943." Such inaccurate recording continued until December 24, 1948, when "the board decided to expel [Yun] for lack of attendance and/or failure to pay tuition."

Imprisonment: Fukuoka Prison

As stated earlier, Yun and Song were tried in the Kyoto trial court and sentenced to imprisonment on April 1 and April 17, 1944, respectively. When were they moved to Fukuoka Prison, their final abode in life?

To date, no record of their transfer has been found. If the usual process were followed, it must have been immediately after the sentencing.

Fukuoka Prison is located at 108 Nishiaramachi, Fukuoka, Sawara-ku, about one kilometer from Hakada Bay, where the Yuen (Mongol) fleet, assisted by the Koryeo kingdom, invaded Japan (in A.D. 1274—Trans.). Geographically, it is a Japanese prison closest to Korea.

Ibuki Gou guesses at the reason for their transfer to Fukuoka Prison:

They were arrested and tried in Kyoto. Why were they sent to Fukuoka Prison? What was waiting for them?

Chronicles of the Prison Terms Carried Out during Wartime, a 1,600-page tome published in 1966, contains "Schedule of Reserved Detention Cases (May 15, 1941–May 31, 1945)" which notes, "Kumamoto and Fukuoka are for Joseon independence movement cases." In other words, did they have a policy to send those found guilty of independence-movement-related offenses to Kumamoto and Fukuoka?[34]

At any rate, Yun and Song began to serve their terms at Fukuoka. The terms were to last until November 30, 1945, for Yun and until April 12, 1946, for Song. All prisoners had their heads shaved and wore red prison uniforms; Yun and Song were no exception.

Their sentence was "prison labor," which is different from mere imprisonment without forced labor. Regular prisoners were assigned woodwork and other factory work, which they worked on together in the prison. Political prisoners in solitary confinement, on the other hand, were given solitary assignments, and they had to finish the quota given to them each day.

All political prisoners in Japan at that time were subject to solitary confinement. Each cell was a windowless room. Presumably, this was to prevent the dissemination of "subversive ideas," but to prisoners, it was a doubly cruel punishment, blocking any human contact. In such a painful environment they had to perform forced labor, which included weaving casting nets, gluing envelopes, and sewing cotton work gloves.

Kim Gwang-seop, the famous poet who served a two-year term as a political prisoner in the Seodaemun Prison in Seoul beginning in 1942, stated that he had to weave casting nets in solitary confinement. In his book *My Prison Diary,* he remembers the experience as follows:

The room had the same dimensions as that of the detention house. The only thing that belonged to me there was my face. Its door never opened, night or day.

I would have gladly worked, but there was no work at first, let alone a book to read. Work was given as punishment, but having nothing to do was also punishment. A month later, I was given work weaving fish nets with silk thread. One stitch, two stitches—as my fingers were chapped and aching, I wondered who would use these to catch fish in the cold river?[35]

In such a room where a faint ten-watt lightbulb was on all day and all night, the so-called political prisoners were forced to do this kind of work. Just imagining their suffering brings the sensation of swallowing a lump of live coal.

Professor Yun Il-ju's writing also sheds light on Yun Dong-ju's prison life:

Sending a postcard written in Japanese was allowed once a month, from which it is difficult to see what went on there. I remember, however, sending him a copy of the English-Japanese bilingual New Testament upon request. I also remember writing to him, "I feel the approach of autumn as the sound of a cricket accompanies the tip of my pen," to which he replied, "I am grateful that your crickets chirp away in my solitary cell, too." He must have counted the days to write home; at the beginning of each month, a postcard filled with tiny prints the size of sesame seeds would arrive. Some sentences were blacked out in ink by prison guards. I could glimpse that some of them were descriptions of forced labor; other parts were completely redacted.[36]

From these descriptions, we can deduce the following about the rules of Fukuoka Prison and Yun's prison life:

1. A postcard written in Japanese by the prisoner was allowed once a month to his family.
2. Reading the Bible was allowed. Yun's specific request that the English-Japanese bilingual New Testament be sent tells us that he wanted to practice reading in English as well.
3. Yun was in solitary confinement.
4. Yun had to work in prison and wrote about it to his family, but such communication with the outside world was prohibited.
5. All writing was censored, and prohibited contents were redacted.

Yet despite these conditions, Yun heeded the chirping of a cricket and was thankful for it, writing, "I am grateful that your crickets chirp away in my solitary cell, too." He was "grateful"; even though he was being treated as subhuman by the treacherous regime, his generous and noble character was not marred by it. He wanted to "love all those / dying" with "a heart that sings the stars," and that was how his spirit stayed pure while enduring the wretched conditions.

The prison labor was harsh. According to Yun Hye-won, upon the death notice, Yun's father and uncle went to Fukuoka Prison to collect the body and any personal effects, which consisted of a bag of clothes he had worn in prison. Examining them, Yun's mother moaned deeply, saying, "They must have put him to so much work that his clothes were worn out in such odd ways." She was holding a thermal undershirt whose left sleeve and left chest area were particularly worn out. Strands from the cloth and small holes were visible, implying that Yun had to use the left side of his body even though he was not left-handed. What kind of work caused a shirt to wear out that way?

During his prison term, no one visited him. His family mailed some food from time to time, as noted by Professor Yun Il-ju: "After Uncle [Yun Yeong-chun] saw him in Kyoto in the fall of 1943, no one was able to see him until after his death on February 16, 1945. My heart aches thinking about his loneliness in the prison far, far away. Mother would sometimes prepare roasted grain powder and taffy and mail them, but there was no way to know whether he received them."[37]

Yun probably never received them. Prison regulations prohibited personal food made outside, for it could be used for poisoning, as a means of illegal communication, or to cause other potential problems.

Song, on the other hand, had one visit. When Yun's father and uncle came to gather Yun's body, they requested a visit with Song. This was the only time Song met with anyone he knew since his arrest by the Special Police on July 10, 1943.

The wretched condition Song was in was described by Yun Yeong-chun. Song had on "a pair of half-broken glasses" and was "unrecognizable because he was just skin and bones." How were his glasses broken? Did he drop them? Was he beaten? Whatever the cause, he had to get by with half-broken glasses. Like blood oozing out from a wound, they speak to the hardship, humiliation, suffering, and inhumane treatment he endured in Fukuoka Prison.

Death: February 16, 1945

Yun's life ended in Fukuoka Prison on February 16, 1945, at 3:36 A.M.

He was just twenty-seven years and two months old. It was nineteen months and two days after his arrest and three years and one month after his lamentation, "I abridged my confessions into one line. / —Twenty-four years and one month: / What kind of joy did I hope for?"

A young Japanese prison guard who was present at his death told his family that Yun "shrieked a high-pitched cry as he died."

The high-pitched shriek at death—what was it? His whole life, his whole heart, his whole joy and sorrow, his whole desire, his whole suffering, his whole love, his whole yearning and lamentation, his whole everything . . . All of these became one shriek, which was shouted out to the world. He could not close his eyes without that last shriek. Grief-stricken, he departed.

A big question remains. Yun was young and healthy, and enjoyed exercise and walking. Why did he die within a year of his prison term at Fukuoka? What was the cause of his death?

Yun's uncle Yun Yeong-chun, who went to Fukuoka Prison with Yun's father to collect the body, left a critical statement:

I heard of Dong-ju's death while I was in Xinjing. By the time Yeong-seok [Yun's father] and I arrived at Fukuoka Prison, ten days had passed since Dong-ju's death. As Mong-gyu was in the same prison, we requested to see him. We thought we'd see the living first and the dead later.

As we waited for the visitation paperwork to be processed, I saw "Independence Movement" written in Chinese characters on the document relating to their case. As we entered the prison, the guard warned us that we must talk with Mong-gyu in Japanese and be composed, avoiding any talk about current affairs. As we passed the corridor, we saw about 50 Korean men in their twenties in prison uniforms. They were lined up for shots before the dispensary.

Mong-gyu ran to me. He was wearing a pair of half-broken glasses. At first, he was unrecognizable because he was just skin and bones. He greeted, "How were you able to come?" and his voice sounded as if from another world. He mumbled something I couldn't hear, and I said, "How'd you end up like this!" He muttered, "I'm like this because they gave me shots, and Dong-ju, too. . . ." Of course, it was said in Korean. He grabbed my wrists. His hands were hot. I thought of the time taking a walk with him in Ueno Park in Tokyo. As I thought of losing him in such a place, tears kept flowing from my eyes, and my heart was filled with indignation. I couldn't talk anymore. We were told that time was up, so we left the place. This was the last time I saw him. (He died a week later.)

We went to the morgue. When the lid was opened, it seemed as if Dong-ju was pleading to me: "How could this happen?" Ten days had passed since his death, but the body had not decomposed because Kyushu Imperial University people embalmed it. A young Japanese guard who accompanied us said sympathetically, "Dong-ju was a gentle person. I couldn't understand what he said, but he shrieked a high-pitched cry as he died."[38]

Over the years, this statement was deemed very important for two reasons: first, the crime listed on Song's document was "independence movement"; and second, both Yun and Song were subject to "shots" administered by the prison.

The statement regarding "independence movement" proved to be accurate, as the court's judgment record published thirty years after Song's death revealed that the "Joseon independence movement" was the crime of which Song and Yun were both convicted.

As for the second point—that Song's and Yun's cause of death was the shots administered by the prison—it has not been officially proven. It is only strongly presumed that Song and Yun were subjected to biomedical experiments. Owing to the nature of the case, however, it is nearly impossible to prove now. It is inconceivable that any documents pertaining to the heinous crime of conducting biomedical experiments on live humans still exist. Nor would any involved individual volunteer such information. Reverend Ra Sa-haeng also stated to me: "It was right after liberation. Mr. Yun Yeong-chun came to see me. He asked me to accompany him to look for Dong-ju's boarding house in North Ahyeon-dong. He said he wanted to get Dong-ju's books and possessions left there when Dong-ju left for Japan. We couldn't find it, actually. But while looking for the house, he told me about what happened when he went to find Dong-ju's body in Fukuoka. Mong-gyu told him that they were forced to get injections. Even though Mong-gyu said, 'I won't get them,' they told him, 'You must.'"[39]

In 1980, a Japanese scholar attempted to construct a concrete theory on Japan's live human biomedical experiments. The scholar was Mr. Konoo Eichi, who was studying Korean literature at Dongguk University Graduate

School after graduating from Chuo University in Japan. He stated that the "unidentified injections" that Yun received might have been plasma-replacing saline solution, which was being experimented with at Kyushu Imperial University at the time.[40]

Chronicles of the Prison Terms Carried Out during Wartime, cited earlier, contains a statistical report on "The Number of Deaths in Individual Prisons (from 1943 to January 1946)." Fukuoka Prison had 64 deaths in 1943, 131 deaths in 1944, and 259 deaths in 1945.[41] The death rate doubled each year; such an increase is not normal. One possible explanation is that a large-scale biomedical experiment was being done to the prisoners at Fukuoka at the time.[42]

Ms. Yun Hye-won described her father and uncle's trip to Fukuoka Prison as follows:

> After Father and Uncle returned with my brother's remains, our relatives paid respects and listened to their stories about Fukuoka Prison. Father and Uncle said, the clerk told them when they arrived at the prison, "Just in time. No one claimed the body for so long that we were about to send it to Kyushu Imperial University. But because of the gasoline shortage, the car wasn't here yet." Kyushu University was going to take the body for dissection practice. Father and Uncle could not be there earlier because of all the paperwork that delayed them.
>
> Father was shocked by how terrible Mong-gyu looked. He dropped on the corridor floor and wailed. Mong-gyu looked like a bag of bones with skin hanging, and his jawbone was protruding, he said. Uncle tried to comfort Father, but after Father stopped crying, Uncle started wailing. When they went to the morgue, they saw many, many coffins. They didn't know whether they were all filled with corpses or not. When they opened Dong-ju's coffin, they saw the body preserved by the Kyushu University Medical School. There was no sign of decomposition and no wounds either.
>
> Father added that Dong-ju had a clean, white shroud on, but I think he lied so that Mother would feel better. Why would the prison put a white shroud on the body.[43]

Song's last days were indescribably wretched. His two relatives broke down in tears after their visit because he was not even recognizable. Yet he was still receiving injections. He knew the injections had already killed his friend and cousin Dong-ju. He knew he was dying, yet he was forced into it. What must have passed through his mind?

Nine days after the visit, on March 7, 1945, Song passed away. Even after Dong-ju's tragic death, Song survived just a little longer to leave testimony about the cause of their death. There is an old Korean expression that when one is egregiously wronged, "one can't close his eyes even at death." When Song's father arrived to claim the body, he saw that Song's eyes were wide open. Mr. Song Chang-hui closed his son's eyes.

Here Lies Yun Dong-ju the Poet

How did the families of Yun Dong-ju and Song Mong-gyu in North Gando hear of their deaths? What happened afterward?

Homecoming

Professor Yun Il-ju remembered:

A postcard from Dong-ju would come by the fifth of each month, but we had not received any by mid-February 1945. It was a Sunday when a telegram arrived. Everyone was in church, and it was just me and my younger brother at home that morning. The telegram read, "Dong-ju died February 16, collect the body." I rushed to church. I came back home with my family and was soon joined by others after the service ended. The house became a place of wake without the deceased. A messenger was sent to my mother, who had been out of town, to bring her home. We were overwhelmed with grief as well as worries. Not only was it a long way from North Gando to Fukuoka, but crossing the Tsushima Strait (now Korea Strait) was very dangerous because of frequent bombing attacks from Americans. Bombing in the mainland of Japan was severe as well. Moreover, the proper paperwork and passport were extremely difficult to obtain. Worried about the safety, others suggested that Father send someone else, but he was determined to go himself. Sending our grief-stricken father off, we were filled with both grief and anxiety. Father first stopped in Xinjing to meet with Uncle Yeong-chun, and the two of them left for Fukuoka via Andong.

After Father left, a notice arrived by mail from the prison. It was a pre-printed form on which necessary instructions were added. It stated, "Dong-ju in critical condition. May be released on bail. In case of death, collect the body. Otherwise, the corpse will be donated to Kyushu Imperial University for dissecting purposes. Reply ASAP." It recorded the cause of illness as cerebral hemorrhage. Even considering that mail would take up to four days to reach us, we could not understand why the notice arrived ten days after his death. Couldn't they have notified us earlier so that we could do something about it? Again, we broke down in tears.

As soon as they arrived in Fukuoka, Father and Uncle went to see Mong-gyu. He was standing in line to get injections when he saw them. He started crying, uttering, "Dong-ju!" He was extremely emaciated. Later, a Japanese guard informed Father and Uncle that Dong-ju had cried out something loudly before breathing his last. When they brought a handful of ashes that had been Dong-ju, we went all the way to Sangsambong Station to receive them. The station was in Korean territory by the Tumen River, about 50 miles from Yongjeong. From there, I took the ashes from my father's arms and crossed the bridge over Tumen on foot. It was frigid and overcast that day. The bridge seemed infinitely long. We kept silent, with pent-up anger deep in our hearts. On that bridge, Dong-ju bid the final farewell to his beloved Korea.

His funeral was held in early March (I cannot remember the date clearly) in the front yard of our home. There was a big snowstorm. Two of his poems, "Self-Portrait" and "A New Road," were recited. They had been published in a school magazine *Munu* before his graduation from Yonhui. The burial place was Yongjeong's East Hill. The ground would be frozen until April in Gando, so we went back there on a warm day in May to lay sod and plant flowers. Around the Dan-o Festival [May 5 in the Lunar calendar—Trans.], Grandfather and Father placed a large tombstone with the inscription "Here Lies Yun Dong-ju the Poet." It was the first time Dong-ju was called a poet by his father and grandfather. An epitaph was composed and calligraphed by a gentleman named Haesa Kim Seok-gwan. The entire epitaph was in Chinese characters, about 300 characters. At that time, the fact that Dong-ju had died in prison could not be revealed. Instead, Mr. Kim used the metaphor of a caged bird that prematurely died. My heart ached as I observed Father and Grandfather standing and caressing the tombstone as the masons worked on it. The grandson and son, now lost forever, they'd never forget. Mong-gyu's death followed within 20 days, on March 10, and the process, including the notice by mail, was similar to Dong-ju's. Mong-gyu was buried in a place called Dailazi in Gando's Helong County.[1]

Ms. Yun Hye-won has more detailed and sorrowful memories of the circumstances, revealing the pain of the family members like a fresh-cut wound.

At the time of Yun's death, Ms. Yun was staying at the Songs' home in Dailazi, the capital city of Helong County. It was about ten miles from Yongjeong toward Hoeryeong. Mong-gyu's father, Song Chang-hui, a former teacher at Myeongdong School and superintendent of a grade school in the area, was a local official in Dailazi then. His wife, Yun Shin-yeong, doted on her niece Hye-won. After Hye-won graduated from Myeongshin Girls' High School, Yun Shin-yeong asked her to stay in their home while she worked as a grade school teacher in Dailazi, and Hye-won had been living there since the summer of 1944. She described the day when the news reached her: "It was a Friday when Dong-ju died. The telegraph arrived at home two days later, on a Sunday. The news did not come to me until the next morning."[2]

She was in the kitchen with her aunt, preparing breakfast before going to work, when a relative of hers who worked in transportation came to see them. He had a telephone at his place, a precious item at the time. She greeted him happily, but he hesitantly delivered the message: "Dong-ju's dead." He had received a telephone call from Yongjeong.

Hye-won recalled, "Ah! I was speechless. My uncle and aunt and me, the three of us dropped down and wailed. How much did we cry!"

While remembering that day, her eyes became moist, filling with sorrow as if it had happened yesterday. "I ran straight home without giving thought to going to work. The whole place was like a sea of tears. Many people from church were there trying to comfort us."[3]

At home, Ms. Yun heard about the telegram from the day before. Her mother had been out of town to help with a relative's wedding feast, and her grandfather had been lying in his room because of his arthritis. Only her randmother and father had gone to church. Shocked by the news, Il-ju showed the telegram to his grandfather and then dashed to church, about two-thirds of a mile away, to pull his father out of the sanctuary.

The telegram stated that the body should be claimed. Her father decided to go first to Xinjing to pick up her uncle Yun Yeong-chun, then head to Japan together. She continued: "But we were surprised by Grandfather. He loved Dong-ju so much, but he was against Father going to Japan to bring the body back. 'The dead is dead. What if something happens to you on the way? Do not go. You are my only son.'"4

It was true that the journey to Japan was dangerous because of America's air raids in Japan, but many people still made trips back and forth. Nevertheless, this white-haired elderly man wanted to stop his middle-aged son from going to Japan because he was his "only son." Here, we can imagine the shock Mr. Yun Ha-hyeon received from Dong-ju's death. He was terrified of the leviathan called Japan, who plucked the young, healthy, beloved life and swallowed it like hair. It was a shock accompanied by real fear, fear great enough to want to give up the remains of his eldest grandson, the apple of his eye. Is the size of one's love proportional to the size of one's shock at its loss? How wretched is it to live through it?

Despite Yun Ha-hyeon's misgivings, Hye-won's father set out: "Father and Uncle took the body and had it cremated at the Fukuoka crematory. They spread some of the ashes on a quiet beach facing the Tsushima Strait and said a prayer. The remaining ashes they put in a porcelain bowl placed in a small wooden box as a symbolic gesture. They said Dong-ju's face was graceful as if he was asleep."5

Yun's funeral was held in the front yard of his home on March 6, 1945. They obtained a coffin and placed in it the wooden box containing Yun's ashes. Reverend Mun Jae-rin of Yongjeong Central Presbyterian Church, the family's church, oversaw the funeral. What made the funeral special was the reciting of Yun's two poems, "Self-Portrait in the Well" and "A New Road."

Ms. Yun Hye-won received a deep impression of her mother during the funeral: "My mother was a benevolent, patient person who was also very strong. During the day, she'd keep busy with all the preparation. In the middle of the night, when everyone was asleep, she'd go to the coffin, caress it, and weep silently."6

Yun's mother did not wail loudly and only wept silently when no one was around during the funeral preparations because she was in the presence of her elderly parents-in-law. Korean customs dictated that a young person's death not be wailed over before the elders. Mrs. Kim Shin-muk, who was present, had a sad story to tell.

The telegram announcing Yun's death had arrived when Yun's mother was at a relative's house. A messenger was sent to bring her home, but the news of

Yun's death was not given to her until she arrived home. Not knowing what had happened, she entered the room filled with grave-faced people and asked, "What happened? Is Grandfather not well?"

Because of her frail health, they were concerned to tell her of her son's death. Yet she looked unperturbed, surprising those around her. She did not cry in front of the others while waiting for the ashes. When her husband returned, she oversaw all the preparations for the funeral, performing her role as the daughter-in-law of the eldest clan leader.

"But sometime after the funeral, when she was doing laundry, she saw a white dress shirt belonging to Dong-ju. She couldn't stand it anymore. She broke down and wailed and wailed. She couldn't stop."[7]

The burial was on March 6. Yun was buried in the church cemetery belonging to Central Presbyterian Church in Yongjeong's East Hill.

Some records say that Yun was "buried in the East Hill church cemetery." This is inaccurate. There were several churches in Yongjeong, three of which were Presbyterian: Central Church, East Hill Church, and Toseongbo Church. Yun's family church was Central Presbyterian, whose cemetery was in East Hill, and that is where Yun was buried. At that time, a body was buried next to the previous one, regardless of gender, age, and status. Even family members would be buried apart from one another unless they died at the same time, adhering to the idea that all Christians are a family.

On the day of burial, snow was falling heavily as if jealous of the imminent spring. It chilled the hearts of those burying Dong-ju's ashes.

Death of Song Mong-gyu

March 7, 1945. The day after Yun's funeral was held in Yongjeong, a telegram arrived announcing the death of Song Mong-gyu.

Song's family wept bitterly. The sorrow and mortification of Song's family were even worse than those of Yun's, as bitter as their feelings were. Yun's family had been waiting for the day of Yun's release from the faraway prison when they were shocked by the news of his death. In Song's case, they had heard of Song's conditions from Yun's father and uncle, who reported that the emaciated Song was dying, having been forced to get mysterious injections. They had been worried sick, without being able to do anything, when the news reached them. Their mortification was indescribable.

The news affected Song's mother in the worst way. Song's friends had often said what a pleasure it was to visit him at home because his mother was such a caring, doting mother. The son she had loved so much and given so much attention to was now gone at such a young age, and under such horrifying circumstances. Mrs. Kim Shin-muk remembered the day like this: "She collapsed on the ground and wailed. She was suffocating with grief. She pounded on her chest and wailed so much that later on, we saw her chest was bruised black and blue. Our hearts were bleeding alongside hers."

While Mrs. Song's bitter tears were flowing over her eldest son's death, Mr. Song Chang-hui went to collect his son's corpse and cremate it in the Fukuoka crematory.

Mr. Kim Jeong-u said that when he returned home from school in the summer of 1945, others told him about Song's funeral, and it left a deep impression on him. After Song's body was cremated in Fukuoka, the remaining bones were ground in front of Mr. Song Chang-hui. Some powder from the bones spattered to the ground, and Mr. Song, uttering, "Even a speck of my son's bone cannot be left in the enemy's land!" collected the soil upon which the powder landed and brought it with the rest to bury at home.[8] The same story was told to Ms. Yun Hye-won and Mrs. Kim Shin-muk.

What does this signify? In the end, Mr. Song ended up burying his son's ashes and ground-up bones along with the soil of the enemy land, resulting in Song's remains resting forever in Japanese soil. How deeply profound can one's indignation and resentment be! The gravity of Mr. Song's resentment was proportional to the degree of loss he suffered.

Because Mr. Song had never been to Japan and did not speak Japanese, unlike Yun's father and uncle, he took Song's second cousin Song Hui-gyu with him to claim the corpse.

They went to the morgue in Fukuoka Prison and saw Song's coffin. Song, with an unkempt beard and an emaciated face, lay there with his eyes open. Kyushu University had also injected preservatives into the body, hoping to use it for dissecting purposes, and the body was not yet decomposed. Strangely, Song had a beard even though the prisoners were not allowed to grow them. Were they observing how facial hair affects the body while Song was being experimented on with injections?

Mr. Song Chang-hui closed his son's eyes, saying, "I am here. You can close your eyes now." Song's body was moved to the crematory in Fukuoka.

Ms. Yun Hye-won recalled: "Uncle [Mr. Song Chang-hui—Trans.] brought all of Mong-gyu's ashes, unlike my father. He had a dream the night before, he said. Mong-gyu appeared to him and said, 'Not even a speck of my bone should be left in the enemy's land!' So he even collected the dirt around where the bones were ground up and brought it back. The box containing the ashes was larger and longer, too. When someone commented, 'It is heavy,' Uncle replied, 'Yes, bones are supposed to be heavy.'"9

Song's ashes were buried in the hill of Jangjaechon in Myeongdong Village, where the family used to live.

Yun and Song expired just like that. They had a deep love for their people and culture and an even deeper sense of responsibility for their fatherland's future. Having given their all, they were sacrificed to the cause of resisting inhumane violence—violence by a nation that stole the soul and spirit of another to satisfy its greed, morphing the other nation into a phantom. They were buried under the sky of North Gando that bore and raised them. Six months later, just as Yun and Song had expected, as recorded in the Special Police's interrogation papers, Japan was defeated and surrendered the war it had started.

On May 20, 1945, when the ground thawed, Mr. Song Chang-hui raised a tombstone that read: "Here Rests Song Mong-gyu, a young writer." Yun's family likewise put up a tombstone, "Here Lies Yun Dong-ju the Poet."

It was rare that descriptions like "young writer" or "poet" were attached to the name on tombstones at the time. These families must have been expressing their deep love for their beloved and grief over their untimely death in this way.

The tombstones were raised before Japan's defeat, and it was a time of savage wartime, ridden with frantic last-ditch efforts by Japan. In light of that, these tombstones are even more moving.

They had endured the humiliation of changing their Korean names to Japanese names in order to pursue higher education in Japan so that they could contribute to Korea's independence. Yet they returned home as cold ashes after their wretched prison sentences killed them. They only regained their true names after death, written on their tombstones by their fathers.

Speaking of Japanese names, a clarification should be made. The telegram sent to notify the family of Yun's death was not quoted correctly by Professor Yun Il-ju, who stated that it read, "Dong-ju died February 16, collect the body." In fact, it must have said "Hiranuma Doojyu died February 16, collect the body." An official notice of death issued by a government agency would not have listed only the first name. Likewise, Song's death notice would have been: "Somura Mugei died March 7, collect the body."

Previously, Professor Yun Il-ju confided with me: "I didn't want to reveal that Dong-ju changed his name, but when *Special Police Monthly* records and others became public, it had to be let known."

However, the poem "Confessions" was written when Yun decided to register his Japanese name and must be read in that context. The lines "Tomorrow or the day after, on a happy day, / I have to write another line of confessions. / —At that young age, / Why did I make such shameful confessions?" form a painful confession. In that sense, poetry is a kind of prophecy.

How the Tomb of Song Mong-gyu Was Found

Here, a special matter must be pointed out. In 1990, confusion and misinformation about the time of Song's death and the burial site were corrected.

Until then, Professor Yun Il-ju's statement that "Song died on March 10, 1945, and his remains were buried in Dailaji where his family resided, with a tombstone that read 'Here Rests Song Mong-gyu, a Young Writer'" was accepted.

However, in 1989, when some Korean Chinese leaders in Yanbian Korean Autonomous Prefecture (formerly North Gando) went to look for the site, they confirmed that no such tomb existed there. After the liberation of Korea, Mr. Song Chang-hui worked for a while as the superintendent of Jishin Middle School in Yanbian, but in early 1948, he and his family moved to North Korea. None of Song's relatives live in Yanbian now, and it was not possible to find out where Song's tomb was.

Those searching for Song's tomb suspected that Professor Yun's statement might be incorrect and asked the surrounding educational organizations and senior citizens' organizations for assistance. They asked the students and senior citizens to look for a tombstone that said, "Here Rests Song Mong-gyu, a Young Writer" and notify them if it was found.

Soon, someone reported that such a tombstone was sighted on the hill of Jangjaechon in Myeongdong Village. When a team was sent there, they found the tombstone knocked over near a tomb on a gentle slope. It was the middle of winter, and the felled tombstone was frozen on the ground. The site indeed turned out to be a Song clan plot where six Song members were buried.

However, there was confusion because the tombstone was about fifteen feet away from a tomb at the bottom of the hill. Which tomb was this tombstone for? For this, the opinions of the residents were divided.

Three men pointed at the tomb farther up from the tombstone. They speculated that about five years previously, grazing bulls had fought there, and the tombstone was knocked over and ended up below. But an eighty-four-year-old woman with a shaking head claimed that the tombstone belonged to the tomb fifteen feet away but fell one year. Neither party was yielding. When the ground thawed in spring, they dug out both tombs and discovered that the tomb at the bottom was Song's. Afterward, it was decided that Song's ashes be relocated next to Yun's tomb on the hill in Yongjeong. The following recounts the details.

On April 5, 1990, the traditional Tomb Sweeping Day, a number of Yanbian community leaders and residents climbed the hill of Jangjaechon. Mr. Yu Gi-cheon, former superintendent of Yongjeong Middle School who initiated the Song Mong-gyu's Tomb Search Project, opened an earlier edition of this book before they began digging the site. He announced, "According to this book, not only his ashes but the dirt from Japan were buried together. Only if the coffin contains dirt mixed in with bone waste, it is the tomb of Song Mong-gyu!"

They first dug at the tomb farther up on the hill. When they noticed a large coffin rather than a small one intended for ashes, they stopped digging and covered it up again. The three men who originally argued that the tomb was Song's now pointed at a different tomb beside it. They started digging again, but the same thing happened. The three wanted another one nearby to be dug, but the rest of the group did not agree.

Instead, they started digging at the tomb fifteen feet away from the tombstone. Soon, a small coffin was found. Four layers of *botchi* covered the coffin,[10] evidence of a careful and caring burial. When the *botchi* was removed, a coffin made of red pine, one of the best materials, appeared. When they opened the lid, a white porcelain jar was revealed. On one side of the coffin was a small pile of dirt mixed with bone waste. Mr. Yu cried out:

"Look! It's just as written in the book! This is the tomb of Mr. Song Mong-gyu!"

When I visited Yanbian in 1992, Mr. Yu guided me to the site of Song's original tomb. Listening to the story of its discovery, I lowered my head and cried for a long time.

On the day they found the coffin, they removed it to Yongjeong and, after preparing a new burial site near Yun's tomb, buried it there. Thus, Song's ashes are now interred near Yun's in the Yongjeong hill.

The tombstone also corrected the date of Song's death. Song was known to have died on March 10. The tombstone, however, recorded the date as March 7. Mr. Song Chang-hui's friend Mr. Haesa Kim Seok-gwan composed and calligraphed the epitaph. Mr. Kim also did the same for Yun's tombstone. Song and Yun even shared the same writer for their tombstones; their lives were interwoven to the last.

Mr. Kim Seok-gwan was one of the five, including Yun's father, who went to Beijing to study. After returning from Beijing, he taught at Myeongdong School alongside Yun's father. He was good at Chinese composition as well as calligraphy. Thus, for his friends' sons, he composed the epitaphs in Chinese and calligraphed them. Yun's epitaph reads as follows:

Ah! The deceased poet Yun Dong-ju's family clan is Papyeong. After graduating from Myeongdong Grade School, he entered Helong Prefecture's First District School. He studied for three years at Eunjin Middle School in Yongjeong and then transferred to Sungshil Middle School in Pyeongyang for one year. He returned to Yongjeong and finished Gwangmyeong's Middle School program with outstanding grades. In 1938, he entered Yonhui Junior College's literature department. He spent four winters there and graduated. Even after that, he yearned to study further, and in the following April went to Japan and studied at Doshisha University's literature department in Kyoto. But who knew! Even in the ocean of learning, great waves hit him. He lost his freedom and became a caged bird. An illness was added, and he passed away on February 16, 1945, at the age of twenty-eight. His talent was abundant, his fame as a poet was about to come, but the cruel spring wind was merciless. Flowers bloomed but no fruit was born. How regrettable! He was Elder Ha-hyeon's grandson and Mr. Yeong-seok's son. He was intelligent and enjoyed learning. He composed many new-style poems, and his pen name was Dong-ju.[11]

June 14, 1945

Composed and calligraphed by Haesa Kim Seok-gwan
Erected by younger brothers Il-ju and Gwang-ju.

[Translation from Chinese into Korean by the author]

CHAPTER 11

The Glory of the National Poet

A Flower in Frigid January

"A flower in frigid January, a carp under the ice."

THIS IS WHAT the great sensualist poet Jeong Ji-yong said of Yun Dong-ju. Of course, this was in 1947, after Korea's liberation from imperial Japan's menacing chains. Jeong was the first to read Yun's poetry, aside from Yun's relatives and friends, and recognize its greatness. As a poet who had first-hand experience of imperial Japan's horrifying fetters, Jeong was deeply moved after reading Yun's poems and hearing about Yun's short and genuine life, and Jeong summarized his assessment of the poet in the one exquisite phrase.

Nowadays, magnificent hothouse-grown flowers fill the shop windows even in the severe January weather; carp swim leisurely in the farming pool, exposing their massive backs. Perhaps the contemporary reader cannot fathom the vivid metaphor in Jeong's praise for Yun.

But imagine the Korea of 1947. A flower that blooms under the severe temperatures of frigid January is a miracle and carries the grace of God in itself; a carp that moves leisurely about in icy water under a thick plate of ice is an awe-inspiring being.

Though time passes, words remain. But sometimes a word's sensitivity changes as time goes by, just as a highly polished silver pot with a beautiful luster becomes gradually tarnished in the china cabinet. When thinking of this, one cannot help feeling wistful.

Three steps are necessary for poetry and poets to exist:

1. First, composition of poems.
2. Second, dissemination of the poems.
3. Third, recognition of the poems' value with due credit

Out of the three, the only step completed in Yun's lifetime was the first. The second and third steps were left for others after his death.

Today, the term "national poet" usually accompanies Yun's name. In order to discuss Yun Dong-ju the poet, we must also discuss his family and friends who remained behind and did their share of work for his poems. This way, we can draw a complete picture of the poet.

Let us travel back to the time of liberation.

On August 15, 1945, the Japanese emperor, who was regarded as a living god by the Japanese people, announced on the air with a trembling voice Japan's unconditional surrender. With this, the curtain fell, and its long wars against America, China, and others ended. If counted from the time of the Mukden incident, it was fifteen years of invasions that ended in the demise of imperial Japan.

What happened to Japan afterward?

On August 30, 1945, the occupation forces led by U.S. Army General MacArthur moved in. From September 2, when the official surrender documents were signed, Japan was under the rule of the American occupation forces.

On October 4, the MacArthur headquarters ordered the abolition of various laws that oppressed human rights, including the Public Order Maintenance Law, and on October 6, it disbanded the infamous Special Police. On October 15, the Public Order Maintenance Law was officially abolished. Special Police officers were laid off and became unemployed.

The Public Order Maintenance Law lasted twenty years, from its creation by the Imperial Diet in 1925 until its abolition in 1945 following the collapse of imperial Japan. During those twenty years, it became the means and tools through which Japan's imperialism committed various wrongdoings under the pretext of "protecting its political system." Its countless victims, sacrificed under this evil law's razor-sharp blade, included Yun Dong-ju and Song Mong-gyu.

The effect of imperial Japan's destruction also rushed in quickly to North Gando. Manchukuo, a puppet state of Japan, disappeared. The Soviet forces entered Manchuria in order to disarm the Japanese and the Manchukuo forces. After the Soviet forces left, North Gando was returned to China and placed under the communist regime.

As days of violent upheaval came and went, Yun's family observed the first anniversary of Yun's death on February 16, 1946. They prepared various dishes and sweet rice drinks as if they were having a wedding reception.

In June 1946, Yun's younger brother Yun Il-ju, then age eighteen, left for the south by himself. The rest of the family—grandparents, parents, Hye-won, and Gwang-ju—remained in North Gando. Arriving in Seoul, Yun Il-ju looked for his brother's friends to find out information about him. First, Gang Cheo-jung handed him some items that he had kept for Yun, such as his books, his Yonhui College senior yearbook, and a portable desk. Yun Il-ju also met Jeong Byeong-uk. This meeting turned out to be very important, as Yun's hand-copied poetry collection, *Sky and Wind and Star and Poem*—one of only three copies—was in Jeong's possession and was the only surviving copy.

Jeong Byeong-uk had been drafted toward the end of the war and survived it. Conscription of Korean students began in October 1943, after Yun's arrest. Imperial Japan, having started a war that was beyond its powers, resorted to drafting young Joseon students, and Jeong had gotten caught in that scheme.

However, Jeong made a prescient arrangement before going to war. He brought the hand-copied manuscript of *Sky and Wind and Star and Poem* to his parents' house in Mangdeok-ri, Jinwol-myeon, Gwangyang-si, Jeolla-namdo. Jeong stated:

> Dong-ju's own, as well as the copy belonging to Professor Yi Yang-ha, could not be found, but my copy was kept safe, hidden deep in the closet of my parents. It was published in 1948 by Jeongumsa, and that is how Dong-ju's poems came to be known.
>
> Six months after Dong-ju's arrest, I was drafted as a so-called "student soldier." I did not know whether I would come back alive. I gave the manuscript to my mother, asking her to keep it safe until either I or Dong-ju returned. If neither of us returned, I added like a last testament, it should be sent to Yonhui College to be published when Korea became independent. Fortunately, I came back home safely. Overjoyed, Mother proudly handed me the manuscript, wrapped several times in silk wrap.[1]

Jeong's younger sister Jeong Deok-hui (who married Professor Yun Il-ju after liberation but had never seen Yun in person) corrected Jeong's statement regarding the hiding place: "It was not hidden in the closet. Byeong-uk went to war and assumed that it was hidden in the closet when my mother gave it back to him. Actually, it was hidden under the living room floor."[2]

Jeong's family home was large. There was a secret hiding place in the living room, where some floor panels could be lifted so that things could be hidden underneath. It was not visible when the floorboards were down. They had dug a deep hole underneath and placed a large urn over straw. The straw was to prevent moisture.

> We stored all our important, precious items there. It was when I was in high school, during my vacation stay there, that my mother showed me the hiding place. No one was home, and she opened the floorboards and showed the hideaways. She had kept precious items for my future wedding, too. She also showed me the manuscript of *Sky and Wind and Star and Poem*. "Your brother asked me to keep it, saying, 'It must not be found by the Japanese police,'" she explained. I opened it but couldn't read it because it was all in Korean. So I closed it. I had only been educated in Japanese and couldn't read Korean. I also saw a notebook that my brothers' friends inscribed farewell before parting. I read some of it because it was in Japanese. After that, we put everything back into the urn and put the floorboards down.[3]

The manuscript, thus kept with so much care, was published by Jeongeumsa later on.

The role of Gang Cheo-jung was pivotal in introducing Yun's poetry to the world after liberation when Gang worked as a staff writer for *Kyunghyang Shinmun*. He printed "An Easily Written Poem" in the February 13, 1947, issue of the *Kyunghyang Shinmun*. And he did so with the introduction written by Jeong Ji-yong, the great poet and the newspaper's then editor in chief. Under the circumstances, this was the most ideal introduction of an unknown poet to the world, and Gang accomplished this.

Jeong Ji-yong's Introduction of Yun Dong-ju to the World

Korean journalism had all been shut down toward the end of annexation under Japan's harsh oppression. After liberation, it was resurrected, and *Kyunghyang Shinmun* started as a Catholic newspaper. Its first issue was published on October 1, 1946, while South Korea was still under the U.S.

military's rule. According to *Kyunghyang Shinmun: A Forty-Year History*[4] published in 1986, it was a time of tension between political forces on the left and the right, even in journalism.

Its CEO was Bishop No Gi-nam, and the editorial staff consisted of only twenty-two people. It only published two tabloid-sized pages per day (publishing four pages only on Thursdays and Sundays) and did not require many staff members.

The editor in chief was the poet Jeong Ji-yong, and the managing editor was the novelist Yeom Sang-seop, both of whom were heavyweight literary writers. Gang Cheo-jung, Yun's Yonhui Junior College friend, joined the original editorial board as a member of its one-person investigation team.

Jeong Ji-yong's editor in chiefship lasted only about nine months, from October 1, 1946, until July 9, 1947. Yun's poem was printed on page 4 of the Thursday issue on February 13, 1947.

Yun's poem in the paper, with its author listed as "The late Yun Dong-ju," was immediately followed by a brief biography written by Jeong Ji-yong:

Born in Myeongdong Village, Gando. While studying English literature at Doshisha University in Kyoto, Yun was arrested by the Japanese police and sentenced to two years' imprisonment. While serving the term in Fukuoka Prison, he was subjected to suspicious injections and died at the mortifyingly young age of 28. During the last desperate period of Japan, in 1945, imperial Japan murdered the flowering poet as a "subversive Korean" on February 26, and itself has perished. The poet Yun Dong-ju's ashes were buried in East Hill, Yongjeong, and his heartbreaking poems, over ten titles, are in my possession. I am proud to print them continuously, as far as the space in the paper allows. —Ji-yong.[5]

Where the introduction begins is the yearbook picture of Yun Dong-ju from Yonhui, wearing the black mortarboard.

The indication that the poet is dead by adding "the late" is also noteworthy. It was intended to show that the young poet was killed in the Japanese prison. Also surprising is Jeong signing his name as only "Ji-yong" even though he was the editor in chief who had written this formal, Chinese-character-studded introduction.

From his introduction, it seems that it was Jeong's intention to print at least ten poems of Yun's in upcoming issues. However, after the second poem, "Another Home," was printed without annotation on page four of the

Thursday, March 13, 1947, issue and the third, "The Boy," on page two of the Sunday, July 27, 1947, issue, no more of Yun's poems were printed in the paper. Jeong had resigned from his post at *Kyunghyang* on July 9 of that year and gone back to Ewha Womans University to teach again.

February 16, 1947, three days after "An Easily Written Poem" was printed in *Kyunghyang Shinmun*, was the second anniversary of his death. On that day, Gang Cheo-jung, Jeong Byeong-uk, and about thirty relatives and friends of Yun and Song gathered at the Flower Hall in Sogong-dong, Seoul. Jeong Ji-yong attended this memorial as well. Yu Yeong, who went to Yonhui together with Yun and Song, recited his own poem titled "Knock on the Window If You Are Outside: Calling the Spirit of Dong-ju and Mong-gyu." Kim Sam-bul also presented his study of Yun's poetry.

Yun's poetry book was planned to be published before February 16, 1948, the third anniversary of his death. Finally, the first edition of *Sky and Wind and Star and Poem* was published by Jeongeumsa on January 30, 1948.

This edition had thirty-one poems, nineteen of which were from the hand-copied manuscript kept by Jeong Byeong-uk and twelve from Gang's possession.

"Prelude" was placed at the opening of the book. The remaining thirty poems were divided into three sections with separate titles:

1. "Sky and Wind and Star and Poem": eighteen poems from Yun's own hand-copied manuscript
2. "White Shadow": five poems Yun wrote while at Rikkyo in Tokyo and sent to Gang Cheo-jung
3. "Night": seven poems selected from Yun's writings kept by Gang, including "Night" and "Confessions"

They also added a foreword written by Jeong Ji-yong, a memorial poem written by Yu Yeog, and an afterword by Gang Cheo-jung.

Among these, Jeong Ji-yong's foreword became a classic must-read among Yun Dong-ju scholars. Jeong's artistry with words is particularly stunning. Gang's afterword vividly describes the deep friendship between Yun and his friends. Both essays were written with the utmost care to honor the tragic unknown poet the world was about to discover. They contributed greatly to opening the door of Yun's poetry to the world, and both essays are reprinted here:

Foreword by Jeong Ji-yong

"Fore"—is not fitting here.

I am obligated to write a few words with great care, but today is a day I loathe to death to take a pen. With the will of heaven upon me, I groan without being ill.

What should I write?

I am prematurely getting old after liberation, having wasted my talent and lost courage.

If someone rebuked me by asking, "Have you even lost your heart?" I would straighten myself and kneel before him, for I know I cannot protest.

Yet I still have the strength to kneel; I take my pen and burn incense before poet Yun Dong-ju's posthumous work.

I have no material to speak to his character as a poet but thirty posthumous poems.

"A tiger dies and leaves a skin [and a man dies and leaves a name]," goes the old saying. If so, should we examine its skin and name it "Su-nam" or "Pok-dong"? For there was no tiger that had a name.

True, I did not know Yun Dong-ju, but his poems were true "poems."

A tiger's skin is no more than a skin. But Yun's poems speak to his character as a poet.

This excessive ordeal, this excessive fatigue—I should not get angry.

(Excerpted from his poem "Hospital")

The questions and answers between me and his brother Il-ju:

"How old would he be now if he were alive?"

"He would be thirty. He died at twenty-eight."

"When did your family move to Gando?"

"In my grandfather's time."

"How did he do?"

"He cultivated land and was a small landowner."

"What does your father do?"

"He was in business and did some office work, too."

My heart ached. "O if things like poetry and grief started to ferment in Gando, it must have been from the generation of Yun Dong-ju!"

. . .

When spring comes
I will commit sin;
My eyes
Will open
After Eve's labor is done

Covering the shame with fig leaves

I will have sweat on my forehead.
(Excerpted from "Again, the First Morning")

The questions and answers with Il-ju again:
"How old was he when he finished Yonhui and went to Doshisha?"
"He was twenty-five."
"Did he date?"
"He was so quiet, I wouldn't know."
"Did he drink?"
"I never saw him drink."
"Did he smoke?"
"I did not see him smoke at home, where elders were."
"Was he parsimonious?"
"He'd give away books or shirts whenever someone asked."
"Was he studious?"
"He'd read a lot, but whenever needed, he wouldn't hesitate to give his
time."
"How was his temper?"
"He was mild and gentle."
"Was he healthy?"
"He played in a soccer team at middle school."
"His discernment?"
"He'd go along with others but would not give himself away."
. . .

Like a rabbit that escaped from the hills of the Caucasus
Let us protect the liver, circling round and round.

You, emaciated eagle, that I raised for so long!
Come and gnaw the meat off me without a care!

You shall be fattened,
I shall waste away, but,
(Excerpted from "Liver")

In *Five Thousand Words of Laozi*, the sage says: "Empty the mind, fill the belly; weaken the will, and toughen the bones."

The young man Yun Dong-ju had weakened his will. That is why he was superb at lyrical poetry, and his bones were tough. Isn't that also why he gave away his flesh to the Japanese and kept his bones?

Didn't you die in horrifying loneliness? Without even an opportunity to publish your poem in your twenty-eight years!

The famous pro-Japanese writers who had their heyday during the colonization—they left writing that deserves good spitting at. The unknown Yun Dong-ju left poems that were honorable and sorrowful and eternally beautiful.

That is what poetry and poets are supposed to be.

. . .

If the cross is allowed to me
Like the happy man Jesus Christ
Who suffered
I will drape my neck,
Quietly shedding
Blood blooming like flowers
Under the darkening sky

(Excerpted from "The Cross")

The young poet of Joseon was like a flower blooming in the middle of winter, like a carp that swims under the frozen river. The Japanese military police murdered the poet and ruined their own country.

Yun died from the sin of having strong bones; his skeletons now rest in Gando, his old hometown.

ANOTHER HOME
The night I returned home,
My skeleton followed me to the room and lay with me.

The dark room connects to the universe;
The wind blows like a sound from heaven.

Observing the skeleton, weathering finely
In the darkness, who is weeping?
Is it I?
Is it the skeleton?
Is it the beauteous soul?

The dog with an unyielding principle
Barks the darkness away all night long.

The dog that barks the darkness away
Must be pursuing me.

Let us go, go,
Go like a fugitive.
Let us go to another beautiful home,
Hiding from the skeleton.

If Yun were alive now, how would his poems progress? That is the issue here.

As his friend Mr. Kim Sam-bul said during Yun's memorial, without a doubt, they will strive resolutely for a new way!

December 28, 1947
Ji-yong

Afterword by Gang Cheo-jung

Dong-ju was neither a talker nor an extrovert, but his room was always filled with friends. Even when busy, if a friend came and said, "Are you there, Dong-ju?" he'd put behind whatever he was doing and greet him with a smile.

When asked, "Dong-ju, want to take a walk?" he'd never refuse it. Whether it was winter, summer, night, or dawn, he'd go. Whether it was to the hills, by the river, or wherever, he'd follow. He'd walk quietly, his face somber. Sometimes he'd let out a grief-stricken groan: "Ah—!"

That "Ah—!" never failed to invoke a feeling of desperate rage in his friends.

"Dong-ju, you got some money to lend?" some poor friends eyed his thin wallet. He never failed to give money if he had any. If he didn't, he'd feel better only after he gave away his coat or watch. So his coat and watch often took trips to pawn shops through his friends.

But Dong-ju was always stubborn with two things. One was about his poems. If someone asked, "Dong-ju, how about editing this line here?" Dong-ju never listened. He would keep quiet for ten days, a month, or two months and think until a poem was born. Until then, he never showed it to others. When he showed it, it had already become a faultless piece of jade. He was extremely meek and mild, but he never yielded when it came to his poems.

Another was the love he had for a woman. But he never confessed this love to her, nor did he reveal her identity to his friends. He only kept the agony and hope for himself, without her knowing it or returning his love to him. Perhaps he was shy, perhaps he was idiotic. But now I think back, perhaps it was not merely a love for a woman but a dream for "another home" that would never come true. At any rate, he kept this a secret.

He was born in Gando and died in Fukuoka. He was born in a foreign land and died in a foreign land, but he loved his fatherland and loved the Korean language. My friend Dong-ju, together with his childhood friend Song Mong-gyu, was convicted of the crime of "independence movement activities," sentenced to two years in prison, and killed there. It happened while they were university students in Kyoto.

"I couldn't understand what he said, but he shrieked a high-pitched cry as he died. It sounded as if he was saying, 'Long live the independence of Joseon.'"

The Japanese prison guard who saw his last moment told this to his family, who went to claim his corpse. The grief-stricken groan! The Japanese guard did not understand Korean, but the sound of the groan must have given him a deep impression. Dong-ju was gone after letting out the groan. He was twenty-eight, and it was the year of liberation. Mong-gyu followed him a few days later, and he was a talented man, too. Their skeletons are resting in Gando, and through the efforts of Dong-ju's friends, his poems are here in a book so that the world can see them.

My calling you won't bring back replies, Dong-ju and Mong-gyu. But I want to call your names again, Dong-ju! Mong-gyu!

Through the concerted efforts of many, Yun Dong-ju's posthumous poetry collection *Sky and Wind and Star and Poem* was thus published.

Who Was Gang Cheo-jung?

Yun Dong-ju scholars, as well as those who love Yun's poems, always praise Jeong Byeong-uk, for he was the ultimate contributor to the establishment of Yun's position in Korean literature by safekeeping Yun's handwritten manuscript of *Sky and Wind and Star and Poem* for publication after liberation.

However, there is another whose role was crucial. Yet he is neither known nor praised for his role. It is Gang Cheo-jung.

The study of Yun's poetry and personal life is incomplete without knowing Gang Cheo-jung and his role. In some sense, Gang's contribution is even more dramatic and enormous.

Comparing his role with Jeong's, we can easily see Gang's importance and status in making Yun's work known to the world.

Jeong Byeong-uk:

· Was given a handwritten manuscript of nineteen poems by Yun and kept it safe until liberation

Gang Cheo-jung:

· Kept all extant poems by Yun that were not part of the handwritten manuscript, including "Confessions," which Yun left in Seoul before going to Japan; we would have none of these poems, except some poems and sketches from middle school and *dongsi*, had it not been for Gang Cheo-jung
· Stored all personal effects of Yun's that Yun left in Seoul before going to Japan, including his books, Yonhui yearbook, and portable desk, and passed them to Yun Il-ju when he came to Seoul after liberation
· Kept all five poems Yun mailed him from Tokyo; this is extremely important to the Yun scholarship because no other poems Yun wrote in Japan survived

Particularly, Gang's contribution to publishing Yun's poetry after liberation is absolute. As a reporter at *Kyunghyang Shinmun*, he used the newspaper to introduce to the liberated Korea the unknown poet who had died in imperial Japan's prison. Not only that, but he managed to accompany it with an introduction by the great poet Jeong Ji-yong, making this debut dramatic and effective. Under his leadership, Yun's posthumous poetry collection was published, securing Yun's name as a published poet.

The first edition of *Sky and Wind and Star and Poem*, published in January 1948 by Jeongeumsa, consisted of nineteen poems from the handwritten manuscript kept by Jeong and twelve poems selected from Gang's possession.

So why is it that Gang Cheo-jung, who is a crucial person in the life and works of Yun Dong-ju, became obscure as if buried?

The reason is directly connected to the tragic history of post-liberation Korea. In 1950, Gang was arrested by the South Korean public security authority as a leftist and was sentenced to death. Therefore, during the Cold War period of conflicting ideologies, even his close relatives and friends dared not mention his name, and naturally, he became forgotten. Among Yun's close friends—aside from Song Mong-gyu, who died in the same prison only a few weeks after Yun—Gang was the most tragic figure.

According to Yonhui Junior College's student records, Gang was born in 1916 in Wonsan, Hamgyeong-namdo. Gang entered Yonhui the same year as Yun. From their initial meeting in the spring of 1938, Yun, Song, and Gang became very close. The three of them began Yunhui as roommates on the third floor of the dormitory.

The late Professor Jang Deok-sun of Seoul National University (Korean literature) was from Yongjeong, North Gando, and went to Gwangmyeong School's Middle Division and Yonhui Junior College's Liberal Arts Division two years behind Yun. Sometime during their Yonhui days, he roomed with Gang Cheo-jung in Yonhui-dong. Professor Jang told me about some interesting episodes that speak to Gang's character.

Gang was twenty-two years old when he started at Yonhui and had already had various life experiences. He was very knowledgeable about snakes. While living in China before he began Yonhui, he had raised snakes in an earthen-floor room there. Once, during a walk with Jang around the hills near Yonhui-dong, Gang caught a snake alive on the riverbank. Gang handled the live snake, and pointing at spots, explained that they evidenced degeneration of the legs. Jang was turned off by snakes but remembered one of the things Gang had said:

"Among all species in the world, the most spiteful is the snake. Most animals are tamed by hands that feed them, but that's not the case with snakes. They'd accept food but won't be tamed. No matter how much you pay attention and feed them, they won't be tamed."[6]

At Yonhui, Gang was a star student. He was gifted in language learning, one of two "best English speakers" at Yonhui, earning the nickname "Guru of English." A natural leader, he was elected during his senior year as president of Munu Association, the student body of the Yonhui Liberal Arts Division.

Yonhui student records reveal that Gang changed his name to Japanese, Shinnong Samashige. Shennong (in Chinese pronunciation) is an ancient mythological god-king of China, one of the sovereigns, as in the legend of the Three Sovereigns and Five Emperors. According to the legend, he had a man's body and a bull's head and managed fire. He was the god of farming, medicine, and music, as well as the creator of sixty-four trigrams. He was also the god of metal casting, brewing, and trading. Shennong's last name was Gang, and it was witty of Gang Cheo-jung to use the ancient mythological king's name for his Japanese name.

Yun's brother Yun Il-ju, at the tender age of eighteen, moved to Seoul in June 1946. Yun Il-ju, knowing no one in the strange city, looked for his late elder brother's friends. Through the grapevine, Yun Il-ju was introduced to Jeong Byeong-uk, who was then a junior and Korean literature major at Seoul National University. Jeong had been drafted at his graduation from Yonhui and did not return home until after liberation in the fall of 1945. The following spring, he was enrolled at Seoul National University as a junior. Yun Il-ju was also able to meet Gang Cheo-jung, who, to Yun Il-ju's surprise, had stored all of Yun Dong-ju's personal effects, which he handed over to Yun Il-ju.

This was a great, unexpected gift to Yun's family. Exactly six months after his death in prison on February 16, 1945, Japan surrendered and Korea was liberated. Yun's family looked for personal belongings of Yun's in Seoul, thinking that they might still be stored in the boardinghouse in North Ahyeon-dong. Yun's uncle Yun Yeong-chun asked other relatives from North Gando and found out that Ra Sa-haeng had once been to the last boardinghouse where Yun had stayed in Seoul. The two of them tried to find the boardinghouse, but Ra, who had only been there once almost four years earlier, could not find it. Afterward, the family gave up on finding Yun's personal effects.

Thus, it was an even greater surprise that Gang Cheo-jung had kept all of Yun's poems and books and handed them over to the family. When Yun Il-ju moved to Seoul in June 1946 and found Gang, Gang was probably working on the launching of *Kyunghyang Shinmun*.

Yun went to Japan in early 1942. This means that Gang had stored Yun's books and writing, not a small bundle, for over four years despite the harsh conditions of living under Japanese rule. The manuscripts saved by Gang carry very important meanings and great weight in evaluating Yun's life as a poet.

The handwritten manuscripts kept by Gang can be sorted into three categories:

1. Poems that were written prior to Yun's selection of nineteen poems and not included in the selection (including "Beatitudes" and "Consolation")
2. Poems that were written after Yun's selection of nineteen poems (including "Confessions" and "Liver")

3. Five poems Yun wrote in Japan ("An Easily Written Poem," "White
   Shadow," "Lovely Memory," "Flowing Street," and "Spring"—So far,
   these are the only poems Yun wrote in Japan that remain; had Gang
   not kept these, no poem from Yun's Japan days would exist)

When all of these things are considered, Gang's preservation of Yun's
poems is just as important as Jeong's.

Following is a list of three people who preserved Yun Dong-ju's manuscripts and their contents:

1. Jeong Byeong-uk: Nineteen poems selected by Yun
2. Yun Hye-won: Poems from middle school days and *dongsi* (Among
   Yun's family members, Yun Hye-won and Yun Il-ju are the only two
   who moved to South Korea. Yun Il-ju, who moved alone to the south at
   age eighteen, did not bring anything belonging to Yun Dong-ju. Yun
   Hye-won, with her husband, moved to the south in December 1948
   after the publication of Yun's poetry in Seoul, bringing with her from
   her parents' home all the poems Yun had written during middle school)
3. Gang Cheo-jung: The rest of the poems[7]

By the second anniversary of Yun's death, Gang was planning the publication of the nineteen poems kept by Jeong, together with a selection from his
possession. Gang set the purported publication date as immediately before
the third-anniversary date, that is, February 16, 1948.

As a reporter at *Kyunghyang Sinmun*, Gang had connections in cultural
and literary circles. Naturally, he pushed the plan forward, for at that time,
Jeong was a twenty-five-year-old student at Seoul National University,
whereas Gang was a thirty-one-year-old reporter in the field.

In the October 10, 1983, revised edition of *Sky and Wind and Star and Poem*,
Professor Yun Il-ju wrote in the introduction: "Professor Jeong Byeong-uk
had the core body of Yun Dong-ju's work in safekeeping and has always been
a guide in publishing the poems since 1955." From this, we see that Jeong
Byeong-uk was involved in the work since the February 16, 1955, revised
edition.

In order to introduce and promote Yun's poems, Gang decided to serialize
them in the newspaper. As stated earlier, Gang requested that Jeong Ji-yong,

the great poet of the time and the newspaper's editor in chief, write an introduction. In February 1947, *Kyunghyang Shinmun* began printing Yun's poems.

A third poem, "The Boy," was printed on July 27, 1947, which was after Jeong Ji-yong's resignation. A short introduction to the poem says, "The late Yun Dong-ju is our gentleman-scholar, who passed away alone at a young age in a Japanese prison." This, too, looks to be the work of Gang Cheo-jung, who wanted to imprint the image of Yun Dong-ju in people's hearts. Through such sincerity and endeavors, the first edition was published on January 30, 1948.

Gang's endeavors in publishing were notable. Again, Gang asked Jeong Ji-yong to write a foreword. Even by way of riding the coattails of the great poet Jeong Ji-yong, Gang wished to promote Yun's poems. Jeong wrote the foreword on December 28, 1947, while he was teaching at Ewha Womans University. Gang even brought Yun Il-ju to Jeong Ji-yong, so that Jeong would hear about Yun and Yun's family from Yun's own brother. That is how the section titled "The Questions and Answers between Me and His Brother Il-ju" was written. That day, Jeong asked Yun Il-ju many questions. Regarding their father's occupation, Yun Il-ju answered, "He was in business and did some office work, too." After the book was published, it was mailed to the family home in North Gando. Yun's father, after reading the foreword, felt hurt. Having prided himself as an intellectual all his life, he did not like the insinuation that he was a trader/merchant. He chided Yun Il-ju, saying, "Why did you give such an answer?"

Gang Cheo-jung wrote an afterword to the book, and the book was finally published in January 1948. Finally Yun Dong-ju was a published poet.

Yet the authors of the foreword and the afterword shared an unfortunate destiny. Two-and-a-half years after the book's publication, the Korean War broke out. The hatred, conflict, and collision between the Left and the Right worsened greatly during the war, casting dark shadows on the lives of Jeong Ji-yong and Gang Cheo-jung. Their connection to the Left made them pariahs.

Consequently, when the revised edition was published by Jeong Byeong-uk and Yun Il-ju on the tenth anniversary of the poet's death in February 1955, both the foreword by Jeong and the afterword by Gang were eliminated. From this moment, Jeong Ji-yong's and Gang Cheo-jung's relationship to the book was severed.

I became deeply interested in Gang Cheo-jung when I first saw the first edition of *Sky and Wind and Star and Poem* in the home of Professor Yun Il-ju.

It was understandable that Jeong Ji-yong's foreword had been taken out. The accusation of Jeong's departure for North Korea during the war resulted in the erasure of his writing and his existence. Until the censorship officially ended in 1987, his name could not be mentioned even in academic journals. Sometimes, his name was allowed to be printed as "Jeong [blank]-yong" or "Jeong Yong." However, I could not understand why Gang's afterword was taken out, and so I asked Professor Yun Il-ju, "What kind of person was Gang Cheo-jung? Why was his afterword taken out in the revised edition?"

Professor Yun hesitated and answered unwillingly: "It was revealed that he was . . . a leftist."

As soon as I heard the answer, I had a hunch and thought, *Ah! This man must be . . .*

In the 1983 revised edition, Professor Yun Il-ju wrote a footnote after the poem "Spring," the last of the five poems from Yun's Tokyo days: "These five poems written in Tokyo were enclosed and sent in letters to a friend in Seoul, but when the letters were destroyed, the end of this poem was also destroyed."

This "friend in Seoul" was someone who had exchanged letters with Yun Dong-ju. If, despite the fact that this friend received and kept the five precious poems, his name could not be revealed, it must have been Gang Cheo-jung, the "leftist."

When I communicated my conjecture to Professor Yun Il-ju, he confirmed it, adding that according to Gang, the letters had to be destroyed because their content, if discovered, could be dangerous. When I asked him if Gang had had more personal effects of Yun's, he answered, "He kept all my brother's books, manuscripts of poems, Yonhui yearbook, a buckle, and a portable desk, all the things my brother left in Seoul when he went to Japan. Gang gave all of them to me."

However, Professor Yun was concerned that Gang's connection to his brother might create negative images and did not wish to discuss him further.

Later, Professor Jang Deok-sun provided me with more details about Gang's life: "He worked as a reporter for the *Kyunghyang* newspaper after the liberation, but was executed later as a leftist. I do not remember if it was before or after the Korean War. I just remember that he was arrested, sentenced to death in the martial court, and executed. I saw a related article on the paper then, but someone told me that he was executed by firing squad."

It was shocking news.

I retraced his career at *Kyunghyang*. At the beginning of *The Forty-Year History of "Kyunghyang Shinmun,"* his name was listed as one of its founding members. On page two of the April 27, 1947, issue of the newspaper on microfilm, an article written by him could be seen. It was about Admiral Yi Soon-shin, commemorating him before his birthday, which is April 28. His writing was very intriguing. The vocabulary and logic he used in the piece revealed his ideology. From this, I believed that the charge of being a leftist was not a false one but truth. The article is reproduced here, as it is a helpful source for understanding who he was:

"Admiral Yi, the Lord Chungmu"

We name many great names from the Yi dynasty: Kim Gweng-pil, Cho Gwang-jo, Yi Hwang, Yi I, Seo Gyeong-deok, Song Si-yeol, and so on. They were embodiments of feudalism, the finest among the aristocrats and giants of Confucianism. Yet, as their systems and their classes disappeared, and even their philosophy waned, their names disappeared from the minds of the Korean people. Even the great Yi I, the descendants of today do not know why he was great; his fate is with the museum, along with other artifacts of the past. So why is it that Yi Sun-shin shines even more brightly as a new period opens?

It is because he protected the land of Korea with love, for the Korean people and with the Korean people. The people do not perish. That is why the great men who fought with the people live in the hearts of the people forever. In the times of life and death, great men overcome the crisis with the people. When a crisis comes upon the people, they think of the great men even more. And this is why we commemorate Yi Sun-shin even more dearly today.

We do not merely long for Yi Sun-shin the hero. We long for the Yi Sun-shin who struggled shoulder to shoulder with the people against the evil. Of course, there are numerous reasons that make him great. Called Zhuge Liang of Korea, he had resourcefulness, tactics, and great management of the troops. He was loyal and brave, just and fair, perfectly prepared and trained for battles. His iron-clad Turtle Ships were brilliant. He cut off the path of the Japanese navy in the southern sea, and prevented them from taking over the granaries in the south.

Examining the state affairs of the time, however, we see the vivid aftermath of the wretched bloodbath caused by political bickering and purge of the scholars. Because of the factional strife between the two major parties, national policies were divided. Instead of defending the nation with war strategy and armament, the king and all his officials took flight to the outskirts of Uiju. They were defeated daily in the battles on land, and Japan was trampling on the whole land. Having no party affiliations, Yi Sun-shin was politically isolated, and every kind of impediment hindered his position.

Under the circumstances, how could a hero's resourcefulness or Turtle Ships alone achieve a great victory in the vast sea? Yi Sun-shin knew this. Therefore, trusting in the people, he consistently carried out the battles with the people and for the people. In his speech and actions, we see him sharing worries and sorrows with the people. Because of the limited space here, I only give one contrasting example showing how closely Yi Sun-shin stayed and fought with the people.

When the king and his officials left Seoul, the people begged the king not to forsake them by staying in Seoul. But they traded hemp shoes with white gold in the palace and left Seoul in the middle of the night as if fleeing. The people were filled with hatred upon learning this and set fire to Jangyewon [the institution overseeing slavery—Trans.] and Hyeongjo [the institution overseeing crimes—Trans.], which they hated. In Gaeseong, they even threw rocks at the king. But what about Yi Sun-shin?

When he was arrested for a bogus crime and taken to Seoul in a cage cart, the roads in every town were lined with people, men and women, old and young, who despaired and wailed at the injustice of it all. When he was released and reappointed as the Chief Commander of the Navy, the people gathered alongside the road to offer their meager food and wept with joy, greeting him. They felt relieved, and Yi Sun-shin comforted them. What a great contrast of night and day do we see here? Here lies his greatness. This is why we still love him today.

I do not call him by his title Lord Chungmu in this article but use his name because he is still alive with the people, and we feel close to him. The king who gave his title is long gone, but the people who called on his name and followed Admiral Yi Sun-shin have not perished.[8]

Gang was said to be a born leader among his friends. He lived a turbulent, eventful life and left only two pieces of writing, one about Yi Sun-shin and the other about Yun Dong-ju, each commemorating a great man continuously beloved by the Korean people. One cannot help but think about Gang's own fate.

I set out to research Gang's life in earnest. However, I could not find any evidence supporting Professor Jang's statement that Gang was "arrested, sentenced to death in the martial court, and executed." Microfilms of several newspapers from the period were examined, but no report of his arrest and execution was found. With the assistance of the Research Data Department of *Kyunghyang Sinmun*, I found a 1953 article reporting a large-scale case—the Jeong Guk-eun Spy Case—in which Gang was mentioned as being involved in the case.

On September 21, 1953, Son Won-il, South Korea's then minister of national defense, held a press conference with regard to the Jeong Guk-eun Spy Case. This was immediately after the ceasefire following the Korean War, and martial law was still in effect. The Defense Ministry directly handled spy cases involving civilians, and it was the defense minister's job to report on them.

Jeong Guk-eun was a journalist who worked for *Jo-Il Shinmun*, a Japanese newspaper during the annexation. After liberation, he continued to be active, serving as a resident special reporter in Japan for *Yonhap Shinmun* until his arrest. Arrested alongside him were a high-ranking police officer in charge of the Security Bureau's Central Division and a businessman from Han'guk Tongsang Incorporated.

This was a big case that warranted special coverage. Yang U-jeong, the CEO of *Yonghap Shinmun* and incumbent congressman, was suspected of involvement and interrogated in custody. Jin Heon-shik, minister of interior, and Yi Jae-hyeong, minister of commerce and industry, were also suspected and, after their resignation from their posts, were also interrogated in custody. An investigative committee was formed in the Congress, and the whole case was blown up.

All eyes were on it, and it caused great turbulence. Because martial law was still in effect, Jeong Guk-eun was transferred to the High Martial Court and tried in a single-trial system. He was sentenced to death on December 2 of the same year.

This case was accompanied by peculiar events. On the morning of January 23, 1954, the execution date of Jeong, people started queueing up near the Hongjewon crematorium, the site of execution by shooting. By 2 P.M., the time of execution, thousands of onlookers crowded the area. A photograph of the large crowd was printed in the January 26, 1954, issue of *Donga Ilbo*. However, the execution was postponed with no further explanation. It was reported that Jeong was executed by firing squad in Susaek on February 18, 1955, but even after his reported death, rumors spread. Some believed that Jeong was still alive in Japan and worked as a double agent under the protection of the Far East Command of the United States. These rumors would not die down. The military authorities had to publish the photograph of the corpse and have reporters who knew Jeong's face identify it.

As seen here, the case was an event of great consequence. On September 22, 1953, *Kyunghyang Shinmun* reported on Defense Minister Son Won-il's first press conference as the main article of the paper's national section: "Jeong Guk-eun, editor-in-chief of *Dongyang Tongshin* and *Yonhap Shinmun*, was arrested in Seoul, on August 31, by the Army Special Task Force. Since then, it has been subject to much speculation and public discussion. The Special Task Force has conducted a thorough investigation of Jeong, which revealed his criminal activities. He was transferred to the High Martial Court [. . .], and the Minister of Defense gave the full account of the case as follows."[9]

In this article, Gang's name is given some importance. The following facts relating to Gang have been summarized by several newspapers reporting on the case:

Gang Cheo-jung worked under Kim Sam-ryong, the chief of the Workers' Party of South Korea (Namrodang—Trans.), as an executive in its special division. Joining the party after liberation, Jeong Guk-eun established *Gukje Shinmunsa* in Sogong-dong in the Jung-gu section of Seoul and became its managing editor. Jeong appointed the party's special division executives, such as Gang, to the newspaper's key positions. Gang, as the party's high-line contact for Jeong, collected information through newspaper organizations and handed it over to North Korea. In June 1949, Jeong Guk-eun, upon Gang's command, established *Gukbang Newspaper* in Myung-dong in the Jung-gu section of Seoul with a fund of one million won from the Workers' Party of South Korea. Under the pretense of news coverage, Jeong obtained information on top secrets in national defense, which was then transmitted to North Korea through the high-line contact, Gang Cheo-jung.

Between 1948 and 1949, Gang Cheo-jung was thirty-two to thirty-three years old. How much historical truth does the Defense Ministry's announcement have? Notwithstanding answers to this question, one thing is clear: In South Korea at the time, Gang Cheo-jung was regarded as the young true power of the Workers' Party of South Korea (WPSK).

The journalist-novelist Song Ji-yeong, who was managing editor of *Gukje Shinmun* before the Korean War, testified at the Jeong Guk-eun trial. During his testimony, he mentioned Gang Cheo-jung, stating that he was recruited by Gang to be *Gukje Shinmun*'s managing editor, that he subsequently met Jeong, and that Jeong was close to leftist individuals such as Gang. According to Song Ji-yeong's testimony, Gang Cheo-jung, even though he was merely a reporter, had the authority to appoint the paper's managing editor.

When and how did Gang's demise come?

According to the military authority's announcement, Jeong Guk-eun, arrested in August 1953, had engaged in intelligence activities "following the command of Gang Cheo-jung, the high-line contact for the Workers' Party of South Korea." In spite of this, there was no mention of personal details or the arrest of Gang.

There is, however, a record that indirectly puts Gang's arrest prior to Jeong's. On page two of the October 28, 1953, issue of *Joseon Ilbo* is the head-line "Jeong Guk-eun Case Investigation Comes to an End," under which the investigation up to that point is reported. Titled "No. 275 of Defense Ministry Report and Public Announcement," it reports on one of the charges against Yang U-jeong, the CEO of *Yonhap Shimun* and incumbent congressman: "Spy Jeong, who is a cell to Gang Cheo-jung, the special military strategist under Kim Sam-ryong, the head of the Workers' Party of South Korea, man-aged *Gukje Shinmun* and *Gukbang Shinmun*, spying on top military secrets to transmit them to the [North Korean—Trans.] puppet group. Yang U-jeong advocated for the spy Jeong by aiding him to move to Japan as *Yonhap Shin-un*'s resident special reporter in Japan when Jeong detected danger to his safety after his high-line contact was arrested by the military investigative net."[10] Both "cell" (the smallest structural unit in the Communist Party) and "high-line contact" are special terms that establish their vertical relationship. The phrase "Spy Jeong, who is a cell to Gang Cheo-jung" means that Jeong worked for Gang, and "his high-line contact" refers to Gang Cheo-jung.

In Defense Minister Son Won-il's first press conference report mentioned earlier, the time of Jeong's move to Japan as *Yonhap Shinmun*'s special reporter to Tokyo is mentioned: "In about February of 4283 [Korean year—Trans.] after the highest executives of the WPSK's special division were arrested by the Army Special Task Force and other investigative bureaus."[11]

The Korean year 4283 is 1950. Newspaper articles from February 1950 onward report only the arrest of WPSK's executives, such as Kim Sam-ryong and Yi Ju-ha. Gang's name is not mentioned. However, it is clear from the circumstances that Gang Cheo-jung was also arrested, tried in a martial court, and sentenced to death.

Thus, in this book's revised edition (published in August 1998), accepting Professor Jang Deok-sun's statement, I wrote that Gang "seems to have been executed by firing squad around the time of the Korean War. If so, Gang passed away at a promising young age of thirty-four years."

After *Donga Ilbo*'s review of the revised edition was printed, however, I was contacted by Yi Gang-ja, born in 1919, who was Gang Cheo-jung's wife. She revealed, "My husband was arrested, tried, and sentenced to death. But he was not executed."[12]

While waiting for his execution date in the Seodaemun Prison, to which he was transferred from the military prison, the Korean War broke out. It was June 25, and the People's Army captured Seoul within three days and freed the prisoners from Seodaemun Prison. Gang returned home on June 28, which happened to be their daughter's 100th Day celebration.

Gang recuperated at home for about two months, but on September 4, he headed north, saying that he was "going to the Soviet Union to study."

By September 4, 1950, the battles were in earnest, with the People's Army advancing south with little difficulty. Yet Gang left his family and his country to go north.

Gang and Yi got married in December 1942 and had two sons and a daughter. After his departure in September 1950, Yi never heard anything about him. She had to destroy all documents and photographs relating to him.

"My in-laws were in Wonsan. My father-in-law practiced herbal medicine successfully, and they were well off," Yi stated. About Gang, she said, "His character was reserved, but he loved his children so much." Then she added in a low voice, "When I went to see him in prison, the guards used to say, 'Oh, you came to see the handsome man from the Hamgyeong province!'"

What impressed me deeply was the strange relationship between Gang Cheo-jung and the WPSK, which almost led him to his death. Only in the newspaper articles about the Jeong Guk-eun case is his relationship to the WPSK as its executive revealed. In all other extant documents relating to the WPSK, there is no mention of Gang Cheo-jung. In memoirs by former WPSK executives such as Pak Gap-dong and Yang Han-mo as well as the three-volume masterpiece *Studies on the Workers' Party of South Korea* by WPSK expert Kim Nam-shik, Gang Cheo-jung is not mentioned at all. Just as in the Yun Dong-ju documents, his existence evaporated into thin air in the WPSK documents. By both rightists and leftists alike, his existence seems to have been denied. How strange is his fate?

Through the materials I was able to gather, we have traced Gang's life and character. Yet how could we assess a person with such meager evidence? It is through the heartfelt caring, faithfulness, and sacrifice he made for his friend Yun Dong-ju that we know him. He truly knew how to love a friend.

Regarding the manuscripts from Yun's middle school years, I mentioned that Yun Hye-won brought them to Seoul. In December 1948, Yun Hye-won moved to South Korea with her husband O Hyeong-beom, whom she had married the previous year in North Gando. When they moved, she brought all the poems and *dongsi* from Yun's middle school years that had remained in Yongjeong. Yun's father had asked her to do this. Did he foresee that his son would one day become the national poet? The collection of Yun Dong-ju, as we see it today, was thus completed.

It is notable that new documents relating to Yun are continuously being discovered by researchers and scholars who love him. Along with documents discovered by Yanagihara Yasuko, another example is the last photograph of Yun Dong-ju, which was discovered by Tago Kichiro, former NHK director in Japan. In January 1995, while co-producing a TV program about Yun Dong-ju with Korea's KBS, Tago unearthed the photograph during interviews with Yun's classmates from Doshisha University. It was taken in May 1943, when Yun and his friends from Doshisha went to the Uji River in Uji, a city south of Kyoto. Many researchers are endeavoring to find additional documents about Yun Dong-ju.

Yun Dong-ju's posthumous poetry book *Sky and Wind and Star and Poem* was first published with only thirty-one poems. Since then, it has been revised and expanded several times to contain 128 pieces of his work. Countless scholarly articles and books have been published, and his poems are more beloved than ever. They have been translated into numerous languages, including English, Japanese, French, Czech, and Chinese.

The appeal of Yun's poetry is not due to particular biographical facts, such as his death in prison in the enemy nation. At the heart of it is the purity, truth, and beauty that his poems contain—that is, the literary triumph he achieved as a poet. Someone spoke about the correlation between a people and its poetry like this: "In order for a great poem to appear, to be sung by the whole people, one generation, or even two, may have to wait." The weight and worth of such a great poet accompany Yun's poetry.

About the great poet of the Song dynasty Su Dongpo, Lin Yutang wrote, "There is a certain characteristic in a great classic that can be called truth, like a precious gem that remains after going through smelting processes. In other words, a classic survives various fashionable literary styles of its time, moving all readers of every period."[13]

This beautiful praise can be dedicated to Yun's poetry. Taking a step forward, we throw out another question: What is the essence of truth in Yun Dong-ju's poems? It is the graceful dignity contained in his poems. Moreover, because this truth was formed by the convergence of his poetry and his life, it contains magnificent purity.

Yun was born during World War I and died during World War II. In the dark prison of one of the chief actors of the war, he became a subject of live medical experimentation and was killed at a young age. It was a short, heartbreakingly sad life. Knowing that the hands that killed him also belonged to humanity, the truth contained in his poems saddens our hearts even more.

Evil intention, hatred, wickedness, greed, the will to dominate, and destructiveness nursed and nurtured by mankind in darkness as its own children—all these and their beastly power and impulse sprang forth at once, destroying this world and violating human dignity. This sums up this period of his life. He was plunged into the whirlwind of such wretched lunacy and filth. Yet like a fragrant lily that blooms in a virulent thorn field, he revealed human dignity of purity and goodness amid ugliness. From that revelation stems the power and appeal of his poetry.

What shape should life form? What quality should life carry with it?

Sometimes we hear the agonizing groan of creation that murmurs darkly in the depths of its soul. We groan together, lost together. That is when Yun Dong-ju's poem approaches us quietly.

> Looking up at the sky to my dying day
> I wished no speck of shame within me,
> But even at the breeze between leaves
> I suffered.

The deeper the darkness gets, the brighter the light shines. As the world gets darker and more turbid, Yun's poems bring out more clearly the beauty of the human spirit, pure and clean.

Again, today, we stand before the terrifying and beautiful lines. As we face them, our eyes are suddenly open and recognizing our own ugliness and sinfulness, which are revealed as if surfacing above water. How divine is the pure and clean spirit of man?

ACKNOWLEDGMENTS

I AM DEEPLY THANKFUL to Professor Young-mee Yu Cho of Rutgers University for introducing me to this important book and suggesting that I translate it. This translation would not have been possible without her initiative, encouragements, and feedback.

Ms. Song WooHye graciously agreed to the publication of my translation even though we have never met or spoken to each other, and I am grateful for her trust in me.

I would also like to thank Rutgers University Press for the DITTA series and for the honor of being one of the inaugural translators for the series. With the invaluable assistance from its editors, this book has taken its current form.

Lastly, a sincere gratitude goes to the Literature Translation Institute of Korea for awarding me a generous translation grant.

NOTES

Foreword

1. For more information about leftist literary culture in Korea during the colonial period, see Sunyoung Park, *Proletarian Wave*.

Chapter 1   Birth of the Poet

1. Author's personal interview with Kim Shin-muk (undated).—Trans.
2. Author's personal interview with Kim Shin-muk (undated).—Trans.
3. Yun Il-ju, "Life of Yun Dong-ju," 152.
4. An iconic pastor, theologian, and poet, Moon Ik-hwan (1918–1994) is most famous for his dissident activities against dictatorship in the 1970s and 1980s in South Korea. His son Moon Sung-keun is a noted actor and politician.—Trans.
5. King Gojong sent three secret emissaries, unsuccessfully, to the Second Hague Peace Convention to declare the invalidity of the Japan-Korea Treaty of 1905, which effectively took Korea's sovereignty away.—Trans.
6. Yun Byeong-seok, *The Biography of Yi Sang-seol*, 171.
7. In Korea, a person's *ho* (art name) was often used with, or in lieu of, the person's full or last name. Chunwon is Yi Gwang-su art name.—Trans.
8. Kim Yun-shik, *Yi Gwang-su and His Time II*, 528.
9. Yun Il-ju, "Life of Yun Dong-ju," 150.
10. Author's personal interview with Mun Ik-hwan (undated).—Trans.

Chapter 2   Myeongdong

1. National Assembly Library of Korea. "Provisional National Council and Provisional Government Documents," 725-726.

2. The *Book of Changes* (or the *I Ching*) is an ancient guide to divination and one of the oldest Chinese texts. Sirhak was a Confucian movement during the Joseon dynasty.—Trans.

3. Author's personal interview with Mun Jae-rin (undated).—Trans.

4. See the entry in National Institute of the Korean Language, *The Standard Korean Language Dictionary.*—Trans.

5. Author's personal interview with Han Jun-myeong (undated).—Trans.

6. Author's personal interview with Han Jun-myeong (undated).—Trans.

7. Yun Dong-ju, *Sky and Wind and Star and Poem.*—Trans.

8. Author's personal interview with Kim Shin-muk and Mun Ik-hwan (undated).—Trans.

9. See Hwang Gu-tae ed., *The Translated Poetry of Du Fu.*—Trans.

10. Kim Gu (1876–1949) was the most influential resistance leader during Japan's annexation of Korea and the president of Korea's Provisional Government in 1940–1947.—Trans.

11. Kim Gu, *Baekbeom Diary*, 59.

12. Author's personal interview with Kim Shin-muk (undated).—Trans.

13. Yun Il-ju, "Life of Yun Dong-ju," 152.

14. *Hangnyeol* characters are fixed characters that denote the kin relationship. First names in each generation of a clan contain the same fixed character, as in Dong-ju and Il-ju in the Yun family.—Trans.

15. Known as Ilhan New in America, Yu Il-han (1895–1971) was an entrepreneur, independence activist, and philanthropist. He founded La Choy Food Products Inc. in America and Yuhan Co. Ltd. in Korea. His entire fortune was donated to public welfare and education purposes.—Trans.

16. Song WooHye, "Studies on the Organization of North Gando 'Korean Citizens Association,'" 115.

17. Author's personal interview with Kim Shin-muk (undated).—Trans.

18. *Goman* seems to come from *geuman,* a word meaning "no more," as in "no more daughters." *Gaettong* literally means "dog dung." As infant mortality was high, crude names were often used for children, with the wish that the evil spirits bypass the child with a lowly sounding name. *Gopdani* is from the word for "pretty and tidy."—Trans.

19. Author's personal interview with Kim Shin-muk (undated).—Trans.

20. Author's personal interview with Han Jun-myeong (undated).—Trans.

21. Kim Jeong-u, "Childhood of Yun Dong-ju," 117.

22. Gang Deok-sang, *Modern History Sources*, 455.

23. Kim Jeong-u, "Childhood of Yun Dong-ju," 117–119.

24. Author's personal interview with Han Jun-myeong (undated).—Trans.

25. White Mountain: Mount Baekdu. The patriots in North Gando had a custom of referring to their area as "the backside of Mount Baekdu," as they always felt a deep affinity to the mountain.

Hanbae-geom: Dan'gun Wanggeom (the king who founded Gojoseon in 2333 B.C. in the foundation mythology—Trans.). The seeds: Descendants of Dan'gun.

26. Words are by Henry Carey (1687–1743). Lyrics copied from New Korean-English Hymnal #79.—Trans.

27. Chunmong, "Righteousness (2)," *Dongnip Shinmun*, November 15, 1919, 4.

28. *Dongnip Shinmun*, January 22, 1920, reprinted in National Institute of Korean History, *History of Korean Independence Movement III*, 573.

29. Author's personal interview with Han Jun-myeong (undated).—Trans.

30. Author's personal interview with Mun Ik-hwan (undated).—Trans.

31. Kim Jeong-u, "Childhood of Yun Dong-ju," 120–121.

32. Author's personal interview with Han Jun-myeong (undated).—Trans.

33. Author's personal interview with Han Jun-myeong (undated).—Trans.

34. Author's personal interview with Han Jun-myeong (undated).—Trans.

35. Author's personal interview with Han Jun-myeong (undated).—Trans.

36. Author's personal interview with Kim Shin-muk (undated).—Trans.

37. Bolshevism refers to the Marxism developed by Lenin during the age of imperialism and proletariat revolutions.

38. Song WooHye, "Studies on the Organization of North Gando 'Korean Citizens Association,'" 127.

39. "The First Lecture of the Association of Korean Students in Japan."

40. Kim Jun-yeop and Kim Chang-sun, "So-Called Gando Communists Incidents," 385–400.

41. Author's personal interview with Han Jun-myeong (undated).—Trans.

42. Author's personal interview with Han Jun-myeong (undated).—Trans.

43. Author's personal interview with Kim Shin-muk (undated).—Trans.

Chapter 3   Yongjeong

1. A pine tree on top of Biam Mountain in Yongjeong. It was a beloved symbol of Koreans in North Gando, and it is said that by 1938, the Japanese officials had killed it. The City of Yongjeong planted another pine tree in 1990.—Trans.

2. Jo Du-nam, "Getting It off My Chest," 217.

3. Jo Du-nam, "Getting It off My Chest," 217.

4. The Fourth Republic of Korea (1972–1979) in South Korea.—Trans.

5. Author's personal interview with Kim Shin-muk (undated).—Trans.

6. Author's personal interview with Jeong Dae-wi (undated).—Trans.

7. Kim Jeong-myeong, "Status Report on Joseon Independence Movement against Japan in Gando," 99 (emphasis added).

8. Yun Il-ju, "Life of Yun Dong-ju," 153.

9. Kim Jeong-u, "Childhood of Yun Dong-ju," 115. Yun's age in Kim's quote is calculated using the traditional Korean age. According to the international system, Yun was thirteen in the fall of 1931.—Trans.

10. Yun Il-ju, "Life of Yun Dong-ju," 153.

11. Reverend Kang Won-yong's memory of this is different. According to Reverend Kang, Yun's classmate, Yun was placed third and he was placed first, with a speech titled "The Fist." Reverend Kang was praised for his oratory skills in various contests and national meetings when he was in school and later became a great Christian preacher, regarded as "one in one hundred years." As the direct testimony of an innately gifted orator, he is likely to be correct.

12. Yun Il-ju, "Life of Yun Dong-ju," 153.

13. Both before and after Manchukuo, English Hill always enjoyed extraterritoriality. Manchukuo was established in March 1932, and Yun, Mun, and others started Eunjin Middle School in April 1932. Thus, in terms of the time frame, they began entering English Hill after Manchukuo was set up. Thus, what is described here about Eunjin Middle School was a special phenomenon because of English Hill's extraterritoriality even under the rule of Manchukuo.

14. Mun Ik-hwan, "Yun Dong-ju, the Poet of Sky, Wind, and Star," 310–311.

15. Mun Ik-hwan, "Yun Dong-ju, the Poet of Sky, Wind, and Star," 310–311.

16. Mun Ik-hwan, "Yun Dong-ju, the Poet of Sky, Wind, and Star," 310–311.

Chapter 4   Song Mong-gyu

1. In Korea, the transliterated French term *conte* refers to flash fiction. In the West, it refers to short tales or novellas.—Trans.

2. *Donga Ilbo*, January 1, 1935.

3. Typos, punctuation, spelling discrepancies, and other mistakes in the original text are not reflected in the translation.—Trans.

4. Author's personal interview with Song Ung-gyu (undated).—Trans.

5. Author's personal interview with Kim Jeong-u (undated).—Trans.

6. This "incident" was staged by the Japanese army as an excuse to demand the Chinese army to evacuate the Shanhai Pass, a major pass in the Great Wall of China near Liaodong Bay.—Trans.

7. Mun Ik-hwan, "Yun Dong-ju, the Poet of Sky, Wind, and Star," 311.

8. Yun Il-ju, "Life of Yun Dong-ju," 153–154.

9. "Complete Records of Imperial Japan's Special High Police Regarding Its Interrogation of Yun Dong-ju," 303.

10. Kim Jeong-myeong, "Status of Seditious Schemes by Rogue Joseon People in China in 1936," 589.

11. Kim Gu, *Baekbeom Diary*, 278–279.

12. Author's personal interview with Ra Sa-haeng (undated).—Trans.

13. Kim Gu, *Baekbeom Diary*, 287–288.

14. Saeki Yuichi and Nomura Koichi, *Modern History of China*, 402.

15. Author's personal interview with Ra Sa-haeng (undated).—Trans.

16. Kim Jeong-myeong, "Status of Seditious Schemes by Rogue Joseon People in China in 1936," 590.

17. Author's personal interview with Song Ung-gyu (undated).—Trans.

Chapter 5   Seven Months in Pyeongyang

1. Yun Il-ju, "Life of Yun Dong-ju," 154.

2. *Sungshil University: A 90-Year History*, 257.

3. Mun Ik-hwan, "Yun Dong-ju, the Poet of Sky, Wind, and Star," 312.

4. Pak Eun-hui, "Formation of Yun Dong-ju's Symmetrical Ideas." The article lists this book in its references. Presumably, then, Professor Pak is familiar with my views on this point but disagrees with them.

5. Pak Eun-hui, "Formation of Yun Dong-ju's Symmetrical Ideas." Professor Pak based this statement on the Japanese translation of *Modern Korean Literary History* by Kim Yong-seong, from which she quoted the part on Kang So-cheon. I quote from the same book in the original in this chapter.

6. Kim Yong-seong, *Modern Korean Literary History*, 397.

7. Kim Yong-seong, *Modern Korean Literary History*, 401.

8. Kim Yong-seong wrote about Kang's stay in North Gando based on Jeon Taek-bu's statement. However, Jeon's statement and Kim's writing were not consistent.

9. Jeon Taek-bu, "So-cheon's Hometown and Me," 312. This statement contains errors. Kang had never published in *Donga Ilbo* and *Joseon Ilbo* up to this point in time. Further, the cessation of the two papers and *Kids' Life* did not take place during the time frame mentioned by Jeon.

10. Kang, who was from South Hamgyeong Province, might have met Yun in Yongjeong when attending church. Kang was a fervent Christian and must have gone to church while in Yongjeong, and it may have been the church that Yun attended.

11. Shin Hyeon-deuk, "Roar with a Child's Heart against Japan," 320. See the list of Kang's published works.

12. What Jeon Taek-bu quoted as Kang's comment on Yun's poems probably concerns the draft of poems Yun had before leaving for Pyeongyang in August 1935. Jeon Taek-bu was Kang's fourth-year classmate and friend from Yeongsaeng High School in Hamheung. Jeon lost touch with Kang when Kang left school in December 1933, and they did not meet again until Kang arrived in South Korea during the Heungnam Evacuation (December 1950). Therefore, by the time Kang made statements about his friendship with Yun and Yun's poems, Yun had a firm status as a famous poet in Korean society.

13. Shin Hyeon-deuk, "Roar with a Child's Heart against Japan," 320. See the list of Kang's published works. Even if titles mentioned in Kim Yong-seong's book are added (including those works pointed out by Shin Hyeon-deuk as "erroneously reported"), the number is barely over ten.

14. *Sungshil University: A 90-Year History*, 361.

15. It was Sungshil University at the time of the Korean Empire but was downgraded to Sungshil Junior College by the Japanese government after the annexation. Japan had a policy of allowing only one university in Korea, and the existing one was Gyeongseong Imperial University.

16. *Sungshil University: A 90-Year History*, 336.

17. *Sungshil University: A 90-Year History*, 338.

18. *Sungshil University: A 90-Year History*, 341.

19. Gwangbokhoe (Liberation Association), established in 1965, is an organization for former independence fighters and their descendants.—Trans.

20. *Donga Ilbo*, August 16, 1982.

21. By "Pyeong · Sang" Yun denotes that he conceived/planned the poem in Pyeongyang.

Chapter 6   Return to Yongjeong

1. The information was gathered from Jang Yun-cheol (b. 1908, former principal at Shinil High School). Mr. Jang was a student at Eunjin Middle School at the time.

2. Han Sang-il, "Continental Wanderers," 6.

3. Mun Ik-hwan, "Yun Dong-ju, the Poet of Sky, Wind, and Star," 321.

4. Led by President Rhee Syngman from 1948 to 1960.—Trans.

5. Seo Byeong-uk, "Park ChungHee's Manchu Officer Connection," 406.

6. Led by President Park ChungHee from 1962 to 1972.—Trans.

7. While the author does not cite the source, a photocopy of the report card is printed on page 203 of the Korean version, which is not included in this book. She seems to have had access to the school materials that Omura Morio collected, as mentioned in the earlier paragraph.—Trans.

8. The Five-Color was Manchukuo's flag, and the Rising Sun was imperial Japan's flag. As Manchukuo was Japan's colony, both flags were hung over each side of the gate on holidays.

9. The pen name has the same pronunciation as his actual name but with a different Chinese character for "Dong."

10. Yun Il-ju, "Life of Yun Dong-ju," 155.

11. Author's personal interview with Yun Hye-won (undated).—Trans.

12. *Sky and Wind and Star and Poem*, 246.

13. Yun Il-ju, "Life of Yun Dong-ju," 155.

14. Author's personal interview with Yun Hye-won (undated).—Trans.

Chapter 7   Yonhui Junior College

1. Jang Deok-sun, "Yun Dong-ju and I," 143–144.

2. After liberation, Yonhui took the new name "Yonsei University."—Trans.

3. Jo Seong-hwan, *Conversations with Beijing*, 255.

4. Yu Yeong, "Yun Dong-ju during the Days of Yonhui Junior College," 122–126.

5. Yun Dong-ju, "Beginning and the End," 187.

6. The "a" in Sun-a is a postpositional particle attached to a name, when the person is addressed familiarly.—Trans.

7. Traditionally, Korean peasants wore white. They called themselves *baekui minjok* (people of white garment).—Trans.

8. Author's personal interview with Yun Hye-won (undated).—Trans.

9. Author's personal interview with Yun Hye-won (undated).—Trans.

10. Author's personal interview with Yun Hye-won (undated).—Trans.

11. Author's personal interview with Yun Hye-won (undated).—Trans.

12. Yun Il-ju, "Life of Yun Dong-ju," 155–156.

13. Yun Il-ju, "Life of Yun Dong-ju," 156–157.

14. The author did not cite the source. However, Yonhui school records (including report cards) of both Yun Dong-ju and Song Mong-gyu, along with other sources, are on display at Yun Dong-ju Kinyeomgwan (Yun Dong-ju Memorial Hall) in Yonsei University.—Trans.

15. Author's personal interview with Jeong Gu-gwan (undated).—Trans.

16. Yun Dong-ju, "Beginning and the End," 187-189.

17. Duus, *Modern Japan*, 243.

18. Won Il-han, "My Curriculum Vitae," 6.

19. Ma Gwang-su, *Study on Yun Dong-ju*, 116.

20. The English version used here is a translation by Constance Garnett. The original poem is thought to have been written in February 1878.—Trans.

21. The English translation used here is by Dante Gabriel Rossetti.

22. Kim Gwang-seop, "Departure for Poetry," 308–309.

23. The author did not cite the source. However, Yonhui school records (including report cards) of both Yun Dong-ju and Song Mong-gyu, along with other sources, are on display at Yun Dong-ju Kinyeomgwan (Yun Dong-ju Memorial Hall) in Yonsei University.—Trans.

24. Won Il-han, "My Curriculum Vitae," 6.

25. Jeong Byeong-uk, "Unforgettable Events concerning Yun Dong-ju," 134–135.

26. Yun Il-ju, "Life of Yun Dong-ju," 157.

27. Ra Sa-haeng, "25-Year History of the Methodist Theological School."

28. Ra Sa-haeng, "25-Year History of the Methodist Theological School," 338.

29. King James Version.—Trans.

30. The author did not cite the source. However, Yonhui school records (including report cards) of both Yun Dong-ju and Song Mong-gyu, along with other sources, are on display at Yun Dong-ju Kinyeomgwan (Yun Dong-ju Memorial Hall) in Yonsei University.—Trans.

31. Won Il-han, "My Curricula Vitae," 6.

32. Jeong Byeong-uk, "Unforgettable Events concerning Yun Dong-ju," 137–138.

33. See chapter 2.—Trans.

34. Jeong Byeong-uk, Unforgettable Events concerning Yun Dong-ju, 140–141.

35. Yun Il-ju, "Life of Yun Dong-ju," 160.

36. Yi Gwang-su, "Tokyo Travelogue," 184.

37. Mizuno Naoki, "Did Yun Dong-ju Do *Changssi Gaemeyong*?," 166.

38. About the name change, Professor Mizuno argued in the previously cited article:

> It is true that Yun's legal sir name became *Hiranuma* by 1942. However, his first name remained the same. The Japanese pronunciation of the Chinese characters for Dong-ju is *Doojyu*, but his first name was not changed since its pronunciation was not legally changed (on the family registry). Therefore, while his surname changed, we cannot say Yun changed his name." (Mizuno Naoki, "Did Yun Dong-ju Do *Changssi Gaemeyong*?," 161)

However, I cannot agree with this view. It is a complacent presumption in contradiction to the circumstances Korea faced at that time. Let us go over them here.

Toward the end of the annexation, all Koreans were forcefully mandated to use Japanese at all times under the National Language (Japanese) Use Policy. Even small children were severely punished if they spoke Korean during playtime at school. When these realities are considered, Professor Mizuno's claim that "his first name was not changed since its pronunciation was not legally changed (on the family registry)" does not stand.

Instead, the focus should be on the correlation between the name change law and the National Language Use Policy. I assume that the name change policy enforced by the governor-general toward the end of colonization, aside from its ideological reasons, guaranteed a practical role of perfecting the National Language Use Policy.

Even the forceful mandate of the National Language Use Policy could not simply make Korean names Japanese. Because personal names were Korean proper nouns, they would be the last traces of the Korean language. If Korean names were changed to Japanese, they could eliminate *all* Korean words from Koreans' speech. This way, Japan's National Language Use Policy could achieve perfect success.

Even commonsensically, it is inconceivable that, while the National Language Use Policy was the supreme policy, anyone would use both Japanese and Korean pronunciations for a Japanese-style name, calling Yun "Hiranuma Dong-ju." In fact, according to his relatives, Yun was called "Hiranuma Doojyu."

For these reasons, after analyzing the facts correctly, we must conclude that Yun acquiesced to *changssi gaemyeong*, unlike the view of Professor Mizuno.

39. Recently, an article examined the issue of why Yun and Song submitted the name change request to Yonhui College at that late date from a new perspective. It is the article by Professor Mizuno at Kyoto University. He wrote:

> It is probably between February and August of 1940 that Yun Ha-hyeon, as the head of the clan, registered the family's new Japanese name Hiranuma with the Registry Office. [According to the *changssi gaemyeong* edict, new names had to be registered between February 11 and August 10, 1940, and Professor Mizuno's assumption is reasonable.]
>
> … In 1940, the Yun family's new name was "Hiranuma," and the Songs' "Somura." But Yun and Song did not report this to Yonhui College and continued to use their Korean names. In December 1941, they graduated from Yonhui with their Korean names unchanged.
>
> … In February 1941, Yun Chi-ho became the new superintendent of Yonhui College. As mentioned in the book by this author, Yun Chi-ho probably did not willingly change his name, but the newspapers reported that he was the front man in propagating the governor-general's *changssi gaemyeong* policy. When Yun Chi-ho took over the superintendent position at Yonhui, Yun and Song might have been against it. Perhaps they did not change their names during that time because of that.
>
> Yun and Song did not change their names until after they graduated, right before they went to Japan to study, and the above are the possible reasons. (Mizuno Naoki, "Did Yun Dong-ju do Changssi Gaemyeong?," 163–167)

Professor Mizuno does not fully understand the extent of humiliation, pain, and agony *changssi gaemyeong* brought to Koreans. His statement that "perhaps they did not change their names during that time because" Yun and Song "might have been against" Yun Chi-ho's appointment is an ill-judged conclusion.

Koreans were forced by the governor-general to change their own unique Korean surnames and given names to Japanese names. By erroneously reducing such a traumatic national event to personal feelings against an individual, Professor Mizuno has changed the essence of the matter.

Moreover, the view is inconsistent with the timing of the event. Yun Chi-ho took over the post in February 1941. Their surnames had already changed between February 11 and August 10, 1940, but they did not report their *changssi gaemyeong* at Yonhui even when their revered Dr. Underwood was the superintendent. This is evidence that *changssi gaemyeong* had nothing to do with Yun Chi-ho. Yun and Song requested their name change only when they had absolutely no other option.

40. Yun Il-ju, "Life of Yun Dong-ju," 155.

41. Yun Il-ju, "Life of Yun Dong-ju," 158.

42. Mun Ik-hwan, "Memories of Dong-ju," 215.

43. The author did not cite the source. However, Yonhui school records (including report cards) of both Yun Dong-ju and Song Mong-gyu, along with other

sources, are on display at Yun Dong-ju Kinyeomgwan (Yun Dong-ju Memorial Hall) in Yonsei University.—Trans.

Chapter 8   Japan

1. Author's personal interview with Kim Shin-muk (undated).—Trans.

2. Yun Yeong-chun, "From Myeongdong Village to Fukuoka," 110.

3. Kim Jeong-u, "Childhood of Yun Dong-ju," 121.

4. A tatami mat is 180 cm wide and 90 cm long, and two tatami mats are equivalent to one *pyeong*. Thus, a six-tatami-mat room is a three-*pyeong* room. (A six-tatami mat room, in turn, is about 106 square feet.—Trans.)

5. Kim Yun-sik, *Yi Gwang-su and His Era*, 480 (quoting Yajima Fumio, *Universities of Japan*, 104).

6. The author did not cite the source, but included an image of the article on page 338 in the Korean version, with a comment that it is from Rikkyo University News dated April 10, 1942.—Trans.

7. Such ideological harassment took place in Korea too. The following is a testimony about that:
"After the Sino-Japanese War started in 1937, Christians were often interrogated or taken to the police station. They were asked, 'Which is higher, your god or the Emperor? Which is more important, the Bible or the Imperial message? Is shrine worship a religious ceremony or secular ceremony?' These questions were ludicrous, a trap." Yi Seong-sam, *Methodism and the History of Seminaries*, 209.

8. Yun Yeong-chun, "From Myeongdong Village to Fukuoka," 109.

9. Jeong Byeong-uk, "Unforgettable Events concerning Yun Dong-ju," 138.

10. Jeong Dae-wi, *Nodakdari Chorok Durumari*, 23–24.

11. Ibuki Gou, "Waiting for the Morning of the Epoch," 351–352.

12. Yun Yeong-chun, "From Myeongdong Village to Fukuoka," 110–111.

13. Ibuki Gou, "Waiting for the Morning of the Epoch," 353.

Chapter 9   Arrest, Trial, Imprisonment, and Death

1. Author's personal interview Yun Hye-won (undated).—Trans.

2. In spring 1942, the Japanese government shut down *Seongseo Joseon* (Bible Joseon), a religious periodical published by Ham Seok-hyeon, and imprisoned dozens of people based on an article printed in its March issue.—Trans.

3. See *Munhak Sasang* 43 (April 1976).—Trans.

4. The facts and quotations in this subsection are based on the author's undated personal interview with Ko Hui-uk.—Trans.

5. Chian Ijiho, *Security Maintenace Law and the Special Police*, 131.

6. See *Munhak Sasang* 63 (December 1977).—Trans.

7. Song was Yun's paternal aunt's son, and they studied together at Myeongdong Grade School, Eunjin Middle School, and Yonhui Junior College. Song's disposition was radical and active, while Yun's was mild and composed.—Author.

8. People's High School was Machukuo's equivalent to middle school, even though Song had already graduated from Daeseong Middle School in Yongjeong.—Author.

9. Myeong, a graduate of Tokyo Imperial University, taught Asian history, Korean history, and Chinese writing at Eunjin Middle School. He infused nationalism into the hearts of his students.—Author.

10. This refers to the Japanese Consulate in the Qing dynasty (later changed to China and then Manchuguo), located in Yongjeong, Gando. The affairs of Koreans in Manchuria were overseen by the consulate's police.—Author.

11. *Munu* was not an alumni publication but the college's literature department publication. Song and Yun each published poetry in *Munu* around the time of their graduation from Yonhui.—Author.

12. This is an error. Yun was in the preparatory program in the English Department at Rikkyo University, which still has records of his enrollment there.—Author.

13. Japanese universities did not recognize the diploma from Joseon's junior colleges, whose graduates, even after passing the entrance examination, were separated in the "preparatory department."—Author.

14. As recorded at the end of this document, Ko, from Gyedong 14–18, Seoul, was first mentioned here.—Author.

15. The Korean name of this individual and his identity are unknown.—Author.

16. This refers to the formal transfer of the suspects to the prosecution after police investigation. As indicated in this list, the three were arrested on July 14, 1943, transferred to the prosecution on December 6 of the same year, and locked up as prisoners under trial until the following June. At the subsequent trial, Song and Yun were sentenced to thirty months' imprisonment and twenty-four months' imprisonment, respectively.—Author.

17. Kim Jeong-myeong, "Status of Seditious Schemes by Rogue Joseon People in China in 1936," 589. The list recorded in this source is most trustworthy, as it was explicitly compiled by the Special Police over the arrests relating to the Nakyang Military School case.

18. Pak Gyeong-shik, *Compiled Records Relating to the Korean-Japanese People*, quoted in Ibuki Gou, "Waiting for the Morning of the Epoch," 303.

19. Ibuki Gou, "Waiting for the Morning of the Epoch," 305.

20. Yun Il-ju, "Life of Yun Dong-ju," 160.

21. Yun Yeong-chun, "From Myeongdong Village to Fukuoka," 112–113.

22. Kim Jeong-u, "Childhood of Yun Dong-ju," 121.

23. Author's personal interview with Kim Jeong-u (undated)—Trans.

24. See *Munhak Sasang* 110 (October 1982).—Trans.

25. The Yun family is not from Cheongjin, but due to an administrative error, his place of origin was recorded accordingly.—Author.

26. Yun Dong-ju was born in 1917, but the birth registry erroneously recorded it as 1918, which appears in all the school and police records.—Author.

27. Miyake Shotaro, "Public Order Maintenance Law," 222–223.

28. Miyake Shotaro, "Public Order Maintenance Law," 207, 211.

29. See Kim Gu, *Baekbeom Diary*, 195–196, 220–221.

30. See Jeong Gwang-hyeon, *History of the March First Independence Movement*, 7–12.

31. See Ju Yo-han, *Biography of An Do-san*, 360–361.

32. Yi Seok-rin, "Joseon Linguistic Society Case and Dr. Choe Hyeon-bae," 129–134.

33. Choe Jong-go, *History of Jurisprudence and Philosophy of Law*, 413.

34. Ibuki Gou, "Waiting for the Morning of the Epoch," 312.

35. Kim Gwang-seop, *My Prison Diary*, 43.

36. Yun Il-ju, "Life of Yun Dong-ju," 161–162.

37. Yun Il-ju, "Life of Yun Dong-ju," 162.

38. Yun Yeong-chun, "From Myeongdong Village to Fukuoka," 113–114.

39. Author's personal interview Ra Sa-haeng (undated).—Trans.

40. Kono Eiji, "Yun Dong-ju and the Mystery of His Death," 323–325.

41. Quoted from Ibuki Gou, "Waiting for the Morning of the Epoch," 312.

42. Here, Mr. Kim Heon-sul's statement must be carefully examined. Mr. Kim was honored in 1977 by the South Korean government as an "independence patriot." He stated that he saw Yun at Fukuoka Prison and that he himself was subjected to live human biomedical experimentation. The content of his statement is as follows:

In August 1942, Mr. Kim was 18 years old and was enrolled in Kyoto Middle School as a fourth-year student when he was arrested in connection with the "Kyoto Foreign Students Case" and tried at Kyoto District Court. He was sent to Fukuoka Prison in June 1943 and stayed there until his term ended in September 1944. During his stay in prison, he saw Yun.

All political prisoners were in solitary confinement. Kim was locked up in Cell 48 of the North Third Wing, and Yun was in Cell 108, across from Kim's cell. The cell, like the prosecution's cells, was hermetic. Kim saw Yun for the first time in the early summer of 1944. He heard a new prisoner being moved into the cell facing his and looked through the watch hole on his door. A young man was led by a guard to Cell 108, holding a thin blue blanket, a pillow, and a food bowl. The guard locked the door after him and hung the sign "STRICT" which meant it held a political prisoner.

Later, when prisoners went out to the yard for exercise, Kim was able to exchange names with the new prisoner, who introduced himself as "Yun Dong-ju from Doshisha University in Kyoto."

Mr. Kim's forced labor in prison was to sew cotton work gloves and cotton work socks. When he left the prison, he received 12 won for compensation. His statement concerns two topics: (1) the live human biomedical experimentation he underwent; and (2) his observation of Yun Dong-ju. (Kim Heon-sul, "Yun Dong-ju, Last Seen," 291–293.)

(1) The live human biomedical experimentation Mr. Kim underwent

Before I first met Yun Dong-ju, in the winter of 1942 [This is a mistake. Mr. Kim was sent to Fukuoka Prison in May 1943], I had a strange experience. In winter, the cell is dark and cold like absolute hell. My hands and feet were frostbitten, bloody, and swollen. Yet, I had to fill the quota for the day's work. That day, I was working hard, stitching the socks with a needle. The guard opened the door and told me to come out. My heart sank, thinking that the prison director wanted to see me. I stopped the work and followed the guard.

Other prisoners were coming out, too. We followed the guard out to the open area in the center. Some had been there before, and I saw my comrade Yi Won-gu. He was in the same wing, but we never had a chance to talk, so our words rushed out. "How's your health?" "When will you be discharged?" "Are your working skills better?" "Are you reading any book?"

Others were following our suit, too. As I talked to other comrades, I received news of others. They were all my seniors by four or five years. [...] The guard came and led us all into the hospital ward.

When we entered the exam room, the prison doctor told us to sit on the wooden chairs there. The doctor, an intelligentsia, seemed sympathetic to us. "You are all promising young men. . . . Will Joseon become independent?" As he looked round at us, he looked sorry for us. He said he used to have his own medical practice but was drafted. He was placed as a prison doctor because he was too old to be a military doctor.

Shortly afterward, he distributed sheets of paper with arithmetic questions and told us to quickly put down the answers. There were several hundred simple adding and subtraction questions. We put down the answers without knowing why we had to do them. About five minutes later, the doctor told us to stop and collected the answers.

One of us, Jo Hui-dal, who had been a medical student at Kyushu University, asked the doctor, "I'm studying medicine, too, but what are you trying to do with this?" The doctor said, smiling, "Nothing special." He then gave each of us an injection of 5 to 10 cc on the arm. We did not know what these injections were. We did not understand and let ourselves be injected. I rolled the sleeves up my bony arm to be injected each day.

It continued for over a week. After a few days, our arithmetic abilities were reduced by more than half. After a week, many answers were wrong, too. We called this the live body experiment.

(2) Yun Dong-ju, Last Seen

The door to the cell opened about five times a day for activities like cleaning, meditation, meals, latrine box exchange, exercise, bringing in and taking out materials for labor, and baths (once in a while). For latrine box exchange, exercise, and baths, the prisoner went out to the corridor. Especially when exchanging latrine boxes, prisoners would bring out the dirty ones and bring the formalin-filled latrine box back in, and that was when we could see each other up close.

I did not see Yun during the latrine box exchange because he took a long time to take it out. He seemed to be in ill health and couldn't move the box quickly. The box was made of wooden pieces shaped like Japanese soy sauce or wine containers. A healthy person can easily lift it with two hands. Yun seemed to have a hard time with it. After he moved the box, he'd go back to his room without looking around.

Yun's face often looked flushed. Most prisoners were pale, but he seemed to have a fever, not just a low-grade fever at that, either.

When our eyes met during the latrine box exchange, he had no expression. Even though we introduced ourselves to each other, he did not seem to bother with anything. It was a face of emptiness and futility.

Yun was tall and well-proportioned. He had a wide forehead which seemed to protrude a bit. He was so emaciated that there was a triangular depression under each temple, and his chin looked sharp. Like other political prisoners at the time, Yun looked like a classical scholar and had an irrefutable air of dignity.

On the bath day, we'd strip in the cell and come out naked to line up to the bathroom. We called this the "parade of skeletons." Yun's parade of skeletons was miserable. He was large-boned, and his shoulders, arms, legs, and chest looked like skin-covered bones. There was an American prisoner in the same wing, and he looked like that, too. Large-framed bodies seemed to reveal emaciation fully, and it was a sight difficult to witness.

Generally, prisoners' health deteriorated noticeably between arraignment and conviction due to the severe torture. The Japanese torture was notorious for being primitive and vicious. I imagined that Yun's body deteriorated in the process as well.

We woke up at 5 A.M. (5:30 A.M. in winter) and wet-mopped the floor. We then had to sit for half an hour to meditate. The lead guard then roll-called. He'd grab the lock of the cell door, shouting "number," and we had to shout back our numbers. Mine was 257, but I do not remember hearing Yun's because his voice was quiet like a mosquito's. No long-term prisoner had enough strength, but Yun's strength seemed even worse. He could not even walk straight.

In the summer of 1944, I had four months left to go, and I endured the bone-breaking pains. Sometimes I begged the guard to transfer me to the infirmary because of pain. Sometimes I begged to be exempt from labor. Summertime was unbearable, too. After twelve hours of labor on the hard floor, the whole body ached. The oppressing heat made breathing difficult, and I felt the urge to kill myself several times a day. [. . .]

Yun did not even come out for exercise at times. Sometimes I thought that he was transferred, but I would notice movement there and see the meal tray being returned. I saw a figure leaving the latrine box and returning to his cell. "He looks terrible," I said to myself.

Once during the roll call, there was a commotion in Cell 108. The guard went into it, followed by someone from the medical room. Silence soon followed, and I deduced that Yun must have fainted while sitting for meditation. Even in such a condition, they wouldn't move him to the infirmary. What can one do but curse the cruel punishment.

The previous account is the statement of Kim Heon-sul. At first glance, his descriptions are dynamic and convincing. However, his description of Yun makes one wonder. In the fall of 1944, Yun had written to his brother: "I am grateful that your crickets chirp away in my solitary cell, too." His style of writing and the spirit reflected in it show the dignity and gracefulness that a weak dying person could not possibly have. But according to Mr. Kim, Yun was on the verge of death. How much of it can we believe?

Additionally, during an interview by the monthly magazine *Bit* [Light—Trans.], published in Daegu, Mr. Kim claimed that Yun's cause of death might have been tuberculosis. The magazine reports:

> Mr. Kim says that it is not likely that Yun Dong-ju died of live human biomedical experimentation.
>
> Kim and his comrades went through the "live body experiment," but while it made them fatigued, it would not have led anyone to death. Instead, he wonders whether Yun was suffering from tuberculosis, judging from the symptoms. Kim himself had the disease later on and is convinced of it. (Seo Dong-hun, "Kim Heon-sul, Who Served His Term in Fukuoka Prison with the Poet Yun Dong-ju," 30.)

This seems to be a ludicrous claim. Mr. Kim was "experimented" on in the winter of 1943, but Yun's death took place in February 1945. Kim's theory may stand only under the premise that experimentation of the same kind and intensity kept repeating over a long period.

But how could that be possible? Experiments lead to other experiments based on the results of the earlier ones. Mr. Kim is only reflecting on his earlier experience in reaching his conclusion. Further, he was released months before Yun's death and could not have known what went on in Fukuoka Prison afterward.

Most crucially, Mr. Kim's conclusion directly contrasts with Song's statement to Yun Yeong-chun. According to Yun Yeong-chun, Song was skin and bones; his voice was hard to hear, as if coming from another world; and his hands were feverish and hot. When asked what happened, Song replied, "I'm like this because they gave me shots, and Dong-ju, too." If one must choose between Song's statement and the statement of Mr. Kim who left the prison five months before that, it will have to be Song's.

How do we evaluate Mr. Kim's statement, then? His narrative seems too dramatically exaggerated and embellished, which is almost fatal to its trustworthiness. Even the examination of his statement about his sentence reveals such a tendency.

Mr. Kim was involved in an incident called the "book club case." The club members, Korean foreign students in Kyoto, were arrested tried for the violation of Public Order Maintenance Law and Lese-Majeste Law. About the sentence term he received, see the following: "Two years' imprisonment. The judge's order that '[Kim] deserves a summary execution. But since this is his first offense, the court only sentences him to two years of imprisonment,' and this was preposterous to [Mr. Kim]. He could no longer trust in their conscience and gave up the idea of appeal. Nowadays, there's an 'inflation of sentence terms,' and even ten years' imprisonment is not uncommon; in those days, however, two years' imprisonment was a rarity. But he accepted it as the suffering he must endure." (Seo Dong-hun, "Kim Heon-sul, Who Served His Term in Fukuoka Prison with the Poet Yun Dong-ju," 26.)

When this author checked the documents filed with South Korea's Ministry of Patriots and Veterans Affairs, Mr. Kim's sentence term was not two years' imprisonment. Rather, it was "1 year and 6 months' imprisonment (including 90 days of pre-trial detention)."

A biographer must examine all sources and testimony before her and investigate facts and values that are trustworthy. This detailed footnote is recorded here for posterity, in the case that Mr. Kim's "tuberculosis hypothesis" becomes a new research subject among Yun Dong-ju researchers in the future.

43. Author's personal interview with Yun Hye-won (undated).—Trans.

Chapter 10   Here Lies Yun Dong-ju the Poet

1. Yun Il-ju, "Life of Yun Dong-ju," 162.
2. Author's personal interview with Yun Hye-won (undated).—Trans.
3. Author's personal interview with Yun Hye-won (undated).—Trans.

4. Author's personal interview with Yun Hye-won (undated).—Trans.

5. Author's personal interview with Yun Hye-won (undated).—Trans.

6. Author's personal interview with Yun Hye-won (undated).—Trans.

7. Author's personal interview with Kim Shin-muk (undated).—Trans.

8. Author's personal interview with Kim Jeong-u (undated).—Trans.

9. Author's personal interview with Yun Hye-won (undated).—Trans.

10. *Botchi* is a large piece of birch bark pressed flat and dried. When used as a covering, it waterproofs the coffin. It is a North Gando custom that filial children prepare *botchi* for their parents' funeral.

11. Same pronunciation but with different Chinese characters.—Trans.

Chapter 11   The Glory of the National Poet

1. Jeong Byeong-uk, "Unforgettable Events concerning Yun Dong-ju," 141.

2. Author's personal interview with Jeong Deok-hui (undated).—Trans.

3. Author's personal interview with Jeong Deok-hui (undated).—Trans.

4. See *Kyunghyang Shinmun: A Forty-Year History.*—Trans.

5. *Kyunghyang Shinmun*, February 13, 1947.—Trans.

6. Author's personal interview with Jang Deok-sun (undated).—Trans.

7. How many poems by Yun Dong-ju survive? Professor Yun In-seok (the late Yun Il-ju's eldest son) stated, "Currently, we have 150 handwritten pieces if we even count a one-page sheet that only bears the title 'Missing Handcuff.' Excluding duplicate versions, the total is 128, of which 124 are poems, and four are essays."

8. Gang Cheo-jung, "Admiral Yi, the Lord of Chungmu," 2.—Trans.

9. *Kyunghyang Shinmun*, September 22, 1953.—Trans.

10. "Jeong Guk-eun Case Investigation Comes to an End."—Trans.

11. *Kyunghyang Shinmun*, September 22, 1953.—Trans.

12. Author's personal interview with Yi Gang-ja (undated).—Trans.

13. From Lin Yutang, *Biography of Su Dongpo.*—Trans.

BIBLIOGRAPHY

Chian Ijiho 松尾洋. *The Public Order Maintenance Law and the Special Police* 治安維持法と特高警察. Tokyo: Kyoisusha, 1979.

Choe Jong-go 최종고. *The History of Jurisprudence and Philosophy of Law* 法史와 法思想. Pakyeongsa, 1980.

Chunmong 春夢. "Righteousness (2)" 義 (二). *Dongnip Shinmun* 독립신문, November 15, 1919.

"The Complete Records of Imperial Japan's Special High Police Regarding Its Interrogation of Yun Dong-ju" 尹東柱에 대한 日警極祕取調文書全文. *Munhak Sasang* 문학사상, December 1977.

Duus, Peter 피터 두으스. *Modern Japan* 日本近代史. Translated by Kim Yong-deok 金容德 譯. Chishik Sanopsa, 1983.

"The First Lecture of the Association of Korean Students in Japan" 留日學友俱樂部의 第一回 講演. *Dongnip Shinmun* 독립신문, March 18, 1920.

Gang Deok-sang 姜德相 , ed. *Modern History Sources* 現代史資料. Vol. 28. Tokyo: Misuzu Shobo, 1972.

Gang Cheo-jung 강처중. "Admiral Yi, the Lord of Chungmu" 충무공 이순신. *Kyunghyang Shinmun* 경향신문. April 27, 1947.

Han Sang-il 韓相一. "Continental Wanderers" 大陸浪人. *A Study on Japan's Imperialism* 日本帝國主義의 한 研究. Kkachi, 1980.

Hwang Gu-tae 황구태ed., *The Translated Poetry of Du Fu* 두시 언해. Seoul: Kkum gwa Bijeon, 2023.

Ibuki Gou 伊吹鄉. "Waiting for the Morning of the Epoch" 時代의 아침을 기다리며. *Munhak Sasang* 문학사상, May 1985.

Jang Deok-sun 장덕순. "Yun Dong-ju and I" 윤동주와 나. *Nara Sarang* 나라사랑 23, June 1976.

Jeon Taek-bu 전택부. "So-cheon's Hometown and Me" 소천의 고향과 나. *The Complete Works of Children's Literature by Kang So-cheon* 강소천 아동문학전집. Vol. 2. Gyohaksa, 2006.

Jeong Byeong-uk 정병욱. "Unforgettable Events concerning Yun Dong-ju" 잊지못할 윤동주의 일들. *Nara Sarang* 나라사랑 23, June 1976.

Jeong Dae-wi 정대위. *Nodakdari Chorok Durumari* 노닥다리 초록 두루마리 [An Old Ox, a Green Overcoat]. Seoul, Jongno Seojeok, 1987.

"Jeong Guk-eun Case Investigation Comes to an End" 정국은 사건 수사 일단락. *Joseon Ilbo* 조선일보. October 28, 1953.

Jeong Gwang-hyeon 鄭光鉉. *The History of the March First Independence Movement* 독립운동사: 판례를 통해 본. Seoul: Beopmunsa, 1978.

Jo Du-nam 조두남. "Getting It off My Chest" 털어놓고 하는말. *The Deep-Rooted Tree* 뿌리깊은나무 31, September 1978.

Jo Seong-hwan 조성환. *Conversations with Beijing* 북경과의 대화. Gyeonggi-do Goyang-si: Hakgobang, 2008.

Ju Yo-han 주요한. *Biography of An Do-san* 안도산 전. Seoul: Samjungdang Mun'go, 1975.

Kim Gu 김구. *Baekbeom Diary* 백범일지. Seomundang, 1984.

Kim Gwang-seop 金珖燮. "Departure for Poetry" 詩에의 登程. In *My Prison Diary* 나의 獄中記. Changjak kwa Bipyeongsa, 1976.

Kim Heon-sul 김헌술. "Yun Dong-ju, Last Seen" 내가 마지막 본 尹東柱. *Jeonggyeong Munhwa* 정경문화, August 1985.

Kim Jeong-myeong 金正明, ed. "The Status of Seditious Schemes by Rogue Joseon People in China in 1936" 一九三六年の在支不逞朝鮮人の不穩策動狀況. *The History of Joseon Independence Movement* 朝鮮獨立運動史. Vol. 2. Japan: Hara Shobo, 1967.

———. "Status Report on Joseon Independence Movement against Japan in Gando" 間島における抗日獨立運動狀況報告の件. *The History of Joseon Independence Movement* 朝鮮獨立運動史. Vol. 3. Japan: Hara Shobo, 1967.

Kim Jeong-u 김정우. "Childhood of Yun Dong-ju" 윤동주의 소년시절. *Nara Sarang* 나라사랑 23, June 1976.

Kim Jun-yeop and Kim Chang-sun 김준엽, 김창순. "The So-Called Gando Communists Incidents" 세칭 간도 공산당 사건. *History of Korean Communist Movement* 한국 공산주의 운동사. Vol. 4. Seoul: Korea University Asiatic Research Center, 1974.

Kim Yong-seong 김용성. *Modern Korean Literary History* 한국 현대 문학사 탐방. Seoul: Hyeonamsa, 1984.

Kim Yun-shik. 김윤식. *Yi Gwang-su and His Era* 李光洙와 그의 시대. Vol. 2. Han'gilsa, 1986.

Kono Eiji 鴻農映二. "Yun Dong-ju and the Mystery of His Death" 윤동주, 그 죽음의 수수께끼. *Hyeondae Munhak* 현대문학, October 1980.

Kyunghyang Shinmun: A 40-Year History 경향신문 40년사. Seoul: Kyunghyang Shin-munsa, 1986.

Ma Gwang-su 마광수. *A Study on Yun Dong-ju* 尹東柱 研究. Jeongeumsa, 1984.

Miyake Shotaro 三宅正太郎. "Public Order Maintenance Law" 治安維持法. In *The Complete Modern Jurisprudence* 現代法學全集 第三十八卷. Vol. 38. Japan: Nihon Hyoronsha, 1931.

Mizuno Naoki 水野直樹. "Did Yun Dong-ju Do Changssi Gaemeyong?" 윤동주는 "창씨개명"을 했는가. *Tasi Ol Munhak* 다시올 文學, Winter 2013.

Mun Ik-hwan 문익환. "Memories of Dong-ju" 동주형의 추억. In *Sky and Wind and Star and Poem* 하늘과 바람과 별과 시, by Yun Dong-ju 윤동주. 6th ed. Jeongeumsa, 1983.

Mun Ik-hwan문익환. "Yun Dong-ju, the Poet of Sky, Wind, and Star" 하늘, 바람, 별의 詩人, 尹東柱. *Wolgan Jungang*, April 1976.

National Assembly Library of Korea 國會 圖書館. "Provisional National Council and Provisional Government Documents" 臨時 議政院 및 臨時 政府 書類. *Documents from the National Council of the Provisional Government of Korea* 大韓民國 臨時 政府 議政院 文書, 725–726. Seoul: National Assembly Library of Korea, 1974.

National Institute of Korean History 국사편찬위원회. *History of Korean Independence Movement* 한국 독립 운동사 三. Vol. 3. National Institute of Korean History, 1967.

National Institute of the Korean Language 국립 국어원. *The Standard Korean Language Dictionary* 표준 국어 대사전. Accessible at https://stdict.korean.go.kr /main/main.do

Office of National History, Kyoto University School of Letters 京都大学. 文学部. 国史研究室. *The Dictionary of Modern Japanese History* 日本近代史辭典. Tokyo: Tōyō Keizai Shinpōsha, 1966.

Pak Eun-hui 박은희. "The Formation of Yun Dong-ju's Symmetrical Ideas: Centering on the Poems from Early Summer of 1936" 윤동주의 對稱. *Tasi Ol Munhak* 70 (Winter 2013).

Pak Gyeong-shik 박경식, ed. *Compiled Records Relating to the Korean-Japanese People* 재일조선인 관계 집성. Samil Seobang, 1975.

Ra Sa-haeng 羅士行. "The 25-Year History of the Methodist Seminary School" 흘러간 감신 동창25년사. *Changhae Ilyeop*.

Saeki Yuichi and Nomura Koichi 佐伯有一, 野村浩一 外著. *Modern History of China* 中國現代史. Translated by O Sang-hoon 吳相勳. Han'gilsa, 1980.

Sunyoung Park. *The Proletarian Wave: Literature and Leftist Culture in Colonial Korea, 1910–1945.* Cambridge, MA: Harvard University Press, 2015.

Seo Byeong-uk 徐炳旭. "Park Chung-Hee's Manchu Officer Connection" 朴正熙의 滿軍人派 *Wolgan Joseon* 月刊朝鮮, August 1986.

Seo Dong-hun 서 동훈. "Kim Heon-sul, Who Served His Term in Fukuoka Prison with the Poet Yun Dong-ju" 詩人 윤동주와 함께 후쿠오카 형무소에서 감옥살이를 한 김헌술옹. *Bit* 빛, August 1987.

Shin Hyeon-deuk 신현득. "The Roar with a Child's Heart against Japan: The World of Kang So-cheon's Dongsi" 동심으로 외친 함성: 강소천 선생의 동시 세계. In *The Complete Works of Children's Literature by Kang So-cheon* 강소천아동문학전집. Vol. 10. Gyohaksa, 2006.

Song WooHye 송우혜. "Studies on the Organization of North Gando 'Korean Citizens Association'" 북간도 '대한국민회'의 조직 형태에 관한 연구. In *Korean Nationalistic Movement* 한국민족운동사연구, vol. 1. Jishik Sanopsa, 1986.

Sungshil University: A 90-Year History 숭실대학교 90년사. Seoul: Sungshil University Press, 1987.

Tajisaki Kenichi 藤崎健一. *Rikkyo Literature* 立教文學.

Won Il-han 원일한. "My Curriculum Vitae" 나의 이력서. *Hanguk Ilbo* 한국일보, January 20, 1982.

Yajima Fumio 矢島文雄. *Universities of Japan* 日本の大學. Osaka: Hoikusha, 1967.

Yi Gwang-su 이광수. "Tokyo Travelogue" 東京求景記. *Complete Works of Yi Gwang-su* 이광수전집. Vol. 9. Seoul: Samjungdang Mun'go, 1977.

Yi Seok-rin 이 석린. "The Joseon Linguistic Society Case and Dr. Choe Hyeon-bae." 조선 어학회 사건과 최현배 박사 *Nara Sarang* 1 (1971).

Yi Seong-sam 이 성삼. *Methodism and the History of Seminaries* 감리교와 신학대학사. Hanguk Kyoyuk Doseo Chulpansa, 1977.

Yu Yeong 유영. "Yun Dong-ju during the Days of Yonhui Junior College" 연희전문 시절의 윤동주. *Nara Sarang* 나라사랑 23, June 1976.

Yun Byeong-seok 윤병석. *The Biography of Yi Sang-seol* 이상설 전. Iljogak, 1984.

Yun Dong-ju 윤동주. *Sky and Wind and Star and Poem* 하늘과 바람과 별과 시. Jeongeumsa, 1948.

Yun Dong-ju 윤동주. "The Beginning and the End" 終始. In *Sky and Wind and Star and Poem* 하늘과 바람과 별과 시. 6th ed. Jeongeumsa, 1983.

Yun Il-ju 윤일주. "Life of Yun Dong-ju" 윤동주의 생애. *Nara Sarang* 나라사랑 23, June 1976.

Yun Yeong-chun 윤영춘. "From Myeongdong Village to Fukuoka" 명동촌에서 후쿠오카까지. *Nara Sarang* 나라사랑 23, June 1976.

Alphabetical List of Interviewees (Author's Undated Personal Interviews)

Han Jun-myeong 한 준명
Jang Deok-sun 장 덕순
Jeong Dae-wi 정 대위
Jeong Deok-hui 정 덕희
Jeong Gu-gwan 정 구관
Kim Jeong-u 김 정우
Kim Shin-muk 김 신묵
Ko Hui-uk 고 희욱

Mun Ik-hwan 문 익환
Mun Jae-rin 문 재린
Ra Sa-haeng 라 사행
Song Ung-gyu 송 웅규
Yi Gang-ja 이 강자
Yun Hye-won 윤 혜원
Yun Il-ju 윤 일주

NOTES ON CONTRIBUTORS

Widely recognized as a national poet, YUN DONG-JU has been one of the most popular poets in post–Korean War South Korea. His life and poetry have been the subject of countless scholarly articles and books, as well as a feature-length film. His poetry collection has been translated into several languages worldwide. In the United States, it was published as *Sky, Wind, and Stars* in 2003.

A historian and novelist, SONG WOOHYE has published biographies, collected essays, novels, and short-story collections. Best known for her work on Yun Dong-ju, she has also published papers on the history of North Gando and the Korean independence movement. She received the Samsung Literary Award in 1984.

FLORA M. KIM, born 1969 in New Jersey and raised in Seoul, is a freelance translator and interpreter. Formerly a lawyer and currently a librarian employed at Princeton University, she taught courses in translation and interpreting at Rutgers University.

DAVID KROLIKOSKI is assistant professor of Korean at the University of Hawai'i at Mānoa.